CIVILIAN INTERNMENT IN CANADA

Human Rights and Social Justice Series

ISSN 2291-6024

Editors: Karen Busby and Rhonda Hinther

2 *Civilian Internment in Canada: Histories and Legacies*, edited by Rhonda L. Hinther and Jim Mochoruk

1 *The Idea of a Human Rights Museum*, edited by Karen Busby, Adam Muller, and Andrew Woolford

CIVILIAN INTERNMENT IN CANADA

HISTORIES AND LEGACIES

EDITED BY RHONDA L. HINTHER
AND JIM MOCHORUK

UNIVERSITY OF MANITOBA PRESS

24 23 22 21 20 1 2 3 4 5

University of Manitoba Press
Winnipeg, Manitoba, Canada
Treaty 1 Territory
uofmpress.ca

Cataloguing data available from Library and Archives Canada
Human Rights and Social Justice Series, ISSN 2291-6024 ; 2
ISBN 978-0-88755-845-0 (PAPER)
ISBN 978-0-88755-593-0 (PDF)
ISBN 978-0-88755-591-6 (EPUB)
ISBN 978-0-88755-594-7 (BOUND)

Cover design by Michael Carroll
Interior design by Karen Armstrong

Printed in Canada

This book has been published with the help of a grant from the Federation for the Humanities and Social Sciences, through the Awards to Scholarly Publications Program, using funds provided by the Social Sciences and Humanities Research Council of Canada.

The University of Manitoba Press acknowledges the financial support for its publication program provided by the Government of Canada through the Canada Book Fund, the Canada Council for the Arts, the Manitoba Department of Sport, Culture, and Heritage, the Manitoba Arts Council, and the Manitoba Book Publishing Tax Credit.

Funded by the Government of Canada | Canada

Contents

Introduction

RHONDA L. HINTHER AND JIM MOCHORUK

Eleven-year-old Myron Shatulsky missed seeing his beloved father, internee Matthew Shatulsky, by a mere two hours when the train transferring Matthew and his comrades from the internment camp in Kananaskis, Alberta, to one at Petawawa, Ontario, passed through Winnipeg earlier than anticipated on a July day in 1941. Myron had not seen his father since the RCMP hauled him away the year before, as part of what historian Reg Whitaker has termed the Canadian government's "official repression of communism" during the war. "When we came to the station and heard that the train had [gone]—no need to write how we felt," said Matthew's wife Katherine in her next letter to him. "The poor boy has so many scars on his heart to heal that he will remember for the rest of his life."[1]

Now in his eighties, Myron Shatulsky's experiences of the internment years and their impact on his family and community serve as a powerful reminder of the fragility of civil liberties and human rights. His story is part of a larger, complex—and contested—conversation on civilian internment in Canada. Internment has affected persons from a variety of political backgrounds and racialized and ethnocultural communities, during times of war and perceived war, with the most well-known being the internments of those of Japanese, Ukrainian, and Italian descent. Experiences of arrest, internment, and displacement remain deeply felt by former internees and their kin.

Modern Canada has an unfortunately rich and shameful record of violating civil rights and liberties through the employment of civilian internment. This is a complicated and, at times, messy and confusing story encompassing arrest, displacement, and confinement. And this story spanned—and still spans—war and peacetimes, having affected persons from a wide variety of political backgrounds and ethno-cultural communities. Civilian internment in this country has not been widely discussed, particularly in comparative ways, despite the well-known impounding of tens of thousands of Japanese, Ukrainians, assorted eastern Europeans, Germans, and Italians as "enemy aliens" during the two world wars, and in spite of the deeply rooted experiences of those directly affected and their kin, as Myron Shatulsky's experience highlights.

In a dictionary sense, internment can be simply defined as the state of being confined as a prisoner without formal charge and conviction, with persons typically incarcerated for political or military reasons. But, as this collection indicates, such a strict definition is too limited for what transpired in Canada. During the Great War (1914–1918), over 5,900 eastern Europeans, primarily from the Austro-Hungarian Empire,[2] were interned in camps across the country, ostensibly for reasons of national security—although part of the official rationale for internment of eastern Europeans quickly came to include the warehousing of the indigent and unemployed foreigner.[3] Approximately 80,000 more were forced to register with, and report on a regular basis to, local authorities. And even after the wartime emergency ended, the Canadian state managed to transfer to other forms of legislation many of the powers of the War Measures Act, which had allowed it to imprison and deport "dangerous foreigners"—and others whose views the state disliked or feared.

As Reg Whitaker, Greg Kealy, Andrew Parnaby, and Dennis Molinaro have pointed out, for most of the interwar period, even when the War Measures Act was not in operation, the civil liberties of many Canadians, but especially those of Canada's "ethnic" leftists, were at great risk.[4] A series of legislative enactments and amendments related to Immigration, Citizenship, and the Criminal Code of Canada effectively extended wartime emergency laws into peacetime.[5] Collectively, these laws made it possible to surveil, harass, arrest, imprison, and even deport those whom the government of Canada and various provincial attorneys general deemed to be members of subversive organizations. Even more to the point, as Barbara Roberts has made clear, unknown—but sizable—numbers of foreign-born radicals were arrested, interned, and then deported via closed door and often secret administrative proceedings between 1919 and 1921—all on barely disguised political grounds.[6] And although it is a commonplace belief that the level of harassment and deportation declined after the election of Mackenzie King's Liberal government in 1921, the 1920s was still not an easy time to be an ethnic leftist. With or without the repeal of the amendments to the Immigration Act, immigrant radicals could be and were arrested, interned, and deported. But matters got even worse after R.B. Bennett's Conservative government came to power in 1930. The new federal government decided to use Section 98 of the Criminal Code to attack the Communist Party, to seize its papers and other property, and to imprison eight of its leaders. It also decided to employ the Immigration Act to not only "shovel out the unemployed" during the Depression but also to get rid of ethnic radicals such as the "Halifax 10." Such actions were truly draconian and sent a chilling message: the government had found—and was more than willing to use—powers which allowed it to arrest, imprison, intern, and deport long-time residents of Canada and to otherwise suspend core civil liberties during the interwar period for those who dared to think and act in ways the government did not approve.[7]

During the Second World War, using the newly enacted Defence of Canada Regulations, federal authorities, in league with local governments, the RCMP, and local police, worked to intern a diverse array of groups. Japanese Canadians (including men, women, and children), were forcibly relocated from the West Coast, and enjoy the dubious distinction of surpassing all other groups in terms of numbers affected (over 20,000 individuals were "evacuated"), loss of property, and the devastating effects on the community and individuals. Hundreds of persons of Italian and German descent were also incarcerated without charge, largely for their alleged pro-fascist and pro-Nazi political orientations.[8] Over a hundred Communists and pro-Communists, many of whom were so-called "ethnic hall" socialists, were also rounded up and interned in 1940 and most remained incarcerated well after the Soviet Union became an ally in the summer of 1941. As several of the contributions to this volume note, Canada also played host to internees on behalf of Britain; among these were German merchant marines, Italian nationals, and a sizable number of European Jews who, despite being early victims of Nazism, were arrested and interned in Britain after the outbreak of the Second World War because they were German nationals. While the common current uniting the internment of these disparate groups was ostensibly a concern for national security and the successful prosecution of the war effort, scholars and others have demonstrated (both in this collection and elsewhere) that in most cases these were not the real reasons these groups were targeted. Rather, wartime served as the perfect excuse to ramp up the racist targeting of groups like the Japanese Canadians. It is no exaggeration to say that ever since the earliest community members' arrival, the lives of Japanese Canadians had been unequally regulated and circumscribed by formal and informal racist manoeuvring on the part of white government officials, union members, citizens' groups, and others. Likewise, national security had little to do with the targeting of the far left; rather, federal and local authorities seized it as an excuse to thwart communist and pro-communist activism in Canada once and for all, making use of the Defence of Canada Regulations to sidestep legitimate legal process that would have—at least potentially—offered some possible semblance of justice served and the accompanying risk that these radicals might be acquitted if charged.

Just as the end of the Great War had not brought an end to internment in Canada, the conclusion of the Second World War was equally problematic in this regard. As the hot war ended, the Cold War began—and some would argue it began right here in Canada with the Gouzenko Affair. In light of his revelations of Soviet spying, the federal government, under authority of the War Measures Act—which had not yet expired in the fall of 1945—issued a secret order-in-council (PC 6444), which allowed authorities to detain without charge several Canadian communists, scientists, and so-called fellow travellers.[9] Authorities continued their surveillance of the far left during the Cold War through Operation Profunc (PROminent FUNCtionaries of the Communist Party), an initiative that endured for some thirty years starting in 1950. Under Operation Profunc, in the event of a Soviet attack or the advent of war, prominent Canadian communist activists and fellow travellers would be apprehended and interned.[10] In 1970, invoking the War Measures Act in a time of peace, Prime Minister Pierre Elliott Trudeau used its provisions to arrest and detain 497 people, all of whom could be held for up to ninety days without bail—at the discretion of the authorities—when the October Crisis gripped Quebec in 1970. And, as in previous episodes of detention and internment, most of those targeted for special attention were not terrorists, but political critics (in this case nationalist and leftist critics) of the dominant order in Quebec and Canada.[11]

As a number of the contributions to this collection remind us, important legal changes came in the 1980s: indeed, we see the formal death of the War Measures Act following the success of the hard-fought Japanese Canadian redress movement; a movement that not only sought redress for what had happened to the community during the Second World War, but had linked this fight to a struggle for broad anti-racist educational initiatives and the protection of the civil liberties of all Canadians. However, despite the changes in Canada's "emergency laws," these have not prevented subsequent governments from finding new ways to detain and hold persons perceived as threatening national security (or the values of the liberal state). In the wake of the 11 September 2001 terrorist attacks on the United States, Canadian authorities became willing participants in the "War on Terror" in many ways, including the creation of a security certificate process that allowed authorities to hold suspected or believed potential terrorists without charge. Like other past internment episodes, this one is inherently racialized; the majority of targets are Muslim men of colour.

Some may very well say that this volume simply dredges up sad memories from a seemingly distant past; memories which are better left undisturbed. However, as the forgoing brief history of Canadian internment indicates, the suspension of civil liberties and de facto internment is with us in the here and now. Indeed, "forgetting" past human rights violations by our governments—such as interning people for no other reason than their ethnicity or racialized background or their religious and political beliefs—is extremely dangerous. It is such forgetfulness which allows governments to claim to be defenders of civil liberties (via the Charter of Rights and Freedoms), while simultaneously trying to find ways to circumvent those rights—usually in the name of allegedly compromised security, or vague notions of the greater good. But the questions bear posing—whose security and whose greater good? The passage of Bill C-51—the Anti-terrorism Act, 2015—by the Harper government (and Prime Minister Justin Trudeau's unwillingness to retract it), the use of Security Certificates to detain and deport non-citizens on the grounds that they may be threats to national security, and the treatment accorded to Omar Khadr, both by our allies and then by the Canadian government, are stark reminders of the fragility of civil rights in Canada and the ways in which authorities use and abuse their power in often violent attempts to reshape undesirable bodies into questionable and politically loaded notions of ideal citizens. In this regard, Mona Oikawa's work linking white settler colonialism, internment (specifically Japanese Canadian internment during the Second World War), and residential schools for Indigenous children expands the conversation in a suggestive and compelling fashion. As she put it, "The genocidal practices utilized against Native Peoples, including forced displacement, incarceration, segregation, dispossession, destruction of community infrastructures, denigration of languages other than English and French, the role of the Christian churches in destroying traditional spiritual practices, and separation of families were forerunners to exclusionary white settler immigration policies and their policing of immigrants, and the eventual formulation and administration of the Internment. Although the processes of colonization and the Internment are not identical, it is essential to see them as linked."[12] Given this, it makes sense that civilian internment in Canada—and elsewhere—needs to be considered as part and parcel of a cultural and political hegemony that grants incredible authority to those in power who can, and do, claim to be restricting the civil liberties of some Canadians "for the common good." We must be ever vigilant and active in questioning the motives and challenging the actions of those who seek to circumscribe human rights.

While the focus of this work is clearly upon Canada, it needs to be said that civilian internment cannot be fully understood in a strictly Canadian context. Internment is really a global phenomenon—practised by regimes around the world in times of both war and peace. Canada's wartime internment operations were transnational from the outset, receiving as they did civilian internees from Great Britain—many of whom were German antifascists or German-Jewish refugees—and merchant seamen who had been captured in ports around the world as well as on the high seas. Then of course there were also the prisoners of war who were shipped to Canada for internment—truly an international brigade. Meanwhile, many of Canada's own internees were transnational citizens of the world—having been born in Germany, Italy, Japan, the Austro-Hungarian Empire, and elsewhere, accidents of birth that ended up justifying their internment. But even more to the point, Canada's internment operations clearly had rough equivalents in the United States, Great Britain, and other Allied nations, to say nothing of the more extreme examples of its wartime enemies (and its sometime ally, the Soviet Union). Indeed, in some ways Canadian internment operations were directly linked to and followed the example of other nations. Because of Canada's ties to Great Britain—and its willingness to serve as a dumping ground for some of that nation's internees—the link to British internment operations was especially close. Beyond this there is no escaping the similarities and differences in the treatment of Japanese Canadians, Japanese Americans, and Japanese Australians during the Second World War—operations that were clearly linked by a shared sense of war-induced hysteria and deep-rooted anti-Asian sentiment. Nor was Canada's use of emergency powers to arrest and intern in times of peace without international parallel. Prime Minister Pierre Elliott Trudeau's use of the War Measures Act to arrest, detain, and intern suspected threats to the state during the October Crisis certainly stands out in Canadian historical memory as an extraordinary use of wartime powers in peacetime. However, it was not unprecedented among the Western democracies—as evidenced by the British government's use of emergency powers during the "the Troubles" in

Northern Ireland. And at the height of the Cold War several Western nations had the equivalent of Canada's "Operation Profunc"—a plan for the arrest and internment of Communists in the case of real or apprehended war with the Soviet Union—ready to be put in place. Again, this situation is not simply a relic of the past. One can see the same sentiments and the same appeals to "security" in the cavalier manner in which U.S. presidential candidate (and subsequently president) Donald Trump proposed interning all Muslims in the United States as solution to terrorist threats, while concurrently minimizing the seriousness of the civil liberties violations that were part and parcel of the treatment of Japanese Americans during the Second World War. This should remind us all of the importance of internment awareness.

The history of civilian internment is a complex one, encompassing as it does arrest, displacement, confinement, and surveillance. Indeed, the phrase itself is complex. Most often it is used to indicate only those individuals who were placed in jails or specially designated internment camps. However, this collection takes a much broader approach. For example, only a small fraction of the Japanese Canadian community was formally interned—782 out of over 20,000 who were "evacuated." Yet one can argue that the entire West Coast Japanese Canadian population experienced a form of internment: their real and chattel property was seized and all were forcefully evacuated from their homes and communities. Those who were not formally interned were relocated to remote towns in the Interior of BC, to work camps throughout mainland Canada, to sugar beet farms on the prairies—and to a host of other such locations—where they remained under RCMP and British Columbia Security Commission supervision, had virtually no freedom of movement, and had no real guarantee of their basic civil rights. This clearly constitutes internment by other means. The same might be said of certain left-wing activists—women in this case—who were not formally interned, but who were imprisoned on charges under the Defence of Canada Act that were much like the "particulars" used to justify the internment of their male colleagues. The term internment can also be used to describe some of the remote Alternative Service camps which housed and "employed" conscientious objectors. Clearly the more formal meaning of civilian internment certainly applies to the German-Jewish refugees and other German antifascists who had the misfortune of being rounded up in their new home of Great Britain and then shipped to Canada for formal internment. The same may be said of the seamen of the German merchant marine who were captured and then sent to Canada. But how does one define the experience of those who were arrested and detained, and in some cases deported—largely on account of their political views? Were they interned? Well, in the immediate aftermath of the First World War when the War Measures Act (WMA) was still operational and internment camps still open, the answer is a simple yes, they were civilian internees. However, in the years between 1920 and 1939, a time when the emergency powers of the WMA were transferred over to the Criminal Code of Canada and the Immigration Act, the answer is a bit less certain. What happened to left-wing ethnics (and a few other radicals) during the interwar period certainly looked like internment, but it was really *only* a removal of rights and liberties for those who subscribed to ideologies which the state declared to be illegal. It is of some note that one of the very few bodies which had sought to offer legal support for the left-wing activists who ran afoul of the Canadian state's notions of political propriety during this period, the Canadian Labour Defence League, was itself declared to be an illegal organization under the terms of the Defence of Canada Regulations in 1940. So much for the tradition of protecting civil liberties!

The crucial point, of course, is that internment and the removal (or severe limitation) of civil rights and liberties are interrelated phenomena which must be considered in tandem—and this is precisely what several of the essays contained in this book do. However, it is also the case that contributors to this collection are interested in a whole host of other internment-related issues. To facilitate explicit comparative dialogue, we have largely resisted grouping articles by internment episode, but rather have attempted to take a more thematic and comparative approach to the presentation of the content.

One entire section is devoted to the question of how the experience of those who were subjected to internment should be represented to the broader public—particularly in museums and other public spaces. Thus, there are essays which detail how—and to a lesser extent why—these episodes are represented in four different Canadian museums. Collectively these essays help us to understand both the difficulties of representing unsavoury or tragic parts of a nation's past to a broader audience, but they also tell us much about the politics of commemoration.

Other essays in this collection not only address the experience of internment through the mechanism of oral history interviews and a careful rereading of internment memoirs, but they also force us to reconsider how factors such as one's age, ideological commitments (or lack thereof), and subsequent life experiences shape memories of what was obviously a traumatic set of experiences. Contributions which deal with the recollections of German merchant seamen who were interned in Canada while particularly young and of Japanese Canadians who were children when their families were forced from their homes provide some completely unexpected—and seemingly positive—stories of the internment experience. But the same collection contains pieces that indicate that the experience for some of the German-Jewish internees, and virtually all of the Canadian left-wing internees, was remembered in vastly different ways. This of course raises the issues of memory and remembrance. Several authors inquire into the way in which subsequent life events have influenced internees' memories of this period in their lives: gender, age, ideological commitments, events on the world stage, and eventual life paths clearly influenced the way in which the internment experience was narrated.

While civilian internment has not made much of a mark on the consciousness of the overall population, it has been a growth industry in certain academic and community circles—thus there is what historians would refer to as a "lively historiography" surrounding various portions of Canada's internment operations. And it is lively precisely because parts of it are matters of intense historical debate. Jack Granatstein, for example, offered a strong defence of the Canadian government's decision to "evacuate" Japanese Canadians from the West Coast long after the consensus view had come to a very different conclusion; a defence which spilled over from the academic to public spheres.[13] Regarding First World War internment operations, which were conducted primarily against eastern Europeans, a very interesting set of debates has arisen between the original scholars of Ukrainian-Canadian internment—who also tended to be important activists in the movement for redress—and researchers such as Francis Swyripa and Orest Martynowych—and now Kassandra Luciuk—who offer important modifications and nuances to the larger narrative.[14] Equally significant for the Italian Canadian experience in the Second World War is the path-breaking volume of articles, *Enemies Within: Italian and Other Internees in Canada and Abroad,* which was an effort by several historians of Italian Canadian history "to facilitate more informed discussion" on the topic of Italian Canadian internment during the Second World War, on which, to that point, the discourse was being largely shaped "by a simplified version of events." Specifically, the collection's editors Franca Iacovetta, Roberto Perin, and Angelo Principe note in their introduction a desire to challenge the simplified explanation of the internment that had developed as a result of the "drawing on selective evidence, ignoring contrary views, and glossing over the fascist history of the Italian immigrant communities," which "has become the orthodox position" on the event.[15] The crucial point here, however is this: there is no single historiography of internment. Rather there are several—as the various internment operations are most typically treated in splendid isolation from each other.[16] Thus, there is the story of the First World War internment of Ukrainian Canadians, which seems to stand alone from all other interpretations of internment; then there is the well-studied case of Japanese Canadians in the Second World War, replete with its own internal debates;[17] the somewhat lesser-known case of German-Jewish internees who spent part of the Second World War in Canada, almost always stands apart from all other internment experiences, and is composed primarily of memoirs of former internees and the work of two of the contributors to this volume.[18] Meanwhile, the growing literature surrounding Italian Canadian internment is typically treated quite separately from all the others, although it is almost always linked to that of the internment of Canadian fascists;[19] the case of the internment of Canadian pro-Communists has always been studied as a separate case, often firmly situated within the lengthy historical trajectory of government surveillance and repression of the left.[20] Likewise is the case with the less frequently studied experiences of religious conscientious objectors and their "alternative service" experience; and then there is the almost completely unstudied matter of German merchant seamen and non-Jewish anti-Nazi refugees from Germany.[21] The only historiography that actually seems to span a broad array of these experiences is the work of those scholars who are examining redress movements, and their historical antecedents.[22]

The chapters in this collection not only address most of these historiographies but actively challenge some of the predominant narratives, ask pointed questions about the linkages between scholarship and redress activism, and broaden the field of study to include groups who have all too often been ignored or lumped into an erroneous category. Perhaps even more to the point, an effort is also being made to link these experiences into a new, more broadly based and inclusive historiography. The chapters in this collection provide readers with a sense of just how profound the impact of internment and the concomitant suspension of civil liberties has been in Canada. Broken down into nine broad categories, these parts each address key thematic issues.

Part 1, a set of broad-based metanarratives, seeks to provide readers with a context for what is to follow in the rest of the collection. It features chapters by Jodi Giesbrecht and Dennis Edney. Vastly different in approach, uniting these chapters is the common concern of placing individual episodes of internment and the suspension of civil liberties into a much broader context—commencing with the First World War and ending, well, with today. As the long-time pro-bono lawyer and confidant of Omar Khadr, Edney's comments about and his passion for the preservation of civil liberties are compelling and serve as a cautionary tale about the fragility of civil liberties in the age of Guantanamo Bay. Giesbrecht, who oversees curation at the Canadian Museum for Human Rights (CMHR), speaks to the way in which the controversial topic of internment has been handled by the curators and other professionals at the CMHR. Her essay not only provides a detailed analysis of how museum professionals operate—a lovely complement to the essays in Part 7 of this collection—but it also has the advantage of taking readers through the first and second world wars and beyond, including the experiences of conscientious objectors, the Gouzenko Affair of the early phase of the Cold War, the October Crisis of 1970, and the "War on Terror."

Part 2, featuring chapters by Kassandra Luciuk and Jim Mochoruk, provides new insights into the nature and surprising impact of internment operations on the founding and operation of left-wing Ukrainian institutions during and between the two world wars. Although it is a commonplace in the literature that ethnic leftists were not singled out for internment in the early days of the First World War, Luciuk's contribution makes it clear that in this first national internment operation it was precisely the proletarianized and radicalized eastern Europeans who were targeted by the Canadian state. Indeed, her work makes a powerful case for the linkage between this experience of internment and the subsequent radicalization of sizable numbers of Ukrainian speakers. Jim Mochoruk's chapter carries the story of some of these radicalized Ukrainians forward into the Second World War and tells the sometimes comic, sometimes tragic story of damage inflicted upon a Winnipeg co-operative that was founded and staffed by the Ukrainian left during the interwar years. Underlying this particular analysis is an understanding of the trials and tribulations of the ethnic left during the interwar period. After examining the experience of those associated with the People's Co-op in the lead-up to the renewal of the WMA and the application of the Defence of Canada Regulations—and the full-out assault on the Ukrainian left in 1940–41—Mochoruk demonstrates that despite all of its weapons, the state failed to destroy any of these agencies. This was not a result of the strength of the Canadian civil liberties tradition, but rather of the incompetence of the state.

Taking two very different perspectives on community interventions and relations with authorities, the chapters in Part 3 explore the important ways grassroots actors and their engagement with authorities impacted the internment experiences of two communities. Marinel Mandres's chapter examines the case of Serbians during the Great War, while Travis Tomchuk's considers Montreal Italians during the Second World War. Mandres explains how Serbian community leaders, through careful quasi-diplomatic manoeuvring, helped to free internees. His study serves as an important piece of recovery history—as he notes, almost nothing of the Serbian civilian internment experience is included in the existing body of knowledge of Canada's first national internment operations. In his contribution, Tomchuk details how, by acting as informants, disgruntled and discredited Italian community leaders helped to create internees. Looking specifically at the interventions of two informants, Camillo Vetere and Augusto Bersani, both active in the Italian community in Montreal during the Second World War, Tomchuk ably demonstrates how revenge and petty rivalries—rather than any semblance of a concern for national security or the war effort—drove informant behaviour. Tomchuk's work highlights the danger that reliance on community informants poses, especially when often questionable assertions become the seemingly sole evidence on which authorities based their decisions on whom to intern.

Part 4 features chapters by Rhonda L. Hinther and Christine Whitehouse. These pieces examine internment via a gendered lens, in the context of two wildly divergent internment experiences. Whitehouse's piece provides a starkly different type of consideration of the "camp boys" (the primarily German-Jewish men shipped to Canada from England for internment, particularly the youngest amongst them) than one finds in most of the scholarly and biographical literature. Her analysis of masculinity and sexual identity construction, coming as it did in a crucial period in the lives of the young men who found themselves confined in these internment camps, offers an important intervention in the discourse on this cohort of internees. Rhonda L. Hinther's contribution, which deals with the well-studied field of the repression of the far left-wing in the early stages of the Second World War, adds an important new dimension to the literature by focusing on women who were arrested, jailed, and in a handful of cases, formally or nearly interned. This is a heretofore vastly understudied group. Her work will cause readers to examine how dominant contemporary gender assumptions played into the choice of who was to be interned. It also reminds one that the gendered understanding of political activism within the left in general and the ethnic left in particular also shaped decisions about and the treatment of the female activists who were interned.

Part 5 includes Aya Fujiwara and Mikhail Bjorge's stimulating and provocative pieces on Japanese Canadians during the Second World War. Both challenge some long-standing interpretations of the Japanese Canadian experience and behaviour during "internment." Dealing with its own specific subject matter, each piece in this section challenges the absence of the workers' experiences in the historiography of Japanese Canadians and the Second World War, especially the lack of attention to detainee resistance to internment and working conditions in the camps and elsewhere in popular accounts and remembrances. In her chapter, Fujiwara considers Japanese Canadian sugar beet farm workers in southern Alberta. Inadvertently sentenced to hard labour (in spite of not having been sentenced at all), in order to stay together as a family, many Japanese Canadians elected to take up sugar beet farm labour. Fujiwara's work challenges an established narrative and views Japanese Canadians as coerced labourers experiencing a different type of "internment." They were not docile, however; as she notes, in several instances Japanese Canadians pushed back against the conditions they encountered, both on the farms, especially in terms of wages, and in the communities in which they lived, particularly where the education of their children was concerned. Mikhail Bjorge, in his piece, likewise challenges the existing narrative of Japanese acquiescence in the face of removal. He views Japanese Canadian evacuees as workers, framing their experiences in the camps in the context of the workplace. In doing so, he demonstrates several key examples of workplace resistance, including strikes and other instances of direct labour action, many incidents of which involved the activism of not only men, but also women and children detainees. Both articles stand as dramatic examples of how specific aspects of the public and private sectors, served by and supportive of institutionalized racism, were complicit—to bolster their own economic interests—in encouraging, defining, and enforcing the captivity and forced relocation of Japanese Canadians. Each chapter here thus offers an important critique of the logic of capitalism and the convenience of racist assumptions for employers and the state alike. This makes clear the economic motivations underpinning wartime civilian internment and forced relocation, a situation evident in other internment contexts.

Part 6 is perhaps the most eclectic of the entire collection; uniting each chapter is a focus on intensely personal stories. In her contribution, Grace Eiko Thomson shares her personal recollections of the experience of forced relocation and internment. It is a beautiful, thoughtful, and wonderfully self-reflexive narrative. But it is even more than this, as Ms. Thomson has interwoven her mother's life experiences into the narrative—via the medium of her mother's written memoir which Thomson translated from the original Japanese. In almost poetic fashion this essay explores themes of alienation and belonging, trauma and its enduring, complex intergenerational legacy.

Clemence Schultze's chapter is a remarkable example of personal and historical reconstruction. The child of a German political refugee father who had lived and worked in England prior to the outbreak of the Second World War who was subsequently interned in Britain and then Canada, she grew up knowing little of her father's wartime internment or of her mother's efforts to remain in contact with him. There were a few amusing stories—suitable for a child to hear—but nothing else. She eventually came into possession of a mass of documentary material from her parents which allowed her to flesh out the wartime experience and feelings of both her parents—both through actual letters sent and received and the far more fulsome journal her mother kept, which recorded not only all the letters she sent to her future husband, but also many of the things she could not put in censored correspondence. In all, a remarkable, compelling, and—as Dr. Schultze herself put it—somewhat ambiguous story emerges. Finally, this section concludes a contribution from Canada's premier archivist of eastern European Canadian source materials, Myron Momryk, who examines the experience of Peter and Mary Prokopchak following Peter's arrest and internment. Based upon a collection of recently unearthed family documents, especially the heavily censored and coded correspondence which passed between the two, Momryk's work provides fascinating insights into Peter's internment experience and its impact on Mary and their relationship, revealing how, if anything, it deepened the couple's commitment to the ideology that had led to his internment in the first place.

Part 7 examines questions of commemoration and the politics of public memory. While academic historians pride themselves on their peer-reviewed publications and their work in the university classroom, the reality is that most people do not get their history from such sources. Instead, a much higher proportion of the public is exposed to history through museums and heritage sites. This lays a heavy and important responsibility upon those working in these contexts to bring history to life in nuanced and yet accessible ways for diverse audiences. As this section makes clear, how history is exhibited in public spaces is an inherently fraught process. And this is especially the case when the subject matter at hand relates to "negative heritage" such as internment. Displays related to internment disrupt and challenge triumphalist national narratives that so typically accompany portrayals of a country's wartime experience—be it a "hot war" like the first and second world wars, a Cold War, or an extremely ambiguous "War on Terror." Chapters here by Ed and Todd Cassie, Emily Cuggy and Kathleen Ogilvie, and Sharon Reilly thoughtfully examine the issues confronting museums seeking to educate a broader public on issues which do not fit into the "heroic" tradition of national or regional history commemoration. The challenges in telling the story of internment is carefully illustrated in this section.

Part 8 examines two distinct groups of international internees whom Canada "hosted" in the context of the Second World War. One of the ways Canada supported the international war effort was by receiving and incarcerating men designated enemy aliens, who had been arrested in Britain and elsewhere outside Canada. These men—drawn from a variety of ethnic and political backgrounds—arrived in Canada through a host of circumstances and, once on Canadian soil, had a multitude of different and complex experiences. Some of these paralleled those of domestic civilian internees; others differed, as an outcome of the intersections of nationality, place of origin, age, and ethnicity in the Canadian context. For many, finding themselves in a Canadian internment camp was baffling; others, though incarcerated, experienced their period here as a time of adventure. Avoiding many of the dangers of wartime Europe and elsewhere was a silver lining many noted in their reminiscences years later, albeit one that left some with remnants of what we might today call survivor's guilt. In her chapter, Paula Draper examines the German-Jewish "camp boys," refugees from Nazi terror who sought sanctuary in Britain but were interned as enemy aliens on account of nationality and later shipped to Canada for ongoing incarceration. Referring to it rightfully as "a little known episode of the Holocaust," Draper situates these men's stories firmly within Canada's larger history of anti-Semitism, reminding us that contemporary Canada "had kept her doors tightly closed against those fleeing Europe, particularly Jews." Following their release, many later remained in Canada (in spite of the roadblocks authorities enacted), making homes, careers, and successful lives for themselves, concurrently processing their internment experiences as scarring but ultimately lifesaving, given what so many Jews and others in Europe endured under Hitler. Judith Kestler's innovative contribution to this section brings to the fore the hitherto largely unexamined case of Second World War German merchant seamen internees. Captured by British warships, Kestler estimates some 3,500 of these men ended up in a number of different internment camps across Canada. Seafaring was largely a young man's game—the vast majority ranged between the ages of fifteen and thirty-five—and this shaped their recollections and the construction of their captivity narratives, which Kestler unpacks through oral histories and autobiographical writings. While they noted their loss of freedom and its accompanying disadvantages as negative, Kestler concurrently finds that "these former internees present their experience in a rather favourable light," largely because of their life cycle position, the educational opportunities camp life afforded, and their exposure to aspects of Canada and "Canadianness."

Finally, the chapters in the book's last section speak to the complexity and challenges of redress, popular memory, and what it means to understand, acknowledge, and attempt to rectify past injustices in light of complicated shared pasts and presents. These processes are fraught, as each of these chapters point out, albeit in very different ways. This section begins with a piece from Franca Iacovetta, who speaks from a position of both personal and professional authority. Here, she revisits her important past work on Second World War Italian Canadian internment by discussing the path-breaking book she co-edited, *Enemies Within: Italian and Other Internees in Canada and Abroad*: a work which consciously sought to challenge the "simplistic story that neglected fascism and anti-fascism in the immigrant communities." Her entry point is the difficult multiyear dialogue in which she engaged with a woman whose father and uncle had been interned. The descendant challenged Iacovetta and her co-editors' assertions in *Enemies Within*, suggesting that the book minimized the suffering internees' families endured. In considering this critic's perspective, Iacovetta reflects on the politics of redress, the construction of popular and collective memory by causes like the Italian internment redress movement (for better or for worse), and the perils of writing activist, engaged history, particularly when it fails to align with broader community agendas and popular beliefs about the past.

This section, and the entire collection, ends with a piece by Art Miki, who revisits the narrative of Japanese Canadian forced relocation and internment during the Second World War, told through the prism of his own experiences as a child on a Manitoba sugar beet farm, a situation his family "chose" in an effort to stay together during the war. He also describes the subsequent struggle, decades later, for redress; a struggle in which he played a prominent leadership role. Miki underscores that redress—the struggle for and the nature of it as ongoing action—is a difficult and complicated process. But it is essential, since, as he concludes, "it is through the recognition of past injustices that we as a country vow never to make those mistakes again and grow to become more inclusive, understanding and welcoming."

It is our profound hope that this collection will serve not as some sort of definitive statement on the various aspects of civilian internment in Canada, but rather as the starting point for an even more rigorous and detailed set of discussions and research projects. Civil liberties, and the violation of the same—be it historical or in the here and now—is a topic that must always be at the forefront of scholarly, community, and personal agendas, at least if we hope to avoid, redress, and reconcile the mistakes and injustices of the past.

Notes

1 Matthew Shatulsky, writing under his pen name, Dyadya, later documented the train journey, during which he and fellow internees attempted to get word to family and friends in Winnipeg that the train would arrive earlier than originally expected. The contents of Katherine's Shatulsky's letter quoted above is included as part of his article. See "The Red Patch: Organ of Hull Anti-Fascists Internees," *May Day Souvenir Issue*, 1942, AUUC Archives, Winnipeg, Manitoba.

2 Peter Melnycky, "The Internment of Ukrainians in Canada," in Frances Swyripa and John Herd Thompson, eds., *Loyalties in Conflict: Ukrainians in Canada During the Great War* (Edmonton: Canadian Institute of Ukrainian Studies, 1983), 3.

3 Ibid., 2. By 28 October 1914 this was made explicit by the government in an "Order-in-Council respecting Enemy Aliens."

4 Reg Whitaker, Greg Kealy, and Andrew Parnaby, *Secret Service: Political Policing in Canada from the Fenians to Fortress America* (Toronto: University of Toronto Press, 2010); Dennis G. Molinaro, *An Exceptional Law: Section 98 and the Emergency State, 1919–1936* (Toronto: University of Toronto Press, 2017).

5 For an excellent and concise discussion of these changes see Barbara Roberts, *Whence They Came: Deportation from Canada, 1900–1935* (Ottawa: University of Ottawa Press, 1988), 22.

6 Roberts, *Whence They Came,* especially 96–97. See also, Barbara Roberts, "Shovelling Out the 'Mutinous': Political Deportation from Canada before 1936," *Labour/Le Travail* 18 (Fall 1986): 81.

7 See Lita-Rose Betcherman. *The Little Band: The Clashes between the Communists and the Political and Legal Establishment in Canada, 1928–1932* (Ottawa: Deneau Publishers), 76–78; Roberts, "Shovelling Out the 'Mutinous,'" and Dennis Molinaro, "'Citizens of the World': Law, Deportation, and the Homo Sacer, 1932–1934," *Canadian Ethnic Studies* 47, no. 3 (2015): 143–61.

8 Robert Keyserlingk, "Breaking the Nazi Plot: Canadian Government Attitudes towards German Canadians, 1939–1945," in *On Guard for Thee: War Ethnicity and the Canadian State,* ed. Norman Hillmer, Bohdan Kordan, and Lubomyr Luciuk (Ottawa: Canadian Committee for the History of the Second World War, 1988). Keyserlingk indicates that 847 Germans were arrested as were 632 Italians.

9 For details on this case, see Ross Lambertson, *Repression and Resistance: Canadian Human Rights Activists, 1930–1960* (Toronto: University of Toronto Press, 2014), 143–95.

10 Operation Profunc has been the subject of several popular treatments, including a Fifth Estate episode and several websites. Frances Reilly's recent PhD dissertation, is the first scholarly treatment of the subject. See Frances Reilly, "Controlling Contagion: Policing and Prescribing Sexual and Political Normalcy in Cold War Canada" (PhD diss., University of Saskatchewan, 2016), https://ecommons.usask.ca/handle/10388/7396.

11 Dominique Clement, "The October Crisis of 1970: Human Rights Abuses under the War Measures Act," *The Journal of Canadian Studies* 42, no. 2 (2008): 160–86.

12 See Mona Oikawa, "Connecting the Internment of Japanese Canadians to the Colonization of Aboriginal Peoples in Canada," in *Aboriginal Connections to Race, Environment, and Traditions*, ed. Rick Riewe and Jill Oakes, 17–26 (Winnipeg: University of Manitoba, 2006), 20. We are grateful to Adele Perry for drawing our attention to Oikawa's important work.

13 See, for example, J.L. Granatstein and Gregory A. Johnson, "The Evacuation of the Japanese Canadians, 1942: A Realist Critique of the Received Version," in *On Guard for Thee*. This debate had been commenced when Granatstein published a lengthy piece on this topic in the pages of the popular Canadian magazine, *Saturday Night*, two years earlier in November 1986.

14 Kassandra Luciuk, whose work is included in this book, makes explicit that the First World War internments were a case of attempted suppression of labour activism, challenging the argument many earlier authors put forth suggesting that internees were targeted primarily for their eastern Europeanness. Meanwhile, both Swyripa and Martynowych have offered nuanced critiques of the redress-inspired work of Lubomyr Luciuk, Bohdan Kordan, and a few others. See Orest Martynowych, "Re: internment of Ukrainian Canadians," reproduced in Lubomyr Luciuk, ed., *Righting an Injustice: The Debate over Redress for Canada's First National Internment Operations* (Toronto: The Justinian Press, 1994), 65; Frances Swyripa, "The Politics of Redress: The Contemporary Ukrainian-Canadian Campaign," in *Enemies Within: Italian and Other Internees in Canada and Abroad*, ed. Franca Iacovetta, Roberto Perin, and Angelo Principe (Toronto: University of Toronto Press, 2000), 355–378. For other perspectives, see Lubomyr Luciuk, *A Time for Atonement: Canada's First National Internment Operations and the Ukrainian Canadians 1914–1920* (Kingston: Limestone Press, 1988); J.B. Gregorovich, ed., *Commemorating an Injustice: Fort Henry and Ukrainian Canadians as "Enemy Aliens" during the First World War* (Kingston: Kashtan Press, 1994); Lubomyr Luciuk, *In Fear of the Barbed Wire Fence: Canada's First National Internment Operations and the Ukrainian Canadians, 1914–1920* (Kingston: Kashtan Press, 2001); Bohdan Kordan, *Enemy Aliens, Prisoners of War: Internment in Canada during the Great War* (Montreal and Kingston: McGill-Queen's University Press, 2002); James Farney and Bohdan S. Kordan, "The Predicament of Belonging: The Status of Enemy Aliens in Canada, 1914," *Journal of Canadian Studies* 39, no. 1 (2005): 74–89; and Bohdan Kordan, *No Free Man: Canada, the Great War, and the Enemy Alien Experience* (Montreal and Kingston: McGill-Queen's University Press, 2016).

15 Franca Iacovetta, Roberto Perin, and Angelo Principe, eds., *Enemies Within: Italian and Other Internees in Canada and Abroad* (Toronto: University of Toronto Press, 2000), 6.

16 A notable exception to this is *Enemies Within*. Although primarily focused on Italian experiences during the Second World War, it also includes a handful of key articles on other internment episodes.

17 The most important works in this regard include: Forrest E. La Violette, *The Canadian Japanese in World War II* (Toronto: University of Toronto Press, 1948); Ann Gomer Sunahara, *The Politics of Racism* (Toronto: Lorimer, 1981); Ken Adachi, *The Enemy That Never Was: A History of the Japanese Canadians* (Toronto: McClelland and Stewart, 1976); Yuko Shibata, *The Forgotten History of the Japanese Canadians: Volume I* (Vancouver: New Sun Books, 1977); Peter Ward, *White Canada Forever:*

Popular Attitudes and Public Policy towards Orientals in British Columbia (Montreal and Kingston: McGill-Queen's University Press, 1978); Takeo Nakano, *Within the Barbed Wire Fence: A Japanese Man's Account of His Internment in Canada* (Toronto: University of Toronto Press, 1980). The revisionist take would include the works of J.L. Granatstein and G.A. Johnson, "The Evacuation of the Japanese Canadians, 1942: A Realist Critique of the Received Version," in *On Guard for Thee,* 101–29; Patricia Roy, J.L. Granatstein, Masako Iino, and Hiroko Takamura, *Mutual Hostages: Canadians and Japanese during the Second World War* (Toronto: University of Toronto Press, 1990); and Patricia Roy, *The Triumph of Citizenship: The Japanese and Chinese in Canada, 1941–67* (Vancouver: UBC Press, 2007). More recent interpretations include Aya Fujiwara, "Japanese-Canadian Internally Displaced Persons: Labour Relations and Ethno-Religious Identity in Southern Alberta, 1942–1953," *Labour/Le Travail* 69 (Spring 2012): 63–89; Stephanie Bangarth, "The Long, Wet Summer of 1942: The Ontario Farm Service Force, Small-Town Ontario, and the Nisei," *Canadian Ethnic Studies* 37, no. 1 (2005): 40–62; Stephanie Bangarth, *Voices Raised in Protest: Defending North American Citizens of Japanese Ancestry, 1942–49* (Vancouver: UBC Press, 2008); Pamela Sugiman, "Passing Time, Moving Memories: Interpreting Wartime Narratives of Japanese Canadian Women," *Histoire Sociale/Social History* 73 (2004): 51–79; Pamela Sugiman, "'A Million Hearts from Here': Japanese Canadian Mothers and Daughters and the Lessons of War," *Journal of American Ethnic History* 26, no. 4 (Summer 2007): 50–68; Pamela Sugiman, "'Life is Sweet': Vulnerability and Composure in the Wartime Narratives of Japanese Canadians" *Journal of Canadian Studies* 43, no. 1 (2009): 186–218; and Carmela Patrias, "Race, Employment Discrimination, and State Complicity in Wartime Canada, 1939–1945," *Labour/Le Travail* 59 (Spring 2007): 9–42. For redress movement-specific commentary, see Roy Miki and Cassandra Kobayashi, *Justice in Our Time: The Japanese Canadian Redress Settlement* (Vancouver: Talon, 1991); Maryka Omatsu, *Bittersweet Passage: Redress and the Japanese Canadian Experience* (Toronto: Between the Lines, 1992); and Roy Miki, *Redress: Inside the Japanese Canadian Call for Justice* (Vancouver: Raincoast, 2004).

18 Paula J Draper, "The Accidental Immigrants: Canada and the Interned Refugees," (PhD diss., University of Toronto/OISE, 1983); Paula J. Draper, "'The Camp Boys': Refugees from Nazism Interned in Canada, 1940–1944," in *Enemies Within*; Christine Whitehouse, "'You'll Get Used to It!': The Internment of Jewish Refugees in Canada, 1940–43" (PhD diss., Carleton University, 2016); Patrick Farges, "Masculinity and Confinement: German–Speaking Refugees in Canadian Internment Camps (1940–1943)," *Culture, Society, and Masculinities* 4, no. 1 (2012): 33–47; Irving Abella and Harold Troper, *None Is Too Many: Canada and the Jews of Europe, 1933–1948* (Toronto: Lester and Orpen Dennys, 1982); Franklin Bialystok, *Delayed Impact: The Holocaust and the Canadian Jewish Community* (Montreal and Kingston: McGill Queen's University Press, 2000); Gerald Tulchinsky, *Branching Out: The Transformation of the Canadian Jewish Community* (Toronto: Stoddart, 1998); Gerhard Baessler, *Sanctuary Denied: Refugees from the Third Reich and Newfoundland Immigration Policy, 1906–1949* (St. John's, NL: Memorial University, 1992); Ernst Zimmerman, *The Little Third Reich on Lake Superior: A History of the Canadian Internment Camp R,* ed. Michel S. Beaulieu and David K. Ratz (Edmonton: University of Alberta Press, 2015); Jaleen Grove, *Oscar Cahen: His Life and Work* (Toronto: Art Institute of Canada, 2016); Henry Kreisel, "Diary of an Internment," *White Pelican* (Summer 1974); Walter W. Igersheimer, *Blatant Injustice: The Story of a Jewish Refugee from Nazi Germany Imprisoned in Britain and*

Canada during WWII (Montreal and Kingston: McGill-Queen's University Press, 2005); Erwin Schild, "A Canadian Footnote to the Holocaust," *Canadian Jewish Historical Society Journal* 5, no. 1 (Spring 1981); Erwin Schild, *The Very Narrow Bridge. A Memoir of an Uncertain Passage* (Toronto: Adath Israel Congregation/ Malcolm Lester, 2001); and Eric Koch, *Deemed Suspect: A Wartime Blunder* (Toronto: Methuen, 1980).

19 Recent work on the Italian experience includes Pamela Hickman and Cavalluzzo J. Smith, *Italian Canadian Internment in the Second World War* (Toronto: James Lorimer, 2012).

20 For the largely first-hand accounts that dominate the literature on this topic, see Peter Krawchuk, *Interned without Cause* (Toronto: Kobzar, 1985); Peter Krawchuk, ed, *Reminiscences of Courage and Hope: Stories of Ukrainian Canadian Women Pioneers* (Toronto: Kobzar, 1991); Peter Krawchuk, "The War Years," in *Our History: The Ukrainian Labour-Farmer Movement in Canada, 1907–1991* (Toronto: Lugus, 1996); William Repka and Kathleen M. Repka, *Dangerous Patriots: Canada's Unknown Prisoners of War* (Vancouver: New Star Books, 1982); Ben Swankey, "Reflections of a Communist: Canadian Internment Camps," *Alberta History* 30, no. 2 (April 1982): 11–20; and Roland Penner, "Transition, Turmoil, and Trouble (1939–1943)," in *A Glowing Dream: A Memoir* (Winnipeg: J. Gordon Shillingford, 2007). In regard to works that focus upon state security matters, see Reg Whitaker, Gregory S. Kealey, and Andrew Parnaby, "Keep the Home Fires Burning, 1939–45," in *Secret Service: Political Policing in Canada: From the Fenians to Fortress America* (Toronto: University of Toronto Press, 2012); Gregory S. Kealey, "State Repression of Labour and the Left in Canada, 1914–20: The Impact of the First World War," *Canadian Historical Review* 73, no. 3 (September 1992): 281; 1; Daniel Robinson, "Planning for the 'Most Serious Contingency': Alien Internment, Arbitrary Detention, and the Canadian State 1938–39," *Journal of Canadian Studies* 28, no. 2 (1993): 5; Reg Whitaker, "Official Repression of Communism during World War II." *Labour / Le Travail* 17 (1986): 135–66; Chris Frazer, "From Pariahs to Patriots: Canadian Communists and the Second World War," *Past Imperfect* 5 (December 1996): 3–36; Reg Whitaker and Gregory S. Kealey, "A War on Ethnicity?: The RCMP and Internment," in *Enemies Within*, 128–47; Joan Sangster, *Dreams of Equality: Women on the Canadian Left, 1920–1950* (Toronto: McClelland and Stewart, 1989); Ivan Avakumovic, *The Communist Party in Canada: A History* (Toronto: McClelland and Stewart, 1975); Merrily Weisbord, "Total War" and "Underground," in *The Strangest Dream: Canadian Communists, the Spy Trials, and the Cold War* (Montreal: Véhicule Press, 1994), 103–10; A. Grenke, "From Dreams of the Worker State to Fighting Hitler: The German-Canadian Left from the Depression to the End of World War II," *Labour / Le Travail* 35 (1995): 65–105; Varpu Lindström, *From Heroes to Enemies: Finns in Canada, 1937–1947* (Beaverton, ON: Aspasia Books, 2000); Ian Radforth, "Political Prisoners: The Communist Internees," in *Enemies Within,* 194–224; Rhonda L Hinther, "'Dear Kate! I Don't Know How You Manage!'" The Ukrainian Left and WWII," in *Perogies and Politics: Radical Ukrainians in Canada, 1891–1991* (Toronto: University of Toronto Press, 2018); Michael Martin, *The Red Patch: Political Imprisonment in Hull, Quebec during World War II* (Gatineau, QC: M. Martin, 2007); Michelle McBride, "The Curious Case of the Female Internees," in *Enemies Within,* 148–70; Cy Gonick, "Underground, Imprisoned, and Interned" in *A Very Red Life: The Story of Bill Walsh* (St. John's, NL: Canadian Committee on Labour History, 2001).

21 For some recent discussion on conscientious objectors, consult *Journal of Mennonite Studies* 25 (2007), which features several articles on conscientious objectors and their experiences during the Second World War. See also Marlene Epp, "Alternative Service and Alternative Gender Roles: Conscientious Objectors in BC during World War II," *BC Studies* 105/106 (Spring 1995): 139–58.

22 In this regard, see Ian Radforth's excellent article, "Ethnic Minorities and Wartime Injustices: Redress Campaigns and Historical Narratives in Late Twentieth-Century Canada," in *Settling and Unsettling Memories: Essays in Canadian Public History*, ed. Nicole Neatby and Peter Hodgins, 369–415 (Toronto: University of Toronto Press, 2012). Also see the introduction—and several of the chapters—in Iacovetta, Perin, and Principe, eds., *Enemies Within*. See also the collection of essays edited by Jennifer Henderson and Pauline Wakeham, *Reconciling Canada: Critical Perspectives on the Culture of Redress* (Toronto: University of Toronto Press, 2013.)

PART I

METANARRATIVES

CHAPTER 1

The Rule of Law and Human Rights in the Twenty-First Century

DENNIS EDNEY

The world today faces grave challenges to the rule of law and human rights. Previously well-established and accepted legal principles are now being called into question in all regions of the world through what I would suggest are ill-conceived responses to terrorism. Many of the achievements in the legal protection of human rights are under attack.

Terrorism does pose a serious threat to human rights and all countries have an obligation to take effective measures against acts of terrorism. Under international law, governments have both a right and a duty to protect the security of all their citizens. However, since September 2001, many countries have adopted new counterterrorism measures that are in breach of their international obligations. In some countries, the post-9/11 climate of fear and insecurity has been exploited to justify long-standing human rights violations carried out in the name of national security. This represents a continuum with patterns evident historically in Canada and elsewhere, as the other chapters in this collection, and perhaps most notably the introduction, demonstrate.

These recent circumstances have led to an intense debate over where the balance lies between the rule of law, human rights, and civil liberties on the one hand and security on the other. In April 2000 U.S. Secretary of State Madeleine Albright described her view of an appropriate balance between security and civil liberties. She stated: "We have found, through experience round the world, that the best way to defeat terrorist threats is to increase law enforcement capabilities while at the same time promoting democracy and human rights."[1]

These remarks would have struck many Western liberal audiences, at the time, as mainstream beliefs, consistent with the rule of law and reflective of values which we prided ourselves on at that time. However, since 9/11, many Western democracies have reappraised the balance described by Secretary Albright and embarked upon a politics of fear to limit civil liberties.

In adopting measures aimed at suppressing acts of terrorism, we are involved in more than a simple utilitarian calculation of security at the expense of our civil liberties or a balancing of the right to security of the many against the legal rights of the few. It is only by upholding our core principles, these standards, these obligations to protect civil liberties that we are able to define the boundaries of permissible and legitimate state action against terrorism.

We are fighting for more than the safety of our citizens, though that is an important objective. We are also fighting for the preservation of our democratic way of life, our right to freedom of thought and expression and our commitment to the rule of law; those liberties which have been hard won over the centuries and which we should hold dear. In our commitment to the rule of law, we cannot compromise on long-standing principles of justice and liberty.

And what do I mean by that lofty phrase "the rule of law"? Simply, that law restrains and civilizes power.

There are those who see the rule of law in negative terms: as a constraint on freedom and creativity; as a series of traps for the unwary; as a set of rules designed to stifle initiative and enterprise. They see the Constitution as a means of enabling courts to frustrate the will of elected bodies (parliaments). To some, the rule of law is thought to require the police to investigate and bring to prosecution every act which infringes upon the "rule book," no matter how harmless or incidental that act might be.

This is not what law is about. The rule of law is meant to be a safeguard, not a menace. I prefer the statement by the political philosopher Edmund Burke, who described civil society as "a partnership not only between those who are living, but between those who are living, those who are dead, and those who are to be born."[2]

Law is not the enemy of liberty; it is its partner.

Those who would place security at the expense of civil liberties could benefit from considering the words of former U.S. Supreme Court Justice William Brennan. As he observed, "There is considerably less to be proud about, and a good deal to be embarrassed about, when one reflects on the shabby treatment civil liberties have received in the United States during times of war and perceived threats to national security. . . . After each perceived security crisis ended, the United States has remorsefully realized the abrogation of civil liberties was unnecessary. But it has proven unable to prevent itself from repeating the error when the next crisis came along."[3] One has to look no further than Guantanamo Bay to understand how easy it is for a nation to fall into lawlessness when it does not get the balance right between security and civil liberties. Guantanamo has been called everything from an off-shore concentration camp to a legal black hole. It is a complex of brutal prisons where hundreds of men and youths from all over the world have been held by the U.S. government under incredibly inhuman conditions and incessant interrogation.

It was in January 2002 that we witnessed the first shocking images of detainees, hooded and shackled for transportation across the Atlantic to Guantanamo Bay, Cuba, much as other human beings had been carried in slave ships 400 years earlier. On their arrival at Guantanamo Bay, we witnessed the humiliation of these anonymous beings, unloaded on the tarmac like so much human baggage to then be transported to open-air wire cages that would be their home for many years—all without access to family, friends, lawyers, human rights organizations, or any semblance of due process or judicial oversight.

Photos of detainees, in orange jumpsuits, crouched in open cages—cuffed, hooded, and masked, while kneeling at the feet of U.S. soldiers, became emblematic of how the United States intended to fight its "War on Terror." For the watching world, no knowledge of international humanitarian conventions was needed to understand that what was being witnessed was unlawful. This was not a manifestation of the Geneva Conventions at work; nor was it an act of deportation or extradition. It was far worse. It was the unlawful transportation of human beings to a world outside the reach of law, and the clear-cut intention of the American authorities was to have them remain so, held indefinitely as internees.

In that world, crimes against humanity were to be carried out in Guantanamo Bay. And, it was into this hellish world that a young Canadian boy, Omar Khadr, was abandoned.

There were simply no boundaries to the human rights violations carried out on Omar and other internees. Organizations such as the International Red Cross, Amnesty International, and Human Rights Watch reported that such violations were standard operating procedures: procedures which included physical and sexual abuse, torture, rape, and even murder.

I would never have envisaged that the history of the new century would encompass such an erosion of moral order. And never in my wildest imagination could I have foreseen in countries such as the United States and Canada the destruction and distortion of fundamental legal and constitutional principles that have been in place since the seventeenth century. We appear to have forgotten the lessons of the Star Chamber, where the accused were submitted to torture, to accusations based on secret evidence, heard by a secret court, while being shackled in extremes of isolation.

During his ten years both at Bagram Theatre Detention Facility in Afghanistan and then Guantanamo Bay, Omar endured repeated interrogations, some by a military interrogation team under the control of Spc. Joshua Claus, who was later implicated in the death of two Bagram prisoners and was convicted of assault, prisoner maltreatment, and lying to investigators in 2005. Claus used a host of torture techniques on Omar; techniques that included beatings, stress positions, water boarding, threats with dogs, hanging in a crucifixion pose on a prison wall for hours at a time, and, of course, psychological terror tactics—all in order to extract evidence.

Claus was eventually given immunity for his abuse of Omar Khadr in return for his testimony at Khadr's trial. His testimony contained statements about what Khadr said to him under duress and abuse. Indeed, in a pre-trial hearing Claus, identified as "Interrogator #1," as much as admitted that Omar had been threatened with the prospect of being "gang-raped to death" in prison if he did not cooperate. Despite this, and despite Claus's own 2005 conviction for assault, prisoner maltreatment, and lying to investigators—which earned him five months in jail—Claus was a star witness against Omar in his murder trial at Guantanamo Bay.[4] Is there any better example of the perversion of the rule of law than this?

I recall my first meeting with a young Omar Khadr in Guantanamo Bay. He was being held in one of the notorious secret prisons, called Camp 5, designated for enhanced interrogation techniques as described by the Pentagon, namely torture.

Shackled to the floor, in a freezing, concrete windowless cell with a harsh fluorescent light bulb on twenty-four hours per day, was the tragic figure of Omar: blind in one eye; partially blind in the other; partially paralyzed on his right side; and his whole body suffering from extensive shrapnel injuries. Meanwhile, his cell was purposely kept cold so that he would never be able to rest, spending much of his time trying to stay warm. In all my years visiting Omar in Guantanamo, he was always restrained by leg shackles.

At some point, I was able to obtain video footage showing American and Canadian intelligence agencies interrogating Khadr while sleep-deprived for three weeks at a time. In a major rebuke to the Canadian government, the

Canadian Supreme Court ruled that the U.S. treatment of Khadr contravened the International Convention on Torture and the Geneva Conventions and that Canada had been complicit in his torture.

There can be no greater rebuke levied against a government that purports to uphold the rule of law than to have participated in the torture of a youth. And what greater betrayal can there be of Canadian values?

The worst excesses of the past years should have sounded loud alarms, not least because of that precise historic parallel to the Star Chamber. We are now witnesses to *Habeas corpus* being abandoned; secret courts being created to hear secret evidence; guilt inferred by association; torture nakedly justified; and vital international conventions consolidated in the aftermath of the Second World War—the Geneva Conventions, the Refugee Convention, the Torture Convention, and more—deliberately avoided or ignored in the "War on Terror" by Western governments, including our own.

International Law

Our generation has had the most sophisticated development of international laws, treaties, and conventions the international community has ever known, all stating that human rights abuses will not be tolerated. These international instruments include the Geneva Conventions, the Convention on Torture, the Convention on the Rights of the Child and many more, all applicable to Omar Khadr and all denied to him. It is no exaggeration to say that the international consensus reflected in the Universal Declaration of Human Rights and the Charter of the United Nations, that no one in the future would fall outside the protection of the law, has been overridden and supplanted by lawlessness.

As a signatory to all these international treaties, Canada has an obligation to protest when they are not being applied to one of its citizens, and yet it refused to uphold its human rights obligations when it came to Omar Khadr. By failing to do so, former Canadian governments have demonstrated a shocking, reckless, and ruthless disregard for those moral and legal laws and principles that are in place to guide us as a civil society, while demonstrating how fragile are laws and their application that we assume are there to protect us when we don't stand up and make our politicians speak out to injustice. As Constance Backhouse, a distinguished Canadian legal scholar, has put it, "some cases enshrine the defining moments of their time. Omar Khadr's case is one. Future generations will rightly judge our shocking dereliction of responsibility in this matter and our collective failure to extend justice and humanity."[5]

In 1941, in his annual State of the Union address, President Franklin Roosevelt told America and the world what he saw as the core values of a democracy, postulating that there were "four essential human freedoms" at the very heart of American democracy: freedom of speech and expression, freedom of worship, freedom from want, and freedom from fear. Most famously he proclaimed that it was protection of, and adherence to, such values which would protect the United States from the illiberal, autocratic, and tyrannical regimes that were then dominating Europe.

While it is easy to see FDR's famous "four freedoms" speech as being about the external threats posed to democracy from fascism and Soviet-style communism, he was also well aware that there were serious internal threats to the ideals of democracy—notably economic inequality. Clearly this is an issue which is with us still—and which has grown as a global problem. But what of "freedom from fear"? It would seem that we are engaged in a battle where fear mongers are trying to convince the citizens of all the democracies that they can only be safe if we limit freedoms—and shut our doors to those in need. In effect, we are facing a new danger from within—and not the sort of fifth column that the purveyors of hatred and fear imagine. Rather, we can no longer assume that our fellow citizens of Western democracies understand the origins of their rights and the importance of liberal democracy.

We are now observing much of the world increasingly responding to a growing international refugee crisis not with compassion, but with xenophobia and racial and religious intolerance. The resettlement of Syrian refugees was a flashpoint in the U.S. presidential election of 2016. Donald Trump's rhetoric on Syrian refugees tapped into many Americans' anxieties about national security and threats of terrorism, particularly when he said, in a 31 August 2016 speech, "we have no idea who these people are, where they come from."

Tragically, the Syrian refugees seeking to move to the United States and other parts of the Western world are amongst the most vulnerable in the Syrian conflict: many are women and children, members of religious minorities, and victims of violence and torture. Yet, the desire to scapegoat and abuse newcomers has become a virus that has affected many countries despite the fact that the refugee crisis is one of the gravest humanitarian crisis to unfold across the world in modern times.

As of late 2016, fully 86 percent of the world's refugees were being hosted by poor and developing countries, near war zones or conflict sites. And more than half of these refugees were children. Indeed, in 2016 one out of every 113 people in the world was classified as a refugee, an asylum seeker, or as an internally displaced person. In all too many ways the situation is sadly reminiscent of refugees fleeing the Nazi onslaught in the late 1930s and early 1940s. Then, too, most Western governments, including Canada's, turned their backs on refugees, and millions who were trapped perished.

These are clearly troubling times. And for those who cherish the rule of law—along with what, prior to 9/11, had been a steadily growing international consensus on human rights and liberties—nothing can be more troubling than recent developments in the United States. President Donald Trump arrived at the White House after a lengthy campaign which witnessed him questioning judicial independence, offering thinly veiled threats to the freedom of the press, promising to resume the use of torture on America's "enemies," guaranteeing that he would build a wall to keep Mexicans out of the United States, insisting that he would impose a de facto ban upon all new immigrants from Islamic states, attacking his fellow Americans based on their gender, race, and religion, and even mocking a disabled reporter for his physical problems. FDR and Eleanor Roosevelt—who knew something about democracy (and about discrimination based upon disability and gender)—must surely be turning in their graves.

While Trump may have emerged as the "Fear Monger in Chief," he has had much support in this endeavour—for fear and resentment "sell" well in politics. And this has come not just from within his inner circle—which included the publisher-in-chief of the "Alt_Right" vehicle *Breitbart,* Steve Bannon—but from his former rivals on the campaign trail as well. Thus, when candidate Trump called for the creation of a database of all Muslims in the U.S., at least three of his rivals for the Republican nomination strove to outdo his Islamophobic rhetoric, but even more to the point, the blogosphere and airwaves were filled with the comments of those who wanted Trump to go even further. It bears repeating: fear sells.

Eroding confidence in public institutions and encouraging fear not only increases public anxiety but fans the flames of intolerance, discrimination, and bigotry. Now, misinformed and fuelled by fear, it is not a difficult step for people to accept that drastic measures must be taken in the interest of national security, even if it means suspending civil liberties, compromising our values, or ignoring the rule of law—we rationalize that it is for the greater good of society. But the deeper objective of such a strategy is to weaken our democratic institutions, as they are obstacles that limit the autocratic powers that the current resident of the White House seems to crave.

Conclusion

The case of Omar Khadr is a landmark for all Canadians to heed so that we preserve our respect for the rule of law. Khadr was a Canadian youth who endured detention in Bagram and in Guantanamo. This young man was charged with multiple offences and in 2010 faced trial in a military tribunal that permitted evidence derived from torture. He accepted legal advice to plead guilty so that he could serve out his time and get out of the legal black hole of Guantanamo Bay, as the alternative would very likely be indeterminate detention. Khadr returned to Canada in 2012 and was released on bail in 2015. He is now married and focuses on his future by attending university.

Although there are tremendous tensions between democratic national sovereignty, open global markets, and mass migration, the answer to resolving those tensions is not to build high walls. Western societies need to educate, innovate, and provide opportunities. In an age of polarization and vilification, this may seem a lofty aspiration. But democracies have a habit of rising to the challenges they face. Human history is a history not only of cruelty but also of courage, kindness, compassion, and sacrifice. What we choose to emphasize in this complex history will determine our lives. If we only see the worst, it will destroy our capacity to do something positive.

I remain convinced that no government, no tyranny can quash forever the human desire to be free and to live under the only form of government consistent with that desire—representative government installed with the consent of the people. We do not have to engage in grand, heroic actions to participate in the process of change. Small acts, when multiplied by millions of people, can transform the world. Anger, vengeance, and violence are exceedingly easy to access and almost effortlessly unleashed. The higher calling is the belief in the ultimate moral justice and the inevitable victory of righteousness over wrong. We may not have control of world events but we do have control over how we respond to the world. We do have control over how we treat each other. So, in the end, it is not about policies that work; it is about forging consensus; fighting cynicism; finding the political will to make change; and discovering the character to open our hearts to one another. Sometimes courage is the little voice at the end of the day that says, "I'll try again tomorrow."

Notes

1 M. Albright, "U.S. Secretary of State, Speech to the University of World Economy and Diplomacy," Tashkent, Uzbekistan, 17 April 2000.

2 Edmund Burke, "Reflections on the Revolution in France," 1790, *The Works of the Right Honorable Edmund Burke,* vol. 3, 359 (1899).

3 William J. Brennan Jr., "The Quest to Develop a Jurisprudence of Civil Liberties in Times of Security Crises," speech delivered at the Law School of Hebrew University, Jerusalem, Israel, 22 December 1987.

4 Anna Mehler Paperny, "And Then There Were Seven: The Jury Who Will Decide Omar Khadr's Fate," *Globe and Mail,* 11 August 2010.

5 Constance Blackhouse, cited in, "Letter Writing Campaign/Justice for Omar Khadr," *Free Omar: The Official Campaign Website*, 4 April 2016. https://freeomar.ca/2016/04/04/letterwriting-campaign/.

CHAPTER 2

Human Rights and the Politics of Freedom: Civilian Internment in the Canadian Museum for Human Rights

JODI GIESBRECHT

The history and legacy of civilian internment in Canada is examined in several exhibits at the Canadian Museum for Human Rights (CMHR), located in Winnipeg, Manitoba. This chapter will provide an overview of these installations, discussing the curatorial strategies used, as well as some of the opportunities and challenges faced in representing these complex issues through exhibition mediums that make heavy use of digital technologies and a limited amount of written text or material artifacts. Difficult content can be challenging to curate, especially within the context of public institutions such as national museums. As the essay in this collection by Emily Cuggy and Kathleen Ogilvie demonstrates, considerable thought and sensitivity must be applied to all stages of the exhibition development process. The "politics of freedom" provides a useful conceptual framework for this discussion of the CMHR's internment-related exhibitions, one that considers the historically specific ways in which discourses of exclusion, citizenship, detainment, and resistance intersect with evolving national debates over the meaning, scope, and consequences of human rights in Canada.

The Canadian Museum for Human Rights opened its doors to the public in September 2014 with the mandate "to explore the subject of human rights, with special but not exclusive reference to Canada, in order to enhance the public's understanding of human rights, to promote respect for others and to encourage reflection and dialogue."[1] Over ten years in the making, the CMHR began as the vision of late media mogul Israel Asper, who desired to establish a centre for human rights and Holocaust education in Winnipeg. In 2008, the museum became a federal institution jointly funded by the City of Winnipeg, the Province of Manitoba, the Government of Canada, and hundreds of private donors. It is the first federal museum to have been built from the ground up since 1967, and the first established outside the national capital region.

The development of exhibition content and the design of the museum's galleries also took place over a number of years. Content development began in earnest in 2009 during a series of cross-Canada public engagement sessions, when museum representatives were joined by a Content Advisory Committee that was comprised of seventeen well-known human rights scholars, activists, and experts, who travelled throughout each province and territory to hear first-hand from Canadians about the kinds of stories and issues they wished to see in a museum for human rights.[2] The results of these meetings were summarized and published in a 2010 report, which guided the continued selection of content at the museum. Content was further researched and developed by the museum's in-house subject matter experts, and was peer reviewed by a large number of external experts.[3] Graphic design, media production, image and artifact sourcing, text writing, and related components of exhibition development occurred collaboratively, as is standard practice in museums, amongst teams of curators, designers, filmmakers, media producers, educational programmers, interpretive planners, and many others.

The museum's ten core galleries, totalling 47,000 square feet of exhibit space, include historical and contemporary content from all parts of the world and provide different perspectives on the expansive subject of human rights. The Canadian Journeys gallery, the largest gallery in the CMHR in which stories of civilian internment are represented, examines over seventy issues in 10,000 square feet of exhibit space. Some of the criteria used in selecting content to represent Canadian history include the representation of stories from all regions of Canada, the examination of Canada's constitutional architecture, the integration of past and present human rights issues, and the acknowledgement of diversity—in terms of region, language, culture, politics, class, gender, sexual orientation, gender identity, ability, race and ethnicity, age, and so on.[4]

Balancing a consideration of both steps and missteps, of rights won and lost, the Canadian Journeys gallery also presents differing perspectives and points of view, often told through first-hand accounts and oral histories. Relying heavily on new media and digital platforms, this kind of narrative storytelling departs from the reliance on grand narratives and fixed conclusions typically contained within museums. Rather, the assemblage of stories, images, films, artifacts, and other exhibit elements are arranged in a non-linear, non-teleological fashion, in order to reflect the complexity and diversity of Canada's human rights history. As reviewers of the gallery have noted, the very idea of a singular perspective or narrative would not be in keeping with human rights practices. An inclusive and decolonized view of Canada's human rights history is instead comprised of multiple views and diverse stories that encompass a range of subjects and issues.[5]

There are several distinct exhibit elements in Canadian Journeys. Along the perimeter of the gallery, eighteen 8' x 8' story niches or alcoves combine text, images, artifacts, digital interactives, and media to examine a variety of human rights issues, including the Winnipeg General Strike, the Chinese head tax, missing and murdered Aboriginal women, language rights in Canada, Indian residential schools, women's rights, the Underground Railroad, and many others. A grid of 8' x 8' panels lines the upper perimeter of the gallery, each panel depicting the face of an individual, historical or contemporary, linked in some way to Canada's human rights history. Details about each of the stories on this "Image Grid" are available in digital kiosk stations, as are additional images. While a portion of these images are fixed, printed panels, those images located along the longest wall in the gallery are digitally projected onto a screen approximately 96 feet long and 16 feet tall. Periodically, the single images on the digital wall fade, and the resulting "Digital Canvas" projects a four- to five-minute production that combines still images with limited moving imagery and text. The gallery also consists of an interactive floor game and a film theatre that plays a short production about the historical evolution of human rights in Canada.

Within this gallery, several stories related to civilian internment are told: First and Second World War internment, Japanese Canadian forced relocation, conscientious objection, as well as arrests and detention stemming from the Gouzenko Affair, the October Crisis, and the so-called War on Terror. While these particular episodes are not the only instances of civilian internment in Canadian history, these examples reveal much about discourses surrounding national security, citizenship, liberty, and rights.

Given the mission and mandate of the Canadian Museum for Human Rights, exhibits on internment are also framed within the broader context of human rights and civil liberties in Canada. Episodes of civilian internment are integrated amidst a variety of other historical and contemporary human rights issues, from Indian residential schools to women's rights in twentieth-century

Canada, from the history of racial segregation and discrimination to the Winnipeg General Strike. This broader methodological and curatorial approach reminds visitors of the rich, layered, and diverse stories that make up Canada's human rights history, contextualizing episodes of civilian internment with broader shifts in the evolution of human rights discourse in Canada.

Exhibiting Civilian Internment

The story of wartime internment is told in the Canadian Journeys gallery at the CMHR through a medium that is primarily visual—the printed image grid and the digital canvas. The printed grid story focuses on First World War internment,[6] while the short, five-minute silent film that plays on the digital canvas addresses internment in both world wars.[7] The key messages we hoped to convey included the historical context within which the Canadian government introduced legislation that criminalized segments of the Canadian population on account of ethnicity and political views, the lived experiences of internment and the impact on families and communities more generally, and the ways in which resistance to internment, from both internees and the broader public, eventually contributed to wider campaigns to advance human rights and civil liberties.

In many ways, the treatment of wartime internment in a museum focused on human rights is challenging. The modern concept of "human rights" did not exist at that time. Notions of natural rights, civil liberties, due process, and related concepts have long been part of the general vocabulary, but there were no international declarations of human rights in the contemporary sense, nor a domestic bill of rights or constitutionally entrenched charter of rights.[8] This historical context, alongside factors like widespread xenophobia and wartime anxiety, is difficult to represent through an exhibit that relies heavily on visual assets and limited text.

Conscientious Objectors

The history, experiences, and significance of conscientious objectors during the Second World War is also examined in Canadian Journeys in a media production on the digital canvas. Through still images and a limited amount of text, this exhibit emphasizes the notion of freedom of religion and conscience in addition to the themes of national security, xenophobia, surveillance, and restriction of liberties. The deeper historical context—such as the Canadian government's promise to Mennonites, Hutterites, Doukhobors, and others upon their migration to Canada that their pacifist beliefs would be respected

Figure 2.1. *Canada's "Enemy Aliens,"* Canadian Museum for Human Rights, Winnipeg, Manitoba. Canadian Museum for Human Rights/Jodi Giesbrecht. Image in the digital production is from Library and Archives Canada, photograph by R. Palmer, PA-170535.

in the form of exemption from military service, as well as the discrimination conscientious objectors faced from wider society[9]—was important to convey in this exhibit, as well as the fact that the alternative service camps set up during the Second World War originated from Mennonite conscientious objectors themselves.[10]

If we look at these two digital canvas productions together, the challenges in curating exhibits on First and Second World War internment and on conscientious objectors become apparent. The various categories of difference and definition—within and between "Enemy Alien" and "Conscientious Objector"—resulted from different histories of immigration, settlement, and negotiation with the state. Questions of free will and conscience, too, are complex subjects. The differences between various groups of internees, the complexities of state motivations and legitimizing discourses, and the distinctive responses of internees and their descendants over issues of collective memory, commemoration, and redress are similarly expansive yet nuanced issues.

Yet, when viewing these digital media productions, we notice that these distinct stories share much in common visually.[11] Images depicting groups of men performing labour-intensive tasks in wilderness settings characterize much of the visual evidence we have on these issues; given the limited amount

Figure 2.2. *Under Suspicion: Japanese Canadians and Wartime Rights*, Canadian Museum for Human Rights, Winnipeg, Manitoba. Canadian Museum for Human Rights/Ian McCausland.

of text we could use in these films, specific aesthetic signifiers such as barbed wire or camp uniforms become central to differentiating the stories of wartime internment and conscientious objection.

Japanese Canadian Forced Relocation

The story of the forced relocation, dispossession, and internment of Japanese Canadians during the Second World War is told in one of the seventeen "story alcoves" located around the lower perimeter of the Canadian Journeys gallery. This exhibit makes greater use of material artifacts than do most exhibits at the CMHR, and the majority of objects displayed in this alcove are currently on loan from the Nikkei National Museum in British Columbia. These artifacts include suitcases, Hudson's Bay blankets, and a hishaku or ladle used for cooking.[12] The use of personal and familial belongings is intended to convey the sense of personal experience, representing the few possessions Japanese Canadians were permitted to take with them when they were ordered to relocate and their properties were confiscated. The alcove also exhibits registration cards from two Canadians of Japanese origin, as well as a facsimile of the 1988 Japanese Canadian Redress Agreement, using photographs to also tell the story of community mobilization and action that brought about a formal apology from the federal government under then prime minister Brian Mulroney.[13]

In representing this story, the challenge was to convey not just the context of wartime concerns over national security, but also the long history of racism, xenophobia, and exclusion that preceded the forced relocations.[14] The ways in which historical processes of racialization—marked by gender, class, and related categories of difference and oppression—intersected with alleged concerns over national security during wartime, as well as the resistance, the struggles for equality, justice, and citizenship that culminated in the movement for redress, were some of the key thematic messages that shaped the development of this exhibit.

The Gouzenko Affair

Also represented on the image grid exhibit is the story of Igor Gouzenko, whose defection and subsequent exposure of a Soviet spy ring in Canada led to the detention of several individuals who were seen as potential threats to national security. The civil rights and freedoms of these Canadians, believed to be supplying the Soviets with classified documents, were suspended, despite the questionable rationale provided by state authorities. Aside from the historical significance of this event, the key messages conveyed through this exhibit speak to the ways in which episodes of civilian internment, defended by some in terms of national security, stimulated civil liberties activists and organizations in their calls for greater legislation to check the abuse of state power.[15]

The October Crisis

The October Crisis is also exhibited in one of the seventeen story alcoves that are located around the perimeter of the Canadian Journeys gallery. Its design reflects the broader theme of individual rights versus national security, using props, film, text, and photographs to examine not just the events of the October Crisis but also the historical context in which it occurred and the impact it had on broader discourses of human rights and civil liberties in Canada.[16]

The exhibit replicates an apartment in 1970 Montreal that has been ransacked by police. Props such as a poster of Che Guevera[17] represent some of the broader international discourses of liberation that influenced FLQ supporters' political ideologies, while the presence of prison bars and security cameras speak to issues of state power and surveillance. Visual assets include a front-page article from *The Ottawa Journal* announcing the government's invocation of the War Measures Act, images of Canadian soldiers stationed in downtown Montreal, political cartoons, newspaper editorials, and other primary documents. Alongside a film that examines the October Crisis through archival

Figure 2.3. *Fragile Liberties: Emergency Measures and Quebec's October Crisis*, Canadian Museum for Human Rights, Winnipeg, Manitoba. Canadian Museum for Human Rights/Ian McCausland.

footage as well as interviews with Louis Haines, who was detained at that time, and Alan Borovoy, the founder of the Canadian Civil Liberties Association, visitors see themselves being watched in a monitor. Overlaid on this live feed are questions that prompt reflection on the tension between individual rights and national security.[18]

The War on Terror

The most recent example of civilian internment represented at the CMHR is the use of security certificates in the context of the so-called War on Terror. Told through the image grid exhibit, visible on the wall of the gallery as well as in the digital kiosks in the centre of the gallery, the key messages conveyed in this story relate to the ways in which the Canadian government has used security certificates to detain non-citizens without charge or trial, and without disclosing evidence used against detainees. This particular issue raises important questions about the role of citizenship in cases of civilian internment, particularly given the 2007 Supreme Court ruling that the use of certificates violated detainees' legal rights under the Canadian Charter of Rights and Freedoms and the later upholding of amended laws allowing the continued use of security certificates.[19]

Curatorial Concerns and General Themes

The ways in which episodes of civilian internment have been represented at the Canadian Museum for Human Rights demonstrate the many and varied forms of storytelling that are available to curators of Canada's human rights history. Material artifacts, photographs, historical documents, text panels, and other conventional forms of museological exhibition are joined in the CMHR by exhibit forms that integrate new media and digital technologies in the effort to examine issues ranging from the internment of enemy aliens during the world wars, to the detention of suspected radical members of the FLQ during the October Crisis, to the recent use of security certificates to imprison suspected terrorists. Represented in physical and digital formats, these stories are important ways in which the history and legacy of civilian internment in Canada continues to be told.

An important curatorial concern was to include a sense of lived experiences and personal perspectives within the exhibition. These stories are present in the Museum's installations in a few different ways: in the personal belongings of Japanese Canadian families who were forcibly removed from their homes, in the photographs of First World War internees as they gaze at visitors from behind barbed war, and in the recorded interviews with those detained more recently, such as Louis Haines, who tells his story of confinement in the context of the October Crisis. These personal narratives encourage visitors to consider the impact of internment on individuals and communities, the ongoing effects of history on contemporary life, and the ways in which current understandings of historical injustice have framed campaigns for redress.[20]

Yet, the CMHR's exhibits on civilian internment also speak to some of the curatorial and methodological challenges museums face in representing difficult subject matter through the exhibition medium.[21] Across these diverse forms, the limited use of written text is a factor that constrains the ability to convey contextual information about complex issues. The global scale of the world wars or the War on Terror, for instance, or the historical evolution of the Quiet Revolution in Quebec, the history of peace churches in Canada—these are some of the broader historical considerations that do much to deepen stories of civilian internment, but are difficult to address given strict word counts and limited visual evidence for museological storytelling.

The kind of high-level overview of civilian internment episodes presented in the Canadian Journeys gallery of the CMHR exposes the historical fragility of human rights as well as the agency of those who have mobilized to defend civil liberties against the abuse of state power. While the perceived sources of public fears of subversion have changed over the course of the twentieth and twenty-first centuries, from so-called "enemy aliens" to so-called "jihadists," invoking national security to legitimatize the exercise of state power has remained consistent. Similarly, the cultural and political meanings of citizenship have evolved over time, yet episodes of civilian internment are stark reminders of the interconnections between discourses of belonging and unbelonging, and of the ways in which citizenship has been, and continues to be, bound by notions of race, gender, class, and related categories of differentiation.

Detaining the allegedly deviant few in order to uphold the liberty of the broader citizenry is an argument long used by the state when enacting technologies of surveillance and regulation. In this way, freedom becomes a legitimizing discourse for disciplinary forms of governance, forms which many scholars have described as characteristic of modern nation-states.[22] Following Foucauldian theories of power and discipline, such notions also parallel Gilles Deleuze's concept of "societies of control" in which the freedom from coercion paradoxically necessitates state power to coerce.[23] Viewed from this perspective, episodes of civilian internment have been integral to the evolution of Canadian statehood, and with this, to the exercise of sovereign power over its citizens and subjects.

Still, these instances of discipline and internment have also led to dissent, protest, campaigns for redress, and similar efforts to hold the state accountable for its actions. Over the course of the twentieth century, the view that states ought to be responsible for protecting the rights and freedoms of its citizens evolved, and the failure of the government to live up to these obligations was rendered most acute during and after episodes of civilian internment. Particularly after the Second World War, civil libertarians reacted strongly to the detention of citizens for reasons of so-called national security, and worked to raise greater awareness of and concern for human rights and civil liberties.[24] The politics of freedom have thus also provided grounds for the contestation of definitions of citizenship and for the growth of human rights through the expression of free will and autonomy.

The politics of freedom, then, refers to a kind of flexible, malleable discourse that has been used throughout episodes of civilian internment by both state and civil actors to suspend rights and to defend rights. Viewed from this perspective, freedom is that which both incarcerates and liberates the modern subject. Framing the history and legacy of civilian internment in this way reveals much about the many intersections between individual rights and national security, between state action and human agency, and between democracy and liberty.[25]

Given the complexity of this subject matter, in many ways museum exhibits can only begin to scratch the surface of such issues. Still, many of the themes emerge only when considering episodes of civilian internment at more of a meta- or macro-level, as part of the broader history of human rights, civil liberties, citizenship, and state formation in Canada.[26] Amongst the many meanings and legacies that have stemmed from civilian internment, we hope visitors take from our exhibitions the notion that human rights are historically specific, contested, and fragile—and as such, that they must be continuously fought for.

Notes

1 Bill C-42: An Act to amend the Museums Act and to make consequential amendments to other acts. Library of Parliament, 22 February 2008. Section 15.2.

2 Content Advisory Committee, *Canadian Museum for Human Rights: CAC Final Report*, 2010.

3 In addition to conventional scholarly research methodologies, from archival study to oral history interviewing, the curators sought input from external advisory councils and scholars. Curators and other museum staff draw on input from the CMHR's Human Rights Advisory Council, Standing Indigenous Advisory Council, Inclusive Design Advisory Council, teachers' groups, stakeholder groups, the museum's Board of Trustees, scholars and activists, and other individuals whose stories are told in the exhibitions. Peer reviews and external audits were also conducted on gallery content at various points throughout the content development process to ensure rigour and scholarly integrity. See also Clint Curle, Rhonda L. Hinther, and Jason Luckerhoff, "L'évaluation formative au Musée Canadien pour les droits de la personne" in *Les musées et leurs publics: Savoirs et Enjeux*, dir. L. Daignault, B. Schiele (Quebec: Presses de l'Université du Québec, 2014).

4 *Canadian Journeys*, Canadian Museum for Human Rights, Winnipeg, MB.

5 CMHR internal document.

6 *The War at Home*, Canadian Museum for Human Rights, Winnipeg, MB.

7 *Canada's "Enemy Aliens,"* Canadian Museum for Human Rights, Winnipeg, MB.

8 For an overview of the historical evolution of human rights in Canada, see Ross Lambertson, *Repression and Resistance: Canadian Human Rights Activists, 1930–1960* (Toronto: University of Toronto Press, 2005); Dominique Clément, *Canada's Rights Revolution: Social Movements and Social Change, 1937–82* (Vancouver: University of British Columbia Press, 2008); David Goutor and Stephen Heathorn, eds., *Taking Liberties: A History of Human Rights in Canada* (Don Mills, ON: Oxford University Press, 2013); Janet Miron, ed., *A History of Human Rights in Canada: Essential Issues* (Toronto: Canadian Scholars' Press, 2009).

9 William Janzen, *Limits on Liberty: The Experience of Mennonite, Hutterite, and Doukhobor Communities in Canada* (Toronto: University of Toronto Press, 1990): 168, 170–188, 198, 210–226; *Alternative Service*, http://www.alternativeservice.ca.

10 *Refusing Violence*, Canadian Museum for Human Rights, Winnipeg, MB.

11 Ibid.; *Canada's Enemy Aliens.*

12 Sakamoto, Kazuta, Saito, and Morishita family suitcases, Hudson's Bay blankets, hishaku (ladle), wooden form for making tofu, redress poster, registration cards, exhibit artifacts from the Nikkei National Museum and Cultural Centre, BC. *Under Suspicion: Japanese Canadians and Wartime Rights*, Canadian Museum for Human Rights, Winnipeg, MB.

13 Ibid.

14 For general overviews of this subject, see Ann Gomer Sunahara, *The Politics of Racism: The Uprooting of Japanese Canadians during the Second World War* (Toronto: J. Lorimer, 1981); Ken Adachi, *The Enemy That Never Was: A History of the Japanese Canadians* (Toronto: McClelland and Stewart, 1991); Patricia E. Roy, *Mutual Hostages: Canadians and Japanese during the Second World War* (Toronto: University of Toronto Press, 1990).

15 Exhibit text, *Spies, Safety and Civil Rights*, Canadian Museum for Human Rights, Winnipeg, MB.

16 *Fragile Liberties: Emergency Measures and Quebec's October Crisis*, Canadian Museum for Human Rights, Winnipeg, MB.

17 *Viva Che* (1968), screen print by Jim Fitzpatrick, 2012, Canadian Museum for Human Rights Collection.

18 Ibid.

19 *Detained Without Charge*, Canadian Museum for Human Rights, Winnipeg, Manitoba.

20 The subject of redress has become particularly popular in recent years, on account of the increase in public apologies and campaigns for apologies. For an excellent overview of this subject in the Canadian context, including many insightful essays about the ways in which contemporary political objectives shape our interpretation of the past, see Jennifer Henderson and Pauline Wakeham, eds., *Reconciling Canada: Critical Perspectives on the Culture of Redress* (Toronto: University of Toronto Press, 2013). See also Franca Iacovetta and Robert Ventresca, "Redress, Collective Memory, and the Politics of History" in *Enemies Within: Italian and Other Internees in Canada and Abroad* (Toronto: University of Toronto Press, 2000), 381–405.

21 Scholars and museum theorists have noted that the field of museums and human rights is only just emerging; issues related to curatorial methodologies and museological practices more generally remain under-theorized. See Jennifer Carter and Jennifer Orange, "Contested Terrain: Defining a Human Rights Museology," *Museum Management and Curatorship* 27, no. 2 (2012): 111–27; Richard Sandell and Eithne Nightingale, eds., *Museums, Equality, and Social Justice* (London and New York: Routledge, 2012); Erica Lehrer, Cynthia E. Milton, and Monica Eileen Patterson, eds., *Curating Difficult Knowledge: Violent Pasts in Public Places* (New York: Palgrave Macmillan, 2011).

22 Thomas L. Dumm, *Michel Foucault and the Politics of Freedom* (Lanham, MD: Rowman and Littlefield, 2002). Elisabeth R. Anker has also analyzed the politics of freedom in the case of American melodramatic political discourse. See Elisabeth R. Anker, *Orgies of Feeling: Melodrama and the Politics of Freedom* (Durham, NC: Duke University Press, 2014).

23 Gilles Deleuze, "Postscript on the Societies of Control," *October* 59 (Winter 1992): 3–7; Anker, *Orgies of Feeling*, 9.

24 For an excellent discussion of these issues in the case of Japanese Canadian relocation and internment, see Stephanie Bangarth, *Voices Raised in Protest:*

Defending Citizens of Japanese Ancestry in North America, 1942–1949 (Vancouver: University of British Columbia Press, 2008). Also see Clément, *Canada's Rights Revolution*, and Lambertson, *Repression and Resistance.*

25 For an analysis of the themes of sovereignty and internment in the case of Canada and World War I, see James Farney and Bohdan S. Kordan, "The Predicament of Belonging: The Status of Enemy Aliens in Canada, 1914," *Journal of Canadian Studies* 39, no. 1 (Winter 2005): 74–89.

26 An excellent collection of essays that speaks to these themes in a broad, national, and international context is Gary Kinsman, Dieter K. Buse, and Mercedes Steedman, eds., *Whose National Security?: Canadian State Surveillance and the Creation of Enemies* (Toronto: Between the Lines, 2000).

PART II

INTERNMENT AND THE UKRAINIAN LEFT IN TWO WORLD WARS

CHAPTER 3

Reinserting Radicalism: Canada's First National Internment Operations, the Ukrainian Left, and the Politics of Redress

KASSANDRA LUCIUK

The traditional narrative surrounding Ukrainian Canadian internment during the First World War, especially when written by Ukrainian Canadian scholars and community activists, has been strongly influenced by the products of the redress campaign initiated by the organized community in the 1980s.[1] The redress campaign, as well as the scholarship it inspired, has been of critical value in establishing a necessary historiographical foundation, which highlights internment statistics, experiences of internees in the camps, state-sanctioned xenophobia, and the imposition of racial hierarchies in Canada. Moreover, this work has been of critical value in gathering both public and government interest in the subject.

At the same time, however, this redress-inspired scholarship has omitted elements of the story. In many ways, this has been a strategic choice. Redress activists and scholars of Ukrainian internment have made calculated decisions about how to package information in order to achieve certain social, political, and economic goals for the community.[2] While understandable, this remains problematic, as this scholarship has become the main vessel through which the public has come to understand internment. In turn, it has impacted how the historicity of Ukrainians in Canada is understood and the development of a collective identity centred on this interpretation of the past. As others have noted, efforts to popularize history can often produce monolithic, even hagiographic, narratives that do not properly account for the past.[3] Drawing on her own experience as a historian of Second World War Italian Canadian internment, Franca Iacovetta's contribution to this collection underscores the challenges and consequences faced by those who complicate dearly held—but factually questionable—historical understandings. The politics of commemoration is a complex and emotionally charged business.

But even critics of the redress campaign have not yielded convincing counter-narratives. Some have rightfully pointed out that Ukrainian internees were not innocent farmers snatched from their homesteads. Rather, most were young, single, and often unnaturalized labourers. Others have also pointed out that, in contrast to the idea that the Ukrainian community was irreparably fractured by internment, most "respectable" community elites cared very little about the plight of internees. In fact, most businessmen, clerics, and wealthy farmers saw the internees as an embarrassment, and viewed them with contempt.[4] Yet this is where the deconstruction of received wisdom ends, exposing the largely depoliticized nature of even those narratives that attempt to complement or modify the redress literature.

The intricacies and issues surrounding the formation of useful myth and constructed memory notwithstanding, this chapter is interested in adding to and enriching the depiction of those Ukrainians interned during the First World War by looking beyond the category of ethnicity. While internment following the Red Scare of 1917 was a blatant political action, and has long been noted as such, the first phase of internment (1914–17) is often assumed as an explicitly racial project and a lesser example of political policing. I argue, however, that to conceptualize the internment of Ukrainians in racial terms alone obscures more than it illuminates. In contrast to the Japanese experience during the Second World War, where the entirety of the population was removed from the Pacific Coast to beyond the 100-mile exclusion zone, only approximately 4,000 Ukrainians, out of a total population of 170,000, were interned. I attempt to account for the discrepancy between those eligible for internment and those who found themselves behind barbed wire by examining the activities of the Ukrainian left from 1907 to 1919. In turn, I underscore the political nature of the internment operations and show how most internees incarcerated during the first phase were proletarianized, if not also members of the organized left.

The relationship between internment and radicalism has received some attention within the body of work produced by the Ukrainian community. In *No Streets of Gold: A Social History of Ukrainians in Alberta,* Helen Potrobenko convincingly argues that the internment operations disproportionately, if not exclusively, targeted working-class Ukrainians. The book, however, was written well before the era of redress and met with significant opposition within the community.[5] Other community studies produced outside of academia also drew connections between internment and the working class. Peter Krawchuk's *Our History: The Ukrainian Labour-Farmer Temple Movement in Canada, 1907–1991* and *The Ukrainian Socialist Movement in Canada (1907–1918)* both note the devastating effects of internment on the organized and unorganized Ukrainian left.[6]

The shift towards social history in the postwar period likewise precipitated the study of a more capacious and inclusive array of topics, including ethnicity, radicalism, and labour. In time, these studies not only became acceptable, but also entered a minor golden age. In Canada, several works emerged to problematize existing narratives of Canada as a multicultural, inclusive, and tolerant place. Scholars began exploring various xenophobic and anti-immigrant policies that emerged in the pre-war and interwar period. These studies ranged from critical to Marxist and tended to reflect ethnic groups through a proletarian lens.[7] Gregory Kealey's study of state repression of labour and the left during the First World War stands out, as it clearly highlights the explicitly political use of internment.[8] More recent studies by historians of labour and the left have also drawn connections between political policing and internment during the First World War.[9]

The smoking gun in this story does not exist. Most of the government records on internment have long been destroyed or remain inaccessible to scholars. Regardless, a rigorous re-interrogation of newspapers, memoirs, community profiles, and private archival holdings—all sources underutilized by those interested in internment—add a new dimension to this history. When put together, they elucidate that the internment operations marked the genesis of the state's long interest in the left, bringing new meaning to the well-worn phrase *in fear of the barbed wire fence.* Seen in this light, internment can be understood, at least in part, as a project of cleaving off one of the most vulnerable pieces of the organized left, utilizing the vast powers of martial law, wartime emergency powers, and xenophobia as convenient accelerants. Jim Mochoruk and Rhonda Hinther's individual contributions to this collection underscore this further, illustrating how what happened in the First World War was a key point on a lengthy continuum of concerted state persecution of ethnic radicals.

The main drive in this essay, however, is not to eliminate ethnicity as a useful analytical or explanatory lens only to replace it exclusively with class. Instead, my hope is that it triggers future scholarship to think about internment in a more capacious manner and draw connections to broader historical themes. In other words, rather than understanding internment as a project of ethnic oppression—although it was that too—I posit that scholars need to see it as emblematic of the Canadian project more generally. Internment was not a regretful anomaly, nor a tale of sin and redemption. Rather, it was a reflection of the regular functioning of the state, particularly as it deals with those it deems to be disposable "others." This is but a first attempt at such a rethinking, but historians of capitalism, the state and law, race/ethnicity/migration, the North and hinterland, prisons and incarceration, agriculture and food, and colonialism would be well served to add their voices and perspectives here. Starting an examination of internment with these sorts of foundational understandings will produce significantly different histories than ones starting with ideas of ethnic particularism.

The Origins of the Ukrainian Left in Canada

While Ukrainian migration to Canada began in 1891, there is no evidence of an organized body of progressive-minded Ukrainians before 1896.[10] Initially, some Ukrainians living in industrial centres joined local branches of political parties and trade unions upon their arrival. Others, especially farmers, participated in reading clubs and enlightenment societies organized around their bloc settlements.[11] Following its formation in 1904, the Socialist Party of Canada (SPC) began organizing Ukrainians under its authority.[12] Recognizing their organizational value, the SPC moved quickly to establish Ukrainian sections of the party in 1906. These branches declared their commitment to organizing the Ukrainian Canadian proletariat and leading them "over the ruins of capitalism."[13]

Ukrainian membership in the SPC grew steadily, with at least seven new branches appearing in 1907 alone. The newspaper *Chervonyi Prapor* (The Red Flag) was concomitantly founded, serving as the liaison between the SPC and its Ukrainian constituents. The newspaper helped promote "a clear understanding of the international idea of socialism" and sought to assist the working masses "in the fight against lawlessness, exploitation, and slavery."[14] An examination of *Chervonyi Prapor* in this period reveals both the priorities and concerns of the Ukrainians under the tutelage of the SPC. The newspaper frequently reported on the plight of disillusioned workers and farmers who had not prospered in Canada as they once had hoped.[15] Indeed, it was clear that many were not finding the freedom of yeomanry that they had been promised by government agents and recruiters.[16] Instead, many were employed in the back-breaking labour of railway construction, mining, lumbering, and manufacturing. Like most other workers, they faced deplorable working conditions, poor wages, insecure employment, and high injury and death rates.

Chervonyi Prapor was also steadfastly committed to promoting a radical consciousness amongst its readership. Its pages exposed the hardships of those who were witnessing "the injustice of capitalism" and called for political action amongst a strong and united proletarian army.[17] Relatedly, the newspaper encouraged its readers to join local unions, including the Industrial Workers of the World (IWW), the Western Federation of Miners (WFM), and the United Mine Workers of America (UMWA).[18] Of note was that these were all industrial unions who espoused varying degrees of radicalism. The IWW—and to a lesser extent the WFM—had an overtly revolutionary agenda. Despite its early popularity, *Chervonyi Prapor* shut down in 1908, a victim of the recession. The embryonic Ukrainian left could only sporadically support a newspaper in its inchoate form.[19] A year later, the movement regrouped and a new newspaper, *Robochyi Narod* (The Working People), was founded.[20] Continuing the work of *Chervonyi Prapor*, it frequently reported on the progress of the SPC and, in particular, its Ukrainian sections.[21]

Even within the SPC, an organization committed to revolutionary internationalism, the Ukrainian membership often felt alienated from their English-speaking comrades. In 1909, *Robochyi Narod* featured an appeal in response to the "tactlessness of some of the more prominent English comrades." The Ukrainian leaders condemned the party for relegating its constituents to the background despite Ukrainians paying party dues that were used almost exclusively for English-language propaganda and literature. This was especially offensive, the Ukrainians claimed, in light of the shuttering of *Chervonyi Prapor*.[22] Troubled by their increasingly marginal role, the Ukrainian sections officially severed their ties with the SPC. On 20 July 1910, they united within the Social Democratic Party of Canada (SDPC) under the designation of the Federation of Ukrainian Social Democrats (FUSD).[23] Branches of the FUSD bourgeoned across the country, especially in rural farming communities.

Nativism, Ethnic Radicalism, and the Great War

Despite the organizational strife that characterized the early years of the movement, the FUSD was flourishing by 1910. With twenty-three branches, the organization was reaching nearly 150,000 members of the Ukrainian-speaking proletariat through *Robochyi Narod*. In addition to its ongoing commitment to working-class consciousness, the movement became increasingly preoccupied with countering growing nativist and xenophobic sentiments amongst Anglo-Canadians. The presence of Ukrainians, and other "foreigners," had long elicited considerable hostility in Canada, but it was especially prevalent when Clifford Sifton, minister of the Interior, opened the Prairies to settlement.[24] While the Immigration Acts of Frank Oliver, who replaced Sifton in 1905, were instituted to appease Anglo-Canadians and control the flow of migrants to Canada, business and political interests ensured that these policies were lightly enforced. The Prairies were being settled, new mineral resources were being discovered, and the building of two new transcontinental railways was underway. Large numbers of migrants were needed now more than ever. As one mining authority noted: "What we want is brawn and muscle, and we get it."[25]

Many Anglo-Canadians were also troubled by what they saw as the social deviance of migrant workers. The relationship between radicalism and foreignness was particularly intense during the first decade of the century. This period saw the rise of socialist industrial unions and widespread labour unrest, some of which was organized, or widely participated in, by foreigners.[26] In fact, the Royal North-West Mounted Police (RNWMP) records indicate that by 1900, they had already established meaningful contact with Ukrainian workers, some of whom had taken to carrying weapons and engaging in violence against their bosses.[27] Concerns about migrant workers also extended to organized labour. As David Goutor notes, labour leaders were deeply concerned about the use of migrants by the state to drive down wages and break strikes.[28] Conservative craft unionists in particular strove to protect the working class against "foreigners." While the most vicious attacks targeted Asian immigrants, southern and eastern Europeans were nonetheless seen as a menace to the wages and job security of Anglo-Canadians.[29]

The leadership of the FUSD was well aware of the nativism running rampant in Canada. These conditions increased the hopelessness of many Ukrainians who, shunned from mainstream socio-political life, began to participate with increasing enthusiasm in the FUSD. Capitalizing on its popularity, and hoping to serve a wider purpose amongst its constituents, the FUSD transformed itself into a broad-based socio-political outfit. While this was not yet fully realized in this period, the leadership had agreed in theory that the organization had to expand to provide social, cultural, and educational relief in addition to building the class struggle.

To mark the shift in organizational structure, the FUSD changed its name to the Ukrainian Social Democratic Party (USDP) in 1914. As part of its platform, the organization established relief programs for downtrodden workers in case of illness, accident, or injury at work. It came out against predatory lending, personal debt, and taxes on the working class. Relatedly, it demanded an increase to the minimum wage and the institution of a forty-four-hour work week.[30] These demands were highlighted in the pages of *Robochyi Narod*.[31] As the recession took hold, the newspaper acutely covered the growing issue of unemployment.[32] The editors asked why, "in today's economic system," there were still unemployed workers. The newspaper attacked employers "who care only about profit," pointing to the rise in bankrupt merchants and closed banks and factories as signs that capitalism was not working. "Millions of workers are left without employment," the article noted; "families are falling apart."[33]

In 1914, with a war looming, the organization, alongside the labour movement, reinforced its long held antiwar position.[34] When the Trades and Labour Congress (TLC) reneged on its promise to launch a general strike in case of Canada's involvement in the war, the USDP was far more resolute.[35] "The horrible indigence and hunger of workers has not ended," one author wrote. "Now there is an all-European war, which will further the hunger and poverty of workers, claim many victims, and fill the rivers with workers' blood."[36] Several days later, the newspaper reprinted statements of international socialist leaders who had not fallen under the spell of nationalist war chauvinism, including Karl Liebknecht, Clara Zetkin, and Sen Katayama. USDP leaders also passed a resolution asserting that the First World War was an imperialist war. "We declare that we continue to stand by the principles of international socialism," the declaration stated. "We censure all socialists who support the war in principle and call on the world proletariat to establish a Third Revolutionary International on the ruins of the Second International."[37] The USDP had solidified its position on the war and was mobilizing its membership against it.

Rounding Up the "Enemy Aliens"

Despite being citizens of the Austro-Hungarian Empire, Ukrainians in Canada had little to fear when Canada officially entered the war. The government had issued a series of proclamations that exposed all citizens of enemy countries to threats of arrest and internment, but noted that as long as people "quietly pursued their ordinary avocations," they would be protected.[38] However, when the War Measures Act was passed on 22 August, it gave the government emergency powers to administer the war without accountability to either Parliament or extant legislation. This included basically unlimited power to arrest, detain, deport, and censor.

As a result, between 1914 and 1921, 8,579 "enemy aliens" were interned across the country. An additional 80,000 others were issued identity papers and ordered to report regularly to their local police authorities.[39] According to General William Otter, who led the internment operations, only 3,138 of those interned could be classified as genuine prisoners of war. These prisoners were segregated from the other internees and placed in "first class" camps. The remaining 5,411 were sent to work camps in remote areas of Canada.[40]

The threat of internment was only made worse in the aftermath of PC 1501, which gave the government the power to apprehend and intern "enemy aliens" found impoverished and without work. While PC 1501 was ostensibly justified because it protected "enemy aliens" from rising levels of patriotically inspired xenophobia, it was more than likely instituted as a means of allowing municipalities, in charge of relief, to rid their rolls easily. In fact, these policies disproportionately targeted the migrant working class.

PC 1501 and rising unemployment were both widely discussed within the USDP. *Robochyi Narod* reported on the growing feelings of bitterness and frustration amongst Ukrainians in the wave of dismissals. "Hundreds of unemployed Ukrainian workers," one article noted, "groan from the blow of hunger, and those who have luckily found work suffer unheard of cruel treatment and mockery from employer benefactors."[41] The party recognized that layoffs as a result of the recession almost always targeted ethnic migrants who were let go for so-called patriotic reasons.[42] In British Columbia, UMWA locals were particularly aggressive, demanding the dismissal of all Austrian workers. Eventually, threats of strike and violence convinced the mining companies and the federal government to dismiss, and subsequently intern, over 300 "enemy aliens" in the spring of 1915.[43] In Coal Creek, English and Italian miners refused to return to work until all "enemy aliens" were dismissed by the Crow's Nest Pass Coal Company.[44] Meanwhile, in Fernie and Michel, 370 USDP members were eventually let go, all targets of incensed Anglo-Canadian union members.[45] Meanwhile, in Nanaimo, another 150 members were fired and then interned. Members in Hillcrest, Alberta, met a similar fate.[46]

While the party could do little to protect its constituents from unemployment or quell PC 1501, it did establish a soup kitchen and sleeping quarters for the unemployed.[47] It also began organizing protests and encouraged its members to join other unemployed workers demanding jobs and bread.[48] The Winnipeg branch was particularly active on this front during the early years of the war. Perhaps the largest protest that the USDP was involved in took place on 14 May 1915, when approximately 900 unemployed workers began a march towards the American border. Some were arrested immediately, while close to 200 others were stopped when they reached the border. Those who were considered to be "enemy aliens" were weeded out and sent to Brandon, Manitoba, where they were interned. Others were sent to Winnipeg, "where they have the right to die of starvation."[49] This included both Canadian born and naturalized members of the party.[50] The arrest and internment of protesters was clearly political in nature. That it was the USDP behind these protests indicates the political sympathies of those interned.

By contrast, the government was disinclined to suppress those Ukrainians who made up the economic, political, and religious elite of the community. For example, efforts to stop Ukrainians protesting the end of bilingual education in Manitoba were superficial at best. When both regional and the chief press censors voiced their concerns over these protests, government officials were unwilling to impose any sanctions, reminding the censors that these Ukrainians were Canadian citizens.[51] Curiously, these standards did not apply to Canadian citizens protesting unemployment. Perhaps the most notable example of this double standard was the case of Nykyta Budka, the first bishop of the Ukrainian Catholic Church in Canada. Before Britain's entrance into the First World War, Budka issued a pastoral letter urging Ukrainians in Canada to return home and defend Galicia. When Britain entered the war a month later, Budka retracted his statements.[52] While Budka was spared—exonerated twice by authorities—less prominent Ukrainians paid the price for what were interpreted as his treasonous comments.

While these cases represent some of the more targeted attacks on "enemy aliens," others were interned without such clear-cut reasoning. Surviving records of the internment operations indicate numerous reasons for internment, including refusing or failing to register, breaking parole, destroying registration cards, travelling without permission, registering under a false name, writing to relatives in Austria, and holding status as a foreign reservist. Other less tangible reasons included acting in a suspicious manner, showing a tendency toward sedition, using seditious or intemperate language, and being unreliable, of a shiftless character, or simply undesirable. In his memoir, a USDP member from Toronto recalled being randomly stopped on the street by the police. When he told them he was from Austria, the officer immediately arrested him and delivered him to the Stanley Barracks where he was held for a week. On Christmas Day, he arrived at the Kapuskasing,

Ontario, internment camp, where he remained for three years.[53] Definitive reasoning as to why he was stopped on the street and subsequently interned remains unclear. The RNWMP was not randomly asking Torontonians their respective nationalities, so to pick one man, a socialist and a Ukrainian, out of a crowd perhaps speaks to more than mere luck.

All the while, military authorities in Regina, Calgary, Edmonton, and Winnipeg were informing ethnic newspapers that they would be suppressed if they "incited feelings against Great Britain." This was justified by claims in surveillance circles that newspapers kept migrants "in a state of unrest."[54] In the case of the USDP, it was not just the newspaper that troubled government officials. Three months into the war, J.A.M. Aikins, a Winnipeg millionaire, prominent Tory, and future lieutenant-governor of the province, warned Prime Minister Borden that "the foreigners in the North End" might take advantage of the war "for the destruction of property. . . . and other crazy wicked things."[55] This, and other warnings, did not go unnoticed. Some USDP leaders, otherwise employed and innocent of any wrongdoing, were interned in 1915. The hardest hit hub of USDP activity was Winnipeg, where all but one member of the executive committee was arrested and interned. In fact, the situation in Winnipeg became so dire that the organization had to form a temporary emergency executive to conduct its affairs.[56]

The organizational structure was deeply affected by internment. In July of 1915, the temporary Central Executive Council of the USDP and the administrative committee of *Robochyi Narod* met to discuss the future of the movement. Of particular significance was the question of what to do with *Robochyi Narod,* which they had planned to move to Winnipeg before the outbreak of the war. The move seemed impossible "in view of the fact that Western branches have been broken up by the mass arrests of comrades by the military authorities."[57] At first, it was decided that the eastern branches, who had been less affected by internment, would run the newspaper. Following a formal referendum, however, the branches agreed to still move the newspaper to Winnipeg, but convert the newspaper into a monthly instead.[58] After only one year of internment, the damage on the movement was clear. As one provincial police report noted, "there has been less trouble amongst them since the beginning of the war." That some had been interned "seemed to have a good effect on the remainder."[59]

By 1915, reports of the widespread internment of USDP members became commonplace in the pages of *Robochyi Narod.* The newspaper noted that USDP members could be found in various camps across the country, including Brandon, Manitoba; Vernon, British Columbia; Lethbridge, Alberta; Kapuskasing, Ontario; and Spirit Lake, Quebec. Writing from Spirit Lake, USDP member Yuri Drobey informed the party that there were over 800 incarcerated Ukrainian workers in the camp.[60] Some USDP members were interned unbeknownst to their family and friends. *Robochyi Narod* ran missing persons ads between 1914 and 1915. The ads were exclusively for young, single men missing from the industrial hubs of Canada. That the ads were being run in the pages of *Robochyi Narod*, as opposed to any other Ukrainian newspaper, reveals something about the sympathies, and even political affiliation, of the missing men and their families.

Organizing the Camps

Daily existence in the camps was difficult.[61] Not only were internees expected to construct their own camps, but they were also required to clear land, build roads, cut wood, and construct railways. For many, internment took a physical toll. Altogether, 107 internees died —69 of them Austrians, which included Ukrainians. Watson Kirkconnell, who served at both the Kapuskasing and Fort Henry camps, observed that amongst the internees there were "few on whom the long years of captivity had not left their mark."[62]

Word of camp conditions spread quickly among readers of *Robochyi Narod*. The 28 August 1915 issue of the newspaper featured an article by an internee. "Who built the railroads and cultivated this wasteland where formerly only wind howled? We, the victims," he bemoaned, "who today are being tortured. Make our cause known so that all Ukrainians and all the nations of the world might see how the blind, 'civilized' English chauvinists and their Canadian hangers on treat foreigners."[63] In September of 1915, the newspaper printed an update from the internees being held at Castle Mountain, Alberta. "The conditions of Canadian slavery . . . are not just shameful and inhumane," he wrote, "they are worse than hell. Hell is nowhere near as bad as the captivity that we are experiencing."[64] A month later, in October, Dmytro Tkachyk wrote to the newspaper that men were being driven at bayonet point, chained, and fed a diet of bread and water for insubordination. Yet another internee described the mistreatment when internees were too sick to work, noting that a guard struck him with his rifle.[65]

General Otter confirmed cases of mistreatment when he noted that the various complaints of prisoners regarding the rough conduct of the guards "is not altogether without reason and is, I am sorry to say, by no means an uncommon occurrence." Samuel Reat, a U.S. consul in Calgary, wrote that incidences of mistreatment "are not only proved but admitted by the authorities. Guards have cuffed prisoners on the slightest provocation and the conduct of some sergeants has been extremely reprehensible."[66]

In several internment camps, ill treatment and exploitation was often answered with insubordination and resistance.[67] In 1915 alone, there were several escape attempts from the Brandon internment camp and, in the spring, three Ukrainians were actually successful at escaping. It was not until February 1916 that one of them was finally discovered hiding in Stuartburn, Manitoba. In May, another internee escaped by jumping over the barbed wire from a second-floor window. He managed to get within nine miles of the American border before being apprehended. Later that month, two more internees also fled the camp. In June, there was another escape attempt by seventeen Ukrainians, resulting in the fatal shooting of one and the pitchforking of several others.[68]

Noncompliance was especially common in Kapuskasing. As one of the largest internment camps, it hosted approximately 1,300 "enemy aliens." The most frequent acts of defiance included slowdowns, sabotage, and work interruptions. This involved breaking tools, throwing axes into the river, and hiding in the woods during work hours.[69] There were also more serious confrontations between the internees and the guards. Three months after its opening, 100 new prisoners were transported from Toronto to Kapuskasing. The next morning, the new prisoners refused to work. When the commandant informed them that they had to work because they had been provided with clothing, the internees took off their camp-issued clothes. As punishment, they were ordered onto the ice, where the soldiers forced them to march. Those who fell were hit with clubs.[70]

A particularly egregious incident in Kapuskasing involved internees who refused to pledge their full obedience to the commandant. Their barracks were stripped of all possessions and their food was thrown in the river. They were then herded into their barracks and guarded by armed soldiers. Every few hours, the men were called to the commandant's office one by one and asked if they would be obedient. The longer they refused, the longer they were deprived of food and water. This exercise was repeated until every internee conceded.

In 1916, a full-scale riot broke out after 1,200 internees refused to work on a religious holiday. The conflict culminated with camp guards opening fire. Fortunately, less than a dozen internees were seriously injured.[71] On the day of the feast of the Virgin Mary, the internees rioted again after they were denied the right to observe the holiday. Deprived of food and forced to march, they exerted what little control they had by praying and singing as they marched.[72]

As the practice of internment was an intrinsically political activity, it concentrated activists and new recruits for the cause in compact locations. This centralization had the predictable effect of allowing organizers to practice their trade in a greenhouse-like environment. Although internees came from different geographic areas, political backgrounds, and work sites, their common experiences in the camps surely made for quick and easy organizing. A miner from British Columbia had a tremendous amount in common with a rail worker from northern Ontario even when outside of the camps, but within, their mutual interests were magnified a thousand-fold. In fact, reporting to *Robochyi Narod* from Brandon, USDP members noted that the 820 Ukrainians interned there were increasingly turning to political organizing and building class consciousness. Of particular significance was the ability of USDP members to organize reading clubs, which served as the basis for organizing and consciousness building in the camps.[73]

The First Red Scare

While some internees remained incarcerated, most were released by 1917 because caring for them was becoming burdensome and expensive. Those who were physically fit, and deemed not dangerous, were paroled to work for private businesses, the government, and railway companies who relied on the internees to solve labour shortage problems. Regardless, hostility towards "enemy aliens" continued. This was, in large part, the result of the Russian Revolution, which heightened the perception of Ukrainians as "radical aliens."[74] This perception was not entirely without merit; the revolution was widely celebrated within the USDP, revitalizing and inspiring many of its demoralized constituents.[75] But the transformation of Ukrainians, and others, into "radical aliens" was also part of a larger pattern of worker militancy that peaked in Canada in 1919.[76] Canadian workers, increasingly troubled by the deterioration of wages and the threat of unemployment, turned to militant industrial unions to protect them.[77] Unlike the early years of the war when radicalism could be blamed on German and Austrian enemy agents and propaganda, rising worker militancy shifted the blame onto Canada's working class, especially those who were deemed "others."

The RNWMP and the Dominion Police diligently investigated the radical elements within the labour movement and organized left more generally.

Borden commissioned Montreal lawyer C.H. Cahan to recommend ways of suppressing Canada's more radical elements.[78] Two months later, Cahan reported there was, in fact, widespread unrest amongst the working class. This discontent, he suggested, was expressed in "labour agitation and strikes, in attempts to avoid the Military Service Act, in mutterings against food prices, in criticism of the treatment of returned soldiers, in the prevalent suspicion that discrimination is shown in the collection of federal taxes, and in general discontent with the administration of the federal departments." Cahan also noted that the "mental unrest" experienced by ethnic radicals was "directly attributable to the dissemination in Canada of the Socialistic doctrines, espoused by the Russian Revolutionary element, and more recently by the Bolshevik Party in Russia." He recommended that all Bolshevik propaganda and political organizations be aggressively suppressed, and all Russian, Finnish, and Ukrainian nationals be treated as if they were "enemy aliens."[79]

Bulletins in *Robochyi Narod* confirmed that Cahan's recommendations were being implemented, as police raids and arrests were being made almost daily. The bulletins also revealed that more USDP members had been interned in Kapuskasing, Lethbridge, Brandon, and Vernon. Some of these internees remained in the camps as late as 1920.[80] Despite these alarming developments, the newspaper urged USDP members not to lose heart over the persecution of socialism because "such acts were [now] taking place all over the world." Nonetheless, the newspaper recommended that its readers carry their registration cards everywhere and be "absolutely careful in conversations, especially when they are not acquainted with the people around them."[81]

When the federal government banned the printing of any publications in an "enemy language," all public meetings in the aforementioned "enemy languages," and fourteen organizations including the USDP, *Robochyi Narod* told its readers that if they did not receive the next issue of the paper "it is a sign that the . . . law has been put into effect."[82] After nearly ten years of propagating socialism to Ukrainian-speaking workers, this would be the final issue of the newspaper. Another wave of arrests swept the USDP shortly after, when a list of "Chief Agitators in Canada" was released. Many were arrested for possessing objectionable literature, belonging to unlawful associations, and attending illegal meetings. They were incarcerated in the final phase of the internment operations.[83]

While the USDP and *Robochyi Narod* were banned, and some members remained interned, the movement carried on, albeit in a different form. Luckily, earlier discussions to transform the organization into a broad-based socio-cultural society were quickly acted on, and the Ukrainian Labour Farmer Temple Association (ULFTA) was born. Through the ULFTA, former members of the USDP continued the work of the organization, including the construction of the first labour temple in Winnipeg.[84]

Branches of the ULFTA spread to other locales. By 1919, its official organ, *Ukrainski Robitnychi Visty* (Ukrainian Labour News), was established. The transformation of the organization, however, did not take the heat off. When the Winnipeg General Strike erupted on 15 May 1919, several thousand Ukrainian workers actively participated, with the labour temple serving as a base for much of the labour action. Eventually, the authorities raided the labour temple and arrested, interned, or deported several individuals. As a result, the mark of "enemy alien" only intensified, with the state and its allies amongst the business elite eager to take advantage of widespread fear of Bolshevism.

Deportation in particular was a real concern amongst members of the Ukrainian left still interned. Many saw what had happened in Winnipeg as a terrifying precedent, as camp commanders were asked to identify internees who they deemed bitter against Canada or Great Britain, agitators, strike fomenters, troublemakers, members of the IWW, and even those who were "decidedly eccentric." Some 1,964 "enemy aliens," 302 of whom were classified Austrian, were found guilty and deported.[85] This only increased the flow of Ukrainians into the ULFTA and related radical outfits.

Conclusion

The internment operations had a lasting legacy on members of the Ukrainian left. For one, internment triggered the creation of the ULFTA. The organization was a clear outcome of the USDP's premonitions of continued government suppression and eventual destruction. The founders hoped that the ULFTA would become a broad-based organization that could dialectically use culture as a recruitment tool and a shield from government repression. Its mandate to accept all Ukrainians, regardless of whether they had accepted revolutionary and socialist ideas, offered the ULFTA an opportunity to expand the movement. As Matthew Popovich, a leading figure in the ULFTA, noted: "It became obvious that [the organization] must take this opportunity to organize a mass cultural-education association, which would attract those workers who until now have not joined our existing organizations but have shown great interest in the building of a Ukrainian labour temple." To turn these people away, he added, "would be a crime against our movement."[86]

Attracting Ukrainians into the new organization was a relatively easy task. For those already invested in revolutionary and socialist politics, the period of 1917 to 1919 saw the increasing normalization of progressive and socialist thought in Canadian society, even as the propaganda of the Red Scare militated against it. Moreover, the quadrupling of union membership provided the ULFTA with a huge number of potential recruits. For progressive and socialist Ukrainians, then, the ULFTA served as a timely vehicle for their hopes and dreams, and as a vector for organized activity.

For those who did not hold revolutionary or socialist politics, continued resentment over state-sanctioned censures, wartime xenophobia and widespread anti-immigrant sentiments, profiteering scandals, inflation, and anti-worker rhetoric pushed them toward embracing the politics of the left. Indeed, the ULFTA became an outlet for socio-economic complaints, a cultural and educational cornerstone, and a vessel for radical change. The organization advanced the interests of workers and, perhaps most importantly, provided its membership with a sense of community and dignity. The ability of the organization to continue this work in the face of continued discrimination accorded it tremendous legitimacy within the community and, eventually, the opportunity to publicly represent what being a Ukrainian in Canada meant and looked like. This deeply influenced the way in which many Ukrainians came to understand their relationship with Canada, each other, and even themselves.

Internment also illuminates the relationship between the government and the Ukrainian Canadian left. That the ranks of internees were drawn mainly from the working class and/or members of the USDP certainly enhances the notion that this was an organized attack. An examination of the strength of pre-war socialist and revolutionary thought, the campaign to arrest and intern "enemy aliens," the sympathies and activities of those interned, resistance in the camps, and the eventual eradication of the USDP leaves little imaginative room as to the ultimate goals of internment. With this in mind, the connection between this early period and later interventions—including the Winnipeg General Strike, the Workers' Revolt, the haunting specter of Section 98, and the internment of ULFTA members during the Second World War and state surveillance of these members well beyond the war—becomes ever clearer.

More generally, internment reveals how the Canadian government has traditionally dealt with those it deems undesirable "others." For state officials, internees were nothing more than instrumentalized bodies meant to build the country but not join the nation. There were many paths to internment—bad luck, poverty, unemployment, political activism—but all internees shared the commonality of being marked disposable by the state.

Notes

1 For a summary of the redress-inspired literature, and its concomitant arguments, see Lubomyr Luciuk, ed., *Righting an Injustice: The Debate Over Redress for Canada's First National Internment Operations* (Toronto: Justinian Press, 1994).

2 For an overview of Canadian redress campaigns, see Ian Radforth, "Ethnic Minorities and Wartime Injustices: Redress Campaigns and Historical Narratives in Late Twentieth-Century Canada," in *Settling and Unsettling Memories: Essays in Canadian Public History,* ed. Nicole Neatby and Peter Hodgins (Toronto: University of Toronto Press, 2012).

3 Orest Martynowych, "Re: internment of Ukrainian Canadians," reproduced in *Righting an Injustice*, 65; and Frances Swyripa, "The Politics of Redress: The Contemporary Ukrainian-Canadian Campaign," in *Enemies Within: Italian and Other Internees in Canada and Abroad,* ed. Franca Iacovetta, Roberto Perin, and Angelo Principe (Toronto: University of Toronto Press, 2000), 355–78.

4 Peter Melnycky, "Badly Treated in Every Way: The Internment of Ukrainians in Quebec during the First World War," in *The Ukrainian Experience in Quebec,* ed. Myroslaw Diakowsky (Toronto: Basilian Press, 1994), reprinted and cited from http://www.infoukes.com.

5 Helen Potrobenko, *No Streets of Gold: A Social History of Ukrainians in Alberta* (Vancouver: New Star Books, 1977).

6 Peter Krawchuk, *Our History: The Ukrainian Labour Farmer Movement in Canada 1907–1991* (Toronto: Lugus Publications, 1996); Peter Krawchuk, *The Ukrainian Socialist Movement in Canada 1907–1918* (Toronto: Progress Books, 1979).

7 The most prominent examples include Ivan Avakumovic, *The Communist Party in Canada: A History* (Toronto: McClelland and Stewart, 1975); John Herd Thompson, *The Harvests of War: The Prairie West, 1914–1918* (Toronto: McClelland and Stewart, 1978); Daphne Read, ed., *The Great War and Canadian Society: An Oral History* (Toronto: New Hogtown Press, 1978); Donald Avery, *Dangerous Foreigners: European Immigrant Workers and Labour Radicalism in Canada, 1896–1932* (Toronto: McClelland and Stewart, 1979); Howard Palmer, *Patterns of Prejudice: A History of Nativism in Alberta* (Toronto: McClelland and Stewart, 1985); Barbara Roberts, *Whence They Came: Deportation from Canada 1900–1935* (Ottawa: University of Ottawa Press, 1988); Gregory Kealey, *Workers and Canadian History* (Montreal and Kingston: McGill-Queen's University Press, 1995); and Donald Avery, *Reluctant Host: Canada's Response to Immigrant Workers, 1896–1994* (Toronto: McClelland and Stewart, 1995).

8 Gregory Kealey, "State Repression of Labour and the Left in Canada, 1914–20: The Impact of the First World War," *Canadian Historical Review* 73, no. 3 (1992): 281–314.

9 Michel Beaulieu, *Labour at the Lakehead: Ethnicity, Socialism, and Politics, 1900–35* (Vancouver: UBC Press, 2011); Reg Whitaker, Gregory Kealey, and Andrew Parnaby, *Secret Service: Political Policing in Canada from the Fenians to Fortress America* (Toronto: University of Toronto Press, 2012).

10 Krawchuk, *The Ukrainian Socialist Movement,* 1–3.

11 James Darlington, "The Ukrainian Impress on the Canadian West," in *A Nation of Immigrants: Women, Workers, and Communities in Canadian History, 1840s–1960s,* ed. Franca Iacovetta, with Paula Draper and Robert Ventresa (Toronto: University of Toronto Press, 1998).

12 It is unclear where the first Ukrainian branch of the SPC was established as three branches appeared almost simultaneously in Winnipeg, Portage La Prairie, and Nanaimo. There was a total of 101 members in the three Ukrainian branches. Of course, these numbers do not account for the Ukrainians who joined general branches of the party in cities where Ukrainian branches were not available. Krawchuk, *The Ukrainian Socialist Movement,* 7.

13 Ibid., 4.

14 Ibid., 5–8. Particularly noteworthy was the circulation of the SPC platform, which, within six months, had been distributed over 8,000 times. See "Platform of the Canadian Socialist Party," *Robochyi Narod,* 1 May 1910, Stavroff-Krawchuk Collection. The collection is a private collection under the care of Larissa Stavroff. The translation is the author's own.

15 For more on early Ukrainian settlers in Canada, see Michael Marunchak, *The Ukrainian Canadians: A History* (Winnipeg: Ukrainian Free Academy of Sciences, 1970); and Orest Martynowych, *Ukrainians in Canada: The Formative Period, 1891–1924* (Edmonton: Canadian Institute of Ukrainian Studies, 1991). Corroborating accounts of early Ukrainian immigration provide some insight into the difficulties of adjusting to life in a new land. See, for example, Potrobenko, *No Streets of Gold,* especially 23–61; and Vera Lysenko, *Men in Sheepskin Coats: A Study in Assimilation* (Toronto: Ryerson Press, 1947).

16 Avery, *Reluctant Host,* 29.

17 *Chervonyi Prapor,* 29 November 1907. Stavroff-Krawchuk Collection. This is perhaps best expressed through its call to action for May Day. See, for example, "The First of May," *Robochyi Narod,* 1 May 1910 and "How to Commemorate 1 May," *Robochyi Narod,* 1 May 1911. Stavroff-Krawchuk Collection.

18 Avery, *Dangerous Foreigners,* 53–59. Indeed, the Winnipeg branch of the IWW was headed by Dmytro Stechyshyn, a Ukrainian SPC member. For more on the IWW and ethnic workers, see Melvyn Dubofsky, *We Shall Be All: A History of the Industrial Workers of the World* (Chicago: University of Illinois Press, 2000); A. Ross McCormack, *Reformers, Rebels, and Revolutionaries* (Toronto: University of Toronto Press, 1977), especially Chapter 6; and Mark Leier, *Where the Fraser River Flows: The Industrial Workers of the World in British Columbia* (Vancouver: New Star, 1990).

19 Krawchuk, *The Ukrainian Socialist Movement,* 9.

20 *Robochyi Narod* proclaimed itself the only Ukrainian periodical on this continent published by and for the working class alone. The title page featured the slogan: "write for a sample and hand it to your Ukrainian neighbor. It will do him good." *Robochyi Narod,* 1 May 1910. Stavroff-Krawchuk Collection.

21 Krawchuk, *Our History,* 6. New branches were formed in Edmonton, Calgary, Hosmer, Brandon, Montreal, Vancouver, Cardiff, and Canmore.

22 *Robochyi Narod,* October 1909. Stavroff-Krawchuk Collection.

23 For more on the break from the SPC, see Krawchuk, *Our History* and *The Ukrainian Socialist Movement.*

24 Avery, *Dangerous Foreigners*; Palmer, *Patterns of Prejudice*; Roberts, *Whence They Came.*

25 Quoted in Donald Avery, *Reluctant Host*, 33.

26 Palmer, *Patterns of Prejudice*, 54.

27 Myron Momryk, "The Royal Canadian Mounted Police and the Surveillance of the Ukrainian Community in Canada," *Journal of Ukrainian Studies* 28 (2003), 1.

28 David Goutor, *Guarding the Gates: The Canadian Labour Movement and Immigration, 1872–1932* (Vancouver: UBC Press, 2007). Goutor is primarily interested in the organizations that were affiliated with the Trades and Labour Congress (TLC). As A. Ross McCormack notes, the TLC was a national labour organization dominated by the larger, more conservative eastern unions. See McCormack, *Reformers, Rebels, and Revolutionaries*. For more on strike breaking and immigrant labour see Avery, *Reluctant Host*, 35.

29 Goutor, *Guarding the Gates*, 5.

30 Krawchuk, *Our History*, 17.

31 For example, updating the readership on national strikes remained critical. For example, "Strike!," 1 April 1911; "Strike in Cobalt," 8 May 1912; and "Strike in Toronto," 14 May 1913. Stavroff-Krawchuk Collection. The newspaper would also report on the working-class experience more generally. "Police Shoot Innocent Man," 21 May 1913; "Bad Times," 13 July 1913; and "Catastrophe in Hillcrest, AB," 8 July 1913. Stavroff-Krawchuk Collection.

32 "Voices of the Tired" and "Unemployment in Calgary," *Robochyi Narod*, 8 July 1913.

33 "Why Are There Unemployed Workers?" *Robochyi Narod*, 2 April 1913. Stavroff-Krawchuk Collection.

34 The organization had long made its antimilitarism and antiwar position known. For example, articles had previously appeared in *Robochyi Narod* condemning capitalist aggression in the Balkans. "The Socialists and the War," *Robochyi Narod*, 27 November 1912. Stavroff-Krawchuk Collection.

35 McCormack, *Reformers, Rebels, and Revolutionaries*, 119.

36 "The Proletariat and the War," *Robochyi Narod*, 2 September 1914. Stavroff-Krawchuk Collection.

37 Krawchuk, *The Ukrainian Socialist Movement*, 56.

38 See, for example, "Proclamation respecting immigrants of German or Austro-Hungarian nationality, 15 August 1914," in *Loyalties in Conflict: Ukrainians in Canada during the Great War*, ed. Frances Swyripa and John Herd Thompson (Edmonton: Canadian Institute of Ukrainian Studies, 1983), 171–73.

39 Lubomyr Luciuk, *Without Just Cause: Canada's First National Internment Operations and the Ukrainian Canadians, 1914–1920* (Kingston: Kashtan Press, 2006), 9.

40 Lubomyr Luciuk, *In Fear of the Barbed Wire Fence: Canada's First National Internment Operations and the Ukrainian Canadians, 1914–1920* (Kingston: Kashtan Press, 2001), 14.

41 Quoted in Donald Avery, "Ethnic and Class Tensions in Canada, 1918–20: Anglo-Canadians and the Alien Worker," in *Loyalties in Conflict*, 80.

42 Avery, *Dangerous Foreigners*, 67.

43 Avery, "Ethnic and Class Tensions in Canada," 80.

44 See Wayne Norton, "Remembering the History of Interned Miners," *The Free Press* (Fernie, BC), 1 June 2015.

45 "News," *Robochyi Narod*, 23 June 1915. Stavroff-Krawchuk Collection.

46 Krawchuk, *Our History*, 24.

47 *Robochyi Narod,* 28 October 1914. Stavroff-Krawchuk Collection.

48 Krawchuk, *Our History,* 18. The IWW was similarly active in organizing unemployment marches. In Edmonton, approximately 600 workers (80 percent of whom were Slavs) took to the streets in 1914. As a result of another protest, thirteen "foreigners" were arrested for eating a restaurant meal and not paying for it. See Potrobenko, *No Streets of Gold,* 93–95; and David Schulze, "The Industrial Workers of the World and the Unemployed in Edmonton and Calgary in the Depression of 1913–1915," *Labour/Le Travail* 25 (1990).

49 *Robochyi Narod,* 19 May 1915. Stavroff-Krawchuk Collection.

50 Krawchuk, *Our History,* 24.

51 Melnycky, "The Internment of Ukrainians in Canada," in *Loyalties in Conflict,* 6, 7.

52 Stella Hryniuk, "Pioneer Bishop, Pioneer Times: Nykyta Budka in Canada," *CCHA: Historical Studies* 55 (1988), 34–35.

53 "In Camp Kapuskasing," n.d. Stavroff-Krawchuk Collection

54 Quoted in Potrobenko, *No Streets of Gold,* 108.

55 Quoted in Avery, "Ethnic and Class Tensions in Canada," 80.

56 Krawchuk, *The Ukrainian Socialist Movement,* 58.

57 Ibid., 59.

58 Ibid.

59 Quoted in Avery, *Reluctant Host,* 73.

60 Krawchuk, *The Ukrainian Socialist Movement,* 58.

61 For an overview of life in the internment camps, see Luciuk, *In Fear of the Barbed Wire Fence* and *Without Just Cause.*

62 Quoted in Lubomyr Luciuk, *A Time for Atonement: Canada's First National Internment Operations and the Ukrainian Canadians, 1914–1920* (Kingston: Limestone Press, 1988), 20.

63 Cited in Orest Martynowych, "The Ukrainian Socialist and Working-Class Movement in Manitoba" (unpublished paper, 1973, in the Archives of Manitoba), 25.

64 "From the Captive Prisoners in Castle Mountain," *Robochyi Narod,* 28 September 1915. Stavroff-Krawchuk Collection.

65 Quoted in Bill Waiser, *Park Prisoners: The Untold Story of Western Canada's National Parks, 1915–1946* (Saskatoon: Fifth House, 1995), 21.

66 Quoted in Luciuk, *Without Just Cause,* 7, 8.

67 Melnycky, "Badly Treated in Every Way."

68 Melnycky, "The Internment of Ukrainians in Canada," 9.

69 "In Camp Kapuskasing." Stavroff-Krawchuk Collection.

70 Ibid.

71 Melnycky, "The Internment of Ukrainians in Canada," 9.

72 "In Camp Kapuskasing." Stavroff-Krawchuk Collection.

73 "News from the Interned," *Robochyi Narod,* 28 September 1915. Stavroff-Krawchuk Collection.

74 For more on the Red Scare, see Daniel Francis, *Seeing Reds: The Red Scare of 1918–1919, Canada's First War on Terror* (Vancouver: Arsenal Pulp Press, 2010).

75 Krawchuk, *Our History,* 26.

76 See, for example, Kealey, *Workers and Canadian History*, especially Chapter 9; and Craig Heron, ed., *The Workers' Revolt in Canada, 1917–1925* (Toronto: University of Toronto Press, 1998).

77 McCormack, *Reformers, Rebels, and Revolutionaries,* especially Chapter 8.

78 For more on Cahan, see Whitaker, Kealey, and Parnaby, *Secret Service*, 71–80.

79 Quoted in Whitaker, Kealey, and Parnaby, *Secret Service,* 74.

80 The last internment camp to close was Kapuskasing on 20 February 1920.

81 Krawchuk, *The Ukrainian Socialist Movement,* 87.

82 Ibid., 90.

83 "Chief Agitators in Canada," in Gregory Kealey and Reg Whitaker, *RCMP Security Bulletins: The Early Years, 1919–1929* (St. John's, NL: Canadian Committee on Labour History, 1995).

84 The ULFTA was initially known as the Ukrainian Labour Temple Association (ULTA).

85 Melnycky, "The Internment of Ukrainians in Canada," 16.

86 Krawchuk, *Our History,* 35.

CHAPTER 4

Collateral Damage: The Defence of Canada Regulations, Civilian Internment, Ethnicity, and Left-Wing Institutions

JIM MOCHORUK

Although this chapter focuses upon the experience of one particular business, the People's Co-operative of Winnipeg, it is also a meditation upon the ongoing harassment of a particular subset of the Canadian political left; a harassment which was based upon ethnicity and politics. However, it is in some ways also a meditation on both the fragility of civil liberties in times of real or perceived crises—and about the inconsistency and incompetency of those who sought to attack the left.

It needs to be observed at the outset that the regulations used to intern civilians in Canada during the Second World War—and to seize the property and materials of organizations which were deemed to be illegal under those regulations—were all too familiar to members of the ethnic left. Eastern Europeans had been the group most commonly interned during the First World War via the operation of the War Measures Act (WMA)[1] and although the literature suggests that ethnic leftists were not singled out for internment in the early days of the war, Kassandra Luciuk's contribution to this volume makes it clear that it was precisely the proletarianized and radicalized Ukrainian-speakers who were targeted by the Canadian state virtually from day one of internment operations. As the Great War progressed, this targeting became more overt: a wave of arrests and internments in 1915 was heavily focused upon industrial regions where Ukrainian-speaking workers and activists were concentrated. Enough members and leaders of the Ukrainian Social Democratic Party (USDP) were arrested and interned at this time that it threw the organization into crisis mode.[2] And the USDP's problems only deepened as both the party and the unions and other organizations it had helped to create received the lion's share of the authorities' attention; attention that increased exponentially during 1918 with raids on USDP offices and meetings all across Canada, the seizure of materials suspected of being seditious and, in at least one case, the seizure (and sale) of the printing press used to produce the offending materials—plus the arrest and internment of several prominent leaders of the party.[3] Later that same year, while the WMA was still in operation, even more dramatic steps were taken to stem the rise of radicalism among Canada's immigrants. On 25 September 1918, all "enemy-language" publications were banned by Order-in-Council PC 2381 while PC 2384 allowed the government to declare any group that advocated economic and/or governmental change by force (a word left undefined) to be an unlawful association.[4] This second order-in-council also made it illegal to be in possession of, or to distribute, the literature which these now banned organizations had produced. So, publications such as *Robochyi Narod* (The Working People) were effectively banned, as were parties such as the Social Democratic Party of Canada—and its ethnic affiliates, including the USDP.

As noted in the introduction to this book, although the WMA lapsed, for most of the interwar period Canada's ethnic leftists still felt the Sword of Damocles dangling over their heads as the state found new ways of carrying forward its emergency wartime powers to harass those whose ideologies and ethnicities were not in accord with those who dominated the state and its institutions. Indeed, during the Winnipeg General Strike of 1919 the original Ukrainian Labour Temple (located at the corner of Pritchard and McGregor in north Winnipeg), the epicentre of the Ukrainian left in Canada, was raided by agents of the RNWMP, who took away all the correspondence and account books they could find and did considerable damage to the print shop and offices.[5] At the same time the homes of leaders such as Mathew Popovich and John Navis—along with at least twenty-eight other leaders and former members of the USDP and the newly created Ukrainian Labour Temple Association (ULTA, later known as the Ukrainian Labour Farmer Temple Association or ULFTA)—were raided and searched for seditious materials.[6] Even more infamously, between 1919 and 1921 large numbers of ethnic radicals were deported from Canada via administrative tribunals of questionable legality.[7]

Despite all of this the ethnic left enjoyed considerable success during the interwar period: thousands of members, innumerable halls, publications, youth groups, educational and cultural programs. and all sorts of ancillary organizations and enterprises flourished under the leadership of the Finnish Organization of Canada, the various predecessor organizations of the United Jewish People's Order, and the ULFTA. As a result, these ethnic agencies became the most visible portions of the pro-communist left. This success, however, also made them the most vulnerable parts of the left—with far more to lose than the Communist Party of Canada (CPC), while their members were in a much more perilous position than Canadian or British-born party members and supporters. As Ian Angus observed in the context of the CPC's move to a more militant stance at the end of the 1920s, "Anglo-Saxon party members arrested at demonstrations received fines or short jail terms: immigrant workers were faced with deportation."[8]

Matters got even worse after the Bennett government came to power in 1930. The use of Section 98 to attack the communist left and the increased use of the Immigration Act to deport foreign-born radicals was keenly felt by members of the ethnic left throughout the early 1930s. So, without meaning to denigrate the impact of the Defence of Canada Regulations (DOC) implemented in September of 1939[9] and the phenomenal powers they granted the government, they really were old hat for most of Canada's ethnic leftists. These people knew from bitter experience just how endangered their rights and civil liberties were at any given moment.

The People's Co-op[10] (and its sister organization the Workers' Benevolent Association or WBA) is a case in point both of the type of harassment which was typical for ethnic leftists during the interwar period and for the dramatic—if indirect—consequences of the operation of the DOC regulations. It is also an example of the ways in which local municipal and provincial officials, assorted red-baiters within the community, and those who had other, more personal axes to grind collaborated with the federal government in an attempt to eradicate the communist left from the political and social scene, using the excuse of a national wartime crisis.

Founded by Winnipeg-based activists within the ULFTA and the WBA in 1928, this co-operative was designed to serve the economic needs of Ukrainian workers and farmers, but it was also meant to serve as a recruiting/educational tool. From the moment it commenced its wood and coal yard operation, but especially after it moved into Winnipeg's highly competitive and politicized milk processing and distribution business in 1931, a major goal of the Co-op was to draw ever more Ukrainian-speaking workers and farmers into the parent organizations (ULFTA and WBA) and into the larger, international socialist movement.[11] Nor did it hide its political orientation: from its inception it was led by such luminaries of the Ukrainian-Canadian left as William Kolysnik and Andrew Bileski—both of whom held elected office (as acknowledged members of the CPC) in Winnipeg while serving as managers of the Co-op. By the same token, the Co-op's first bookkeeper was legendary Communist alderman "Red Jake" Penner, while leading proponents of its founding were from among the executives of the ULFTA and WBA, and the members of its various boards of directors and auditor's commissions, and even its roster of employees, read like a who's who of Winnipeg's Ukrainian left. Given this, it is hardly surprising that the RCMP was spying on its activities from its founding in 1928 onwards.[12]

Despite the vicissitudes of conducting business in the maw of a depression, both parts of the Co-op's enterprise were surprisingly successful. By 1940 the People's Co-op employed over 100 people, owned its own fuel yard along with its own dairy and ice-cream plant in Winnipeg, had acquired an existing creamery in Minnedosa, Manitoba, built a new butter-making plant in Glenella, Manitoba, and had launched the first of a planned set of five co-operative grocery stores in Winnipeg. It even acted as an ersatz financial institution—complete with passbooks—for many of its members, shareholders, workers, suppliers, and patrons, who collectively had over $100,000 lodged in Co-op deposit accounts.[13]

This ability to survive and even thrive through the worst days of the Great Depression was all the more remarkable because of the Co-op's well-known political orientation. As noted elsewhere,[14] this orientation was a two-edged sword, as the dedication, self-sacrifice, and hard work of those associated with the Co-op in its early years stemmed primarily from their commitment to the cause of transforming capitalist society into a new socialist world order. On the other hand, though, this political orientation created some unique problems.

Long before the implementation of the DOC regulations, the Co-op had had to deal with problems which its political affiliation brought in its wake. To begin with, it was almost certainly the only coal and wood yard in Winnipeg that had the RCMP spying upon its operations.[15] And it is just as certain that the executives of other city dairies never had to find strategies to win back customers who had quit taking their milk because they were afraid of what "the church organization" they belonged to might say about getting milk from the "Red Dairy."[16] Nor did other fuel yards and creameries routinely have to deal with internal political crises, such as those resulting from criticisms from leaders of the CPC—alleging that the Co-op was too bourgeois and reformist—or to confront the political and economic consequences of internal ideological splits.[17] Nor did the managers of the Co-op's competitors feel duty bound to find jobs for "comrades" who were facing deportation if they could not find work, or for those who would have to spend longer periods in prison for their political activism if they did not have a guaranteed position with some employer.[18] And while there might have been some questions raised over the stability of their lending institutions, the Co-op's competitors never had to deal with the full-blown investigation of their mortgage holders, as was the case when the WBA had all of its records seized and was charged with violating the terms of its charter in 1933—for among other things, lending money to the Co-op.[19] In short, the Co-op's leaders, workers, and shareholders knew there was a price to be paid for being ethnic leftists—and for trying to occupy the complicated space between political activism and business "success." That price would become even more overt after Canada entered the Second World War: the Co-op was about to experience considerable collateral damage.

Unfortunately for the Co-op, just as a new round of politically inspired persecution was about to descend upon it, the institution was in a particularly precarious financial situation. First of all, it was dealing with a rapidly rising debt load, occasioned by the Co-op's ambitious expansion plan of 1938–40. General Manager Andrew Bileski and Director of Education and Publicity Mitch Sago had argued that simultaneous expansion on several different fronts would not only yield positive economic results, but would be a powerful demonstration of the ability of workers and producers to challenge the existing system of production for profit. So convinced were they of this that they overruled the well-taken objections of the Co-op's Internal Auditor on major aspects of the expansion and launched the Co-op into several new ventures simultaneously (ice-cream production in Winnipeg, butter production in two rural plants, and the stocking and operation of up to five retail grocery stores in Winnipeg), strictly on the basis of borrowed funds.[20]

Beyond this self-inflicted problem of overexpansion the Co-op faced a new crisis of competition that arose suddenly in the fall of 1939. To begin with, a new, non-union dairy was established right in the Co-op's backyard and because it was to be run by Ukrainian-speaking managers and employ Ukrainian-speaking drivers/salesmen, the Co-op's management believed this new creamery's goal was to take away the Co-op's core Ukrainian-speaking customer base in Winnipeg's north end.[21] Even more damaging, however, was the unilateral decision of a much larger firm, Modern Dairies, to ignore a Milk Control Board (MCB) of Manitoba order to raise the price of milk to

Winnipeg consumers for the winter season. Although the Co-op and other dairies protested to the MCB, the 1 September 1939 decision of Modern Dairies to hold the line on consumer prices—announced as a patriotic move in the face of the growing threat of war—had to be matched by all other dairies if they did not wish to lose market share.[22]

The situation was ruinous for the Co-op: its overall revenues fell precipitously just as many of the costs of expansion had to be paid out, leaving it in a full-blown financial crisis by the winter of 1939–40.[23] As the Co-op had done when facing financial problems in the past, it turned to its members, its workers, and to the constituent parts of the Ukrainian left for support. The WBA was particularly important in this regard. Between late 1939 and early 1940 it converted some of its "on-demand loans" to the Co-op into a mortgage, provided the Co-op with a second mortgage, and helped to arrange another $20,000 line of credit via another financial institution.[24] But if the Co-op was to survive, the board believed that it needed to deepen its share capital base. Thus, a membership and fundraising campaign was planned for January and February of 1940: a campaign that would start with a request for Co-op employees to purchase shares.

The idea was that the employees would agree to have a portion of their wages deducted and converted into Co-op shares over a period of six months—usually two shares per week ($4.00). After a meeting between the Co-op's Board of Directors and the workers, a standing vote was taken and the plan approved. In all, sixty-six of the approximately 100 staffers ended up participating.[25] The Co-op's management team and board were pleased with what they viewed as the first step in the larger share sales campaign, completely unaware of the political land mine they had just triggered.

The unintended consequences of this share-purchase plan began to unfold in January of 1940 when Edward Drage, business agent for Local 119 of the Teamsters Union, stopped by the Co-op to pick up union dues from the membership. Drage was informed by a couple of Co-op workers that they couldn't afford both union dues and share purchases. He then interviewed a few more men, including a recently laid-off driver, and came to the conclusion that the share-purchase plan was a compulsory contribution to the employer and, as such, a violation of the union contract.[26] Drage leapt into action. On 25 January 1940 he had the Co-op's representative on the executive of Local 119—John Seter—removed and then suspended the Co-op's entire workforce from the union.[27] Attempts by the shop committee of the Co-op employees to have the Teamsters reverse this decision—through the agency of the Winnipeg Trades and Labour Council (TLC)—were ignored by Drage and Local 119.[28]

But if the Teamsters showed no interest in the plight of the Co-op's workforce, there was one local politician who saw a golden opportunity in this situation: Alderman Charles Simonite. Simonite, a conservative member of City Council, knew that because the Co-op had a contract to provide milk to City of Winnipeg relief recipients and also held the 1939–40 contract to supply milk to the city's tuberculosis patients, it was subject to the city's fair wages and practices regulations.[29] He reasoned that if the Co-op was in trouble with its own union for supposedly unfair labour practices then it might be possible to find the Co-op in violation of city regulations, which would be the perfect pretext for stripping the Co-op of this business. That the loss of what accounted for 27 percent of its milk sales would have killed the Co-op, thrown 100 employees out of work, and left the Co-op's more than ninety-five milk and cream suppliers in dire straits was not something which worried this now self-described "friend of the working man."[30] On 1 April 1940 Alderman Simonite gave notice that at the next meeting of City Council he would be requesting that the Public Welfare Committee be empowered to launch an investigation into the "alleged unfair treatment of employees of the People's Co-operative dairy."[31]

This move was hardly surprising. Simonite was a well-known anti-communist and had often used his position on council to try and prevent the Co-op from getting city business. He had a particular distaste for his former City Council colleague, Co-op manager Bileski. Of course almost everyone connected with the Winnipeg labour movement knew the alderman was anything but a friend of labour. R.G. Anderson of the Winnipeg TLC could point out with some justice that Simonite had been known to "use all skullduggery to circumvent the fair wage laws and was never known to employ a trade union man in his life," while another TLC member was even more blunt, describing the Alderman as "an enemy of labor of all descriptions"—but Alderman Simonite believed he could make common cause with some of the more conservative trade unionists in that fateful spring of 1940.[32]

Simonite's timing was impeccable. To begin with, the CPC had done itself no favour by first coming out in support of the Canadian war effort, only to reverse its decision a few days later. Communists, and those people and institutions which supported the Communist left, were now subjected to much overt hostility.[33] Indeed, there is little question that the CPC's position on the war effort and the revelation of the German-Soviet Non-Aggression Pact of

1939 had contributed to some of the Co-op's loss of business in 1939–40. In this context, the opportunity to launch an attack upon an agency headed by so prominent a communist as Andrew Bileski was too great for Simonite to resist. Beyond this, he had an ace up his sleeve: Simonite was well aware that a split was occurring in the Winnipeg labour movement over the issue of the DOC regulations and their use against communists. In fact, just as the Alderman was calling for a special investigative committee on the Co-op, the Winnipeg TLC was protesting the government's use of the DOC regulations to arrest the editors of the Winnipeg-based (and CPC-affiliated) *Mid-West Clarion* in March of 1940—for an editorial critical of the Canadian war effort. The executive of the TLC had seen this as an issue of freedom of speech and press, but several of the TLC's more conservative member unions left the TLC in protest, charging that the body was too much influenced by communists.[34] Simonite believed he could work with—or at least use—trade unionists such as these and the overtly anti-communist Edward Drage of the Teamsters.

Given all of this, Simonite was easily able to convince his colleagues on City Council to create a subcommittee to conduct a public inquiry into the Co-op's labour practices. As he put it to his colleagues on 15 April 1940, he believed that it was the Winnipeg TLC's job to take action against the Co-op for its labour practices, but it had failed to do so for one of two possible reasons: "Either they are too weak, or they are rotten with communism."[35] And there was little doubt in anyone's mind that Simonite believed the latter to be the case.[36]

The alderman's intention was clearly to put the Co-op on trial for its political orientation just as much—if not more than—for its labour practices. Thus his witness list included people who had never worked at the Co-op, but who were "experts" on communism and had second- and third-hand information on the Co-op's hiring practices, such as the head of the Valour Road Branch of the Canadian Legion.[37] Moreover, the questions that Simonite put to witnesses—former and current Co-op employees—went far beyond the share purchase agreement or other work-related issues, and dealt with matters such as which Co-op officials were CPC members, whether preference was given to communists in hirings at the Co-op, and to what sort of political causes Co-op employees were contributing and to what newspapers they subscribed. In much the same way Edward Drage of the Teamsters (working with Simonite) spent much time in his cross-examination of driver/salesman Jack Pearlmutter, trying to establish that Pearlmutter had once told Drage that he was a communist.[38] The already overtly political tone of the inquiries' questions intensified when

Bileski was on the stand: Simonite wanted him to "name names"—in particular he wanted Bileski to provide the inquiry with a list of the names of the Co-op's Board of Directors, annotated to indicate which ones were party members.[39]

The inquiry provided some excellent political theatre. The largely pro–Co-op crowd in the balcony of City Council's chamber was given to cheering Co-op witnesses—some of whom gave eloquent testimony about the nature and dedication of the Co-op's worker-members—while others displayed a flair for lampooning the claims of the dismissed workers—particularly the almost comic ineptitude which had led to the firings or layoffs of some of Simonite's star witnesses. Percy Herschberg had them "rolling in the aisles" when he declared that he just wished the share-purchase agreement had been commenced earlier, as it was the best way he had yet found to save money,[40] while Jules Pynoo's "confession" that he had in fact made political contributions while an employee of the Co-op—to the CCF—must have brought a smile even to Andrew Bileski's worried face.[41] (The ideological divide between the CCF and the CPC was well-known to everyone in that highly partisan crowd.)[42] But no matter how well the Co-op's witnesses did, and no matter how strong its case,[43] it really did not matter. Simonite and the conservative majority of the subcommittee were not paying attention: indeed, one committee member, Alderman Morrison, simply stopped attending the hearings when the Co-op's case was being presented.[44] It was virtually a foregone conclusion what the final verdict would be when the inquiry wound up late in June—although the Co-op's leaders seemingly believed that the institution would be found not guilty, simply because justice was on their side.[45]

This cognitive dissonance, or more charitably, naiveté, is all the more remarkable given that those Co-op leaders were well aware that the crackdown on leftists—and the growing press and public support for that crackdown—had reached a series of new highs just as the inquiry was hitting its stride. On 10 May, while Simonite was still calling his anti-Co-op witnesses to the stand, the *Winnipeg Free Press* ran an article entitled "Red Threat: Communistic Plot in Canada Charged." Citing an unnamed, but "high provincial government official," the piece claimed that the CPC was "now regarded as the No. 1 menace to Canada's internal security." This source argued that it would be "national suicide" for Canada "to cling to peace-time [legal and civil] rights which were being used to the advantage of the enemy."[46] This sort of rhetoric was frightening enough—particularly because it almost certainly came from the office of the provincial attorney general—but matters became much worse when the rhetoric was matched by action just days later.

On 15 May, a judge of the Ontario Supreme Court handed down a ruling declaring the CPC to be illegal. Asked his opinion on this ruling, Manitoba's attorney general told the local press that he not only approved of it, but that his department had "started action some months ago to have the Communist party outlawed in Manitoba."[47] It was for good reason then that the *Free Press*—in a front-page story of 16 May—questioned what was to become of the five "known and admitted Communists" holding elected offices in Winnipeg—a group including school trustee Andrew Bileski and the Co-op's only overt friend on the Simonite inquiry, Alderman Jake Penner.[48]

The wheels of official government repression of the pro-communist left were being greased quite effectively. The most telling blow, however, was delivered two weeks later. On 4 June 1940, using the DOC regulations, the federal government submitted a list of organizations that were to be banned, which included the CPC and a series of ethnic organizations that the government deemed to be controlled by the party, including the ULFTA. The ban was announced in Parliament on 5 June and by the time Winnipeg newspapers reported on this action the following day, they could run banner headlines proclaiming that "Provincial Authorities Approve Outlawing of 16 Societies," and assure readers that, through the good offices of Attorney General Major, Manitoba had been "one of the first provincial administrations to voice approval of the ban."[49]

This was a huge blow for everyone involved with the Ukrainian left, as the ULFTA's halls, contents, related assets and records were now potentially subject to seizure by the government. In an interview with the local press, Peter Prokopchak (a.k.a. Prokop), then the secretary of the Central Executive Committee of the ULFTA, made clear just how serious this was. With over 200 Canadian branches, eighty temples—five of them in Winnipeg—a couple of hundred orchestras and choirs and hundreds of thousands of dollars' worth of assets on the line, he could only express incredulity at the action of the government in declaring this "cultural and educational" association illegal.[50] Over the next few days, in order to comply with the DOC regulations, the local branches of the ULFTA were disbanded and many of the halls shuttered.[51] Then, on 20 June 1940, a new order-in-council was issued calling for the "control and management" of all properties belonging to "illegal" organizations by the custodian of enemy property—a prelude to the seizure of the properties two weeks later.[52]

While neither the People's Co-op nor the WBA were on the list of banned organizations, subsequent actions by the RCMP and the attorney general of

Manitoba indicated that both believed that the Co-op and WBA were so closely connected to the CPC and ULFTA that not only could they be attacked with impunity, but that they should be attacked.[53] For the Co-op the impact of this new use of the DOC regulations first hit home on 12 June when Alderman Penner, the Co-op's greatest City Hall advocate, was arrested and detained.[54] With Penner in custody and James Litterick, the Manitoba leader of the CPC (and a sitting MLA), being sought by police, it was only a question of when, not if, the authorities would be coming for Bileski and perhaps others at the Co-op.[55]

Because of some uncharacteristically careful planning, it took a while for the authorities to launch their broader roundup of communist activists. Thus, Bileski had enough time to present the Co-op's final submission to the inquiry on 28 June 1940.[56] But the axe did fall: early on the morning of 6 July the RCMP and local police launched a coordinated raid that was focused heavily on members of the Ukrainian-Canadian left. That morning Bileski was picked up, as was Mike Kostanuik—creamery manager and president of the Co-op's Board of Directors. At the same time police arrested J. Dubno, member of the board and manager of the Co-op's new grocery store; M. Biniowsky, former board member and currently the Co-op's night man; J. Prossak, a storeroom worker; and T. Bilecki, one of the Co-op's newest deliverymen.[57] Bilecki was actually arrested while out on his milk route and insisted that he be allowed to finish his deliveries and return his horse and wagon to the creamery—leading to a most unusual parade through the streets of north end Winnipeg as Bilecki and his two car police escort made their way back to the dairy.[58] Mitch Sago, although slated for arrest that morning, had already gone into hiding—becoming the subject of a lengthy manhunt.[59]

The loss of these seven men was just the tip of the iceberg of the Co-op's troubles. For example, the man chosen to set up and run the new Co-op operation at Minnedosa, Emil Miller, fearful of being caught up in the impending roundups, had already gone into hiding, forcing the Co-op to scramble to find another candidate for that job.[60] Beyond this, at least six former or current members of the Co-op's Board of Directors and audit commissions were among those arrested and interned, as was its first general manager, William Kolysnik, as well as many of those from the ULFTA and WBA who had been instrumental in its founding in 1928.[61] Indeed, one would have been hard-pressed to find any of the Manitoba internees (or those in hiding) who were not tied to the Co-op in one way or other, if only as shareholders or "depositors." All in all, the Co-op had suffered a staggering loss of leadership.

Nor was this the full extent of the authorities' assault upon the Co-op. While planning the 6 July roundup, the provincial attorney general had called a special conference with representatives of the RCMP, local police, and several former members of the Ukrainian left. The purpose of this meeting was to ensure that the raids against CPC and ULFTA targets would not only be well coordinated, but would also target institutions not included in the official "illegal list"—most notably the WBA and the People's Co-op—in order to obtain information that would prove that they too were communist agencies.[62] To this end, Attorney General Major invited an interesting troika of advisors to this meeting: M.W. Horbay, the real estate agent who had arranged for the original purchase of the Co-op's fuel yard location and who had subsequently been found to have "flipped" the property for personal gain;[63] Emil Chomicki (a.k.a. Omelian Chomitsky), a former national secretary of the WBA; and Toma Kobzey, a former Central Executive Committee member of the ULFTA and its national secretary, as well as a key figure in the Ukrainian-Canadian left's fight against the CPC leadership in the late 1920s and early '30s.[64] In the cases of Chomicki and Kobzey, both men had been important figures in the Lobay faction fight of 1935–36 which had almost completely torn apart the Ukrainian-Canadian left.[65] In effect, the authorities had recruited a set of informants who not only had axes to grind with their former comrades but who knew where the financial "bodies," so to speak, were buried—or at least had known a few years earlier.[66]

As the transcripts of this conference make clear, the authorities wanted detailed information on how money might have been transferred between the ULFTA, the WBA, and the Co-op on the one side and the CPC on the other.[67] Addenda to the transcripts of this meeting indicate that the authorities were already convinced that the ULFTA and People's Co-op were "2nd line Communist Organizations" and that the WBA "is, or has been, one of the chief organizations for the raising of money for the purposes of the Communist Party of Canada."[68] They simply wanted more information to make the case officially.

For their part, the informants—at least Chomicki and Kobzey—claimed that they wanted to help the authorities in their investigations so that they could regain control of the organizations and look after the interests of the vast majority of the organizations' members who, they noted, were not communists. Indeed, Chomicki had approached the attorney general a few days earlier claiming that many members of the WBA were afraid that because of the ban on left-wing organizations, the communist leadership of the WBA "would dissipate the moneys of the organization and the members will be the losers."[69] Whether or not this was a completely accurate characterization of the source of the members' fears, many members of the WBA were undoubtedly worried about the fate of their organization and its assets in the summer of 1940—and for good reason.

In the days following this meeting the authorities planned and, with expert on-site help from former high-ranking members of the WBA and an unnamed former Co-op board member,[70] executed their 6 July raids on the homes of its targets, the ULFTA hall and print shop, and the WBA and Co-op offices. In the process, the provincial authorities confiscated all of the business records and papers of both institutions—as well as any "subversive" material on hand.[71]

Strangely enough there was a completely unintended benefit to this particular action for the Co-op. While the seizure of all of their business records made life difficult for the relatively junior staff members who would now be running the Co-op and the WBA,[72] the fact that the government of Manitoba wanted to conduct a full audit of the books of both institutions—to prove that they were funnelling money to the CPC and ULFTA—caused the City of Winnipeg to defer making any final judgement on the Co-op's labour practices until the province had completed its investigation.[73] The RCMP also suspended its investigation of the Co-op while the province was conducting its audit—although individuals who worked for, or were associated with, the Co-op were still subject to individual investigations.[74] This provided a de facto stay-of-execution for the Co-op, as the provincial auditor, Mr. Harrison, who had been thwarted in his 1933 attempt to prove that the WBA had violated its charter, was an extremely thorough man. Indeed, according to the RCMP he allowed his investigation to drag on too long as he waited for the Co-op to produce a ledger that had not been caught up in the raids.[75] Thus his audit was not completed until November of 1940. At that point the city's investigative subcommittee came to its preordained conclusion that the Co-op had indeed acted in violation of its fair wages and practices regulations.[76] Although it made no formal recommendations to the rest of the council the implication was clear: the Co-op had violated city employment policy and should be stripped of its relief milk business.[77] However, by the time that the entire City Council got around to reading the report and got advice from the city solicitor on how best to proceed,[78] the decision to strip the Co-op of this business could not be implemented until 1 January 1941. By that time, because of enlistments and the growth of war-related employment opportunities, Winnipeg's unemployment rate had fallen so drastically that the impact of losing the city's relief milk business was nowhere near as dramatic as it would have been in the spring of 1940.

Of course, in the immediate aftermath of the 6 July raids no one at the Co-op could have predicted this particular outcome. Everything was in crisis mode. On 9 July, with the results of the City Inquiry still pending and only three days removed from the arrests and the seizure of the Co-op's records, Walter Sawiak—up to this point only the Co-op's bookkeeper—was appointed interim general manager and president of the board, effectively taking on the roles of both Bileski and Kostanuik. And of course he was also still the one who was responsible for the maintenance of financial records which the Co-op no longer possessed.[79] But this was not the end of his problems and responsibilities, for in addition to the loss of Bileski, Kostanuik, Dubno, and Sago from the management team, the Co-op's sales manager had recently resigned to serve as the manager of a rival dairy[80]—so Sawiak had no sales manager, no creamery manager, no fuel yard manager, no publicity director, no executive board members, and no business records. Indeed, there was no one in Winnipeg who had signing authority for Co-op business. To make matters worse, Sawiak was also dealing with a personal set of crises. His father Michael, a long-time activist on the Ukrainian left, but now a very sick older man, was one of those who had been arrested and interned, while Sawiak's wife Helen had recently been released from a tuberculosis sanitarium and was far from well. Trying to secure his father's release and caring for his family would have to be balanced with his attempts to save the Co-op.

The enormity of the crisis was brought home forcefully to Sawiak by Mr. Fleming of the MCB when he visited the Co-op offices shortly after the raids. Fleming informed the new manager that the milk producers who held official quotas from the MCB for supplying the Co-op were greatly disturbed that they hadn't yet been paid for their June shipments. Sawiak was told that if they were not paid promptly the dairy would forfeit its MCB surety bond of $12,500 (which would most assuredly drive the Co-op out of business and still not cover all the money that was owed to the shippers).[81] As Sawiak explained to Fleming, he had just gotten back from the official opening of the Co-op's butter plant at Minnedosa, and found this whole situation "on his doorstep" with signing officers available to send out the necessary cheques—but he hoped to have new ones assigned within a few days.[82] What Fleming didn't tell Sawiak was that the MCB was also well aware that the Co-op had a large number of "depositors" whose money was crucial to the operations of the dairy and that the MCB was worried that given the current circumstances, those depositors might start "a run," which would cause the dairy to go out of business. What is even more interesting—and also not disclosed to Sawiak—is that the head of the MCB, J.D. Cameron, was inclined to find some way to allow the Co-op to stay in business, largely for the protection of the dairy's ninety-five milk suppliers.[83] Thus, there was at least one government official who was looking at the Co-op in something other than a strictly political light.

Sawiak quickly pieced together a new interim executive and board of directors and called an emergency meeting of the Co-op's membership in order to formally recognize the new board and appoint officers. He also needed to give a report on the recently concluded city inquiry and to try and explain the events of the past few days and what it all meant for the future of the Co-op—if for no other reason than to calm the fears of shareholders and depositors. Fortunately, the Hebrew Sick Benefit Hall had already been booked by the Co-op for 10 July when Bileski had planned to give his report on the city inquiry to the shareholders. This was now transformed into an emergency membership meeting.

At this gathering Sawiak followed the script that he and Bileski had been preparing before the raids and gave a remarkably upbeat report to the assembled crowd, assuring them that there was no reason to think that the Co-op would be found guilty of unfair labour practices.[84] He was a bit more careful in how he described the impact of the arrests and the seizure of the Co-op's records, but he was able to announce that the Co-op's employees had met on July 8th and had agreed, unanimously this time, to extend their share-purchase agreement for another six months.[85] Sawiak and the new board clearly hoped that this internal display of faith in the future of the Co-op—which amounted to the purchase of $9,000 worth of shares by Co-op employees—would inspire confidence among the other shareholders and depositors.[86]

Still, even when this was added to new shares being purchased by farmers and cream shippers from the Glenella and Minnedosa regions (by his own account, the manager of the new Glenella plant, Jim Larkin, had been quite successful at signing up new shareholders even as the City of Winnipeg inquiry was proceeding)[87] it was not going to be enough to keep the Co-op in business. As the head of the MCB knew, it was entirely likely that the Co-op's very public problems would lead depositors to pull their money out of the Co-op for fear that the funds would be seized or frozen, as had happened with the assets of the ULFTA. And, with the WBA also under investigation, there was no chance that the Co-op could turn there for a new loan.

The Co-op desperately needed money to cover the ongoing losses until a longer-term strategy could be developed. One long-time Co-op supporter, J. Koral—father of Michael Koral, one of the emerging leaders of the ULFTA—gave the Co-op a personal loan of $4,800 on the basis of a chattel mortgage on all of the dairy's horses, harnesses, and wagons.[88] But even this was nowhere near enough, as the Co-op's milk department, the Minnedosa plant, and the new grocery store in Winnipeg were all losing money, while mortgages held by the WBA were coming due. As a result, Sawiak was forced to pledge all of the Co-op's accounts receivable as security in exchange for an increase in the Co-op's line of credit at the Canadian Imperial Bank of Commerce. At this point, there wasn't a single solitary asset that the Co-op could call its own. As Attorney General Major put it to Sawiak a few months later, "it would appear that the assets [of the Co-op] are not sufficient to justify the company continuing in business."[89] Indeed, according to the provincial auditor's report, by 30 June 1940—a week before the raids were carried out—the Co-op's "assets would not permit of the payment of more than 50 cents on the dollar of current obligations."[90]

Still, Sawiak and the Co-op were not about to throw in the towel. With the new finances lined up the Co-op set out to rebuild its volume of sales and institute a new regime of economy that would allow it to weather this seemingly perfect storm of legal, political, and economic woes. Unfortunately, no sooner had these new financial arrangements been made than a series of new crises erupted in August—all related in one way or other to the DOC regulations.

Sawiak's greatest fear—a sudden and large-scale withdrawal of depositor funds—was realized in August of 1940 when the Co-op's single largest depositor decided to withdraw her entire $5,000 from the Co-op.[91] The Co-op did not have those funds and had no hope of raising them on short notice so Sawiak flew out to Vancouver, where the depositor, a Mrs. Shandrova, lived, and somehow or other managed to convince her to withdraw only $1,000, which the Co-op managed to cover.[92]

Unfortunately for Sawiak, the moment that he returned from Vancouver problems began erupting at the Co-op's two rural plants. As already noted, Emil Miller, who had been slated to be the manager at Minnedosa, had gone into hiding to avoid internment and had to be replaced—in this case by the inexperienced John Boychuk/Boyd.[93] At first he was aided by Miller's lover, Octavia Kraikiwaska—a ULFTA activist and Miller's de facto co-manager—who had remained at Minnedosa to help with the transition.[94] Among other problems, they found they had to cope with the plant's former owner, who had been retained as the plant's butter-maker as part of the purchase agreement and quickly proved to be an individual who had some decidedly atypical attitudes for a member of the People's Co-op.

This fellow, Mr. Anderson, was not only pro-Nazi in his sympathies but was sharing his views with everyone who came into the plant. The dual risk of alienating cream suppliers and (ironically) of running afoul of the DOC regulations for harbouring a Nazi in that troubled summer of 1940 (France had just fallen) was far too great for the Co-op to take. However, it was initially felt that Anderson could not simply be fired, as the Co-op still owed him money for the purchase of the plant. So, the road-weary Sawiak headed off to Minnedosa on 14 August to try and convince Anderson to cease his pro-Nazi proselytizing.[95] Clearly this chat had no lasting effect, for a few days later it was reported that Anderson was doing it again. This time the former owner was fired and, as expected, he immediately demanded payment of the $1,600 that the Co-op owed him. However, because this debt had been secured by Co-op shares, the board did not have to refund the value of these immediately.[96] Under both provincial law and the Co-op's constitution there was a far more protracted process involved in redeeming shares. And it was certainly no coincidence that at a 5 September meeting of the board it was decided that all requests for share redemptions would be held in abeyance until December (and perhaps beyond).[97]

The almost comical problem of a Nazi working for the Co-op paled in comparison to the situation that was developing at the Co-op's facility at Glenella. Not long before the 6 July raids, plans had been laid by Sago and Bileski for a major shake-up at this new plant. Jim Larkin (a.k.a. Mike Pesklyvec), the plant's inaugural manager and a former Co-op board member, was to be removed from this post and brought to the city as a milk route driver in Winnipeg. Larkin was assured that it wasn't a demotion, but simply a move intended to bring an experienced organizer back to the "centre" to help bolster the CPC's and ULFTA's much depleted forces in Winnipeg.[98] Sawiak and John Seter—who was now acting as de facto assistant manager of the Co-op—ended up following through on this plan early in the fall of 1940, with some very serious consequences.[99]

Larkin did not accept the rationale for this reassignment and expressed his frustration in writing, offering a biting and highly personal critique of the way Co-op business had been handled. This caused some consternation in

CPC, ULFTA, and Co-op circles, but this was a minor problem compared to what happened next. Larkin's detailed critique of how the Co-op's expansion was being financed and handled (among other things, Larkin claimed the expansion was the brainchild not of Co-op officials but of the provincial leader of the CPC, James Litterick) had been intended solely for internal consumption—meaning the party, the ULFTA, and the Co-op. However, the "Larkin document" fell into the hands of the provincial and federal authorities in the course of additional raids carried out under the authority of the DOC regulations in October 1940.[100] For anyone seeking to prove that the Co-op (and its mortgage holder, the WBA) was part of an illegal communist organization, this was an extremely useful document, a point not lost upon the RCMP. In fact, after perusing Larkin's critique in conjunction with the provincial auditor's report on the Co-op and the final report of the civic inquiry, an RCMP Intelligence Section report of November 1940 indicated: "It has now been definitely established that the Co-operative, was primarily a business enterprise, with a control of policy being exercised by the Communist Party. The vast majority of the employees of the Co-operative Dairy are listed on our subversive files. In fact, we are quite certain that no less than 59 of the employees are either Communists or strongly sympathetic to the Communist Party."[101]

At this point the authorities had the Co-op and the WBA right where they wanted them. What is amazing in retrospect is that neither the federal nor provincial authorities took the actions they might have, particularly given the latitude allowed under the DOC regulations. For its part, the City of Winnipeg did deprive the Co-op of its relief milk sales, but as noted above, that was not made effective until 1941 when the impact of this loss of business was considerably diminished. More perplexing was this: given the information provided to the provincial attorney general concerning both the Co-op and WBA by Horbay, Chomicki, and Kobzey, many more active members of the Co-op could have been rounded up. There were also allegations made that "many people who were on relief but who had saved sums of money ranging from $500.00 to $1000.00 were induced by the Co-operative to loan this money to it rather than deposit it in a bank so as to cover up the fact that they had any money."[102] This too could have been pursued but wasn't. It was also revealed in the provincial audit that somehow or other John Seter, former route foreman, head of the Co-op's union committee and—in the wake of the 6 July raids—new sales manager for the Co-op, had lent the Co-op $11,000 to help keep it afloat. The RCMP was very curious as to where this money might have originated, but once again never followed up on it.[103] Constable Slee of the RCMP's Intelligence Section certainly felt in November of 1940 that the Co-op's various "Stores, Fuel Yards etc. throughout the province . . . should be investigated as being possible sources of subversive activities such as meetings, distribution of literature, etc.," but again there is no indication that such an investigation was launched.[104]

The provincial authorities actually did pursue both the WBA and the Co-op a bit further, but they did so through the far less dramatic mechanisms of existing provincial law.[105] In the case of the Co-op, several months after the provincial auditor had concluded his audit, the attorney general indicated that he believed the Co-op's lack of proper assets and its methods of raising funds through deposit loans not only violated the Co-op's charter but also several sections of the provincial Companies Act. Moreover, from his perspective the Co-op was essentially insolvent. As a result, in February of 1941 Attorney General Major called Sawiak and the Co-op's lawyer to a closed-door hearing in his office to make representations as to why the People's Co-op should not be shut down.[106] Adding insult to injury, in the same letter Major informed the Co-op that it would have to pay all the costs of the audit and investigation—$1281.28—due immediately.[107]

Miraculously, the Co-op's lawyer, Joe Zuken, and Sawiak convinced Major to give them some time to prove that the Co-op was capable of meeting its obligations—and keeping people employed and shippers paid. They recognized that an important decision had been made that worked to the Co-op's advantage: because the investigation was now being carried out by provincial authorities under the terms of the Companies Act the question no longer seemed to be one of communist affiliation. Perhaps this was because Provincial Auditor Harrison's report had indicated that the Co-op's accounting system was so convoluted that he could not prove conclusively that money was being siphoned off to the CPC,[108] but whatever the reason, it seemed that the question now related to the Co-op's financial bottom line. Thus, the Co-op, which had already been seeking buyers for some of its properties, stepped up its efforts to make a quick sale of assets in order to bring down its level of indebtedness.

No one wanted the somewhat decrepit plant at Minnedosa but by 18 February 1941 the Co-op had found a purchaser for its new plant at Glenella.[109] This sale was carried out at a loss,[110] but it did stop some of the financial bleeding and, along with other economies, was enough to satisfy the attorney general.[111] One suspects that Major assumed that the Co-op (and the

WBA) would soon die a natural death and that there was therefore no need to pursue any more action. Meanwhile the activists associated with the Co-op would be right there in plain sight—so it was probably better from a security perspective to keep them where they were so that the RCMP could keep an eye on them. And aside from the time that Sawiak, Seter, and Boyd packed a five-gallon container of Co-op cream cheese for the internees—with a radio receiver at the bottom so they could get news from the outside world[112]—the Co-op and its employees tended to be so focused on saving the institution that they remained out of any serious trouble.

There was a relatively happy ending to all of this for the Co-op. Not only was the institution in a somewhat better financial situation by the midpoint of 1941, but it benefited immensely when the trajectory of the Second World War altered in June of that year. When Germany invaded the Soviet Union the pro-communist left—and the Co-op—entered into a whole new period of activity and popularity. True, the Co-op's internees were not released until 1942, but the Co-op itself ceased to be the object of any overt harassment—and emerged as one of the most patriotic of all Winnipeg institutions. It and its employees and members certainly worked hard on the campaign to have all of the internees released, but the Co-op and the entire pro-Communist left became massive supporters of the war effort and earned a whole new group of friends and supporters during the war years. (This would of course all change with the onset of the Cold War, but that is another story.)

In the final analysis, it is clear that the People's Co-op had suffered considerable damage as a result of the operation of the DOC regulations, the subsequent internment of its leaders, and the leeway that those regulations provided for red-baiters such as Alderman Simonite. But interagency delays, decisions to use existing legal measures instead of the emergency powers that were readily available, and some very hard work on the part of Co-op workers, supporters, and leaders had allowed it to avoid the fate that Alderman Simonite and so many others had hoped for. Then, in the aftermath of the German invasion of the Soviet Union, there was very little political will to go after the Ukrainian-Canadian left. As a result, the People's Co-op would soldier on for another half century—having another set of halcyon days in the 1940s and again in the late 1950s and early 1960s.

In a strange fashion, the Co-op story actually contains a very small silver lining for those concerned with civil liberties in Canada. While there is little doubt that federal, provincial, and municipal officials were quite willing to disregard core civil liberties—based upon which political ideologies and ethnic groups they thought acceptable or "Canadian"—the handling of the Co-op case suggests that these agencies were so incompetent that they were nowhere near as effective as they might have been. Given the undeniable level of anti-communist fervor that existed within police agencies and almost every branch of the municipal, provincial, and federal governments, given the weaponry available to them via the DOC regulations, and given the public mood in 1939–41, it is quite remarkable that the Co-op, the WBA, the ULFTA—and all other pro-communist ethnic organizations in Canada—were not smashed beyond repair. Considering the obvious linkages between the Co-op, the WBA, the ULFTA, and the CPC—with more than enough in the way of a documentary trail to satisfy the minimalist evidentiary requirements of the DOC regulations via seized internal party documents, detailed audits, and the testimony of disgruntled former members—it is astonishing that the federal Department of Justice did not simply add the People's Co-op and the WBA to its list of banned organizations, which most assuredly would have destroyed both. But then again, as anyone who has looked at the history of Canadian internment knows, the government was not particularly good at either rounding up or identifying enemies. With the exception of Norman Freed and Thomas McEwen (Ewen), the entire national executive of the CPC was able to go underground or flee the country before the mass arrests were made under the DOC regulations. Meanwhile, many of those interned from the Ukrainian-Canadian left were far from being dangerous—or by 1940, even influential. Why the authorities would have bothered to round up so many of what can only be described as yesterday's men—the almost blind and completely powerless W.N. Kolysnik; the rapidly fading and soon to die Michael Sawiak; the completely ostracized (from the CPC and ULFTA leadership) and seriously ill Mathew Popovich—is almost beyond comprehension. This is particularly the case when one considers that younger, more dynamic and energetic leaders such as Michael Koral, John Boyd, William Kardash (arrested but released), and a whole cohort of well-trained and intelligent female organizers and activists such as Mary Kardash, Mary Skrypnyk, Mary Prokop, and Helen Weir were left on the outside. Still, this really should provide little solace. Sexist attitudes and government incompetence, while perhaps constants of sorts, should not have to be relied upon to protect institutions or people from the state.

Notes

1 See, for example, Francis Swyripa and John Herd Thompson, eds., *Loyalties in Conflict: Ukrainians in Canada during the Great War* (Edmonton: Canadian Institute of Ukrainian Studies Press, 1983). In particular, see Peter Melnycky, "The Internment of Ukrainians in Canada," in *Loyalties in Conflict,* 1. See also Norman Hillmer, Bohdan Kordan, and Lubomyr Luciuk, *On Guard for Thee: War, Ethnicity, and the Canadian State, 1939–1945* (Ottawa: Canadian Government Publishing Centre, 1988); and Lubomyr Luciuk, *A Time for Atonement: Canada's First National Internment Operations and the Ukrainian Canadians, 1914–1920* (Kingston: Limestone Press, 1988).

2 Peter Krawchuk, *Our History: The Ukrainian Labour-Farmer Movement in Canada, 1907–1991* (Toronto: Lugas Publications, 1996), 23–25.

3 Orest T. Martynowych, *Ukrainians in Canada: The Formative Period, 1891–1924* (Edmonton: Canadian Institute of Ukrainian Studies Press, 1991), 435.

4 Donald Avery, *"Dangerous Foreigners": European Immigrant Workers and Labour Radicalism in Canada, 1896–1932* (Toronto: McClelland and Stewart, 1979), 75. For copies of these orders-in-council see Appendix II, in Swyripa and Thompson, *Loyalties in Conflict*, 190–96.

5 Martynowych, *Ukrainians in Canada,* 441.

6 Krawchuk, *Our History,* 31–32; and Donald Avery, "The Radical Alien in the Winnipeg General Strike of 1919," in *The West and the Nation: Essays in Honour of W.L. Morton,* ed. Carl Berger and Ramsay Cook (Toronto: McClelland and Stewart, 1976), 223.

7 Barbara Roberts, *Whence They Came: Deportation from Canada, 1900–1935* (Ottawa: University of Ottawa Press, 1988), Chapter Five, especially 96–97. See also Roberts, "Shovelling Out the 'Mutinous': Political Deportation from Canada before 1936," *Labour/Le Travail* 18 (Fall 1986): 81.

8 Ian Angus, *Canadian Bolsheviks: The Early Years of the Communist Party of Canada* (Montreal: Vanguard Publications, 1981), 291.

9 These were implemented under the terms of the War Measures Act on 3 September 1939, a week prior to Canada's actual declaration of war.

10 Before 1938 the People's Co-op was known as the Workers and Farmers Co-operative Association.

11 For an analysis of the politicized nature of the milk trade and the "milk wars" in Winnipeg, see Jim Mochoruk with Nancy Kardash, *The People's Co-op: The Life and Times of a North End Institution* (Halifax: Fernwood Publishing, 2000), 28–32 and 39–47. For more on the goals of the Co-op, see Ibid., 12–21.

12 Library and Archives of Canada (hereafter, LAC) Record of the Canadian Security and Intelligence Service, RG146, vol. 4089.

13 See Mochoruk, *The People's Co-op,* 74–75 and passim.

14 Ibid., 49–53.

15 See, for example, LAC, Record of the Canadian Security and Intelligence Service, RG146, vol. 4089, "Report re: Workers-Farmer Co-operative Association," 12 September 1928.

16 AUUC Archives, PCL Minute Book 1, "Minutes of the Executive Meeting, December 27," m1931 and ibid., 3 January 1932. (These records are now all housed in the Archives of Manitoba as "The People's Co-operative Limited Fonds,"

P7134/1 – P7144/17, but I have retained the original citation references to the AUUC Archives.)

17 This relates particularly to the Lobay crisis of 1935–36. See Mochoruk, *The People's Co-op*, 49–51; Jim Mochoruk, "'Pop and Co.' versus Tim Buck and the 'Lenin School Boys': Ukrainian-Canadians and the Communist Party of Canada, 1921–31" in *Re-Imagining Ukrainian-Canadians: History, Politics, and Identity*, ed. R.L. Hinther and Jim Mochoruk (Toronto: University of Toronto Press, 2011); and Andrij Makuch, "Fighting for the Soul of the Ukrainian Progressive Movement in Canada: The Lobayites and the ULFTA," in Ibid.

18 Mochoruk, *The People's Co-op*, 51. For example, Myron Kostanuik was released from Burwash prison in Ontario on condition that employment was provided for him by the Co-op. There are several references scattered throughout the PCL Minute Books of people being given short-term work in the fuel yard in order to avoid having to go on relief and perhaps face deportation.

19 Archives of Manitoba (hereafter AofM), AO064, GR 244, K-17-3-2, file 3. This file contains both details on the civil suit and a detailed report of the provincial auditor and memos from the attorney general's office.

20 AofM, RG 3 C1, box 4, RCMP file W945-1-105, Division D, Intelligence Section, Nov. 14, 1940, transcript copy of "Larkin" statement. See also, Mochoruk, *The People's Co-op*, 79–81.

21 See AUUC Archives, PCL Records, Minute Book #2, "Semi-Annual Membership Meeting, March 19, 1940 – Temple Theatre – General Manager's Report."

22 See Mochoruk, *The People's Co-op*, 82–83. Instead of fining Modern Dairies the MCB endorsed Modern's pricing plan—leaving the price to consumers at the summer rate, while insisting that the creameries pay producers the higher winter rate for their milk and cream. As a result, throughout the fall of 1939 the Co-op lost money on every quart of milk it sold.

23 For the three months when this price structure was in effect, the Co-op lost over $7,500 worth of revenue. See Mochoruk, *The People's Co-op*.

24 Ibid., 83.

25 Ibid., 84.

26 City of Winnipeg Archives, file A-47, "Memorandum re Meetings of Committee People's Co-operative Society, #2, April 29th, 1940 – Statement by Mr. Drage."

27 AUUC Archives, PCL Records, "Memorandum: Copies of Documents and Materials bearing upon the wages, union relations and share purchases of employees of People's Co-operative Limited," copy of letter "E.G. Drage, Secretary, International Brotherhood of Teamsters, Chauffeurs, Stablemen and Helpers of America to Members of Local 119, People's Co-op Dairy, Feb. 1, 1940."

28 See, for example, ibid., copy of letter, "J. Seter, Co-op Delegate to the Executive Board, Local 119, ITCSH to Executive Committee, Winnipeg and District Trades and Labor Council, February 5, 1940"; and ibid., "Copy of Resolution: Protesting Suspension of Employees of People's Co-operative Ltd. From Local 119. . . . February 7, 1940."

29 City of Winnipeg Archives, Minute Book, Committee on Health, 1935–40, Minutes, 31 May 1939.

30 The 27 percent figure comes from Co-op, not city, sources. See AUUC Archives, PCL Records, Minute Book #2, "Board of Directors Meeting, April 25, 1940."

31 *Winnipeg Free Press*, 2 April 1940, 1.

32 *Winnipeg Free Press*, 8 May 1940, 1.

33 For a detailed discussion of the CPC's dramatic volte face, and its impact on popular perceptions of the party, see Norman Penner, *Canadian Communism: The Stalin Years and Beyond* (Toronto: Methuen, 1988), 161–65.

34 Regarding the raid of the offices of the paper and the arrest of its editors, see *Winnipeg Free Press*, 6 March 1940, 1. For the decision of some affiliates of the TLC to leave over this protest, see Ibid., 17 April 1940, 1.

35 Cited in City of Winnipeg Archives, file A-47, "C.W. Foster, Secretary of the Winnipeg and District Labour Council to the City Clerk, May 13, 1940."

36 It is indicative of Simonite's overall attitude that on 8 July 1940 he spoke in favour of a resolution that called for interning all aliens and others opposed to the war effort and for prohibiting from public office all former members of the organizations banned under the DOC regulations on 4 June 1940. See *Winnipeg Free Press*, "Council Differs on War Measure," 9 July 1940, 1 and 11.

37 City of Winnipeg Archives, file A-47, "Memorandum re Meetings of Committee People's Co-operative Society, #6, 15 May 1940, Mr. CV Combs, Valour Road Legion."

38 Ibid., #10, 20 June 1940, J. Pearlmutter. See also *Winnipeg Free Press*, "Evidence Finished: People's Co-operative Salesman Denies Charges of Union Head," 21 June 1940, 12.

39 City of Winnipeg Archives, file A-47, "Memorandum re Meetings of Committee People's Co-operative Society, #7, May 28, 1940; Ibid., #8, June 3, 1940"; and *Winnipeg Free Press*, "Dairy Workers Not Coerced, Bilecki States," 4 June 1940, 13.

40 *Winnipeg Free Press*, "Dairy Probe Hears Denial of Charges," 8 June 1940, 23.

41 *Winnipeg Free Press*, "Evidence Finished," 21 June 1940, 4.

42 For an analysis of the struggle for the leadership of the working class, see Jim Naylor, *The Fate of Labour Socialism: The Co-operative Commonwealth Federation and the Dream of a Working Class Future* (Toronto: University of Toronto Press, 2016).

43 That one-third of Co-op employees had not participated in the share-purchase plan was proof that the scheme had not been compulsory, which was the primary charge against the firm.

44 *Winnipeg Free Press*, "Evidence Finished," 21 June 1940, 4.

45 AUUC Archives, PCL Records, Minute Book #2, "Special Meeting Board of Directors, June 24, 1940." At this meeting Bileski remained convinced that because the charges against the Co-op were groundless the institution would be found not guilty.

46 *Winnipeg Free Press*, "Red Threat: Communistic Plot in Canada Charged," 10 May 1940, 3.

47 *Winnipeg Free Press*, "W.J. Major Approves New Ruling," 16 May 1940, 1.

48 Ibid.

49 *Winnipeg Free Press*, "Provincial Authorities Approve Outlawing of 16 Societies: Blackout Government List Names of Groups," 6 June 1940, 1.

50 Ibid., "Big Victim: Ukrainian Group Hard Hit by Ban," 6 June 1940, 10.

51 Ibid., "Boards over Doors: Three Labour Temples Closed as Banned Group Breaks Up," 14 June 1940, 3.

52 Ibid., "Seize Property of Illegal Bodies," 24 June 1940.

53 For the impact of the seizure of the ULFTA halls on the WBA, see Anthony Bilecki, William Repka, and Mitch Sago, eds., *Friends in Need: The WBA Story* (Winnipeg: Workers Benevolent Association of Canada, 1972), 199–201.

54 *Winnipeg Free Press*, "Ald. Penner Arrested," 12 June 1940, 1.

55 Litterick went underground and was never arrested or interned. Others were not so fortunate. See Ibid., "Round-up: Navis and Israel Arrested in Drive," 14 June 1940, 1.

56 AUUC Archives, PCL Records, Minute Book #2, "Special Meeting Board of Directors, June 24, 1940."

57 He had been an editor with the *Ukrainian Labour News* and the CPC organizer in Winnipeg. He had only started working for the Co-op when the party was declared illegal in June.

58 Mochoruk, *The People's Co-op*, 88. For Tony Bilecki's "parade" and his work just prior to working at the Co-op, see William Repka and Kathleen Repka, *Dangerous Patriots: Canada's Unknown Prisoners of War* (Vancouver: New Star Books, 1982), 50–51.

59 Sago and Bill Ross (a.k.a. Cecil Zuken) were the subject of a three-month-long manhunt. See Repka and Repka, *Dangerous Patriots*, 180–183.

60 Personal communication with the author, John Boyd to J. Mochoruk, 13 March 2001. (Boyd, a.k.a. Boychuk, served as the manager of this creamery from 1940 to 1942.) Miller had been instrumental in arranging the purchase of the Minnedosa plant in October 1939. See AUUC Archives, PCL Records, Minute Book #2, "Executive Board Meeting, October 1, 1939 – Report of E. Miller," 1 October 1939.

61 This list included John Navis, Mathew Shatulsky, A. Petrash, D. Moysiuk, N. Kaschcak, P. Lysets, N. Stefanitsky, M. Sawiak, and several others. Mathew Popovich, who had been living in eastern Canada for several years by this point—and was no longer a leader in the ULFTA or the CPC—was also arrested and interned.

62 AofM, RG 3 C1, box 4, file 41 "Report of Conference Held in Office of Attorney General at 3 pm Friday, 21st June, 1940."

63 This was part of a bitter dispute. He had been taken to court by the Co-op in 1936 and agreed to repay the Co-op $3,200 in 1937 as part of an out-of-court settlement. See Mochoruk, *The People's Co-op*, 49–50.

64 Mochoruk, "'Pop and Co.' versus Tim Buck and the 'Lenin School Boys,'" 348–66.

65 Makuch, "Fighting for the Soul of the Ukrainian Progressive Movement in Canada," 387.

66 AofM, RG 3 C1, box 4, file 41 "Report of Conference Held in Office of Attorney General at 3 pm Friday, 21st June, 1940," 1–3.

67 Ibid., 3–6.

68 Ibid., 3 and 1.

69 Ibid., addenda, 1940, 2–3.

70 See Peter Prokop's account of how he was located and identified in Repka and Repka, *Dangerous Patriots*, 86.

71 *Winnipeg Free Press*, "Communists, Other Groups Arrested," 6 July 1940, 1 and 6; and Ibid., "New Clean-up of Communist Activities," 8 July 1940, 1.

72 For the difficulties confronting the WBA, see Stella Seychuk's comments in *Friends in Need*, 200–1. For the Co-op, see AUUC Archives, PCL Records, Minute Book #2, "Special Board Meeting, July 9, 1940."

73 City of Winnipeg Archives, Minute Book, Special Committees, May 1937–May 1945, "Meeting of the Special Committee to Enquire into the People's Co-operative Limited," 18 September 1940. See Ibid, "Minutes of the Meeting of the Public Welfare Committee," 12 December 1940.

74 AofM, RG 3 C1, box 4, RCMP file W945-1-105, Division D, Intelligence Section, "Re: Workers-Farmers Co-operative Association, Winnipeg, Manitoba," 16-10-40.

75 Ibid.

76 *Winnipeg Free Press*, "Labour Policies of Creamery Found Unfair," 13 November 1940.

77 AofM, G8078, file #41, "Report of the Special Committee appointed by Council to investigate charges into the treatment of its employees by the People's Co-operative Limited," 8 November 1940.

78 City of Winnipeg Archives, Minute Book, "Minutes of the Meeting of the Public Welfare Committee," 12 December 1940.

79 AUUC Archives, PCL Records, Minute Book #2, "Special Board Meeting, July 9, 1940."

80 Abe Greenberg had been hired in 1936 as part of an earlier Co-op expansion and had never been part of the inner circle of CPC-affiliated Co-op leaders. He had never been at risk of arrest, but he also felt no compunction about fleeing what looked like a sinking ship in 1940. For more information on his arrival at the Co-op, see Mochoruk, *The People's Co-op*, 71–72.

81 AofM, GR 1528, Rg 30, J.D. Cameron Papers, box 3, file #20 – Mr. Cameron's handwritten notes on the Co-op, n.d. [almost certainly 9 July 1940, given Sawiak's promise that a meeting to establish signing officers would be held by "Wednesday"—which would have been 10 July].

82 Ibid.

83 Ibid.

84 AUUC Archives, PCL Records, Minute Book #2, "Special Membership Meeting of the Shareholders of the People's Co-operative Limited at the Hebrew Sick Benefit Hall," 10 July 1940.

85 For details of the July 8th meeting, see AUUC Archives, PCL Records, Minute Book #2, "Special Board Meeting, July 9, 1940."

86 AUUC Archives, PCL Records, Minute Book #2, "Special Membership Meeting of the Shareholders of the People's Co-operative Limited at the Hebrew Sick Benefit Hall," 10 July 1940.

87 AofM, RG 3 C1, box 4, RCMP file W945-1-105, Division D, Intelligence Section, Nov. 14, 1940, transcript copy of Larkin statement.

88 Where he acquired these funds is unknown, as he certainly was not a wealthy man.

89 AofM, G8078, Co-op #41 "Attorney General of Manitoba to The President of the People's Co-operative limited, February 10, 1941."

90 Ibid.

91 AUUC Archives, PCL Records, Minute Book #2, "Executive, Board of Directors Meeting, August 6, 1940."

92 AUUC Archives, PCL Records, Minute Book #2, "Board of Directors Meeting, August 29, 1940."

93 According to Boychuck/Boyd's own account he had very narrowly missed arrest himself as he had been staying with Myron Kostanuik just a few days before his

home was raided. Boyd claims that he spent the next two years hiding in plain sight in Minnedosa—even playing golf with the local police.

94 Personal communication with the author, John Boyd to J. Mochoruk, 13 March 2001. See also John Boyd, *Reflections on my Life-Long Commitment to Socialism* (Toronto: the author, 2015), 6.

95 AUUC Archives, PCL Records, Minute Book #2, "Board of Directors Meeting, August 29, 1940."

96 Ibid.

97 Ibid., "Board of Directors Meeting, September 5, 1940."

98 He had been an activist in both the ULFTA and the CPC and had served as an organizer for the Farmers' Unity League in Saskatchewan before working for the Co-op.

99 AofM, RG 3 C1, box 4, file #41, RCMP file W945-1-105, Division D, Intelligence Section, 14 Nov. 1940, transcript copy of Larkin statement.

100 AofM, RG 3 C1, box 4, file #41, RCMP file W945-1-105, Division D, Intelligence Section, 14 November 1940, transcript copy of Larkin statement.

101 Ibid., Report re Workers-Farmers Co-operative Association, Winnipeg, Manitoba, 14 November 1940.

102 Ibid., "Conference held in Office of Attorney General at 3:00 pm Friday, 21st June, 1940," addenda, 4–5.

103 AofM, RG 3 C1, box 4, RCMP file W945-1-105, Division D, Intelligence Section, 14 November 1940, 3.

104 Ibid., 4.

105 For the WBA this was the Manitoba Insurance Act.

106 AofM, RG 3 C1, box 4, RCMP file W945-1-105, Division D, Intelligence Section, copy of letter, "Attorney General of Manitoba to The President of the People's Co-operative limited, February 10, 1941."

107 Ibid.

108 AofM, RG 3 C1, box 4, RCMP file W945-1-105, Division D, Intelligence Section, 14 November 1940, 3.

109 Ibid., Joseph Zuken to W.J. Major, Attorney General, February 18, 1941.

110 The Co-op realized only $17,000 on what had been a $27,000 investment.

111 AofM, G8078, Co-op #41 "Walter Sawiak, President of People's Co-operative Limited, to Hon. W.J. Major, April 12, 1941."

112 Personal communication with the author, John Boyd to J. Mochoruk, 13 March 2001.

PART III

AUTHORITIES, INTERNMENT, AND COMMUNITY INTERVENTIONS

CHAPTER 5

An Unprecedented Dichotomy: Impacts and Consequences of Serbian Internment in Canada during the Great War

MARINEL MANDRES

During the Great War, an immigrant's classification and treatment were determined by place of origin rather than ethnicity. Members of Canada's Serbian community were paradoxically considered to be both "friendly aliens" and "enemy aliens." Those born in Serbia and Montenegro were considered to be allies while those born in the Habsburg and Ottoman Empires were deemed to be enemies. While the latter were aliens, they were not enemies. This unprecedented dichotomy divided communities and families. Some ethnic Serbs were stigmatized, monitored, arrested, and interned while others supported the war effort by gathering humanitarian aid and/or enlisting in the Canadian, British, Serbian, and Montenegrin armies.

Providing a critical context for interpreting the complex wartime experiences of this particular ethnic minority, this essay examines the impacts and consequences of this dichotomy in terms of diplomatic interventions, organizational involvement, and community engagement. It complicates our understanding of this internment episode, as Kassandra Luciuk in her essay in this collection challenges us to do when approaching the history of Canada's first national internment operations. In the case of the Serbians, the unique combination of diplomatic mediation and organization formation challenged the arrest and internment of particular community members. These activities were also fundamental to shaping the experiences of Serbian men with wartime internment in Canada.

Aside from cursory remarks acknowledging the imprisonment of Serbs, none of the published literature on civilian internment to date provides substantially meaningful details on Serbian experiences.[1] A special census revealed that 165,775 enemy aliens were living in Canada during 1915.[2] At the time, 5,954 of the 8,579 interned enemy aliens were Austro-Hungarian citizens. Several hundred ethnic Serb men were among those Austro-Hungarians.[3] Until now, most of what little is known about the internment experience among ethnic Serbs comes from a 1938 newspaper article and some brief paragraphs in books. The former is drawn from the experiential knowledge of Božidar M. Markovich, which is recounted in a 1938 newspaper article while the latter comes from segments of a book on Serbs in Canada written by Olga B. Markovich, his daughter, and sections of a chapter on Serbs in Ontario by Nikola R. Pašić. The majority of original records relating the Canada's internment operations were destroyed during the early 1950s, upon the directive of the Treasury Board, due to an apparent lack of storage space at the Public Archives of Canada in Ottawa.

The recently discovered diplomatic correspondence of Antun Seferović, consul general of Serbia in Montreal, held at Arhiv Jugoslavije (Archives of Yugoslavia) in Belgrade, contains relevant and substantial information that provides the basis for primary research on the internment and treatment of ethnic Serbs in Canada during the Great War. Letters and documents contained in the Seferović files provide new information that connects existing pieces of the historical puzzle, bridges gaps in knowledge, and gives a voice to these "enemy aliens" and internees. Collectively, these materials provide information that answers the following critical questions: How many Serbians were interned? Where were they interned? Who intervened on their behalf? What were their experiences? What happened to them after being released? These questions are being addressed by an ongoing research project entitled "Loyal Enemy Aliens: The Internment of Ethnic Serbs and Romanians in Canada during the Great War (1914–1920)."[4] This chapter presents some preliminary findings associated with selected segments of the four-year project.

Migratory Waves

Two waves of Serbian emigration to Canada occurred before the Great War began: 1850–1900 and 1900–1914.[5] Both waves were economically and/or politically motivated and originated primarily from Balkan territories occupied by Austria-Hungary. Very few migrants came from independent Serbia. Each wave produced a distinct settlement pattern. The first wave emerged from the Dalmatian and Montenegrin coasts and their immediate hinterlands. It was a numerically small, demographically young, highly nomadic, and male-dominated cohort. Sojourners came, often via the United States, to earn additional income for their families.[6] Attracted by the gold rush, this initial movement was directed to mining and timber camps of British Columbia's Kootenay and Cariboo regions.[7] In coastal British Columbia, Serbians could be found in Prince Rupert, Anyox, Victoria, Nanaimo, and Vancouver.[8]

The second wave involved emigrants (and often families) arriving directly from the Balkans to support colonization efforts in Western and Central Canada. These settlers comprised the majority of Serbian internees. In Saskatchewan, the newcomers took up agricultural activities.[9] In Alberta, they worked in coal mines and on railways.[10] Communities emerged in Regina, Lethbridge, Edmonton, and Calgary.[11] Sizeable populations also developed at Atlin, British Columbia, and Dawson, Yukon Territories.[12] Within Ontario and Quebec, Serbs gravitated to urban areas providing employment in the industrial sector such as Welland, Niagara Falls, Hamilton, Toronto, Windsor, and Montreal.[13] By 1914, the Montreal, Toronto, and Hamilton Serbian communities grew to approximately 50, 500, and 1,000 members, respectively.[14]

When the First World War broke out, Austrian-born Serbs in Canada suffered the same sanctions as other internees under the War Measures Act (1914), the Alien Enemy Registration Ordinance (1914), and the Wartime Elections Act (1917).[15] Non-naturalized subjects were placed under restrictions (e.g., mobility and association), issued special identity cards that were to always be on their person, and compelled to register as enemy aliens with the police on a regular basis or face fines, arrest, and internment.[16] An estimated 80,000 men of military age were obligated to report their address and/or occupation on a weekly or monthly basis.[17] They were subject to surveillance and prohibited from being near critical infrastructure (e.g., bridges, harbours, and railways) and from gathering to demonstrate against their maltreatment. Local authorities could restrict aliens and citizens naturalized since 1911 from living and/or visiting any location where it was believed they could compromise public safety and national security.[18]

Besides attempting to leave Canada, enemy aliens were also interned for "suspicious" conduct and being of "unreliable" or "undesirable" character. Economic factors played a key role in shaping how these men were characterized; nearly all of the internees were poor and unemployed civilians who gravitated to urban areas in search of work and relief. Thus, the enemy aliens only posed an imaginary threat to national security. No subversive acts, such as espionage or sabotage, were ever proven.[19] Nonetheless, undesirable people, namely unemployed ethnics, were exposed to hostile treatment and subjected to imprisonment.

Deprived of their properties and civil liberties, prisoners were exiled to camps situated in the remote wilderness where they languished until after the war ended. Internment camps were traumatic environments, featuring inhospitable surroundings, confined quarters, substandard housing, harsh working conditions, meagre food rations, and inadequate winter clothing. Despondence was compounded by isolation from families, friends, and ethnic communities. Reading materials (e.g., letters and newspapers) were censored. Internees also had to endure verbal and physical abuse from prison guards. These appalling and desperate conditions resulted in shattered nerves, deteriorating health, and even deaths due to injuries, sickness, suicides, and attempted escapes.[20]

Diplomatic Interventions

Serbian communities in Canada were in a unique position because their Austrian-born members could theoretically obtain assistance from Serbia, which was an Allied nation. Dr. Mihajlo Pupin (1858–1935), a physicist at Columbia University, served as Serbia's consul in New York during the Great War.[21] The Federation of United Serbs – Unity (FUS), an American-based fraternal organization that provided insurance and protection to its members, brought the internment of Serbs in Canada to his attention in 1915.[22] At the time, FUS lodges were located in Hamilton, London, Niagara Falls, Edmonton, Britannia Beach, Prince Rupert, and Rossland. A significant number of Canadian Serbs were FUS members.[23] Pupin gained the approval of Britain's ambassador to the United States, Cecil Spring-Rice, to send representatives to the camps and advocate the release of Serbian prisoners.[24] Djordje (George) Smiljanić, president of the FUS Edmonton chapter, facilitated the release of forty-two Serb internees from the Vernon, British Columbia, camp on 17 July 1915, fifty "Slavonians" from Morrissey, British Columbia, on 20 January 1916, and ten Serbs from Mara Lake, British Columbia, between August and September 1916.[25] Before its formation in Canada in 1916, the Srpska Narodna Odbrana (SNO; Serbian National League) in the United States worked with FUS branches in Canada during Pupin's presidency in both of these organizations from 1914 to 1917.[26] It should be noted that Pupin's advocacy was always in his capacity of a diplomat rather than as the president or executive committee member of the Serbian organizations. Thus,

1089.-

Arhiv Jugoslavije Beograd

The Royal Legation of Serbia in Washington certifies ewith that

Captain A n t o V l a d i m i r S e f e r o v i t c h ,
travelling to Montreal, Canada, in the service of the Serbian Go- nment and the Legation is recommending him to the Civil and Mili- y Authorities of both the United States and Canada to allow him e passage into Canada and grant him protection if needed.

The photograph on this certificate and signature are se of Capt. A. V. Seferovitch.

The Chargé d'Affaires,

Figure 5.1 Antun Seferović became the honorary consul of Serbia in Montreal on 5 September 1918. Arhiv Jugoslavije (AJ371-44-59-15).

the reputation and duration of his consular appointment outweighed and outlived his organizational involvement.

Captain Antun Seferović (1871–1953) was appointed as the honorary consul of Serbia in Montreal on 5 September 1918 (see Figure 5.1).[27] Seferović actively liaised with the federal government in order to advocate and intervene on behalf of enemy aliens and internees. Archival material reveals that Seferović communicated extensively with the Dominion Police Office, the Register of Aliens, the Internment Operations Office, and External

Affairs.[28] He pressed the federal government to include ethnic Serbs among the friendly aliens who were exempt from monthly reporting. Seferović succeeded in exempting SNO members from carrying parole cards and from registering as enemy aliens. He personally endorsed and registered all SNO membership certificates as personal identity documents and as evidence of loyalty to Canada. By 1919, Seferović was issuing passports to citizens of the newly formed Kingdom of Serbs, Croats, and Slovenes as well as Czechs, Slovaks, Romanians, and Bulgarians as identity documents and to facilitate their emigration or repatriation.[29] These other ethnic groups did not have their own diplomatic representatives in Canada at the time. Throughout the 1920s, Seferović advocated on behalf of ex-internees, regardless of their whereabouts, to obtain financial compensation for confiscated property, unclaimed balances, unpaid work, and personal injury. He tracked down the ex-internees and corresponded on their behalf with the Internment Operations Office to seek financial reparations.[30] Diplomatic correspondence discloses that Seferović was tactful yet unyielding and uncompromising in his pursuit. Seferović also sought compensation on behalf of the next of kin, whether in Canada or abroad, for deceased ex-internees. His efforts prompted the Internment Operations Office to forward lists of unpaid balances to the diplomatic representatives of other affected communities (e.g., the Polish Consulate in Montreal), who were instructed to identify their own citizens.

Organizational Involvement

Mihajlo Pupin served as president of the Srpska Narodna Odbrana (Serbian National League), a patriotic and humanitarian, yet apolitical organization established in New York on 22 July 1914.[31] In Canada, a distinct entity was created on Pupin's initiative. The Srpska Narodna Odbrana u Kanadi (abbreviated hereinafter as SNO) formed in Toronto on 17 July 1916 and in Welland, Ontario on 23 July 1916.[32] Its name translated into English as the Serbian National League of Canada.[33] Both names are included on its official rubber stamp (see Figure 5.2). Chapters soon formed across the country: Montreal, Toronto, Welland, Falls View (Niagara Falls), Thorold, Port Colborne, Hamilton, Windsor, Fort William, Winnipeg, Regina, Edmonton, Calgary, Drumheller, Vancouver, Princetown, Rocks, Tramville, Phoenix, Anyox, and Prince Rupert.[34] Membership was estimated to be at least 400 by July 1918.[35]

The SNO's advocacy activities, often in partnership with Serbian diplomatic missions, prevented the internment of many Serbs and facilitated the expeditious release of others. Correspondence from the personal files of

Figure 5.2 The Srpska Narodna Odbrana u Kanadi translated into English as the Serbian National League of Canada. Both names are included on its official rubber stamp. Božidar M. Markovich Files (via Olga B. Markovich).

Božidar M. Markovich (1890–1970), the SNO's general secretary, provides examples of such initiatives. On 25 March 1917, Markovich wrote to the Serbian Legation in Washington advising about the predicament of Austrian-born SNO members residing in Ontario, who were classified as enemy aliens. He requested mediation on their behalf, such as exemptions from carrying a parole card and reporting monthly.[36]

Canadian legislation introduced in May 1918 required all foreigners to prove their identity and citizenship with a passport. Those unable to produce a passport were subject to a $50 fine or imprisonment.[37] This order was ignored by most Serbs due to language barriers, the absence of a Serbian diplomatic mission in Canada, and the assumption that they were not subject to the new law on the grounds of their ethnicity (i.e., all Serbs were allies). A group of about fifty ethnic Serb men was arrested for not carrying their passports during an inspection of the Beograd Café in Toronto on 4 June 1918.[38] Since the Serbian Consulate in Montreal was not yet established (it would open in September of 1918), Božidar M. Markovich, the SNO's general secretary, contacted Mihajlo Pupin about the matter. The following day, Pupin advised Markovich that a telegram seeking the release of the jailed SNO members was dispatched to the local police chief.[39] Within twenty-four hours, Toronto's mayor received instructions from the federal government to immediately release all men carrying an SNO membership card. With the exception of two non-SNO members, all of the men were released and exempt from paying the $50 fine. Pupin's intervention resulted in SNO membership cards being accepted in lieu of passports; they shielded holders from harassment and imprisonment. Not surprisingly, SNO membership increased rapidly following this incident.[40]

Some of these new members signed up in jail, which secured their release. A few days after the Toronto incident, on 7 June 1918, Gajo (George) Vasiljević, the SNO's vice-president, and some other Serbs were arrested on the accusation of being enemy aliens.[41] The next day, Markovich informed Pupin about the incident and sent the arrested twenty-two applications for SNO membership certificates. Vasiljević and the other Serbs were released on the grounds of possessing an SNO membership certificate and Pupin's mediation.[42] To date, the only certificate found, which includes a photograph of the bearer and was legitimized by the Royal Serbian Consulate in Montreal, was issued by the SNO of Canada (see Figure 5.3). Copies of this certificate were sent to RCMP detachments where SNO branches existed.

On 16 August 1918, the federal government announced that certain enemy aliens aged sixteen to sixty were no longer required to register themselves every month with the local police chief. This exception applied, at the discretion of local authorities, to Czechs from Austria-Hungary and to Armenians, Greeks, and Syrians from Turkey who were considered friendly aliens.[43] Many Austrian-born Serbs mistakenly assumed that this exemption applied to them and that their SNO membership card or certificate would be recognized in lieu of a passport. This was not the case, as some magistrates did not instantly accept an SNO membership card as proof of identity and loyalty. On 18 September 1918, for example, Martin Dosen [Došen] of Edmonton was charged with being an enemy alien and failing to report. Dosen denied the charges, claimed that he was an Austrian-born Serb, and produced an SNO membership card.[44] His case was referred to the Minister of Justice in Ottawa for consideration.[45] Antun Seferović, Serbia's consul in Montreal, wrote to Sir Joseph Pope, Canada's under secretary of state for Foreign Affairs, on 16 September 1918 to argue that "only those that are members of the SNO should be in the future exempt from all formalities and be considered loyal subjects and placed under special protection and control of this consulate."[46] On 30 September 1918, SNO members were exempted from reporting but still had to carry their parole card.[47] Dosen was never fined, jailed, or interned. Although his case set a precedent and propelled the SNO's importance, some local police authorities did not immediately apply the new directive.

In addition to helping those in the immediate aftermath of arrest, SNO officials also visited internees to help secure their release. On 2 January 1919,

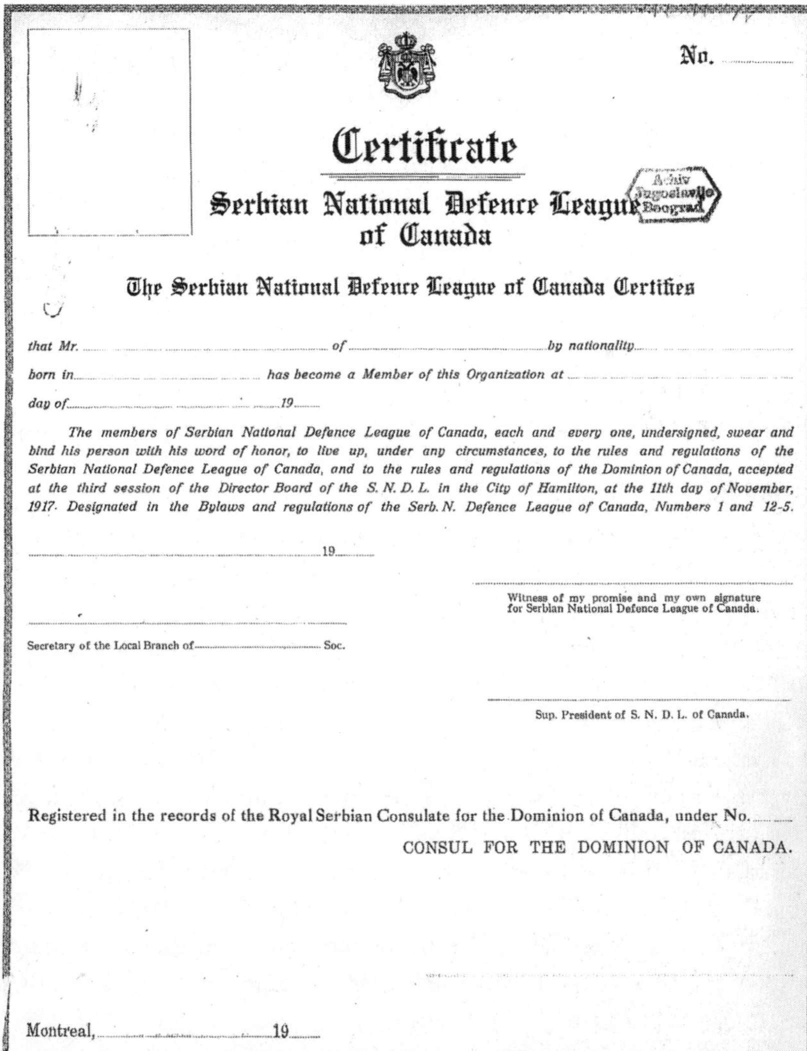

No. ....

Certificate

Serbian National Defence League of Canada

The Serbian National Defence League of Canada Certifies

that Mr. .... of .... by nationality ....

born in .... has become a Member of this Organization at ....

day of .... 19 ....

The members of Serbian National Defence League of Canada, each and every one, undersigned, swear and bind his person with his word of honor, to live up, under any circumstances, to the rules and regulations of the Serbian National Defence League of Canada, and to the rules and regulations of the Dominion of Canada, accepted at the third session of the Director Board of the S. N. D. L. in the City of Hamilton, at the 11th day of November, 1917. Designated in the Bylaws and regulations of the Serb. N. Defence League of Canada, Numbers 1 and 12-5.

.... 19 ....

Witness of my promise and my own signature for Serbian National Defence League of Canada.

Secretary of the Local Branch of .... Soc.

Sup. President of S. N. D. L. of Canada.

Registered in the records of the Royal Serbian Consulate for the Dominion of Canada, under No. ....

CONSUL FOR THE DOMINION OF CANADA.

Montreal, ... 19 ....

Figure 5.3 The only found certificate legitimized by the Royal Serbian Consulate in Montreal and issued by the SNO of Canada. Arhiv Jugoslavije (AJ371-44-59-197).

Božidar M. Markovich, the SNO's general secretary, received instructions from Seferović to visit the internment camp in Kapuskasing, Ontario, to identify the detained Serbs and to request their release.[48] Božidar Markovich spent two days interviewing the internees in the presence of two armed guards. He recorded the name, place, and date of birth, and date of arrival in Canada of each internee along with information about the date and reason for their arrest.

Many were reduced to tears during their interview, partly because they could not comprehend why they were harshly judged as traitors, ruthlessly rounded up, and needlessly detained, some for up to four years.[49] Above all, there was resentment at being imprisoned without a trial. SNO membership cards were issued to internees who expressed antagonism toward Austria-Hungary. Following the interviews, Markovich presented the camp superintendent a list of those qualified for liberation. Markovich secured the release of 164 of these men by proving that their loyalty was firmly with the Allied nations.[50] Markovich was personally held accountable for each of the liberated internees. The released prisoners' names were reported to Seferović. The SNO Vancouver chapter also assisted Serbs and other South Slavs who were arrested or interned for not reporting as enemy aliens by vouching for their identity and loyalty.[51]

Community Engagement

Enemy aliens, in general, and internees, specifically, typically remained silent about their vilification and mistreatment for fear of retaliation, detention, deportation, and other forms of retribution. Wartime marginalization compelled them to renegotiate their place within Canadian society in terms of identity, loyalty, and aspirations. It was not until early 1918 that the Serbian community had the courage to begin expressing grievances about its wartime experiences. Lt. Bud Protich (Budimir Protić, 1875–1938), a Serbian-born court interpreter from Regina, emerged as the community's most forthright advocate. Himself a symbol of Canadian loyalty, Protich had enlisted in the Canadian Expeditionary Force on 13 March 1916 in Winnipeg and was wounded at Vimy Ridge in 1917. Protich questioned the double standards applied to the Serbs along with the treatment of all enemy aliens, irrespective of their ethnicity. Despite his being lauded by the media for his patriotism, the RCMP kept a file on Protich during the war.[52]

On 31 January 1918, Austrian-born Serbs from Regina initiated actions, through Bud Protich and Maj. Dr. Walter D. Cowan (1865–1934), their member of Parliament, to have themselves removed from the "enemy alien" classification.[53] The effectiveness of this initiative and the extent of Cowan's activism are confirmed by the correspondence of May 1918 between William M. Martin (1876–1970), the premier of Saskatchewan, and Aylesworth B. Perry (1860–1956), Commissioner of the Royal North-West Mounted Police (RNWMP), regarding the reporting of Serbs as enemy aliens.[54] The RNWMP instructed Austrian-born Serbs residing in Regina to obtain SNO certificates as confirmation of their identity and loyalty.

Nearly one year later, Protich judiciously voiced his opinion regarding the paradoxical designation and unprovoked mistreatment of Canadian Serbs as enemy aliens during the war. The *Morning Leader* reported on Protich's address to the Great War Veterans in Regina on 6 February 1919, stating that Austrian-born Serbs were forced to report as enemy aliens despite the fact that they were working steadily and loyally for the Allies by assisting with every patriotic endeavour, including enlisting in the Canadian military and relinquishing their jobs to returned veterans. The article highlighted the indignity and incongruity faced by Austrian-born Serbs by citing the case of two brothers. One of them "had to report regularly to the police as an Austrian subject" while the other was "a returned veteran who enlisted with the 195th battalion."[55]

Protich also publicly assessed the absurdity of denaturalization and the manipulative aspect of disenfranchisement. Although arguing for the Serbian case, he gave a voice to all enemy aliens who were involved. Again, the *Morning Leader* took interest and stated that "a blanket disenfranchisement" of all naturalized citizens from enemy alien countries, especially those who are "bitterly hostile" to Austria and Germany, is an "injustice" to their allegiance.[56]

Protich's assessment conveys the prevailing sentiment, perhaps oblique disillusionment, shared by countless Canadians who were stripped of their citizenship, disenfranchised, dispossessed, watched, fined, and interned. After relocating to Vancouver, Protich continued to assist Serbs and other South Slavs with various legal matters. As secretary of the Serbo-Yugoslav Association, he petitioned on behalf of George Davis, former president of the local SNO chapter, to reduce his sentence for an infraction in 1921.[57] Protich helped an ex-internee named Louis Kasum [Kasumović] (1888–1934), a Croatian member of the SNO Vancouver chapter, to become naturalized by vouching for his loyalty.[58]

Effective Advocacy

The internment experiences of Canada's Serbian community remain largely unknown in the mainstream and ethnic media while memoirs of experiential knowledge, personal memory, and survivor testimony are either sparse or lacking. This research is unique in that it reconstructs and interprets the Serbian narrative, thereby contributing to historical accuracy, public awareness, and social memory. It also changes our perspective on civilian internment during the Great War by relating how an ethnic group, during its formative stage, effectively addressed the marginalization of a segment of its members as enemy aliens on the basis of their nationality. The distinction between an "enemy alien" and a "friendly alien" was unintentionally obscured by (mis)use of the term "nationality," which was legally interpreted as referring to a person's citizenship rather than ethnicity.[59]

Serbian communities throughout Canada dealt with their paradoxical wartime treatment as "frenemies" by initially reaching out to representatives of their native home and, eventually, to those of their adopted home. Acting collectively, they also established an organization, the SNO, which actively and effectively facilitated various advocacy initiatives on behalf of members who were considered to be "enemy aliens" and/or affected by the internment operations. These meaningful initiatives often involved collaboration with Serbian diplomats who engaged their network of personal contacts to intervene on behalf of the SNO and to legitimize its activities, especially being the guarantor of its members' loyalty to Canada. Regulatory dispensations for, and the expeditious release of, SNO members are noteworthy products of this partnership.[60]

Notes

1 Various aspects of the internment operations and experiences are examined by: Lubomyr Y. Luciuk, *Internment Operations: The Role of Old Fort Henry in World War I* (Kingston: Delta Educational Consultants, 1980); Lubomyr Y. Luciuk, "Ukrainians and Internment Operations in Ontario during the First World War," *Polyphony* 10 (1988): 27–31; Lubomyr Y. Luciuk, ed., *Righting an Injustice: The Debate over Redress for Canada's First National Internment Operations* (Toronto: Justinian Press, 1994); Lubomyr Y. Luciuk, *Searching for Place: Ukrainian Displaced Persons, Canada, and the Migration of Memory* (Toronto: University of Toronto Press, 2000); Lubomyr Y. Luciuk, *In Fear of the Barbed Wire Fence: Canada's First National Internment Operations and the Ukrainian Canadians, 1914–1920* (Kingston: Kashtan Press, 2001); Lubomyr Y. Luciuk, *Without Just Cause: Canada's First National Internment Operations and the Ukrainian Canadians, 1914–1920* (Kingston: Kashtan Press, 2006); Bohdan S. Kordan and Peter J. Melnycky, eds., *In the Shadow of the Rockies: Diary of the Castle Mountain Internment Camp, 1915–1917* (Edmonton: Canadian Institute of Ukrainian Studies, 1991); Bohdan S. Kordan, *Enemy Alien, Prisoners of War: Internment in Canada during the Great War* (Montreal and Kingston: McGill-Queen's University Press, 2002); Bohdan S. Kordan, "They Will Be Dangerous: Security and the Control of Enemy Aliens in Canada, 1914," in *Security, Dissent, and the Limits of Tolerance in War and Peace, 1914–1939*, Canadian State Trials, vol. 4, ed. Brian Wright, Erick Tucker, and Susan Binnie (Toronto: University of Toronto Press, 2015), 42–70; David Saunders, "Aliens in Britain and the Empire during the First World War," in *Loyalties in Conflict: Ukrainians in Canada during the Great War*, ed. Frances Swyripa and John Herd Thompson (Edmonton: Canadian Institute of Ukrainian Studies, University of Alberta, 1983), 99–124.

2 "Alien Enemies in Canada," *New York Times*, 10 October 1915, 16.

3 A discriminatory system was used whereby 3,138 German-speaking prisoners, including a few genuine POWs, were detained in urban areas and not required to

work while the other 5,441 "Austrian" civilians were interned in remote locations and obligated to perform hard labour. For details, see Luciuk, *Searching for Place*.

4 The research project has been made possible by grants from the Endowment Council of the Canadian First World War Internment Recognition Fund, the Serbian National Shield Society of Canada, Wilfrid Laurier University, and the University of Minnesota's Immigration History Research Center.

5 Academic sources dealing with Serbian immigration to Canada include: Pero Bulat, *Srbi u Kanadi: Njihovo Doseljavanje, Društveni i Ekonomski Život* (Windsor, ON: Avala, 1952); Olga B. Markovich, *Doseljavanje Srba u Kanadi i Njihova Aktivnost* (Windsor, ON: Avala, 1965); Marko Mladenović, *Encyclopedia Canadiana* (Toronto: Grolier, 1972) s.v., "People of Serbian Origin"; Sofija Škorić and George V. Tomashevich, eds., *Serbs in Ontario: A Socio-Cultural Description* (Toronto: Serbian Heritage Academy, 1987); Paul Pavlovich, *The Encyclopedia of Canada's Peoples*, 1999 ed., s.v., "Serbs"; Vladislav Tomović, *Canadian Serbs: A History of Their Social and Cultural Traditions* (Fonthill: Batlik, 2002). Prior to 1850, limited migration to Canada occurred on an individual and isolated basis.

6 While most of the migrants intended to return home after acquiring sufficient funds, many chose to remain when it proved difficult to simultaneously accumulate cash to pay for debts in, and transportation to, their homeland.

7 Markovich, *Doseljavanje Srba*.

8 Niko Musić, "O Istoriji Naših Emigranata u Kanadi," *Glas Kanade* (Toronto), 21 April 1938, 3.

9 Markovich, *Doseljavanje Srba*.

10 Djordje Dj. Smiljanić, "Istorija Jugoslovenskih Kolonija u Alberti," *Glas Kanade* (Toronto), 25 August 1938, 2; Markovich, *Doseljavanje Srba*.

11 The first Canadian parish of the Serbian Orthodox Church (Holy Trinity) was organized in Regina in 1912 and its church was built in 1916.

12 Olga B. Markovich, "Formation of the Srpska Narodna Odbrana (SNO) 80 Years Ago," *Voice of Canadian Serbs* (Toronto), 26 September 1996, 10–11.

13 The second oldest parish (St. Nicholas) was organized in 1913 at Hamilton and its church was built in 1916.

14 Boža [Božidar] Markovich, "Istorija Jugoslovenske Kolonije u Torontu, Ont.," *Glas Kanade* (Toronto), 20 January 1938, 2; Bulat, *Srbi u Kanadi*; "Austrians Get Amnesty; May Flock to the War: Notification to Toronto Men Who Left Home Under a Cloud – Servians Restless to Serve, but Somewhat Helpless," *Toronto Globe*, 31 July 1914, 7; "Local Serbs Unlikely to Aid Native Land: Their Country Being Cut-Off Would Prevent Their Joining Forces," *Toronto World*, 28 July 1914, 3; "Servians of Toronto Ready to Go Home to Wars," *Toronto Daily Star*, 28 July 1914, 1; "Patriotic Servians Ready for the Fray: Toronto Colony Will Answer Call to the Front," *Toronto Globe*, 28 July 1914, 9. Regarding Montreal, see Michael Lefebure, and Yuri Oryschuck, eds., *Les Communités Culturelles au Québec de L'Europe Centrale et de L'Europe du Sud*, vol. 1 (Montreal: Fides, 1984). Regarding Toronto, see "If War Call Comes Many Men are Ready: Toronto Servians Sent Message to Consul in New York," *Toronto Globe*, 30 July 1914, 8. Regrading Hamilton, see "Toronto Serbs Offer Services to the Consul: 200 Declare Their Readiness to Leave at Once for War," *Toronto Daily Star*, 30 July 1914, 3. Regarding Windsor, see Stanislava Marković, "Serbs in the City of Roses," in *Serbs in Ontario: A Socio-Cultural Description*, ed. Sofija Škorić and George V. Tomashevich (Toronto: Serbian Heritage Academy, 1987), 99–127.

15 The War Measures Act distorted and disrupted civil rights. The Wartime Elections Act disenfranchised all enemy aliens naturalized after 31 March 1902 along with those in the process of becoming Canadian citizens.

16 Luciuk, *Searching for Place.*

17 Legal aspects and local impacts of alien registration and internment are examined by Kordan, "They Will Be Dangerous."

18 Jeffrey A. Keshen, *Propaganda and Censorship during Canada's Great War* (Edmonton: University of Alberta Press, 1996).

19 Desmond Morton, *Years of Conflict, 1911–1921* (Toronto: Grolier, 1983); Bill Waiser, *Park Prisoners: The Untold Story of Western Canada's National Parks, 1915–1946* (Saskatoon: Fifth House, 1995).

20 A total of 107 internees died. Some of them had pre-existing conditions. Most of the sources listed in the first endnote address the death of internees. To date, three ethnic Serbs are known to have died in internment camps: Milan Kladar, Steve Peskovich [Pešković], and Samuel Vulovich [Savo Vulović]. Kladar was interned at Kapuskasing (POW # 991) and died of tuberculosis on 22 June 1918 in Hamilton, ON. Peskovich was interned at Vernon (POW # 266), transferred to Mara Lake (POW # 266), and died on 11 December 1916 at New Westminster, BC. Vulovich was interned at Vernon (POW # 979) and died of hemorrhage from a gastric ulcer on 2 December 1918. For details, see Library and Archives Canada, "Prisoners of War, 1914–18 – List of Names," in *Office of the Custodian of Enemy Property* (LAC, RG117, vol. 20, file 225), Library and Archives Canada, "Milan Kladar," in *War Graves Registry: Circumstances of Death Records* (LAC, RG150-4, vol. 278); Archives of Ontario, "Milan Kladar" in *Registrations of Deaths, 1869–1935* (AO MS 935, reel 251); Library and Archives Canada, "Steve Peskovich," in *War Graves Registry: Circumstances of Death Records* (LAC, RG150-4, vol. 278); Library and Archives Canada, "Samuel Vulovich," in *War Graves Registry: Circumstances of Death Records* (LAC, RG150-4, vol. 278).

21 Pupin served as honorary consul (1912–1915), with full consular powers, and then as consul general (1915–1920). Until the establishment of a consulate in Montreal in September 1918, Pupin's jurisdiction included Canada.

22 Pupin established the FUS in 1909 after the amalgamation of various fraternal organizations. Following a series of further mergers, the FUS became the Serb National Federation in 1929.

23 *Toronto Daily Star*, 30 July 1914, 3; *Toronto Globe*, 31 July 1914, 7.

24 Ivan Čizmić, *Jugoslavenski Iseljenički Pokret u SAD i Stvaranje Jugoslavenske Države, 1918* (Zagreb: University of Zagreb, 1974).

25 "Released from Vernon," *Phoenix Pioneer*, 17 July 1915, 2; "Concentrates," *Phoenix Pioneer*, 29 January 1916, 3; "News of the Kootenays," *Creston Review*, 28 January 1916, 5; Library and Archives Canada, Mara Lake Release of Servians in *Secretary of State* (LAC, RG6-H-1, vol. 767, file 3478). To avoid identifying themselves as Austrians, some Serbs used the term "Slavonians" since many Canadians were aware of the Slavs.

26 Žarko Vasiljević, "The American South Slav Attitude towards the Creation of Yugoslavia, 1914–1918" (MA thesis, University of Wisconsin–Milwaukee, 1976).

27 D.M. Pavlović, "Srpski Konsulat u Kanadi," *American Srbobran* (Pittsburg), 27 September 1918, 2; "Named Serbian Consul," *Edmonton Bulletin*, 5 October 1918, 3. Antun Vladimir Špiro Seferović was born in Odessa, Ukraine. His surname is

transliterated Seferovi(t)ch. Seferović served as Montenegro's consul general in New York between 1915 and 1917. He was asked to be Serbia's honorary consul in Montreal on 21 November 1917 but he declined due to an offer from the Romanian government.

28 Information provided in this paragraph is drawn from various files held at Arhiv Jugoslavije (Archives of Yugoslavia) in Belgrade, Serbia.

29 Library and Archives Canada, "Repatriation of Aliens; Diplomatic Representatives of Poland, Czechoslovakia, Jugoslavia, and Finland Empowered to Issue Passports, 1919" in *Department of Justice* (LAC, RG13-A-2, vol. 240, file 1919–1938). The Kingdom of Serbs, Croats, and Slovenes was established on 1 December 1918 and recognized by Canada on 1 June 1919. The diplomatic mission in Montreal officially became the Consulate General of the Kingdom of Serbs, Croats, and Slovenes on 30 May 1921. Legally, all Austrian-born Serbs ceased being enemy aliens upon recognition of statehood. Civilian passports of the Kingdom of Serbs, Croats, and Slovenes began to replace those of the Kingdom of Serbia in 1921. This process was completed by 1924.

30 Arhiv Jugoslavije, Razna Arhiva F-3 (1924–1939), in *Generalni Konzulat Kraljevine Jugoslavije u Montreal* (AJ 420-3).

31 The namesake of the American organization, the Narodna Odbrana, was formed in Belgrade on 8 October 1908 in reaction to Austria-Hungary's annexation of Bosnia-Herzegovina. Pupin resigned from the SNO's executive committee in July 1917.

32 Bulat, *Srbi u Kanadi.*

33 The SNO's name went through various translations, including "Serbian National Defence League of Canada." The SNO was reactivated in 1943 as the "Serbian National Shield Society of Canada."

34 Bulat, *Srbi u Kanadi*; Vladislav Tomović, "The Serbian Press in Canada, 1916–82," *Polyphony* 4, no. 1 (1982): 87–93; Markovich, "Formation of the Srpska Narodna Odbrana."

35 Boža [Božidar] Markovich, "Prposlano: Odgovor iz Kanade," *American Srbobran* (Pittsburgh), 7 November 1918, 2.

36 Boža [Božidar] Markovich, Letter to Ljubomir Mihajlović, Serbian Legation (Washington), 25 March 1917.

37 According to the Bank of Canada's inflation calculator, $50 in 1918 is equivalent to $734 in 2016.

38 Markovich, *Doseljavanje Srba.* The Beograd Café, established in 1912, was the focal point of Toronto's Serbian community. During the war, people met to exchange information, express opinions, and share anxiety. The local SNO chapter held its meetings there.

39 Mihajlo Pupin, Letter to Božidar Markovich (C 11/135/18), 5 June 1918.

40 Boža [Božidar] Markovich, "Istorija Jugoslovenske Kolonije u Torontu, Ont: Stroge Mere Protiv Stranaca," *Glas Kanade* (Toronto), 8 March 1938, 2.

41 Bulat, *Srbi u Kanadi*; Markovich, *Doseljavanje Srba*, Nikola R. Pašić, "Brief Historical Review of Serbs in Ontario and Their Immigration to Canada," in *Serbs in Ontario: A Socio-Cultural Description*, ed. Sofija Škorić and George V. Tomashevich (Toronto: Serbian Heritage Academy, 1987), 13–61. Vasiljević originated from Bjelovar, which was in Austria-Hungary. It is now located in the Slavonia region of Croatia.

42 Bulat, *Srbi u Kanadi*; Markovich, *Doseljavanje Srba*; Pašić, "Brief Historical Review."

43 "Enemy Aliens over 16 Must Register: Czechs and Some Other Friendly Aliens Now Exempt from This," *Montreal Gazette*, 17 August 1918, 1.

44 "City Police Court," *Edmonton Bulletin*, 18 September 1918, 2.

45 "City Police Court," *Edmonton Bulletin*, 20 September 1918, 4.

46 Arhiv Jugoslavije, Letter from Antun Seferović, Honorary Consul of Serbia, to Sir Joseph Pope, Under Secretary of State for External Affairs, 16 September 1918, in *Poslanstvo Kraljevine Jugoslavije u Sjedinjenim Američkim Državama – Vašington; Međunarodni Odnosi - Kanada (1917–1944)* (AJ 371-44-59-118).

47 Arhiv Jugoslavije, Letter from W.H. Walker, Acting Under Secretary of State for External Affairs, to Antun Seferović, Honorary Consul of Serbia, 30 September 1918, in *Poslanstvo Kraljevine Jugoslavije u Sjedinjenim Američkim Državama – Vašington; Međunarodni Odnosi - Kanada (1917–1944)* (AJ 371-44-59-120).

48 Markovich, *Doseljavanje Srba*; Draga Dragasevich, "Povodom Sto Godina Srpske Narodne Odbrane: U Službi Svoga Roda," *Voice of Canadian Serbs* (Toronto), 28 August 2008, 1, 4.

49 Markovich, *Doseljavanje Srba.*

50 Dragasevich 2008; Olga B. Markovich, "Istorijska Uloga Srpske Narodne Odbrane u Kanadi za Vreme Prvog Svetskog Rata: Veličanstvena Pomoć Srpskih Iseljenika," *Voice of Canadian Serbs* (Toronto), 29 May 2014, 4–5.

51 Djordje Dj. Smiljanić and Nikola Plećaš, "Srbi u Britiš Kolumbiji," *American Srbobran* (Pittsburgh), 3 July 1918, 2; Library and Archives Canada, "Jugoslavs in British Columbia; The Protection of as well as Proposed Method to Control Entry and Departure in Canada, 1919," in *Royal Canadian Mounted Police* (LAC, RG18-A-1, vol. 575, file 204).

52 Library and Archives Canada, "Bud Protich, Regina," in *RCMP, Commissioner's Office*, 1914–1918 (LAC, RG18-B-1, vol. 1870, file 170, p. 853).

53 "Regina Serbs Start an Agitation: Don't Want to Belong to 'Alien Enemies,'" *Toronto Daily Star*, 31 January 1918, 12. At the municipal level, Cowan served as councillor, alderman, and mayor of Regina (1915–17). At the federal level, he served as the member of Parliament for Long Lake (1917–21, Unionist) and Regina (1930–34, Conservative).

54 Library and Archives Canada, Serbians Reporting as Enemy Aliens in *RCMP, Criminal Investigations Branch*, 1919 (LAC, RG18-B-5, vol. 2168, file 15/21).

55 "Position of Serbians Is a Hard One: Many of Them Were under Austrian Yoke When They Came to Canada; Always Pro-Ally; Comrade B. Protich asks G.W.V. to Interest Themselves in These People," *Morning Leader* (Regina), 7 February 1919, 11.

56 "Naturalization and the Franchise," *Morning Leader* (Regina), 8 February 1919, 4.

57 British Columbia, "Historical Orders-in-Council, No. 1663, 1921," in *BC Laws*, 2015. http://www.bclaws.ca/civix/document/id/oic/arc_oic/1663_1921.

58 "Enemy by Birth, Ally in Spirit: Case of Croatian Seeking Naturalization Enlists Judge's Sympathy," *Vancouver Daily World*, 3 May 1921, 15.

59 Likewise, the term "reservist" obscured the contrast between "military" and "civilian."

60 While not examined in this paper, the outcomes of Serbia's humanitarian and military missions within Canada were also facilitated by the participation and coordination of the SNO of Canada.

CHAPTER 6

The Ex-Minister and the Fascist: A Tale of Two RCMP Informants during the Second World War[1]

TRAVIS TOMCHUK

Italian dictator Benito Mussolini declared war against the Allies just after 1:00 p.m. eastern time on Monday, 10 June 1940. Immediately following this declaration, members of the Royal Canadian Mounted Police (RCMP) and municipal police forces across Canada appeared in Italian Canadian neighbourhoods and began taking suspected fascists and fascist sympathizers into custody. Men and a few women were seized from their homes or places of work.

For Vincenzo Monaco, that day in June began as another typically long day of bread deliveries for Corona Bakery—a business he and his brother Donato had started in the early 1930s. He loaded his horse-drawn cart with bread and left the bakery at 7:00 a.m. expecting to complete his route and return by 6:00 p.m. Whether Monaco was aware that the Italian government had declared war against the Allies that afternoon is unknown. At some point along the way, however, Monaco was stopped by plainclothes officers of the RCMP and taken into custody as a suspected fascist. Unable to return the horse and cart to the bakery, it was left to wander the streets of Montreal. Monaco was taken to Fort Sainte-Jean in present-day Sainte-Jean-sur-Richelieu and held for three weeks before being transferred to the Petawawa Internment Camp.[2] The roundup of Italian Canadians was carried out in the name of national defence as it had in 1939 when German Canadian civilians had been interned following the outbreak of the Second World War. In total, almost 600 Italian Canadians from across Canada were interned during the war.[3]

An operation of this size takes a great deal of planning. Suspects need to be identified and their detention needs to be coordinated. Obviously, the RCMP had been prepared well in advance of 10 June 1940 in order to begin taking Italian Canadians suspected of fascist activities into custody. Yet, for the majority of the interwar period, the RCMP felt the real threat to Canada's national security came from the Communist Party of Canada (CPC), which had formed in the early 1920s following and inspired by the 1917 Bolshevik Revolution in Russia. As has been well documented by a number of scholars—most notably Greg Kealey and Reg Whitaker—the RCMP placed more of its resources on the surveillance of communists than fascist groups during the interwar period.[4] Though the RCMP first noted the presence of Italian fascism in Canada as early as 1923, it did not consider this political ideology to pose the same threat as communism—a position it would maintain even as late as September 1939.[5] In a letter to Norman A. Robertson of the Department of External Affairs, Charles Rivett-Carnac, the head of the RCMP's Intelligence Section, explained that the communists were a greater danger to Canada because they wanted to eliminate capitalism while fascism did not. Further, Rivett-Carnac wrote that "fascism is the reaction of the middle classes to the Communist danger."[6] The RCMP's greater emphasis on the CPC meant that officers of this police agency went undercover and infiltrated different branches of the party.[7] It appears as though this tactic was not used during the surveillance of Italian fascist groups in Canada. The RCMP's focus on the CPC led to a reliance on informants from Italian Canadian communities to identify fascists who were potential threats to national and public safety. This was done because the RCMP did not have agents of their own directly involved in Italian Canadian fascist organizations.

There were two notable Italian Canadian informants in Montreal working for the RCMP: Augusto Bersani and Camillo Vetere. Bersani was a former minister of the (Protestant) Italian Church of the Redeemer who became involved in the Italian Canadian antifascist movement. Camillo Vetere was active in Montreal's fascist movement and at some point prior to Italy's entrance into the Second World War began informing on comrades. Both men worked together to provide information to the RCMP. Their histories provide some insights into the RCMP's selection of informants during this time of conflict and the power that these men had over others in Montreal's Italian Canadian community.

Little is known about Augusto Bersani's life prior to his arrival in Montreal. Born in Italy, he was believed to have trained in the seminary to become a priest but, for reasons unknown, he did not finish his studies and boarded a ship to New York City. When exactly Bersani arrived in the United States has not been determined though it appears that he may have run into some kind of trouble that necessitated his departure for Montreal in the late 1920s. Once in the city, Bersani began to teach at the Point aux Trembles Protestant School and was later appointed minister of the Italian Church of the Redeemer in 1930. He served as minister until 1938 when he resigned from this position, stating health concerns.[8]

After Italy's declaration of war on 10 June 1940, a number of parishioners from the Italian Church of the Redeemer were arrested and interned. This included church elders such as Vincenzo Monaco, Giovanni Fasano, Giuseppe Raco, and Vincenzo "James" Greco. Reverend Domenico Scalera, who had replaced Bersani, was also interned.[9] The allegations against these men included being a fascist or a member of fascist organizations such as the Casa d'Italia, Dopolavoro, and the Italian War Veterans' Association. Giuseppe Raco, for instance, was alleged to be a member of Montreal's Fascio Giovanni Luparini and was "considered to hold very radical views and [be] a convinced Fascist [*sic*]."[10] Some internees were also accused of having donated gold to Italy and/or made anti-British comments in public. An examination of existing RCMP security reports and the personal papers of Justice J.D. Hyndman reveal that all of these interned parishioners were either informed on by Bersani or believed the former minister had played a role in their internment. Why was this the case? Was this particular Protestant church a hotbed of fascist activity?

Bersani had begun to work as an RCMP informant in 1937 while he was still minister at the Italian Church of the Redeemer. In RCMP security records he was known as S.A. 203 (Special Agent 203).[11] How Bersani became involved in this type of employment is not known. Nor is the amount he was paid for this work. It is also unclear whether the RCMP screened potential informants and what that process might have entailed. As an informant, Bersani was required to provide a report, known as a "personal history file," on those Italian Canadians involved in fascist activities. The information collected on these forms included biographical information about the subject's place and date of birth, vocation, marital status, and the number of children he or she had. It also noted their involvement in the Order Sons of Italy or any other so-called "patriotic institutions," such as the fascio or Dopolavoro, and whether the subject had donated money to the Casa d'Italia or the Italian Red Cross.[12]

Bersani also scoured the pages of the Italian-language press in Canada. In Bersani's collection of personal papers there are hundreds of articles clipped from Montreal's *L'Italia Nuovo* and Toronto's *Il Bolletino Italo-Canadese*. The names of Italian Canadians mentioned within these publications are underlined. Bersani did not only focus his attention on the communities of Montreal and Toronto but also much smaller Ontario urban centres such as North Bay and Timmins.[13]

In addition to collecting his own information on former parishioners and the Italian-language press, Bersani also received information from other RCMP-employed informants such as Camillo Vetere.[14] Vetere was the editor of the Montreal-based Italian-language fascist newspaper *L'Italia*. He was also president of the Italian War Veterans' Association and "a member of the Directorate of the Fascio of Montreal," to quote from an RCMP document.[15] According to Reverend Libero Sauro, who himself was interned during the war, Vetere told him he was sent to Canada for the express purpose of supervising and establishing fascist groups among Italians.[16] In 1925, Vetere helped found Montreal's Fascio Giovanni Luparini and then helped establish another group—Fascio Principe Umberto—in Toronto.[17] Vetere was well known among Montreal's Italian Canadian community and acted as an agent for *Il Progresso Italo-Americano*, an Italian-language newspaper from New York City. Before the Second World War, he was working on a publication called *Oltremare*, a who's who of the Italian community in Canada. People who were interested in being featured in this book were required to fill out a prepared form and pay a certain fee in advance. Vetere was always in need of money, possibly due to his having a large family, so many of the Italian Canadians who knew him subscribed to his newspaper or agreed to be a part of *Oltremare* to help him out financially. Sauro believed that those who had filled out an *Oltremare* form were implicated as fascists as a result.[18]

When and how the relationship between Bersani and Vetere began is unclear. Bersani began working as an RCMP informant in the late 1930s and it is likely that Vetere began around the same time. Vetere's involvement in Montreal's Italian fascist movement made him an important asset to the RCMP, who believed he was well positioned to "know the activities and membership in the Fascio and allied organizations."[19] He continued his fascist activities while providing Bersani with information on fellow comrades.

The RCMP's reliance on informants to identify known or suspected fascists meant that those who provided them with information had a great deal of power to implicate members of their own communities. In a letter written by Clementina Sauro on her husband Libero's internment, she stated that "anyone can sign an affidavit against anyone, and authorities will proceed to the arrest of the accused without further investigation. You can readily see how a certain type of individual would use this scheme to put out of his way whoever may stand between him and any sinister purpose he may have in mind. This is the case with my husband."[20]

Montreal lawyer and former internee Mario Lattoni also felt that informants could make accusations without any requirement of proof. As he stated in an oral history, "The affidavit justifying my arrest claimed that I was planning to blow up the central post office next to the Bank of Montreal in Place d'Armes. It was because of sham affidavits like that, drawn up by people like Vetere and [Antonino] Spada, that the police moved in to arrest hundreds of Italians."[21]

After four months of internment, Vincenzo Monaco was interviewed by Justice James Duncan Hyndman. Hyndman was a former Supreme Court of Alberta judge appointed by the federal Minister of Justice Ernest Lapointe to review the cases of internees who objected to their internment.[22] When Justice Hyndman asked Monaco why he thought he had been interned, the Montreal baker replied that someone seeking revenge had given authorities false information against him. When pressed further, Monaco told the judge that he believed Augusto Bersani, the former minister of the Protestant Italian Church of the Redeemer, to which he belonged, was responsible for his present predicament. After interviewing Vincenzo Monaco and his character witnesses, Hyndman concluded that Monaco was "a decent, honest law-abiding man incapable of committing subversive acts with which he has been charged." And that "it is my absolute conviction that this man is entirely innocent of any subversive act or intentions, and that justice can only be done by ordering his immediate release from internment."[23]

In two other cases, the evidence provided to justify internment was so unconvincing that Justice Hyndman asked for more information from the RCMP. Michele Tamiglia, for instance, was alleged to be associated with the Fascist Party, the Dopolavoro, and the Italian War Veterans' Association. RCMP also believed that he had donated gold to Italy and held anti-British views. During his interview with Justice Hyndman, Tamiglia did admit to being a member of the Italian War Veterans' Association and attending its meetings at the Casa d'Italia. However, Hyndman did not feel this in itself was enough to warrant Tamiglia's internment. The judge interviewed eight others who could testify on Tamiglia's behalf, and no proof that the man was a fascist was revealed. As a consequence, Hyndman requested that the RCMP supply him with more intelligence or witnesses to prove the allegations against the man. If no new evidence was forthcoming, Hyndman recommended that Tamiglia be released immediately. The RCMP appears not to have provided further proof against Tamiglia because he was released from Petawawa on 30 March 1941—two months after Hyndman's recommendation of release.[24]

Nick Jerome was another internee from the Italian Church of the Redeemer whose case was reviewed by Justice Hyndman. Jerome denied any involvement in fascist organizations and, again, Hyndman asked the RCMP to provide him with more evidence. The RCMP forwarded the judge a lengthy report that in Hyndman's opinion "add[ed] nothing of evidential value to the case." The judge then declared, "I am forced to say that I regard [Jerome's] further detention as a rank injustice."[25]

The questionable evidence against parishioners from the Italian Church of the Redeemer and the recurring mention of Bersani during interviews with internees led Justice Hyndman to seriously doubt the former minister's reliability as an informant.[26] This prompted the judge to conduct an investigation into Augusto Bersani in late November 1940 that included interviews with the family members of internees as well as non-Italians involved in the United Church of Canada. The exact number of people Hyndman interviewed is unknown but there are surviving transcripts for eight interviews. The oral testimonies reveal much about Bersani's personality and his motivations.

Shortly after the arrests of 10 June 1940, Bersani contacted the families of his former parishioners and feigned concern for the men's well-being. He approached Anne Jerome and Filomena Monaco, the wives of internees Nick Jerome and Vincenzo Monaco, and said he would seek their release. In a letter written on Chateau Laurier letterhead dated 18 June 1940, Bersani told Anne Jerome that he was in Ottawa on her husband's behalf. He ended his letter on a positive note by stating, "I have good hopes for you."[27] However, that was the last time Anne Jerome heard from the former minister. In Filomena Monaco's case, Bersani promised to deliver clothing to her husband while he was held at Fort Sainte-Jean. She put together a package that included socks, underwear, a sweater, and a jacket which she gave to Bersani. A few days later Bersani paid Filomena a visit and told her that the clothes had been delivered and that her husband and his brother Donato were doing well. Yet, when Filomena wrote to her husband to ask whether he had received the clothing his response was that he had not.[28]

But Bersani's act as the caring former minister did not last long. He paid a visit to Mary Monaco, daughter of Donato Monaco, two weeks after her father had been interned. According to Mary Monaco's testimony, Bersani asked if she had heard any news about her father. When Mary Monaco replied in the negative, Bersani stated that all those who had raised a hand against the former minister at the church would be interned.[29] During a similar visit to Filomena Monaco, Bersani was alleged to have said, "Remember when I was put out of the church and how I suffered, well now you are suffering."[30]

Hyndman's investigation also revealed Bersani's controversial behaviour while minister of the Italian Church of the Redeemer—actions that deeply angered members of the church. One incident involved Roman Catholic children attending Protestant schools. Since the Catholic school system in Quebec was francophone, Catholic Italian Canadians who wanted their children to learn English were in a difficult situation. Walter A. Watson, inspector of taxes for the Protestant school board, discovered that there were roughly 100 Catholic children at Protestant schools in Montreal. When he asked these students why they were attending Protestant schools they told him that Reverend Bersani had sent them. How Bersani became involved in facilitating this is unclear but he wrote letters to Protestant school principals claiming that Catholic children were actually members of his Protestant church, which allowed them to attend English-language classes. In a conversation with Watson, the principal of one of these schools, whose name was not recorded, described Bersani as a "racketeer" who used his position as minister for his own gain.[31] This suggests that Bersani may have received payment or some other kind of favour for getting Catholic children into the Protestant school. Unfortunately, the sources are silent regarding any repercussions for Bersani regarding this incident.

Bersani was also involved in falsifying the church's register of births. By doing so, he could bestow Canadian citizenship to a child born in Italy by changing the child's place of birth to a Canadian town or city. It also appears that Bersani had implicated fifteen-year-old Antonietta Forcillo in this endeavour by having her make changes to the register.[32] When Bersani was confronted about this irregularity by Reverend Robert George Katsunoff, minister of the Church of All Nations and superintendent of the Non-Anglo Mission of the United Church of Canada in Montreal, he simply explained that it had been a mistake.[33]

The most serious charge against Bersani, however, was his inability to prove that Christmas cheer funds earmarked for the parish's poor was received by them. The first incident occurred in 1936. The elders of the Italian Church of the Redeemer brought this to the attention of Reverend Katsunoff. Katsunoff approached Bersani to determine the veracity of this allegation. He discovered that the majority of vouchers that recipients of the relief were to sign actually contained Bersani's signature. Katsunoff told Bersani that if this happened again he would go to the authorities.[34]

The following year, the payment of Christmas relief was again in doubt. A vote was held by members of the church to determine if Bersani's actions should be brought to the attention of superiors in the United Church of Canada. The majority of voters were in support of this course and the result was conveyed by Vincenzo Monaco to Reverend Katsunoff. The reverend then met with Bersani and demanded that he provide the receipt vouchers, which he refused to do. When Katsunoff reported what had happened to the head of the United Church of Canada, Bersani was ordered to produce the vouchers or face the consequences. According to Katsunoff's sworn testimony, after he delivered the ultimatum Bersani flew into a rage and ordered his secretary to burn the vouchers. The disgraced minister formally resigned from the church in early 1938 citing ill health as the reason.[35]

During the sworn testimonies of Reverend Katsunoff, Walter Watson, and Reverend Munroe, each was asked by Hyndman to comment on Bersani's trustworthiness. None of these men trusted the former minister. Both Watson and Munroe declared that they would not trust Bersani even under oath.[36] Even Italian antifascists did not trust Bersani. Ottawa's Anselmo Bortolotti visited the former minister in Toronto after Bersani had relocated to the city during the Second World War. Bortolotti noticed a file with his own name on it in Bersani's apartment. As the antifascist recounted, "When I pointed out to him that this file could prove a danger if the political situation ever changed, he said in a very unconvincing way that it only contained personal information."[37]

Hyndman's investigation of Bersani revealed the former minister's questionable and criminal behaviour. It also raises questions about the RCMP and how it located and selected informants during the Second World War. Bersani's main motivation for becoming an informant appears to have stemmed from his desire to exact revenge against those parishioners of the Italian Church of the Redeemer who he believed had ruined his career. His actions had dire consequences for the men he identified as fascists to the RCMP. Not only did these men lose their freedom, and in many cases, their livelihoods; their families also bore the brunt of Bersani's vindictiveness. Vincenzo and Donato Monaco almost lost their bakery while interned. And in their absence, the bakery was not making as much money as it had in the past, which caused economic hardship for their families.[38] Financial considerations must also have played a role in Bersani's becoming an informant. While the amount of money the former minister was paid by the RCMP is unknown, his departure from the United Church of Canada meant that he needed to find work to support himself.

But what caused Camillo Vetere to become an informant? According to Montreal antifascist Antonino Spada, the RCMP preferred fascists as informants.[39] If it was true that Vetere was sent to Canada by the Italian government to organize fascist organizations, he was likely a devout fascist. This makes his actions somewhat surprising. Did Canadian authorities have something on Vetere that forced him to cooperate? Or was he simply in need of money to support a large family? Existing documents are silent on the reason. However, contemporaries of Vetere, such as the fascist Piero Bracci, believed that it was the money that Vetere earned as an informant that acted as an incentive.[40] The Ottawa-based antifascist Anselmo Bortolotti believed that Vetere received as much as $2,000 from Augusto Bersani for the information he supplied.[41]

Regardless of the reasons for Vetere turning informant, a number of those who either knew Vetere or were interned because of him were surprised that he cooperated with the RCMP. Piero Bracci, himself a fascist who was never interned, admitted in an oral history that he and Vetere had been friends but admitted how surprised he was by Vetere's actions. "I didn't expect the secretary of a *fascio* to denounce and betray his friends," Bracci stated.[42] Vetere continued to live and work in Montreal up to 10 June 1940—the day when Italy declared war against England and France. On the night of 9 June, Salvatore Mancuso later recalled, he and Vetere stayed up until midnight talking at the Casa d'Italia—Montreal's Italian cultural and social centre. Vetere informed those at the Casa d'Italia that he would be leaving for Toronto the next day to look for work. At the time, no one was suspicious of Vetere's impending exit from Montreal. Many still thought him to be a down-on-his-luck fascist. As Mancuso explained, "the people present that evening gave him money and personally I gave him a cheque for five dollars which he never had the nerve to cash."[43]

What happened to Camillo Vetere after he relocated to Toronto is unknown. It is also unclear when his relationship with the RCMP came to an end. It is similarly difficult to pinpoint when Augusto Bersani's role as S.A. 203 ceased. By April 1942, Bersani was living in Toronto and editing and writing articles for the city's antifascist Italian-language newspaper *La Vittoria*. His role was changed to associate editor in January 1943 and it appears as though

Bersani ceased contributing content to the newspaper after that point.[44] Very little is known about Bersani's life after the war. According to Michael Monaco, son of internee Vincenzo Monaco, the disgraced minister turned informant moved to Buffalo, New York, where he co-owned a motel. He would send the Monacos postcards on a regular basis inviting them to stay at the motel. The Monacos, however, never accepted the offer.[45]

The stories of Augusto Bersani and Camillo Vetere, though incomplete, give us some insight into their roles as RCMP informants during the Second World War as well as their reasons for engaging in such work. Bersani sought revenge against the parishioners he held responsible for his troubles at the Italian Church of the Redeemer. But he also appears to have put a great deal of effort into keeping tabs on Italian Canadian fascists prior to and during the war, as evidenced by his personal papers. Whether it was personal conviction or opportunity that led him to join the antifascist movement, is hard to discern. Perhaps it was both. Justice Hyndman's investigation into Bersani revealed a dishonest personality. Yet, Bersani was employed by the RCMP and in a position where he received information from other informants, such as Camillo Vetere, who were part of the fascist movement. We cannot say with certainty how many Italian Canadians were interned because of Bersani but we do know that eleven members the Italian Church of the Redeemer were sent to Petawawa. These men were eventually released after Justice Hyndman could find no evidence to justify their continued incarceration.

Vetere was in a better position to identify fascists within Montreal's Italian community but not all active fascists were taken into custody and interned. Piero Bracci is a prime example. Nearly 600 Italian Canadians were interned during the Second World War, yet only a minority were active fascists. If revenge and money are the main reasons that individuals became informants, then this should give pause to authorities when surveilling a segment of the population. The RCMP does not appear to have questioned the reports submitted by informants. And it was not until investigations were carried out by Justice Hyndman that a serious examination of the allegations was carried out. Up to that point, informants wielded a great deal of power.

Justice Hyndman's investigations also raise questions regarding the danger Italian Canadian fascism posed to Canada. Whether these Italian men and women were active fascists or not, not one was ever charged with a crime. The Canadian government's "intern first" policy judged Italian Canadians before a proper examination of allegations could be proven. This did irreparable damage to the internees and their families. As repugnant as fascism is, believing in this political philosophy is not a crime in itself. This type of pre-emptive action is still being utilized in Canada. Following the 11 September 2001 attacks in the United States, the Canadian government detained five Arab men living in Canada who it claimed were sleeper agents of Al-Qaeda. The detention of Mohammad Zeki Mahjoub, Mahmoud Jaballah, Hassan Almrei, Mohamed Harkat, and Adil Charkaoui was made possible under a security certificate, which falls under the Immigration and Refugee Protection Act (IRPA). A security certificate allows the Canadian government to deport non-citizens because they have violated human and/or international rights, are involved in organized crime, or are considered a threat to national security.[46] All of these men spent years in prison without any formal charges being laid against them. Neither they nor their lawyers were able to see the evidence Canadian Security Intelligence Service (CSIS) used to justify their detention.

The internment of Italian Canadians during the Second World War shows us how quickly Canadian citizens can become enemies of the state during times of crisis. It is a complicated history, as Franca Iacovetta underscores in her essay in this collection. As Italy moved closer to a formal alliance with Nazi Germany, Canadian authorities, led by the RCMP, made plans to arrest and intern hundreds of Italian Canadians. The RCMP acted on the information supplied by men such as Augusto Bersani and Camillo Vetere. Though the financial motivation for Vetere's turn against his fascist comrades can only be surmised, Bersani's behaviour, at least initially, was fuelled by his need for vengeance. Until the outbreak of the Second World War, Canadian authorities had not directed their resources toward the surveillance of fascist groups in the same way they did with communists. This forced the RCMP to rely on members of the Italian Canadian community to help them identify suspected fascists. Yet, the experiences of the Monacos and others demonstrate the dangers that can occur when security agencies place their apparently unquestioned trust in informants. More research needs to be done into the RCMP's vetting process of informants during this period. And, it may be worth examining this in a comparative manner. For example, Jim Mochoruk's contribution to this collection illustrates that prejudiced informants played a key role in the apprehension of at least some of the far leftists interned during the Second World War. It is reasonable to assume this was the case for other internment-affected groups. However, this is challenging research to pursue. Considering how difficult it is to obtain information of this nature from governmental archives, in the case of the Italian Montreal community, we may never know how the relationships between Bersani and Vetere and the

RCMP began. What we do know is that the information these men supplied Canadian authorities resulted in mass arrests and internments for citizens without criminal charges in a court of law. Livelihoods were ruined and families suffered because of hearsay and secret evidence.

Notes

1 Parts of this chapter appeared previously as "Special Agent 203: The Motivations of Augusto Bersani" in *Beyond Barbed Wire: Essays on the Internment of Italian Canadians*, published by Guernica Press in 2012.

2 Michael Monaco, personal interview, 23 June 2011.

3 "Internee List," *Italian Canadians as Enemy Aliens: Memories of World War II*, http://www.italiancanadianww2.ca/tour/internees.

4 Gregory S. Kealey and Reg Whitaker, eds., *RCMP Security Bulletins: The Depression Years, 1933–1939*, vols. 1–5 (St. John's, NL: Canadian Committee on Labour History, 1993); Gregory S. Kealey and Reg Whitaker, eds., *RCMP Security Bulletins: The War Series, 1939–1945*, vols. 1 and 2 (St. John's, NL: Canadian Committee on Labour History, 1989–1993); Gregory S. Kealey, "Spymasters, Spies, and Their Subjects: The RCMP and Canadian State Repression, 1914–1939," in *Whose National Security: Canadian State Surveillance and the Creation of Enemies*, ed. Gary Kinsman, Dieter K. Buse, and Mercedes Steedman (Toronto: Between the Lines, 2000), 18–34; Michelle McBride, "From Indifference to Internment: An Examination of RCMP Responses to Nazism and Fascism in Canada" (MA thesis, Memorial University, 1993).

5 RCMP, "The Organization and Activities of the Italian Fascist Party in Canada," Ottawa, 1937, 13, Canadian Security Intelligence Service (hereafter CSIS), LAC, RG146, vol. 97, file AH-1999/00227; Reg Whitaker, "Official Repression of Communism during World War II," *Labour/Le Travail* 37 (1996): 137.

6 Whitaker, "Official Repression of Communism during World War II," 137.

7 John Leopold, for instance, was an undercover RCMP officer who infiltrated the Communist Party of Canada in the 1920s. Kealey, "Spymasters, Spies, and Their Subjects: The RCMP and Canadian State Repression, 1914–1939," 25–28.

8 "Evidence of Walter A. Watson," Montreal, n.d., LAC, JDHF, MG 30, E 182, vol. 14; "Evidence of Reverend Robert George Katsunoff," Montreal, n.d., LAC, JDHF, MG 30, E 182, vol. 14.

9 These were not the only people involved with the Italian Church of the Redeemer who were interned. Donato Monaco, Nick Jerome (born Nicola Girolamo), Michele Tamiglia, Canio Nicolini, Gennaro Placito, and Costanzo D'Amico were also taken to Petawawa in the summer of 1940. See LAC, JDHF, MG 30, E 182, vol. 14.

10 J.D. Hyndman, "In the matter of the Defence of Canada Regulations and in the matter of Giuseppe Raco, 40-D-269-4-D-126," to Minister of Justice, Ottawa, 17 Feb. 1941, LAC, JDHF, MG 30, E 182, vol. 14.

11 Luigi Bruti Liberati, "The Internment of Italian Canadians," in *Enemies Within: Italian and Other Internees in Canada and Abroad*, ed. Franca Iacovetta, Roberto Perin, and Angelo Principe (Toronto: University of Toronto Press, 2000), 84. Bersani's identity as S.A. 203 is revealed in the papers of James Duncan Hyndman. In a memo to the Minister of Justice written on 17 February 1941, Hyndman attributed the following quote to Bersani: "In recent times [Giuseppe Raco] has ceased all connections with Fascism [*sic*] and all his sympathies have turned to the British people and to the allies [*sic*]. He never held any office in the Fascio nor was

he active in any organization." In a second memo dated 15 March 1941, Hyndman quotes S.A. 203 as follows: "[I]n recent times [Giuseppe Raco] has ceased all connections with Fascism [*sic*] and all his sympathies have turned to the British people and to the Allies. He never held any office in the Fascio nor was he active in any organization." Both the quote attributed to Bersani and the one to S.A. 203 are dated 24 May 1940. J.D. Hyndman, "In the matter of the Defence of Canada Regulations and in the matter of Giuseppe Raco, 40-D-269-4-D-126," to Minister of Justice, Ottawa, 17 Feb. 1941, and J.D. Hyndman, "Memorandum Re: Giuseppe Raco – 40D-269-4-D-126," 15 Mar. 1941, LAC, JDHF, MG 30, E 182, vol. 14.

12 Contact No. 17, "Personal History File: Giuseppe D'Amato," 24 Oct. 1940, Montreal, RCMP, LAC, RG18, F-3, vol. 3563.

13 See the Augusto Bersani Papers, Multicultural History Society of Ontario Archives (hereafter MHSOA), Kelly Library, University of Toronto.

14 RCMP, "The Organization and Activities of the Italian Fascist Party in Canada," Ottawa, 1937, 11–12, LAC, CSIS, RG146, vol. 97, file AH-1999/00227.

15 RCMP, "The Organization and Activities of the Italian Fascist Party in Canada," Ottawa, 1937, 11–12, LAC, RG146, vol. 97, file AH-1999/00227.

16 Libero Sauro, Toronto, to Peat and McBride, Canadian Bank of Commerce, Hamilton, 16 Feb. 1942, Sauro Collection, Columbus Centre (North York, Ontario).

17 Angelo Principe, *The Darkest Side of the Fascist Years: The Italian Canadian Press, 1920–1942* (Toronto: Guernica Editions, 1999), 228.

18 Libero Sauro, Toronto, to Peat and McBride, Canadian Bank of Commerce, Hamilton, 16 Feb. 1942, Sauro Collection, Columbus Centre.

19 "Secret Memorandum to The Inter-Departmental Committee Re: Rev. Liborio [*sic*] Sauro, Toronto, Ont." 27 June 1940, Ottawa, LAC, RCMP, RG18, F-3, vol. 3563.

20 Clementina Sauro, Toronto, to Rev. IG Perkins, Sault Ste. Marie, 22 Sep. 1940, Sauro Collection, Columbus Centre.

21 Montreal's Antonino Spada was a founder of the Italian-language antifascist newspaper Il Risveglio Italiano. Filippo Salvatore, *Fascism and the Italians of Montreal: An Oral History, 1922–1945* (Toronto: Guernica, 1998), 213 and 214.

22 Section 26 of the Defence of Canada Regulations (DOCR), a series of regulations introduced as part of the War Measures Act, allowed an internee to formally object to his or her incarceration within thirty days of being interned. When an appeal was made, the Minister of Justice appointed a judge who conducted an investigation. Government of Canada, *Defence of Canada Regulations* (Ottawa: Government of Canada, 1939), 36.

23 J.D. Hyndman, Ottawa, to Ernest Lapointe, Ottawa, 25 Nov. 1940, "In the matter of the Defence of Canada Regulations and in the matter of Vincenzo Monaco, 40D-269-1-D-751," LAC, JDHF, MG 30, E 182, vol. 14.

24 J.D. Hyndman to W.R. Jackett, "Memorandum Re; Michele Tamiglia – 40-275," 10 Feb. 1941, LAC, JDHF, MG 30, E 182, vol. 14, and Custodian of Enemy Property, LAC, RG117, vol. 656, file 3850, "Tamiglia, Michele."

25 J.D. Hyndman to Minister of Justice, "In the matter of the Defence of Canada Regulations and in the matter of Nicola Di [*sic*] Girolamo (Nick Jerome), 40D-269-4-D-46," 1 Mar. 1941, LAC, JDHF, MG 30, E 182, vol. 14.

26 J.D. Hyndman, "In the matter of the Defence of Canada Regulations and in the matter of Vincenzo Monaco, 40D-269-1-D-751," to Minister of Justice, Ottawa, 3 Dec. 1940, LAC, JDHF, MG 30, E 182, vol. 14.

27 Augusto Bersani to Anne Jerome, 18 June 1940, and "Evidence of Anne Jerome," Montreal, n.d, LAC, JDHF, MG 30, E 182, vol. 14.

28 "Evidence of Filomena Monaco," Montreal, n.d, LAC, JDHF, MG 30, E 182, vol. 14.

29 "Evidence of Mary Monaco," Montreal, n.d, LAC, JDHF, MG 30, E 182, vol. 14.

30 "Evidence of Filomena Monaco," Montreal, n.d, LAC, JDHF, MG 30, E 182, vol. 14.

31 "Evidence of Walter A. Watson," Montreal, n.d., LAC, JDHF, MG 30, E 182, vol. 14.

32 "Evidence of Reverend Robert George Katsunoff," Montreal, n.d., and L. Colucci, Giuseppe Fasano, and Vincenzo Monaco to Dr. Katsunoff, 26 May 1938, LAC, JDHF, MG 30, E 182, vol. 14.

33 "Evidence of Reverend Robert George Katsunoff," Montreal, n.d., LAC, JDHF, MG 30, E 182, vol. 14.

34 "Evidence of Reverend Robert George Katsunoff," Montreal, n.d., and "Evidence of Reverend Lloyd A. Smith, Montreal, 22 Nov. 1940, LAC, JDHF, MG 30, E 182, vol. 14.

35 "Evidence of Mary Monaco," Montreal, n.d, and "Evidence of Reverend Robert George Katsunoff," Montreal, n.d., LAC, JDHF, MG 30, E 182, vol. 14.

36 "Evidence of Walter A. Watson," Montreal, n.d., and "Evidence of Reverend William Munroe," Montreal, n.d., LAC, JDHF, MG 30, E 182, vol. 14.

37 Salvatore, *Fascism and the Italians of Montreal,* 37.

38 Michael Monaco, personal interview, 23 June 2011.

39 Salvatore, *Fascism and the Italians of Montreal,* 213.

40 Ibid., 89–90.

41 Ibid., 38.

42 Ibid., 89–90.

43 Ibid., 122–123.

44 See *La Vittoria*, MHSOA, Kelly Library, University of Toronto.

45 Michael Monaco, personal interview, 23 June 2011.

46 "Security Certificates," Public Safety Canada, http://www.publicsafety.gc.ca/cnt/ntnl-scrt/cntr-trrrsm/scrt-crtfcts-eng.aspx (accessed 27 May 2016); "Hassan Almrei: Case Spotlights Fundamental Justice Concerns of the Security Certificate Process," Canadian Civil Liberties Association, 24 Mar. 2011, https://ccla.org/hassan-almrei-case-spotlights-fundamental-justice-concerns-of-the-security-certificate-process/.

PART IV

GENDER, IDENTITY, AND INTERNMENT IN THE SECOND WORLD WAR

CHAPTER 7

"Camp Boys": Privacy and the Sexual Self

CHRISTINE WHITEHOUSE

Taking the opportunity of his third camp transfer in two years to reflect upon the perplexing experiences of life as a Jewish refugee from Nazi oppression in Canadian internment camps, Franz Krämer penned, "Two years of internment have led to one positive experience: culture can neither be maintained nor grow without liberty. This liberty is composed of certain qualities, such as uncensored speech, privacy, irregularity of life, the possibility of saying to a woman 'Take it or leave it' (While we cannot even get one). . . . In consequence, culture in Camp 'A' was a poor, wornout and underfed lady."[1] Several things are telling about Krämer's analysis of camp culture. First is the very act of his self-reflexivity within the broader framework of late modernity.[2] Where a struggle for physical survival was far from the reality of daily life in Canadian internment camps, internees' general good physical health afforded them the discursive space to dwell on the mental strain of incarceration. Above all else, the interned men lamented the loss of their liberty, a right belonging to all citizens of any "cultured" state, and they reflected on their collective case as one small consequence of the unfolding war between democracy and dictatorship, the line between which at least some saw as blurred.[3] The second major theme apparent in Krämer's analysis of camp life is the importance of the absence of women. Here men's access to women as objects of their desire appears as a right of the modern condition equivalent to freedom of speech, self-determination, and the division of public and private spheres. At the same time, given the absence of these liberties in camp, culture becomes embodied in the form of an imagined sickly woman, revealing an intimate and unspoken relationship between the values of modern democracy, power, and the (sexed) body. It is this axis that incarceration makes apparent that is the subject of this article.[4]

Drawing his observations of camp culture to a close, Franz Krämer queried his readership, "Have I grumbled too much?" And in response, "Certainly. Our cultural life wasn't so bad compared with the activities in those countries which are already at war. And the refugees are at war with Hitler much longer than anybody else, some of them for eight years."[5] His sentiment that internment was experienced as a period of cultural deprivation, administrative confusion, and as an instance of deliverance from a worse fate in Nazi-occupied Europe reflects the myriad ways internees comprehended their fate in Canada as they awaited release, but especially in the decades following, as many former internees became Canadian citizens and some published memoirs providing a narrative framework through which the history of their internment has been remembered.[6] And yet, the refugees were not simply cast out from one homeland, experiencing tremendous displacement and violent loss, to be assimilated into a new national community—a successful story of immigration. This would be to forget that within Canada the refugees were victims of ongoing, structural discrimination as Jews and not as members of an enemy nation. It is worthwhile, instead, to dwell in the historical moment when the messiness of Krämer's emotions captured the uncertainty of their futures as they were pulled between new lives in the United Kingdom, the United States, or Canada, and familial and cultural connections in central Europe and beyond.

The refugees' double consciousness as persecuted Jews and as potential immigrants in the English-speaking world is mirrored in their experiences as interned men, compelled by the gendered contract of modern nationhood to perform one masculinity while their status betwixt and between afforded them more flexibility. Sexuality during incarceration, I therefore argue, became one crucial site for constructing and making sense of the modern self. More specifically, the absence of privacy in internment camps heightened internees' anxieties over how "normal" masculine desire should be performed, while imagining the female body as an object of male yearning, through storytelling and artworks, became one way internees attempted to regain self-determination lost through incarceration. By examining how internees thought about and performed their sexual identities as a subconscious expression of their disenchantment with the realities of late modernity, I aim to consider the consequences for intimacy and the self when the right to privacy and civil society are non-existent.

In thinking about how the internees constructed and represented their varying masculinities without women to affirm their identities, this essay takes up the issue of hegemonic masculinity versus non-hegemonic or subordinate masculinities. R.W. Connell popularized the term "hegemonic masculinity" to refer to the negotiation of male power within social frameworks.[7] Initially this was limited to the ways in which men exercise their dominance over women, but, as the case of male-segregated societies helps make clear, hegemonic masculinity also includes the exercise of power over non-hegemonic or subordinate forms of masculinity.[8] Because masculinity is constructed socially and historically, it is fluid and contingent upon other selfhoods, such as ethnicity and class, intersecting in specific contexts. Rather than form clear binaries, masculinities develop in relation to one another and are frequently performed as hierarchical. Hence, hegemonic masculinity "as the historically and culturally stable and legitimised form of masculinity" is negotiable.[9] Conditioned by the experience of camp life, then, the Jewish refugees tested and deployed their masculinities in a multitude of ways, with the possibility that any given internee could choose to express his masculinity along a moving continuum.

"Camp Boys"

In the summer of 1940, when fears of a German invasion of the British Isles were at their peak following the evacuation of Dunkirk, hundreds of male Jewish refugees found themselves incarcerated in British prisons at a critical juncture in their lives: the transition from schoolboys to men.[10] The youth of the youngest refugees made them especially apt to embrace and adapt to their transient status as they were moved from local holding cells to temporary internment camps outside of London and on the Isle of Man, to Canada and Australia, where many would remain for the duration of the war.[11] One former internee recalled with laughter greeting the policemen who came to arrest him, seeing his incarceration as a way out of shovelling manure on a farm, his only means of subsistence in Wales.[12] Unlike internees over the age of twenty-five, the "camp boys," as they called themselves, had fewer familial ties and obligations in the United Kingdom, many having left Germany and Austria before Kristallnacht in 1938 to enroll in prestigious universities, while others' internment stories began with a more desperate flight from Nazi-occupied Europe following the beginning of state-sanctioned violence against Jews.

Regardless of how they came to be in Britain in the summer of 1940, the common characteristic of their youth only partly explains why most remembered their first encounter with Canada with a mix of nostalgia and resentment. One could also see their narration of the self within the context of what it meant to be a modern man: "To be modern . . . is to find ourselves in an environment that promises us adventure, power, joy, growth, transformation of ourselves and the world—and, at the same time, that threatens to destroy everything we have, everything we know, everything we are."[13] This juxtaposition of adventure and catastrophe was exaggerated in internment camps that became, at least for the youth among them, an experiment in socialization; the absence of the right to privacy quickly exposed men's character and desires in a condensed and enforced collectivity. Theirs, in other words, is a coming-of-age story that, heightened by the conditions of incarceration, reflects some of the anxieties over what it meant to be masculine in late modernity.

What is clear about the story of the "camp boys" is that the bonds of belonging they formed early in their internment experience with one another were powerful identity markers within any given camp, and these bonds often followed them through post-release life as well. When youth were picked up in the United Kingdom, they were frequently arrested alongside friends they had made working as labourers on farms or, most notably, as students at Oxbridge. With their limited autonomy in British camps, they made life-changing choices about which ocean liner to board in order to stay together.[14] Once interned in Canada, they organized themselves into huts based on common interests, backgrounds, and age.[15] Upon their staggered release, former internees would help their still-interned friends secure Canadian sponsors, often settling in the same Canadian cities after the Second World War.[16] And it is with the nostalgia of a class reunion that former internees reflected upon their internment experience nearly forty years later during a gathering of "camp boys" in Toronto. Fraternity, or their close relationships with other men, helped shape who the former internees would become. At least part of their schooling in masculinity included important lessons about managing their sexualities, which ranged at varying times from homosocial to heteronormative. Yet despite the obvious role homosocial or fraternal bonds played in the constructing of selfhood, internees foregrounded their heterosexual desires in visual representations of camp life and the loss of liberty.

Fraternity and Same-Sex Desire

Cities were important sites of modernity, especially for effeminate or same-sex-desiring men who used the anonymity of urban life to conceal what the state judged to be their amoral behaviour. Indeed, cultural historians have successfully made the case for the city as an actor in the making of twentieth-century sexual identities, constitutive of modernity more broadly.[17] But where the alienation of cities served the expression of so-called deviant sexualities under the mores of citizenship and respectability—clubs, rooming houses, and sometimes the cityscape itself providing enclaves for gay social and private lives—the intimacy of incarceration subjected same-sex-desiring men, or those who blurred the lines of friendship, to an altogether different kind of policing of sexual morality. Namely, prisons are sites of hyper-masculinity where "unnatural" desires are policed more directly by fellow internees than by representatives of the state. The regulatory force of the state institution serves as a lens into the joint histories of difference and normalcy under modernity.[18] For the "camp boys," incarceration in Canada could be sexually liberating in that without citizenship the state had even less to say about their sexual proclivities as long as they occurred behind closed doors. At the same time, overcrowding in mass dormitories and communal lavatories meant that no such doors existed and the right to privacy was one of the greatest deficiencies internees had to endure. The "camp boys" were seen by both the state and fellow internees as particularly vulnerable to the advances of homosexuals, likely due to their perceived feminine innocence in a world of men. We see similar patterns of desire, vulnerability, and policing in other instances of same-sex isolation—prisons serving as the most obvious example—but also in migrant worker camps.[19]

Recalling his internment in an exchange of letters with fellow former internee and author Eric Koch, who was writing a book on the subject, John Bardach wrote, "I learned," among other things, "some amenities of homosexuality," but after release, "[I] quickly got over my penchant for boys, developed in Camp and returned, full tilt, to ladies but with greatly heightened understanding and sympathy for gays."[20] In response Koch joked, "My book will be a smash hit. It will be called JEWS WITHOUT WOMEN. Good title, eh?"[21] Homosexuality as a temporary state, an abnormality caused by the absence of women and equally cured by the restoration of "normal" gender relations, echoes Victorian literature linking deviant sexualities with a medical condition. But John was far from the only one who saw homosexuality as a coping mechanism for unsatiated "normal" sexual urges.[22] The problem of privacy mediated all expressions of sexuality, some opting to treat it as a distraction from more worthwhile intellectual pursuits and others substituting a different fetish in its place.[23]

However, though time may have seemed to be standing still for the internees awaiting release, their camp sexual practices should not be considered a time apart, detached from the performance of sexual identities on the outside. Whereas the internee John explained his "penchant for boys" as "situational homosexuality," this analysis reinforces a dichotomy between homo and hetero sex as "natural" rather than acknowledging the instability of sexual identity. In other words, the link between sexual acts and sexual identity might not be so simple to delineate. After all, as Michel Foucault first pointed out, penal complexes are sites for exercising modern power partly through observing and studying sexuality, a relationship and system that presumes homo sex is deviant and, in some cases, subject to medical intervention. Instead of analyzing the sexual acts between internees as "situational," it would be more fruitful to see them as revealing of the fissures and fault lines in modern notions of sexual identity.

The visibility of same-sex desire in camp life caused the greatest anxiety over what becoming a man should look like for the younger internees. Worried that the friendships the "camp boys" developed early on in their internment experience, sometimes beginning in the dormitories of Oxford or Cambridge universities, would become sexual under the constraints of incarceration, older internees apparently took it upon themselves to act as the boys' moral guardians: "The older men took steps to see that the friendships formed were healthy and natural and succeeded in maintaining a high moral tone in this respect. In one hut at one time they formed themselves into a voluntary guard at night, each remaining on watch for an hour till he was relieved by another. Subsequently they found this quite unnecessary and abandoned it."[24] Had the boys wanted to arrange late night encounters in their bunks, they would have faced more practical obstacles to their rendezvous in addition to the sexual morality guard. First, internees were housed in huts accommodating approximately forty men in double bunks, if one was lucky, and in dormitories of three to four hundred men if one was not.[25] To say that the rhythm of tens, if not hundreds, of other men snoring would be an intrusion on an otherwise private and intimate encounter would not be an overstatement. Of course, interested parties could arrange hook-ups during the day when at least some roommates could be expected to be busy attending the camp school, participating in work parties, or enjoying one of the few leisure activities available to internees. However, even those internees willing to make do with life as it unfolded around them in the sleeping huts encountered a second obstacle; building makeshift privacy curtains around individual bunks was forbidden by camp administration and subject to daily inspections by the camp commandant.[26] With these conditions in mind, it is entirely possible that the kind of older gentlemen's guard that formed to police the friendships of young men abandoned their nightly posts not because the internees were not engaging in sexual activities with one another, but because the lack of privacy in their sleeping quarters forced them to turn to other spaces.

Where the alienation of modern cities provided sexual "deviants" at least some opportunity to form and perform their sexual selves using the covert spaces of bars, train stations, and public lavatories, the closeness of internment did not provide internees with the same anonymity or privacy.[27] Like those of modern prisons and concentration camps in Eastern Europe, camp lavatories became important sites for expressing desire and wielding force, a place where internees might hope to escape the gaze of guards but certainly not that of fellow internees. To some, the lavatories came to symbolize internment as a whole, the physical nakedness of communal shower rooms a metaphor for the stripping of their identities as free youth: "Then we were all herded into the shower room and made to strip, you know. . . . Some of these huge naked men, and I was 16 and sort of thrown in with them and I kind of hated the, I mean, I sort of, perhaps ever since then I always rather disliked men because I saw such an assortment of them in those shower rooms where we were all herded, one after the other, you know."[28] Whether consensual sexual acts occurred in the shower rooms is uncertain, but as the sixteen-year-old above learned, regulation of the (sexed) body through the absence of privacy was intimately tied to how young internees began to think about themselves, especially in relation to other, often older, men—"huge" not only in physical size, but also in the discursive space they occupied in camp life.

The bonds of belonging "camp boys" developed likely blurred the lines between friendship and romantic relationships to any onlookers, whether these homosocial encounters occurred frequently or not. This is not surprising given the close living quarters and the movement of cliques from one internment camp to the next over the course of several years. While those in charge of policing the men's behaviour, and those internees who initially stood guard overnight, concerned themselves with the impressionable youth, it seems as though the reality of the relationship between these "mature men" and the younger internees may have been more nefarious than Alexander Paterson reported to the Home Office in the United Kingdom.[29] The focus of his one-on-one interviews with internees was the issue of release and, more to the point, their potential return to the United Kingdom if they found joining the Pioneer Corps more desirable than remaining incarcerated in Canada (many did not). Given the criminalization of homosexuality in Canada and Britain at the time, it is not hard to imagine that such encounters would not be reported to a representative of the Home Office when "good behaviour" and cooperation with the authorities were central to any future immigration plans.

While it is possible that older men saw themselves as moral guardians of the sexual acts between "youngsters," at least one internee recalled in his unpublished memoirs that it was the older men who became especially cozy with the "camp boys": "There was, however, the problem of homosexuality which always raises its head in such situations. It was a known fact that a few of the mature men struck up close friendships with the younger boys. They were constantly together."[30] He goes on to assert that in all likelihood these friendships remained platonic, though some of them were "suspected of homosexual tendencies."[31] Here Harry Loewy's understanding of sexual acts and sexual identity echoes the same sort of language that we see used to describe sexuality in other instances of male-segregated communities such as prisons or mining camps. Sexual intercourse between men was not necessarily a precursor to being labelled gay. Instead, it mattered more whether one performed his gender identity as male or female, was sexually dominant or submissive, masculine or effeminate. Who gave Loewy and his friends the "creeps," then, was "Fritzi," a man who no one else thought of as a man.[32] Not only was his gait feminine, according to Loewy, but he took on typically feminine roles in camp life such as mending other internees' clothes. It was his gender performance as female that gave Fritzi the title "homosexual" by his fellow internees rather than his actual sexual behaviours.

Former internee Gerry Waldston recalls protecting one of his good friends in camp from the unwanted advances of older internees who were "regular" or "creepy" homosexuals (as opposed to those who "turned" during internment as a solution to the absence of women), "who added a lot more of the youngsters to their ranks."[33] It seems as though the perceived innocence of the "camp boys" made them targets, as Waldston understood things, and as one internee penned them in a "A Love Song to a Boy": "Your virginal lips/ Still dreaming their kiss/ And clumsy small hips/ That lover's weight miss/ And childish large eyes/ And unreproved look/ That make me surmize/ You dreamt of

Figure 7.1. Major Racey, commander of Canadian internment Camp "I" inspects the bunks and chats with an internee, c. 1940–43." Boulkind Family Fonds (pr017710), 1062, Jewish Public Library Archives (Montreal, Quebec).

love's book."[34] These older gay men formed their own social groups within the camps and were frequently identified by their sexual preferences above all else.[35] On occasion, Waldston joked in an interview, signs reading "I'm gay" were taped to the back of men's shirts, signifying a warning to others to stay away or approach, depending on one's inclinations.[36]

Age was but one indicator of power relations that existed between internees, the produced effect of which was not inevitably coercion or force. Undoubtedly, real desire between various groups led to harmonious relationships, unequal power dynamics sometimes even serving as a source or enhancer of said desire. However, the examples of both Loewy and Waldston give a good indication of how "camp boys" were perceived as sexually vulnerable and as needing to be protected or to band together in order to ward off "legitimate" homosexuals, who were usually remembered as being older. Given their recollection, one might consider the relationships between "camp boys" and other men they would have encountered in camp, namely the guards who as members of Canada's Veterans Guard—too old for active service overseas—mainly served in the POW and internment camps across the country during the Second World War. Little evidence exists to propose that sexual relationships between guards and the younger internees was a regular occurrence. Unlike the internees, the guards could and did make regular visits to neighbouring towns where they often drank in excess and met local women when stationed far from their own families. Still, the internees' segregation from outside life and their precarious fate would have made camps the perfect place to act out "deviant" sexual behaviours. The photograph of Major Racey and an unidentified internee in Camp "I" (Figure 7.1) alludes to the power structures at work behind the barbed wire prisons. Officially a depiction of the camp commandant's daily inspection of the internees' sleeping quarters, the stance of the guard over the internee seated by his bunk bed suggests his ultimate authority and intrusion in all matters of daily life. Here the internee's bedding is free for the touching, as one of the most intimate private spheres—the bed—becomes subject to command.

Alfred Bader recalls one particular French-Canadian guard who was especially interested in helping the internees in whatever way he could, particularly when it came to securing them extra luxury items such as cigarettes and wood for Bader's religious group to build an ark for the Torah.[37] Not making the connection himself between the guard's helpfulness and his sexual advancements, Bader remembers the guard Bruno: "Unfortunately he really took a liking to me. We arose at 6.45am, to be ready for roll call at 8 o'clock after prayers and breakfast, but around 6.00am, while Julius Kastner in the lower bunk was still fast asleep, Bruno would appear at my bedside and start playing with my penis. He wanted me to go outside the camp with him and walk around the island in the afternoon. What was I to do?" Sensing his vulnerability to Bruno's will, Bader took measures to defend himself by requesting that his good friend and former cattle dealer be allowed to join them. Not interested in having the extra company, Bruno dropped the issue of leaving the camp together. By relying on bonds of friendship, Bader was able to discourage Bruno from further assault.

Other internees were not so fortunate. According to the diary that one internee maintained in secrecy to record the injustices of camp life, the exchange between Bruno and Bader was not an anomaly.[38] Bornemann documented how the guards would enter the internees' sleeping huts at night and pull away their blankets to see who was naked. When the guards became drunk on special occasions such as New Year's Eve, the level of bodily violence escalated to rape. While the men's "situational" homosexuality has been joked about in their postwar correspondence and interviews, none touch on the very real danger of sexual violence, heightened by the uneven power dynamic between guards and internees. It is unclear how often such incidences occurred, but regardless of frequency, bringing them to light shifts the internment narrative away from one of "blunder" and "adventure" to something more harmful and participatory on the part of the Canadian guards.

Stripped of other identity markers such as profession and civilian clothing, sexuality was amplified in internment as one key way of knowing and of being known. With the morality of young men hanging in the balance as they came of age, "camp boys" in particular were subject to policing by fellow internees to ensure that their sexual desires remained "natural," and at least some were also the objects of their desire. As cultural theorists have demonstrated over the last two decades, the regulation of sexual morality is one way that the state mirrored back to its citizens the state's expectations of them in solidifying a national identity, especially during times of war and other crises. Perhaps that is why, in the backwoods and abandoned railway sheds of Canada, most internment guards paid scant attention to the sexual activities of internees so long as they stayed out of sight; no longer German and Austrian citizens and certainly yet to be Canadian or British, internees were stateless, no longer contributors to any "moral" nation. At the same time, this is perhaps why internees policed homosexuality themselves—to maintain some semblance of the modern condition behind barbed wire. Meanwhile, their reactions to sexual behaviours and gender performance indicates that the modern equation of sexual acts with sexual identity is in need of further deconstruction.

"Don Juans": The Heterosexual Male Gaze[39]

If same-sex desire played out under the blanket of the early morning's darkness and in the spaces whose visibility was eclipsed by moments of privacy, the expression of "normal" sexual desire was voiced within everyone's purview. From nearly the beginning of their internment, the men were permitted to write two letters weekly to loved ones and to receive an unlimited amount in return, the distribution of letters the highlight of any given day. In one letter a young woman, an English schoolgirl named Daria, asked her interned friend,

> Tell me, excuse my vulgar curiosity, do men discuss women almost exclusively when alone together? For lately it has struck me, that almost the sole topic of conversation among young women is men. They discuss them endlessly, personally, in every trivial detail, what they wear, what they say, their behaviour, work, success or failure socially, in fact the topic never exhausts itself. And even admitting

> that the important and perhaps chief aim of women is to marry and to have children and that therefore her interest will always lie in the world of men, which had for her a kind of mysterious fascination because it is impenetrable on equal terms, I still think it is curious, very curious.[40]

Next to the subject of their release, internees did indeed discuss women almost exclusively, but perhaps not in the way or for the simple reasons Daria naively assumed in her query. Where the women in her letter discussed men's social and financial standing as prospective husbands, the internees thought about women as objects of their desire, pointing to the upholding of gender inequality. If policing same-sex desire was one way internees expressed anxiety over their masculine identities in a world without women or privacy, communal fantasizing of the female body helped to restore men's power lost through incarceration. Through late-night chatter and especially through shared images of the imagined female body, men sought to restore normative gender relations, making women's sexuality the site for exercising and regulating their male authority. At the same time, the sexual banter may have had the added effect of further eroticizing the relationship between men, demonstrating how one moment could be experienced along a spectrum of masculine desire and dominance.

Camp artists were especially popular men during internment because they were capable of translating to internees images of their lost worlds beyond the wire. Their most popular subject or muse was undoubtedly young beautiful women. But where Daria described the role of women in relation to men according to Victorian norms of respectability—women's primary purpose in life to get married and have children—the internees fantasized about the modern "New Woman," perhaps unsurprisingly, as sexually promiscuous. Emerging from the women's suffrage movement at the turn of the century, the "New Woman" of the 1920s was imagined by many as a threat to existing moral codes and the supposedly "natural" gender hierarchy. However, through incarceration women's independence and sexual liberation are seen as both a source of humour and potential pleasure.

To keep the spirits of his friends high, Gerry Waldston took on the role of camp comedian, in addition to artist, posting a weekly joke on the bulletin board of Camp Sherbrooke for all to see. The source of his audience's laughter was the juxtaposition of sexually liberated women and the internees' inability to access their unrestrained bodies. Visualizing women's bodies as a commodity of

Figure 7.2. "Untitled," Joke of the Week created by internee Gerry Waldston, 1941. Private collection.

the modern world lost through internment demonstrates how men fashioned their evolving sense of self in such intimate domains as sexuality and the body. For Gerry and other artists, women are constructed for their erotic impact on the see-er, establishing a hierarchical relationship between those who see and those who are seen. In Figures 7.2 and 7.3 four women are depicted in a similar manner of dress, accentuating tiny waists, large breasts, and exposed legs. Donning victory curls and painted lips, the two sets of women hint at their sex lives and the expectations put upon them by men.

Although the intent was humour, the images would have also allowed internees to imagine themselves as "Alfred" or the young woman's date with the possibility of a sexual encounter around the corner; the figure of a woman also standing in as a symbol of freedom. For this reason, the male gaze did not simply reinforce an existing power dynamic between men and women, though it did that too. The women created in the artist's eye also possessed power over the internees by being the subject of their desire and not someone or something else.[41] They held the power, in other words, to make "rational" men lose control sexually and intellectually by taunting them with their freedom. And

Figure 7.3. "Untitled," Joke of the Week created by internee Gerry Waldston, 1941. Private collection.

in at least one case, the woman imagined on paper by the men was not a work of fiction, but the likeness of a young woman who gazed back at the interned men as she passed Camp Cove Fields on her way home from school each day.

"Blondie," as she was nicknamed, like the women in Figures 7.2 and 7.3, appears on paper confident and attractive. A girl of just fifteen or sixteen, Blondie would pass by the curious camp overlooking Quebec City on her daily walk home from school in the early fall of 1940 before the refugees were moved to Sherbrooke in October.[42] Believing the internees to be Nazi POWs, she waved to those watching her pass, hoping to attract the attention of the forlorn soldiers. At least one internee made the daily ritual of approaching the barbed wire fence by the pedestrian path to watch her go. Although the woman pictured in Figure 7.5 is not blonde, we might imagine this was the dynamic between Blondie, the soldier on guard, and internee Peter Field when he waited for her to pass. The internee leans forward inquisitively to get a better look at the attractive woman who, despite her interest in the internees, maintains an aloofness about her as she strolls by casually. Unlike the unassuming guard pictured, the actual guard on duty noticed Peter's interest in Blondie, and perhaps taking advantage of an opportunity, asked Peter whether he would like to exchange his pocket knife for the young woman's address.

Figure 7.4. (left) Behind Barbed Wire Scrapbook, LAC Eric Koch fonds, MC30 C-192, vol. 2.
Figure 7.5. (right) "Untitled," internee observes a young woman from behind wire while a guard stands near by. Gerry Waldston, private collection.

And so began a yearlong correspondence between the two, which, on account of Blondie's family connections to William Lyon Mackenzie King, even led to Peter receiving special passes to visit her.[43]

The case of Blondie and Peter shows more implicitly how power dynamics between men and women shift or are complicated when women, quite literally, gaze back at men. The internees who created the images of women as objects of male desire and those who gazed at them undoubtedly wielded power over the female body. Solidifying what they would have considered "natural" gender relations, with men in the power position, the internees subverted their own position as prisoners. Yet the fragility of the internees' power over women's imagined bodies was tested early in internment when the refugees were first housed in camps within city limits and within range of the female gaze. Although Peter fantasized about Blondie and shared stories of their experiences together with other internees, Peter was romanticized by Blondie as a caged man worthy of her sympathy.[44] It was she who fantasized about him as a passive soldier in need of saving through her affections. The power of seeing, in other words, does not belong just to men but is in constant flux according to social circumstances.

The internees' gender identities undoubtedly intersected with their religious and cultural selfhoods. The archival documents do not make explicit the extent to which being Jewish, and the stereotype of Jewish masculinity as effeminate, in particular, affected their sexual proclivities, if at all. It is possible that a broader or alternative understanding of masculinity impacted their sexualities, allowing for a greater spectrum of desire. However, without documented evidence, drawing such conclusions risks advancing stereotypes rather than actual scholarship on Jewish masculinity. It seems apparent that the greatest factor in the men's self-expression was place and the loss of privacy afforded by it.

Conclusion: Privacy and the Return to "Normalcy"

When internees daydreamt what life after internment might look like, the return to a "normal" private life was cause for considerable anxiety. After months, or in some cases years, of a regimented, soldierly routine, would they know what to do with their autonomy or, importantly, how to interact with women? In a drawing titled "Roll Call," Gerry Waldston depicts a former internee standing attention at the foot of a bed, linens rolled and luggage orderly, as his lover looks on in shock. The quotation marks surrounding "Private Life"

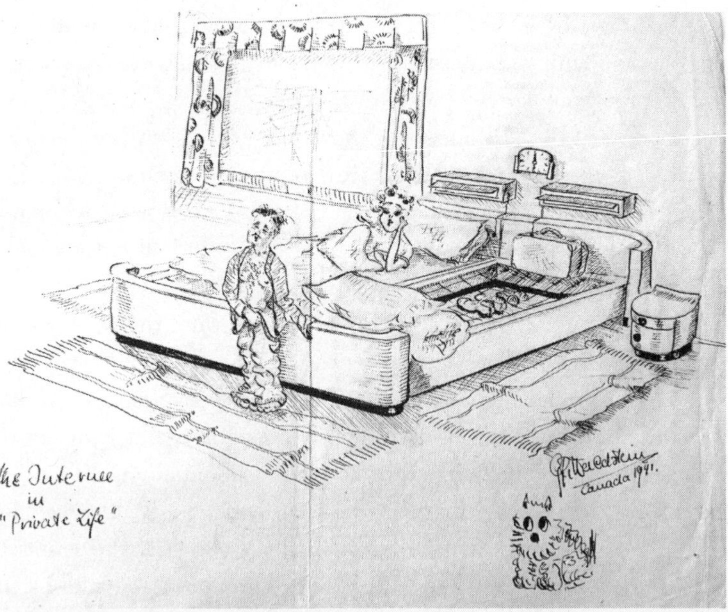

Figure 7.6. "Roll Call." Gerry Waldston, private collection.

betray his fears that the breakdown of private and public life in internment would follow him home, into the bedroom where he would be caught, literally and figuratively, with his pants down.

Therefore, thinking about and performing sexual acts in camp was much more than a way for the young men to pass their time. Making sense of the sexual self was a key way to make sense of the modern self under the conditions of incarceration. Flexing their limited power through policing "unnatural" sexual acts and imagining the "natural" submissive status of women and subordinate men to hegemonic men, internees expressed anxieties over their varying masculinities, governmental authority, and individuality. The conditions of Canadian internment afforded the men the space to express their fluid sexualities from "normal" to "deviant" while still policing effeminate men, in particular, as amoral. That "situational" homosexuality and a more aggressive brand of masculinity seemed to transpire simultaneously, sometimes represented by the same actors, disrupts any notion that gender performance is stable. The absence of privacy in camp made the turn inward that much more difficult but also crucial to re-evaluating the modern condition.

Notes

1 Franz Krämer, "Culture," in *The* Stacheldraht *Farewell Number* (Farnham, QC, Nov. 1941), Library and Archives Canada (hereafter LAC), Department of National Defence, War Diaries, RG24-C3, vol. 15397, file 2282.

2 "Modernity" refers to both the period of time that followed the Enlightenment (roughly from the French Revolution to the postwar years) and a framework of thought that characterized the period. Most importantly to this study, reflexivity was a central feature of modernity so that identity was constructed from a series of shifting self-narratives in response to, among other factors, the tension between nationalism and globalization.

3 "Do you Remember?," in *Camp L Chronicle*, issue 2 (Cove Fields, Oct. 1940), LAC, Erich Koch fonds, MG30 C-192 vol. 1.

4 This article is part of a larger study that situates the history of Jewish internment in Canada within a broader national narrative of ethnic and class discrimination. Christine Whitehouse, "'You'll Get Used to It!': The Internment of Jewish Refugees in Canada, 1940–43" (PhD diss., Carleton University, 2016).

5 Krämer, "Culture."

6 Eric Koch, *Deemed Suspect: A Wartime Blunder* (Toronto: Methuen, 1980); Walter W. Igerscheimer, *Blatant Injustice: The Story of a Jewish Refugee from Nazi Germany Imprisoned in Britain and Canada during World War II* (Montreal and Kingston: McGill-Queen's University Press, 2005); Harry Loewy, "Days behind Barbed

Wire" (unpublished manuscript, Canadian Jewish Congress Charities Committee National Archives, CJC ZB, 164); Erwin Schild, "A Canadian Footnote to the Holocaust," *Canadian Jewish Historical Society Journal* 5, no. 1 (Spring 1981): 31–44.

7 Raewyn Connell, *Masculinities* (Crows Nest, NSW: Allen and Unwin, 1995).

8 Patrick Farges, "Masculinity and Confinement: German-Speaking Refugees in Canadian Internment Camps (1940–1943)," *Culture, Society, and Masculinities* 4, no. 1 (2012): 33–47.

9 Farges, "Masculinity and Confinement," 34.

10 Jewish women categorized as "friendly aliens" during the spring alien tribunals were also interned for a brief period following the roundup of men, but they were quickly released following a public outcry and were never sent to Canada and Australia.

11 About a third of the total number of refugees who were rounded up were aged 16–25. Interview with Gerry Waldston (Toronto, 27 April 2015).

12 Interviews by Harry Rasky, 1980: Gregory Baum, LAC, MG30 C-192, vol. 3.

13 Marshall Berman, *"All that is Solid Melts into Air": The Experience of Modernity*, 2nd ed. (New York: Simon and Schuster, 1982), 13–15.

14 Gerald Frey, Letter to Mary Meyer (June 1940), LAC, Gerald Frey fonds, MG30 c252, vol. 1, "Correspondence, 1940"; Interviews with Harry Rasky: Prof. Ernst Oppenheimer, LAC, MG30 C-192, vol. 3.

15 Appendix 1, War Diary no. 70, entry 20 August1940, LAC, RG24-C3, vol. 15404, file 2287.

16 Irving Sherman, Letter to American Consul General (1 May 1941), LAC, Heinz Warschauer fonds, MG31 D-129, vol. 1, "Correspondence (English) 1938–1941."

17 For examples of the spatial turn in different contexts, see: Jennifer V. Evans, *Life among the Ruins: Cityscape and Sexuality in Cold War Berlin* (New York: Palgrave MacMillan, 2011); Matt Houlbrook, *Queer London: Perils and Pleasures in the Sexual Metropolis, 1918–1957* (Chicago: University of Chicago Press, 2005); Barry Reay, *New York Hustlers: Masculinity and Sex in Modern America* (Manchester: Manchester University Press, 2010).

18 Regina Kunzel, *Criminal Intimacy: Prison and the Uneven History of Modern American Sexuality* (Chicago: University of Chicago Press, 2008).

19 See, for example, Ibid.; T. Dunbar Moodie, *Going for Gold: Men, Mines, and Migration* (Berkeley: University of California Press, 1994).

20 John Bardach, Letter to Eric Koch (20 February 1980), LAC, MG30 C-192, vol. 1, "Correspondence between Koch and former internees 1979–1980 (A-F)."

21 Erich Koch, Letter to John Bardach (13 March 1980), LAC, MG30 C-192, vol. 1, "Correspondence between Koch and former internees 1979–1980 (A-F)."

22 Henry Kassel, "Autobiography 1993," Ontario Jewish Archives (Toronto, ON), fonds 93, vol. 1, file 1.

23 Interviews by Harry Rasky, 1980: John Newmark and Professor William Heckscher, LAC, MG30 C-192, vol. 3.

24 Alexander Paterson, "Report on Civilian Internees Sent from the United Kingdom to Canada during the Unusually Fine Summer of 1940," LAC, MG30 C-192, vol. 2.

25 Accommodation varied significantly between camps depending on whether existing structures, such as army barracks and warehouses, were used, or if new H-huts were constructed. International Red Cross Reports on camps A, I, N, B, & Q.

LAC, Department of National Defence, Directorate of Internment Operations, RG24-C5, vol. 11249, files 9-5-3-23, 9-5-3-40, 9-5-3-41, 9-5-3-42, and 9-5-3-70.

26 War Diary no. 70, entry 20 August 1940, LAC, RG24-C3, vol. 15404, file 2287.

27 Robert Lamprecht, "Chester Railway Station Lavatory" (8 May 1939), LAC, MG30 C-192, vol. 1.

28 Interviews by Harry Rasky, 1980: Arturo Vivante, LAC, MG30 C-192, vol. 3.

29 Interview with Gerry Waldston (Toronto, 27 April 2015).

30 Loewy, "Days behind Barbed Wire."

31 Ibid.

32 "Fritzi Ritz" was an American comic strip from the 1920s, but the internees would have bestowed the nickname "Fritzi" due to its feminization of the German "Fritz," short for Friedrich.

33 Interview with Gerry Waldston (Toronto, 27 April 2015).

34 Robert Lamprecht, "Love Song to a Boy" (10 April 1940), LAC, MG30 C-192, vol. 1.

35 Gerry Waldston estimated that there were one to two dozen "normal" homosexuals in his camp, but that more "youngsters" were recruited. Interview with Gerry Waldston (Toronto, 27 April 2015).

36 Ibid.

37 Alfred Bader, "Autobiography," CJCCC P09-17, pp. 29–30.

38 "Bornemann: A diary containing notes on everyday life in the camps, n.d.," LAC, MG30 c192, vol. 1.

39 Loewy, "Days behind Barbed Wire," 164.

40 Daria, Letter to Eric Koch, LAC, MG30 C-192, vol. 1, "Correspondence to Otto Koch July 1941."

41 Joan B. Landes, *Visualizing the Nation: Gender, Representation, and Revolution in Eighteenth-Century France* (Ithaca, NY: Cornell University Press, 2001): 15–17.

42 War Diary no. 42, entry 15 October 1940, LAC, RG24-C3, vol. 15399, file 2284.

43 Interviews by Harry Rasky, 1980: Peter Field, LAC, MG30 C-192, vol. 3.

44 Ibid.

CHAPTER 8

"Likely to be Hampered and So She Prepared for the Worst": Far Left Women and Political Incarceration during the Second World War

RHONDA L. HINTHER

Authorities caught up with Regina Communist Party activist Gladys MacDonald on 3 June 1940, along with two men, John Slavkowsky (whom the press identified as a Hungarian relief recipient) and Clifford Peet, another local party organizer. According to news reports, the three were "accused of printing a pamphlet known as the *Saskatchewan Factory and Furrow*, containing materials intended or likely to cause disaffection to His Majesty; likely or intended to interfere with the success of His Majesty's forces and intended or likely to be prejudicial to the efficient prosecution of the war." Her arrest was a serious blow to the party locally. Shortly after, an RCMP secret bulletin noted that "the Communist Party of Canada in the Province of Saskatchewan appears to be seriously disorganized as a result of the outlawing of the Party and other left-wing organizations and the arrests of Clifford Peet and Gladys MacDonald, leading Communists." Slavkowsky's wife, Susie, was later charged and convicted with the trio, as the pamphlet's printing allegedly took place in her home. Susie received a suspended sentence, while her husband and Peet received jail terms of six months and one year, respectively, of hard labour served in Regina jail.[1]

MacDonald was convicted and sentenced to a year of hard labour at Battleford Women's Jail. Upon completion of her sentence on the morning of 11 July 1941, according to her lawyer, "she was informed that orders had been issued for her to be held in jail." A short time later, the RCMP supplied her with an internment order, though it listed no grounds to hold her. A week later, she was finally furnished with the particulars justifying her continued incarceration. MacDonald was forced to stay in Battleford Gaol for over a month beyond the completion of her sentence while waiting for a government committee to arrive and hear her internment order appeal on 19 August 1941. Despite a host of positive character witnesses and MacDonald's own testimony that she now supported the war (in keeping with the party's new position), she did not fare well during the proceedings. "Throughout the hearing the hostility of the chairman towards Miss McDonald and her counsel was marked," noted her lawyer, John Stanton. A month later she found herself interned in Kingston Penitentiary, completely unbeknownst to Stanton. A year later, in a memo to another attorney sent to represent MacDonald, he explained, "To this date I have not received from the committee or from the Department of Justice any official notification as to what stand the Committee took on Miss McDonald's case. However, I have no doubt that since she is still interned, the Committee did not recommend her release."[2]

During the Second World War, the Canadian government imprisoned, in jails and internment camps, hundreds of far-left activists. Their detention was part of a broader climate of repression and intimidation that hung over many leftists in wartime Canada. Authorities here, as in other Western states, used the war as an excuse to criminalize radical activism, most notably involvement in a host of leftist "ethnic hall" socialist organizations and support of the Communist Party of Canada (CPC), which, at the time, had grown to considerable strength thanks to its Depression-era activism among the working class and unemployed. The state took aim at these radicals, focusing on the CPC's antiwar position adopted following the German–Soviet Pact in August of 1939. Fearing disruption to the war effort and seizing the opportunity to silence Canadian radical groups (a constant thorn in the government's side), Prime Minister Mackenzie King in the spring of 1940, via the newly inaugurated Defence of Canada Regulations (DOCR), banned a number of organizations linked to and including the CPC, granting state authorities the right to confiscate these groups' property and to arrest their leadership.

Taken together, those apprehended were of diverse ethnic backgrounds. Alongside Anglo Celtics were "ethnic hall" socialists—Jews, Finns, Ukrainians, and others (often labelled "dangerous foreigners"). Indeed, as Jim Mochoruk and I discuss in the introduction to this volume and as his and Kassandra Luciuk's respective chapters demonstrate, this internment episode should be viewed as part of a decades-long continuum of state persecution and detention of radicals, particularly "ethnic" leftists. During the Second World War, despite the obvious civil liberties violations, dubious legal justifications for their detention, and the eventual marshalling of widespread, vocal, national support for their release, their incarceration continued, for most without formal charges ever being laid or proven in court, long after the Soviet Union joined the Allied cause. Most served an average of two years behind bars or barbed wire in a variety of jails and internment camps across the country. That these political incarcerations struck an immediate blow to these activists' communities and kin is certain. However, resistance within and outside the jails and internment camps ensured that political solidarity and individual morale endured. A combination of personal and public resistance was essential to the prisoners' individual and collective sustenance, survival, and eventual release.

The majority of those incarcerated—and all but one of the 100 or so leftist internees—were men. Most were arrested in the spring of 1940, with a second roundup of almost exclusively Ukrainian men occurring on 6 July 1940. Most men accused of violating the DOCR faced internment and ended up together in one of two internment camps—Camp Kananaskis in Alberta or Camp Petawawa in Ontario. There, as manifestations of both resistance and self-care, they recreated aspects of their lives on the outside by holding political talks, language classes, and special events mirroring the far left's activist calendar. During the summer of 1941, authorities transferred the Kananaskis prisoners to Petawawa. In spite of the Soviet Union's becoming an ally and the CPC's changed position in favour of the war, the men remained behind barbed wire. About a month after their consolidation at Petawawa, because of conflict with fascist internees there, the antifascists were transferred to Internment Camp "H"—Hull jail.

On the outside, wives and other supporters (largely through the National Council for Democratic Rights, the organization that replaced the Canadian Labour Defence League, which was banned under the DOCR) staged a valiant campaign for the prisoners' release, all the while dealing with difficult day-to-day circumstances that the absence of their menfolk created. They amassed a groundswell of diverse public support, putting immense pressure on federal authorities. Authorities began releasing the internees in early 1942; the last of them were freed by that October.

The male internees' powerful stories of unjust incarceration have dominated our understanding of this period. This is thanks largely to the dedication of the men and their wives in documenting their personal and collective memories of their ordeal.[3] As such, this group has received the bulk of scholarly and popular attention and it is through the lens of their experience that this period in the far left's history has been understood.[4]

Women prisoners—as a minority group in this story—come off as outliers. Some, like MacDonald (the sole woman internee) and prominent party organizer and labour activist Annie Buller are occasionally mentioned, but their stories—and those of the other women who did time—have never received the same level of treatment or memorialization as the men's. Looking at these women political prisoners complicates the predominant internment narrative. Gender intersected with other categories of identity and oppression (most notably ethnicity) to shape the carceral trajectory and the individual and collective experiences of imprisoned persons in particular ways. Taking an intersectional approach, then, this essay attempts to centre women in this history in order to paint a clearer picture of the extent to which the DOC regulations and the criminalization of radical dissent impacted women of the far left in Canada. To do so, I examine several of the women prisoners' experiences in detail, while also considering a number of other women caught up in the spectre of political policing. I also consider those who managed to avoid detention, in spite of, in some cases, substantial records of long-term radical political activism.

This chapter—and the larger project of which it is a part—builds on my past work on the Ukrainian left in Canada.[5] It also expands on a compelling body of secondary literature dealing with internment generally—in Canada and elsewhere—and the Canadian government's Second World War internment of leftists specifically.[6] Within this, a rich array of sources, many of which I have recently unearthed, make this new examination of wartime political incarceration—and women's experiences with it—possible. These include innumerable letters exchanged between prisoners and their loved ones that expose the public and private dimensions of internment and oral history interviews which I have carried out. RCMP surveillance files have proven especially valuable, as have lawyer's files, court records, government internment and prison records, newspapers, and other materials.

Gladys MacDonald enjoyed the dubious honour of being the only leftist woman internee. Her activist journey was a typical one many left-wing women (and men) followed. Coming from humble beginnings, she was born in 1910 in the small agricultural community of Willen, Manitoba. Her family later relocated to Moosomin, Saskatchewan, where she attended high school until 1926 before returning to the farm for a few years. After taking a business course, she moved to Regina in 1929 where she found work for a lumber company as a stenographer. During that time, she explored left politics, through the Independent Labour Party and the CCF, before eventually settling on membership with the Communist Party, which she joined in 1936. In 1937, she quit her job at the lumber company and went to work as a stenographer in the party's Regina office. She began taking on additional responsibilities by acting as organizational secretary, managing records, recruiting members from her social network, handling office work, and communicating with local branches and party headquarters in Toronto.[7]

She continued in this capacity until her arrest in early June of 1940. At that time, Macdonald was renting a room at 1346 Rae Street and living under the alias of Miss G. McRae. Cheaper rent was one motivation that precipitated her relocation there, along with a desire for concealment. According to her then lawyer John Stanton, when asked in court "why she felt it necessary to live secretly . . . she replied that the Defence of Canada Regulations made it clear that anyone who did not agree with the Government policy was likely to be hampered and so she prepared for the worst."[8] While she carried out work for the now-illegal party from there, she supported herself by working part-time in the office of the Weyburn Fur Company until her apprehension and conviction.

Evidence documenting Macdonald's time in prison is limited. What is known is that shortly after her August 1941 internment appeal hearing, she was shipped from Battleford Gaol to Kingston Penitentiary, arriving "on 25 September 1941, sick and anaemic."[9] According to evidence Michelle McBride uncovered, MacDonald "was a model prisoner," who "refused to associate with the other internees (mostly fascists) and volunteered to work in the prison kitchen."[10] MacDonald remained in jail in Kingston for nearly a year.

Finally, on 26 August 1942, as public support for the leftist prisoners' release intensified, and after yet another hearing, Macdonald's release was recommended. Her early fall liberation was concurrent with those of many of the male leftist internees still held in Hull jail. That being interned was constructed as a manly activity is evidenced in the 19 September 1942 letter Deputy Minister of Justice Vance sent to MacDonald's lawyer, John Stanton, notifying him of her impending release. It stated, "Re: Gladys MacDonald. The Minister of Justice, on the recommendation of the Advisory Committee which heard this **man's** objection to detention under the Defence of Canada Regulations, has directed that **he** be released subject to certain conditions."[11] So few women internees were dealt with that it was apparently too much trouble to change the pronouns appropriately—one last indignity applied to MacDonald's wartime carceral journey.

Concurrent with Macdonald's carceral experience were those of fellow CPC activists and Winnipeggers Margaret Mills and her close friend Ida Corley. Mills was a lower-echelon party worker who helped to keep the party afloat during the early months of the DOCR ban. She served as a secret party courier, assisted with the publication and distribution of clandestine party newspapers, and maintained party records. For this work, she was charged with six breaches of the DOC regulations, including membership in an illegal organization (the CPC) and distributing illegal literature (the party's *Manitoba Worker* newspaper). Mills pleaded guilty on all counts and was sentenced to twelve months on each to be served concurrently in Portage Gaol.[12]

The extent of Corley's role in the party is unclear, but, according to information that came out during her trial, it would seem that she acted at the very least as a minor functionary. During a visit to Mills's home, Mills, who had been under the weather, according to Corley, asked Corley to address and mail a series of sealed envelopes. Prior to leaving, Corley finished addressing the twenty-eight letters but, on her way home, apparently forgot to mail them. She left them on the buffet in her parents' home where she lived, where police discovered them, along with three other likewise seditious parcels ready for mailing, during a search. Corley pleaded ignorance to the letters' contents; when opened, police found each contained a copy of the CPC's *Manitoba Farmer* and a pamphlet entitled "Government War and Hunger Policy Ruins Farmers." This, and the fact that her name was listed in party records found in Mills's possession, sealed Corley's fate. She was tried and convicted on 9 November 1940 for breaching the DOC regulations by being a member of the Communist Party. Magistrate R.B. Graham sentenced her to one year of hard labour.[13]

Fortunately for Corley, Graham's imposition of "hard labour" exceeded penalties permitted under the Criminal Code. A few days after she arrived in jail, the mistake was caught and Graham instructed the clerk of the city police court to substitute her original warrant with new ones, omitting "hard labour." Her lawyer, E.J. Murray, appealed her conviction. Justice Donovan, who heard the case, insisted that Graham "having imposed a sentence in excess of that permitted by law, could not cure this illegality by the substitution of a proper warrant, after the prisoners had been taken to jail." Donovan refused to "amend a conviction not authorized by a statute after the sentence thereunder or part thereof had been served by the accused" and ordered Corley's release on 12 June 1941.[14]

In Portage Gaol, Mills and Corley enjoyed the company of colourful and passionate party activist Annie Buller, there serving a twenty-four-month sentence. Buller was convicted of violating the Defence of Canada regulations for her continued membership in the then illegal Communist Party of Canada. She was also convicted on several counts of publishing subversive literature connected with her role at the party's *Mid-West Clarion* newspaper in February 1940. Buller and Mills became close in jail, continuing to stay in contact after Mills's release in early 1942. Buller remained behind bars until widespread public protest forced the government to finally liberate her several months later in the fall of 1942.[15]

Other women were likewise caught up in the political policing fervor of 1940–41. Authorities in Saskatchewan and Manitoba (with Quebec not far behind) appeared particularly virulent in their pursuit of key women as well as male leaders. This was particularly the case for those women who were working within the "mainstream" wings of the Canadian far left, most notably directly for the CPC and especially its press. For example, appearing in court with Margaret Mills on 18 October 1940 was Anastoria Hrankowski and her husband John. Like Mills, both wife and husband were charged with violating the DOC regulations for being members of the Communist Party and distributing subversive literature.[16] The charges against the Hrankowskis were later dropped.[17] Several other women were convicted of specific DOC regulations violations and served time for their connections to the party, though again none were incarcerated as long as Buller and MacDonald. These two served the most time; Buller because of the length of her two-year sentence, and MacDonald because of the combination of jail sentence and internment order. Also picked up and convicted in Regina like MacDonald were Florence Theodore, Ella Gehl, and Jane Kenilworth, who respectively were handed three-, one-, and six-month sentences.[18] In Montreal, Yvonne Richard received a one-month sentence, and Angéline Dubé paid a $500 fine in addition to her six-month sentence.[19] It is unclear why, unlike MacDonald, women like Winnipeggers Ida Corley and Margaret Mills, the Regina trio of Theodore, Gehl, and Kenilworth, and Montreal's Dubé and Richard escaped internment upon the completion of their shorter sentences. Perhaps these women's apprehensions and convictions represented a kind of collateral damage—bonus prizes picked up in the course of the apprehension of other, supposedly more dangerous or troublesome activists. Or perhaps authorities, disorganized or overtaxed with the management of so many criminalized radicals and others, merely neglected to issue the internment orders that would have ensured continued incarceration in these women's cases.

There is some evidence that at least some women faced particular gender-based indignities at the time of their arrest. Picked up and charged jointly with John Weir and Bill Tuomi when police raided the offices of the *Mid-West Clarion* in Winnipeg on March 5, 1940 were stenographers Edna Shunaman and Bertha Smith.[20] Both women, according to Weir, were subjected to particular humiliation at the time of their arrest. Speaking a week later on 12 March at a political meeting in support of Leslie Morris's run as Communist candidate in Winnipeg's North End, Weir alleged that police strip-searched the women in the *Clarion*'s office. According to Weir, "The police took the two girls and had them stripped naked in search of nobody knows what. . . . This disregard of human indignity is practised by the German secret police, and this incident gave all the appearance of the presence of fascism right here."[21] Winnipeg police denied the allegation. As the *Winnipeg Free Press* noted, "Mrs. Clara Donaldson, the policewoman who accompanied the city detectives and mounted police in the raid on the Clarion offices, said Mr. Weir was mistaken."[22] This is one of the only points of evidence speaking to instances of abuse women left activists encountered while in the carceral system; undoubtedly many more occurred but were omitted from state evidence or the contemporary material and documentary culture produced by these women and their supporters.

The two women were released the morning following their arrest on $400 bail each, and their cases, along with those of Tuomi and Weir, were remanded several times throughout the spring. Eventually, authorities made the decision to simply intern Weir and Tuomi, largely, it seems, to circumvent the potentially risky and costly work of undermining due process. As A.A. Moffat, Crown prosecutor, explained in correspondence to Manitoba's attorney general, "There are a great many communists [in the region] and it would be unsafe to have a communist on the jury." Additional jurors would therefore need to be imported, adding expense. As such, Moffat preferred internment as "it would save a great deal of time and money if they were duly interned."[23] So, an internment order was executed on Tuomi and Weir, and the two were sent to Kananaskis. Concurrently, authorities suspended the charges against Shunaman and Smith.[24] This, plus the fact that the police did not bother to take mug shots of them at the time of their arrest and the lack of coverage of their cases following Tuomi and Weir's internment, suggests that the two women were not on the state's list of dangerous leftists but rather represented collateral damage to the movement for being in a criminalized space.

Most of the prairie women arrested seemed to come from either Anglo Celtic (like Mills and Macdonald) or Jewish backgrounds (like Buller). Interestingly, Ukrainian women, as "ethnic hall" socialists focusing their activism most firmly within the Ukrainian labour temples, managed to avoid being targeted for internment. This was possibly because of pre-existing gender stereotypes within and external to the community. As Jim Mochoruk indicates in his chapter in this collection, the former disgruntled male ULFTAers who acted as informants assisting the Manitoba attorney general, with their axes to grind with the existing ULFTA leadership (which was entirely male) and their own sexism about women from their community, focused their ire clearly on the men. As I have documented elsewhere, women in the ULFTA faced considerable sexism from their male comrades, many of whom held the mistaken idea that these women were "backwards" because often they chose not to express their activism through proscribed male forms.[25] It should come as no surprise, then, that the men formerly in these positions now acting as informants would fail to recognize these women as serious activists or realize that they should have been targets for arrest as well if the Ukrainian component of the far left was to be taken down. The Ukrainian women activists, and the Ukrainian left as a whole (which these women managed to sustain during the worst years of the war and the male leaders' internment), then, seem to have been saved by sexism.

This was perhaps the biggest tactical error red-baiting authorities made in their attempts to decimate the Canadian far left during the war. It would not have been hard to pin the same charges on women like Mary Prokopchak, Mary Skrypnyk, and Helen Weir as those laid against their arrested male counterparts (and, in the case of Prokopchak and Weir, their husbands, both of whom were interned). All of these women were equally as or even more than publicly active than the Ukrainian labour temple men who were interned, and Prokopchak and Weir would go on to play fundamental roles in the NCDR's campaigns to free the prisoners. This speaks to the importance of informants—and their personal baggage—in shaping internment in practice. Likewise, it also speaks to systemic sexism inherent to the security state, as Steve Hewitt and Christabelle Sethna have well documented in their groundbreaking work on surveillance of women's groups in the 1960s and 1970s. As they explain, "Surveillance was deeply influenced by the fact that the RCMP was traditionally an all-male and all-white institution which prized heterosexual masculine comportment; that the Mounties, in both their mandated security and criminal duties, were more accustomed to dealing with male dissent."[26] The absence of women security agents, then, meant that left women's activities were likely considerably under-watched and therefore under-documented compared with the men's in all but the most exceptional of cases.

What is also curious is that some other prominent women (and obvious targets), most notably Becky Buhay (a close friend of Buller), also avoided arrest. In Buhay's case, it may have been because she was based in Ontario and the hunt for CPC leader Tim Buck and several other prominent men who had gone underground in the wake of the imposition of the DOC regulations may have dominated authorities' imaginations there. Or perhaps her prominent role in the leadership of the NCDR with A.E. Smith afforded her some protection. Certainly, more research in Buhay's case is warranted.

Certain women's ability to avoid arrest also speaks to the haphazard nature of internment operations, as other contributions to this volume demonstrate. Authorities were often sloppy and under-resourced, given the level of repression they were attempting to enforce. The creation of so many boogeymen—and, in this case, boogeywomen—made follow up, detention, and even conviction a challenge. Authorities had to pick and choose which activists they might successfully convict and, barring that, decide in whose case application of an internment order could be justified.

In any case, upon completion of their sentences, all of these women, like their criminalized male counterparts, seem to have resumed their activism throughout the war and in the decades beyond. Following her release Margaret Mills frequently turned up as a speaker at progressive events in Edmonton during the war. Flo Theodore, too, continued her activism, eventually running as the candidate for the Labour Progressive Party (the LPP, the successor party to the CPC) for the Saskatchewan provincial legislature in 1945. Likewise, MacDonald—upon her release from Kingston Penitentiary—re-engaged, involving herself with the LPP in Regina when she was not busy at her day job at the Army and Navy Department Store. Buller also carried on as she had prior to the war, remaining an active leader and party stalwart to the time of her death in 1973.[27]

By considering women, this essay has attempted to paint a richer and more nuanced picture of wartime leftist persecution. While there are many parallels between the experiences of women and men caught up under the DOC regulations, there are some important differences that help to enrich our understanding of this period. Women had the potential to be especially vulnerable given the paid positions they took on, sometimes (though relatively rarely) as organizers, like Buller, but more often as secretaries, stenographers, and in other "support" roles that put them into contact with and made them responsible for the preparation for distribution (or actual distribution, via the act of mailing) of illegal materials. The fact that so few women had paid work for the party and its fellow travelling organizations is probably at least one of the reasons why so few women were incarcerated.

Those women who were incarcerated, unlike the majority of the male left prisoners, did not have the benefit of a large comradely critical mass. At best, they might serve part or all of their sentence in the company of one other leftist woman. Buller and Mills were lucky to have had one another in jail. Other women, like Gladys MacDonald, were not so fortunate. And, unlike the majority of the men, all of these women served their time in jails, as opposed to internment camps. Finally, unlike most of the men, these women came out of this experience with criminal records, a fact with the potential for lifelong consequences.

Women did enjoy at least one potential advantage over the male internees. Because the women worked their way through the court systems, they often (depending on the nature of their case) had access to legal means the interned men did not. Corley's ability to appeal her inappropriate sentence serves as one example of this.

The women incarcerated do seem to have been "exceptional" in some fashion. Most held senior leadership roles (though certainly not all women leaders were arrested) or carried out their activism in some of the most visible, public ways—transgressing often what, at the time, were proscribed mainstream gender roles for "respectable" women. Others were caught up in police raids because of the critical support roles they played in the organizations of the far left. Women office workers could be especially vulnerable since their work was so fundamental to maintaining—often clandestine—communications between party leaders, members, and other supporters. Most women managed to avoid incarceration, even some high-level leaders. In some cases, the outcome of the intersection of gender with ethnicity served to protect these women, as in the case of Ukrainian left-wing women who were entirely ignored by authorities.

Examining women enriches our understanding of this particular episode of political policing and expands our understandings of responses to the repression of dissent. Studying the incarceration of these radicals is important. It offers critical insight into a significant but little-known episode where the state enacted regulations to suppress dissidents and detain them, most without charge and for an indeterminate amount of time under the guise of unsubstantiated security concerns. Although a minority of Canadians were touched by this internment episode, studying it is nonetheless important. Like all internments, this one has present-day resonance, serving to inform the debate on the War on Terror and particular legislation such as Bill C-51, the Anti-terrorism Act, which has far-reaching implications for anyone who might be deemed a "security threat." A gendered approach to this research is especially critical, as I hope these women's stories underscore. Their experiences demonstrate how state authority and power have been and can be applied unevenly and inequitably on women.

I am grateful for the assistance and input of Marie Roberge (daughter of internee Bill Tuomi), Larissa Stavroff (daughter of internee Peter Krawchuk), Randy James (and the other volunteers at the Winnipeg Police Museum), Christabelle Sethna, Anne Toews, Andree Levesque, Jim Mochoruk, Debbie Haddad, and the staff at the Archives of Manitoba and Library and Archives Canada.

Notes

1 "4 Persons Rounded Up in Regina Raid," *Medicine Hat News*, 6 June 1940; "Sask. Trio Held under War Act," *Winnipeg Free Press*, 3 June 1940; "War Act Violators Sentenced to Jail," *Winnipeg Free Press*, 12 September 1940; Joan Sangster includes some discussion of Macdonald and several of the other leftist women arrested at this time—see Joan Sangster, *Dreams of Equality: Women on the Canadian Left, 1920–1950* (Toronto: McClelland and Stewart, 1989). For more information on women internees and other women (of varying circumstances and political stripes) rounded up seemingly without rhyme or reason under the DOC regulations, see Michelle McBride's path-breaking article, "The Curious Case of Female Internees," in *Enemies Within: Italian and Other Internees in Canada and Abroad*, ed. Franca Iacovetta, Roberto Perin, and Angelo Principe (Toronto: University of Toronto Press, 2000), 128–47. On page 164, McBride provides important commentary on MacDonald's wartime circumstances.

2 John Stanton to J.L. Cohen, "Memo Re: Gladys McDonald," in vol. 31, file 2917 NCDR: Correspondence, Evidence re: Gladys MacDonald, J.L. Cohen fonds, MG 30 A94, Library and Archives Canada, Ottawa, Ontario (hereafter LAC).

3 For some examples, see Peter Krawchuk, *Interned without Cause* (Toronto: Kobzar, 1985); Peter Krawchuk, ed., *Reminiscences of Courage and Hope: Stories of Ukrainian Canadian Women Pioneers* (Toronto: Kobzar, 1991); Peter Krawchuk, "The War Years," in *Our History: The Ukrainian Labour-Farmer Movement in Canada, 1907–1991* (Toronto: Lugus, 1996); William Repka and Kathleen M. Repka, *Dangerous Patriots: Canada's Unknown Prisoners of War* (Vancouver: New Star Books, 1982); Ben Swankey, "Reflections of a Communist: Canadian Internment Camps," *Alberta History* 30, no. 2 (April 1982): 11–20; Roland Penner, "Transition, Turmoil,

and Trouble (1939–1943)," in *A Glowing Dream: A Memoir* (Winnipeg: J. Gordon Shillingford, 2007).

4 A notable exception in the literature is the important act of recovery history that is Michelle McBride's article, "The Curious Case of Female Internees."

5 See Hinther, *Perogies and Politics: Canada's Ukrainian Left, 1891–1991* (Toronto: University of Toronto Press, 2018).

6 For a list of the key sources, please consult note #20 in the introduction to this volume.

7 John Stanton to J.L. Cohen, "Memo Re: Gladys McDonald," in vol. 31, file 2917 NCDR: Correspondence, Evidence re: Gladys McDonald, J.L. Cohen fonds, MG 30 A94, LAC.

8 Ibid.

9 Ibid. McBride, "Curious Case of Female Internees," 164.

10 McBride, "Curious Case of Female Internees," 164.

11 Deputy Minister of Justice to J.L. Cohen, 19 September 1942, in vol. 31, file 2917 NCDR: Correspondence, Evidence re: Gladys McDonald, J.L. Cohen fonds, MG 30 A94, LAC. Author's emphasis in bold.

12 John Boyd, interviewed by author, 22 July 2015; "Woman Admits Six Breaches of Defence Act," *Winnipeg Free Press,* 30 October 1940. See also entries on 30 October 1940, Winnipeg Police Arrest Record Book, 1 December 1939–27 June 1941, Winnipeg Police Museum.

13 Bass, Bilinsky and Cory [*sic*] file, Joe Zuken fonds, P3144/2, Archives of Manitoba; "$20,000 in Bail is Demanded for McEwen," *Winnipeg Free Press*, 24 October 1940; "Sago, McEwen Go to Jail for 2 Years," *Winnipeg Free Press,* 9 November 1940.

14 See "Three Held under Defence Act Released," *Winnipeg Free Press*, 13 June 1941; Bass, Bilinsky and Cory [*sic*] file, Joe Zuken fonds, P3144/2, Archives of Manitoba.

15 Detective D. Nicholson to Chief Constable George Smith, 4 March 1941, RCMP file, Annie Buller, LAC, A201600180_2016-12-21_09-44-13, p. 39. See also *Winnipeg Free Press,* 1 March 1941 and 21 May 1941, and Louise Watson, *She Was Never Afraid: The Biography of Annie Buller* (Toronto: Progress Books, 1976), http://www.socialisthistory.ca/Docs/History/Buller/AB01.htm.

16 *Winnipeg Free Press*, 18 October 1940.

17 Ibid., 16 November 1940.

18 Michael Martin, "The Red Patch: Political Imprisonment in Hull, Quebec during World War II," *Socialist History Project*, 2007, http://www.socialisthistory.ca/Docs/History/RedPatch.pdf, 131–32.

19 Ibid. Relatively little has been written on Dubé and Richard. Andrée Levesque provides valuable commentary on Dubé's husband and the movement of which both were a part in her article "Évariste Dubé, un Gaspésien communiste," *Magazine Gaspésie* 187 (November 2016–February 2017): 41–43. I am grateful to Levesque for drawing my attention to this piece and other resources to help document these Québécoises' experiences.

20 See *Winnipeg Free Press,* 6 March 1940.

21 John Weir, as quoted in "Police Slap: Women Stripped, Editor Maintains," *Winnipeg Free Press*, 11 March 1940.

22 "Police Slap: Women Stripped, Editor Maintains," *Winnipeg Free Press*, 11 March 1940.

23 A.A. Moffat, Crown Prosecutor, Attorney General Major, 29 August 1940, Bill Tuomi RCMP file, LAC, A201500408_2016-02-23_14-31-16.

24 See entries on 5 March 1940, Winnipeg Police Arrest Record Book, 1 December 1939–27 June 1941, Winnipeg Police Museum.

25 See Hinther, *Perogies and Politics,* and "'They Said the Course Would Be Wasted on Me Because I Was a Girl': Mothers, Daughters, and Shifting Forms of Female Activism in the Ukrainian Left in Twentieth-Century Canada," *Atlantis* 32, no. 1 (2007): 100–10. For additional discussion on this subject, see Joan Sangster, "'Robitnytsia,' Ukrainian Communists, and the 'Porcupinism' Debate: Reassessing Ethnicity, Gender, and Class in Early Canadian Communism, 1922–1930." *Labour / Le Travail* 56 (2005): 51–89.

26 Christabelle Sethna and Steve Hewitt, "Clandestine Operations: The Vancouver Women's Caucus, the Abortion Caravan, and the RCMP," *Canadian Historical Review* 90, no. 3 (September 2009): 463–95.

27 See Parliament of Canada History of Federal Ridings since 1867, https://lop.parl.ca/About/Parliament/FederalRidingsHistory/hfer.asp?Language=E&Search=R; Report re Gladys McDonald, 27 January 1943, Department of Justice file, vol. 3, "Gladys McDonald," Records of the Canadian Security Intelligence Service (CSIS), RG146, LAC, A-2016-00217; See Watson for commentary on Buller's post-internment activism.

PART V

JAPANESE CANADIANS: RESISTANCE AND INTERNMENT BY OTHER MEANS

CHAPTER 9

Informal Internment: Japanese Canadian Farmers in Southern Alberta, 1941–1945

AYA FUJIWARA

The internment of Japanese Canadians during the Second World War is one of the most heavily explored fields in Canadian history. Scholars on both sides of the Pacific have produced a number of insightful studies that provide detailed accounts of life in the internment camps in interior British Columbia.[1] This volume includes a number of important recent pieces, including work by Art Miki, Grace Eiko Thomson, and Mikhail Bjorge. This essay deals with a much less studied aspect of the wartime internment, focusing on the approximately 4,000 evacuees who chose to come as family units to sugar beet farms in southern Alberta. As they were not formally interned in government-administered camps, scholars have hitherto paid little attention to the lives of the Albertan evacuees.[2] This chapter argues that their situation was similar to incarceration or internment for several reasons, despite the fact that wire fences did not separate them from the outside world. First, once assigned to reside on specific privately owned farms in certain communities, the policies made it very difficult to relocate to other locations in search of better economic opportunities. Second, their lives were governed by the strict labour agreement established by the federal and provincial governments and the Alberta Sugar Beet Growers Association (ASBGA), leaving little room for negotiation. Third, their activities were under close surveillance of the Royal Canadian Mounted Police.

The project to send Japanese farming families from the West Coast of British Columbia to the sugar beet fields of Alberta was unique in that it was not only government bodies that were coordinating this action—such as the federal Ministry of Labour, the Alberta government, and the British Columbia Security Commission (BCSC), a government-appointed agent created specifically to carry out the evacuation. Private stakeholders, such as ASBGA and Canadian Sugar Factories, were also involved in this mobilization of labour; a project which clearly sought to take advantage of the wartime situation. This essay argues that the sugar beet internment in southern Alberta, though based on human rights violations of the Japanese evacuees, was viewed by sugar beet farmers as an economic boon.

While Albertans were not uniform in their acceptance of Japanese Canadians from British Columbia and evidence suggests that some people, including the members of the Lethbridge City Council and the Lethbridge Board of Trade, opposed the plan,[3] many saw their economic value as labourers. It was well-known that the Government of Alberta took a very cautious approach to accepting evacuees, largely to avoid giving the public the impression that it had yielded to pressure from the federal government or British Columbia. However, farming communities in southern Alberta, facing a worker shortage, were most keen on receiving extra labourers and saw Japanese evacuees as an attractive commodity. Patricia Roy points out the division between the farmers and city dwellers in their opinions of the Japanese.[4]

Japanese evacuees, on their part, showed very mixed feelings toward their new home, both refusing and accepting their surroundings. While they were not satisfied with their living and working conditions, it was the first time that their contribution was valued in Canada despite the fact that their human rights were not protected. By the end of the Second World War, Japanese labourers were well integrated into the region's economy.

Sugar Beet Labour and Internment

"Internment" takes various forms. While its main purpose is to confine people who are considered to be harmful to the public, it is often designed for profit, namely to secure labour. During the Second World War, Canada sent enemy aliens to road camps, logging camps, and farms on which "serious labour shortages developed."[5] In southern Alberta, the shortage of sugar beet farm workers did not begin with the outbreak of the Second World War. The severe nature of sugar beet farming, which John Herd Thompson and Allen Seager described as a workload that needed "more than ten times the labour required for an acre of grain," alienated many workers. Discontent among them had been widespread long before the Japanese arrived, and obtaining a steady source of labour was very difficult.[6] In addition, they were often looked down upon in farming communities. "The beet workers" were "at the bottom" of the company's hierarchy. They were fieldworkers, who acquired contracts from the growers.[7] Immigrants and ethnic minorities constituted the majority of this workforce, making this occupation somewhat racialized.[8] Their living and working conditions often were quite primitive. During the Great Depression, the reduction of sugar beet prices, which Canadian Sugar Factories controlled in order to maintain their profit, caused a number of political agitations and labour strikes.[9] Such movements deepened the social, economic, and political gulf between the growers and farm workers.[10]

It was in this context that the ASBGA actively encouraged the arrival of Japanese evacuees after 1942. Their concern was more about labour disputes, economic discontent, and Marxist agitation than the Japanese imperialism on which British Columbians focused.[11] Its members regarded Japanese workers as similar to low-cost prisoners or internees, with the advantage that the federal government would monitor any political activities and ideologies that could lead to strikes. As enemy aliens, these workers, the growers believed, should be deprived of any civil rights, including the one to protest. At the same time, the growers expected BCSC to make every arrangement to secure the necessities of life for the Japanese, thereby removing financial burdens that might otherwise be incurred while simultaneously providing some economic security for the Japanese.[12] In this way, the ASBGA expected to avoid the contract disputes that they had encountered in the past and secure a fixed source of labour during the war.

ASBGA, the sugar company, and BCSC were active players in this unofficial internment project. The "Japanese" district was defined around the boundaries of southern Alberta's irrigation farms, including Raymond, Taber, Picture Butte, and Coaldale. Several restrictions were imposed on Japanese farm workers, thereby making conditions similar to those of the internment camps. First, the evacuees "could not purchase or acquire land," and second, they were "prohibited from engaging in normal business enterprises."[13] Yet different bodies had different approaches to the Japanese question, depending on their interests.

Negotiations: Government of Alberta, BCSC, Department of Labour, and ASBGA

The BCSC, which was responsible for the Japanese who chose to go to southern Alberta, played a significant role in linking local growers with the federal government and Japanese evacuees. Its commissioners often saw their role as protectors or guardians of the Japanese, as well as facilitators who wanted this project to proceed as smoothly as possible. As middlemen, they developed a certain level of cooperation with the Japanese. As a result, Japanese evacuees to Alberta had favourable memories of the BCSC commissioners. An evacuee described one of the commissioners, W. Andrews, as having "a very deep understanding of the situation in which the new settlers found themselves."[14] Indeed, the BCSC representatives investigated the composition and fitness of the families to the prairie farming thoroughly before they sent Japanese farmers to Alberta. For the BCSC, whether or not chosen families could actually contribute to the sugar beet farming was a top priority. Thus the commissioners sent very positive messages to both Japanese and growers in Alberta. They hosted several meetings at *Nokai* (farmers' association) halls, to recruit "ideal farming families."[15] To the experienced, relatively young, and healthy farmers who lived in the Fraser Valley region, the commissioners pitched the project as an economic opportunity. "Families are to be provided with [an] individual cottage and small plots of land for their own use and cultivation in addition to the sugar beet farms on which they will work on the basis of five members to a family." "Each family" would be guaranteed "an income of at least $1,000." At the same time, "added income of $2 to $4 per day is assured during the harvesting season on the grain fields."[16] They also told potential Japanese farmers, "Each family will contract to work for a private farmer for the beet season, but the Security Commission officials declare, will continue to watch over them for the duration. Although they will be in private employ, their welfare will continue to be a responsibility of the Government."[17] To the growers in Alberta, the BCSC stressed that Japanese were "experienced" and were "all satisfied with the plan."[18] Thus, one of the commissioners argued, "they (the Japanese) are a very adaptable, industrious race and if they are treated humanely, and with reasonable accommodation, I see no reason why this should not prove a successful undertaking."[19]

The ABSGA was most interested in detailed procedures for this project. It was the organization that would meet the evacuees on an everyday basis. At the same time, this association included some Japanese farmers who came to settle in southern Alberta before the Second World War. As they did not live in the protected zone of 100 miles from the West Coast, they were never interned, while some kept Japanese nationality and thus were "enemy aliens." As a result, some Japanese were able to offer the evacuees assistance. First, the association had to deal with the Canadian Sugar Factories Ltd., which had a monopoly over sugar production and remained suspicious about the idea of mobilizing enemy aliens. Given the fact that many Japanese growers, who had settled in southern Alberta before the Second World War, owned their farms, the company insisted that "no increased acreage" would "be offered to enemy aliens, unless the beet grower who is an enemy alien has an immediate family member in his family in Active Service in the Canadian Forces." It also demanded that any extra acreage should be "offered to desirable Canadian Citizens, who will be able to handle a small acreage of beets, and provide their own labour or local labour to care for such acreage."[20] Such comments indicated that the company did not trust any Japanese, including the pre-war settlers, regarding their loyalty to Canada as questionable. The ASBGA, on the contrary, argued that the additional acreage should be opened to anyone who was capable of cultivating land, whether or not they were enemy aliens. For the ASBGA, which regarded economic gains as more important than people's loyalty issues, "it (the war effort) should be equal sacrifice for all."[21] As the war proceeded, the company became slightly more tolerant toward Japanese as labourers, but remained somewhat cautious in terms of their contracts. Indeed, it drew up a number of clauses that imposed restrictions on how the evacuees could be employed. It insisted that Japanese farm workers were not allowed to move "between or outside of the Factory districts" of the Raymond, northern Lethbridge, and Taber-Coaldale areas.[22] In other words, the company had tremendous power to confine these workers to a certain area.

Second, the ASBGA worked very closely with the BCSC, making sure that the federal government would cover all costs of this project. It agreed to receive Japanese farm workers only after the federal government promised to pay for housing, education, and medical care. The association also requested that the BCSC's local representative be someone who was familiar with the interests of the growers.[23] Above all, its main concern was how to integrate the mass influx of Japanese evacuees into their small communities. Housing issues became quite pressing in the first few months of 1942. The ASBGA was clearly frustrated by the lack of materials to build evacuees' housing. The growers repeatedly requested that the BCSC send more resources, including lumber to build houses for the evacuees. W.F. Russell, secretary of the Growers' Association Development Committee, wrote that "the building of a room 10 x 12" would require much more than the BCSC provided."[24] These requests were then sent to the Department of Labour. Austin C. Taylor, chairman of the BCSC, also wrote to Arthur McNamara, deputy minister of labour, stressing the lack of building supplies. The letter argued that the BCSC could not "throw these evacuated Japanese back on our hands when 30 to 40 degrees below zero winter weather arrives on the prairies."[25] The slowness of such bureaucratic processes and the lack of communication between the BCSC and the ASBGA often increased frustration among the growers. By the end of June 1942, the growers were very much disillusioned by the BCSC, stating that both "Japanese and Growers have lost confidence" in the organization.[26]

The Growers and the Welfare of Japanese Workers

The relationship between the growers and Japanese workers was a very complex and sensitive one. The ASBGA produced somewhat contradictory statements regarding the Japanese throughout the war. The ASBGA, as an organization, rarely showed any sympathy toward Japanese evacuees. Rather, it saw them as something between indentured workers, who were bound by a contract, and POWs who did not possess political rights or the freedom of expression. Protecting the welfare and rights of the evacuees fell under the jurisdiction of the BCSC. The growers judged their work performance by acres that Japanese farmers cultivated and the amount of sugar beets they produced. While evacuee families were paid individually per acre, their collective effort was often discussed in the growers' meetings. After the first season, it was announced that the Japanese were "harvesting a record-breaking Alberta sugar beet crop," which was "estimated between 350,000 and 400,000 tons."[27] In terms of productivity, therefore, the growers were quite satisfied with evacuees' labour.

However, when individual Japanese labourers began protesting the terms of their contracts after the first year—confronting growers over the fact that they were paid less than other fieldworkers—some growers wanted to replace them for the next season with the POWs who were kept in internment camps in Alberta.[28] Such demands were passed to the Department of Labour via the commissioner of the BCSC, who inquired about the availability of POWs as farm labourers, writing, "approximately ten farmers have already advised the Japanese that they do not want them next season."[29] The growers were determined not to raise rates. A BCSC commissioner wrote to A. MacNamara, quoting Philip Baker's comments. "The Beet Growers," in his words, "had to have some assurance from this Commission (BCSC) or the Japanese that they were prepared to enter into contracts next spring at the same labour rate." If such promises were not to be made, the growers would "demand that the Japanese be moved from the area at once."[30]

The BCSC was much more positive about the work that was done throughout the war. Its reports and surveys portrayed the whole project as a great success. Approximately a year after the arrival of Japanese farmers, it cited the sugar company's remark that "Japanese families will show increased earnings over last year."[31] In addition, it claimed that some 200 POWs who were sent to sugar beet farms had not "proved satisfactory," and could not "compete with Japanese labour to any serious extent." Despite the fact that Japanese evacuees were only placed in southern Alberta temporarily, the BCSC also mentioned the possibility of these farmers "establishing themselves on a more permanent basis."[32]

Japanese evacuees, in general, showed very mixed feelings in terms of the treatment they received in southern Alberta. Evacuation as family units appeared very attractive initially. Yet the reality was not always what they had expected. Economically, this type of unofficial internment imposed a lot of pressure on males as breadwinners. At the same time, just as in the interior camps, education of children was also a source of concern. The BCSC was instrumental in securing enough earnings for the families, banning the use of child and senior labourers, and educating children.

In several cases, however, the BCSC failed to achieve its goal of responding to Japanese evacuees' family needs. In late 1943, approximately a year after the Alberta project began, more than one-third of the entire evacuee population consisted of children under sixteen years old.[33] The overpopulated schools, which were caused by the influx of Japanese children into the area, became a major concern in Raymond. According to the initial agreement between the BCSC and the Alberta government, the former was responsible for educating evacuee children if local public schools were unable to accommodate them. Yet the Royal Canadian Mounted Police indicated that such support was very slow to come, reporting that the district got some 1,200 students, and thus "all space and teachers" were "fully occupied."[34] Japanese parents were concerned about their children's high school because they regarded continued education as significant for their successful resettlement in the future. A heated discussion took place when the BCSC refused to cover the tuition of their children who were over fifteen years old on the grounds that they were "not strictly eligible for public school."[35] This decision was taken as "a change in the policy on the part of the Commission," and thus as a betrayal.[36] Twelve Japanese representatives argued that due to the fees, "in many instances our children were forced to sacrifice education."[37]

On the one hand, the evacuees were pleased with the financial opportunities that they found on the vast prairie land. There were signs of mutual understanding between the Japanese settlers and some growers regarding how to best make profit for both sides under the restricted circumstance. In this regard, the Albertan evacuees had some room for negotiation in terms of occupation. Reports in the *New Canadian* revealed that some individual farmers, as opposed to the ASBGA and the sugar company, were quite flexible, letting Japanese families produce vegetables such as "corn, potatoes, and beans," with which they were more familiar than sugar beets.[38] One evacuee indicated the potential of vegetable and fruit farming for the Japanese in Alberta, noting that "if Japanese farmers should make a specialty of cultivating vegetable farms here and keep cows, pigs, and sheep at the same time, there are excellent opportunities for them."[39] In one reported case, a Japanese family was making approximately "$175 in less than a month," which was "sufficient income" for the summer season.[40] This amount was quite high, given that in the 1930s, $200 annually was considered a good income.[41] Evacuees were also quite proud of Japanese contributions to the sugar beet farming industry, as production increased in both its quantity and quality after the first year of relocation.[42]

On the other hand, the evacuees could not hide a sense of humiliation at being the lowest class of labourer. In general, the average wages that they could earn were lower than what they had made in British Columbia.[43] One report indicated difficult living conditions, including "poor housing," "inadequate transportation for the purchases of their groceries," and "insufficient or poor water supply."[44] One farmer also commented that the hardest thing was the lack of reading materials.[45] For others it was the work itself that caused discontent. As one evacuee put it, "The day seems like ages until we become accustomed to the long monotony of working in the sugar beet fields."[46] Another farmer wrote that sugar beet farming was "the hardest labour that he had taken over thirty years in Canada,"[47] and yet another called it "backbreaking and arduous, entailing considerable hardship."[48] At the same time, the Japanese were very frustrated with the general attitudes of the ASBGA, which did not enforce their labour contracts. For example, amount of wages and labour seemed to have varied, depending on the growers who hired the Japanese. One evacuee stressed the exploitative nature of his employment, indicating that he was paid "$27 an acre for the whole summer's work and the hours of work are from around 6 am till 10 at night."[49] Japanese evacuees' representatives tried to demand the right to find a new contract when their original employers did not pay enough wages. The issue of "labour transfer" between farms was indeed one of the major causes of disputes between the growers and the Japanese.[50] At the negotiation table, the Japanese representatives argued that "Mr. Baker and the growers desire only financial gains through the exploitation of the evacuees."[51]

Ironically, the relocation of Japanese brought a very detailed picture of difficult working and primitive living conditions among sugar beet farmers in southern Alberta to official attention for the first time. According to a Japanese Canadian newspaper the government issued several regulations concerning farm labourers after the relocation of the Japanese. One of these prohibited the exploitation of Japanese farm labourers beyond working hours.[52] In 1943, George Collins, BCSC commissioner, provided the Department of Labour with very detailed accounts of the hardships that the Japanese farmers were facing. The report revealed the difficulty of producing sugar beets in this irrigation district and indicated that some Japanese families "might conceivably not receive any returns for their season's work, whereas if they contracted on a labour basis they would at least be paid for whatever work they had done on the property up until the time the failure occurred."[53] Needless to say, such situations had already existed for sugar beet workers, and the federal government had rarely intervened in the labour negotiations between the growers and contract fieldworkers before the war. Collins also pointed out the lack of a "modern (sugar) plant" in the area, which would process sugar more efficiently.[54] He also mentioned that the growers opened up "more acreage" than their workers could "handle."[55] The BCSC representative also stressed that seniors, children, and some women should not be counted as farm labourers. Its Albertan officer reminded the chairman of the BCSC that the majority of Japanese evacuees were children under sixteen years of age or "too young for a full day's work." Interestingly, he also paid special attention to gender, describing women who were "required to do housework" or "about to become mothers within a few months" as "out of class of the workers."[56] Undoubtedly, the ASBGA was not pleased with such intervention. Yet it also tried to take advantage of this situation, negotiating with Ottawa directly in terms of labour supply for the improvement of working conditions. It demanded that the federal government should arrange the same number of labourers on the sugar beet farms in Alberta in 1944.[57]

The wartime mobilization of Japanese Canadians as sugar beet labourers, thus, offers several significant insights that are important in conceptualizing "internment." First, although the wartime internment of Japanese Canadians has often been examined as a state project, some public sectors, as this essay has shown, played a crucial role in defining the policies that regulated their lives. The ASBGA and the sugar company regarded these Japanese labourers as significant but accepted them only with very strict caveats, including that they would be closely surveilled and their movement restricted, and also that their economic security would be guaranteed. It is an illuminating example in which civilians collaborated to deprive Japanese Canadians of freedom by confining their living spaces and defining their duties.

Second, Japanese evacuees who went to Alberta have received little scholarly and public attention, as they did not experience life in internment camps and could live as family units. Their experience was situated outside of the "mainstream" traumatic narrative of Japanese Canadians who lived in interior camps. A closer look at their situation, however, reveals that their life was not very different from that of others who were surrounded by the fences. They lived in a confined space to which they were tied by strict labour contracts. At the same time, the BCSC could not keep many of its promises, including the provision of education, proper housing, and sufficient salary to support all members of the family.

Third, Alberta's sugar beet project during the Second World War suggests that internment was not simply a means to segregate Japanese Canadians from the public for national security. While both federal and British Columbia governments often used surveillance as justification for the internment of Japanese Canadians, economic motivations were apparent in this case. Ironically, the fact that a sizable Japanese Canadian community existed in southern Alberta did not raise any issues for the BCSC's security concerns. It intended to engage Japanese labourers in the most useful way, mobilizing them in the fields that struggled with a labour shortage for the region's profit. Yet throughout the war, Japanese Canadians coped with their situation, establishing better relationships with the BCSC and the ASBGA for their own benefits. The expansion of sugar beet farming was largely due to their effort to maintain family life and to better prepare for the postwar reestablishment to which they looked forward.

Notes

1 For the collection of historic images, see Pamela Hickman and Masako Fukawa, *Righting Canada's Wrongs: Japanese Canadian Internment in the Second World War* (Toronto: James Lorimer and Company, 2011). For the collection of memoirs, see for example, Keibo Oiwa, ed., *Stone Voices: Wartime Writings of Japanese Canadian Issei*, 2nd ed. (Montreal: Véhicule Press, 1994). For analysis of internment memories, see Mona Oikawa, *Cartographies of Violence: Japanese Canadian Women, Memory, and the Subjects of the Internment* (Toronto: University of Toronto Press, 2012). For the general studies of the internment policies, see, for example, Patricia Roy, J.L. Granatstein, Masako Iino, and Hiroko Takamura, *Mutual Hostages: Canadians and Japanese during the Second World War* (Toronto: University of Toronto Press, 1990); and Patricia E. Roy, *The Triumph of Citizenship: The Japanese and Chinese in Canada, 1941–67* (Vancouver: University of British Columbia Press, 2007).

2 Some of the few examples that incorporate the history of evacuees in Alberta into the narrative include Roy's *The Triumph of Citizenship*, 80–88; Ann Sunahara's

Politics of Racism: The Uprooting of Japanese Canadians during the Second World War (Toronto: James Lorimer and Company, 1981), 69–73; and Shelly D. Ketchell's "Relocating Japanese Canadian History: Sugar Beet Farms as Carceral Sites in Alberta and Manitoba" (MA thesis, University of British Columbia, 2005).

3 Roy, *The Triumph of Citizenship*, 84–86.

4 Ibid., 81

5 Carmela Patrias, "Race, Employment Discrimination, and State Complicity in Wartime Canada, 1939–1945," *Labour/Le Travail* 59 (Spring 2007): 33.

6 John Herd Thompson and Allen Seager, "Workers, Growers, and Monopolies: The 'Labour Problem' in the Alberta Sugar Beet Industry," *Labour/Le Travail* 3 (1978): 154.

7 Ibid., 158.

8 Ibid.

9 Ibid., 159–60.

10 Ibid., 174.

11 The author discussed this point in her article, "Japanese-Canadian Internally Displaced Persons: Labour Relations and Ethno-Religious Identity in Southern Alberta, 1942–1953," *Labour / Le Travail* 69 (2012): 63–89.

12 For the consultation between BCSC and the ASBGA, see Roy, *The Triumph of Citizenship*, 83.

13 Library and Archives Canada (hereafter LAC), RG27, vol. 170, Placement of certain Japanese Families in the Province of Alberta, Letter to BCSC to A. MacNamara, Deputy Minister of Labour, 21 August 1943.

14 Chiyo Tonomura, letter to the editor, *New Canadian*, 5 September 1942, 2; see also "Daichi ha hahadeari, haha no chibusa," *New Canadian*, 30 November 1942, 7.

15 "Keep Paternal Eye on Beet Field Workers," *New Canadian*, 2 April 1942, 1.

16 "Alta. Beet Fields for Families, Women, Children to Ghost Town, Nisei to Ont. Camps," *New Canadian*, 28 March 1942, 4.

17 "Keep Paternal Eye on Beet Field Workers," *New Canadian*, 2 April 1942, 1.

18 Glenbow Archives, M3774-3, file 9, J. Shirras, BCSC, letter to W. F Russell, Secretary of the Growers' Association Development Committee, n.d.

19 Ibid.

20 Glenbow Archives, M3773-3, file 9, Manager, Canadian Sugar Factories Ltd., letter to W. F. Russell, 19 March 1942.

21 Glenbow Archives, M3774-3, file 9, 5 March 1942. W.F. Russell, letter to S.R. Noble, 5 March 1942.

22 LAC, RG27, vol. 170, T. George Wood, Canadian Sugar Factories Ltd., letter to George Collins, BCSC, 10 May 1943.

23 Glenbow Archives, M3774-3, file 9, W.F. Russell, letter to Austin Taylor, 24 March 1942.

24 LAC, RG27, vol. 170, Placement of certain Japanese Families in the Province of Alberta, W.F. Russell, letter to Austin Taylor, 22 May 1942.

25 LAC, RG27, vol. 170, Austin C. Taylor, letter to A. McNamara, n.d.

26 Glenbow Archives, M3773-3, file 9, ASBGA, letter to BCSC, 30 June 1942.

27 "Farmers Busy in Harvest," *New Canadian*, 3 October 1942, 1.

28 LAC, RG27, vol. 170, Placement of certain Japanese Families in the Province of Alberta, Report on Japanese Evacuee Settlement Alberta Project, 30 November 1943.

29 LAC, RG27, vol. 170, Placement of certain Japanese Families in the Province of Alberta, George Collins, letter to A. MacNamara, 21 August 1943.

30 LAC, RG27, vol. 170, Placement of certain Japanese Families in the Province of Alberta George Collins, letter to A. MacNamara, 29 October 1943.

31 LAC, RG27, vol. 170, Placement of certain Japanese Families in the Province of Alberta, J.N. Lister, BCSC Report, 9 July 1943.

32 Ibid.

33 LAC, RG27, vol. 170, Placement of certain Japanese Families in the Province of Alberta, A.E. Russell, Report on Japanese Evacuee Settlement, Alberta Report, Period Ending 30th November 1943.

34 LAC, RG27, vol. 170, Placement of certain Japanese Families in the Province of Alberta, Royal Canadian Mounted Police, Alberta, 4 June 1942, re: Japanese Conditions.

35 LAC, RG27, vol. 170, Placement of certain Japanese Families in the Province of Alberta, A.E. Russell, Report on Japanese Evacuee Settlement, Alberta Report, Period Ending 30th November 1943.

36 Ibid.

37 LAC, RG27, vol. 170, Placement of certain Japanese Families in the Province of Alberta, letter to George Collins from delegates for evacuees in Southern Alberta (signed by 12 Japanese), 11 April 1944.

38 Tosuo K. Ohama, letter to editor, *New Canadian*, 4 July 1942, 2; see also "Faith in a Future in Canada," *New Canadian*, 29 July 1942, 1.

39 G. Takahashi, "Farmers Urged to Stay in Alta. after War's End by Employers," *New Canadian*, 27 June 1942, 2. See also, "Ichigo zukuri ya yasaisenmon no nokyo mo," *New Canadian.*, 25 July 1942, 3.

40 "Alberta Folk Don't Mind Staying," *New Canadian*, 15 July 1942, 1.

41 Thompson and Seager, "Workers, Growers, and Monopolies," 158.

42 Joe Ohashi, letter to the editor, *New Canadian*, 3 October 1942, 2.

43 K.M., letter to the editor, *New Canadian*, 8 August 1942, 2.

44 LAC, RG27, vol. 170, Placement of certain Japanese Families in the Province of Alberta, letter from the North and South Japanese Committee to George Collins, 28 March 1944.

45 "Yomimono ga fusoku," *New Canadian*, 9 May 1942, 3.

46 Mas Fujita, letter to the editor, *New Canadian*, 4 July 1942, 2.

47 "Amefuri de komatta arubata shu," *New Canadian*, 4 July 1942, 3.

48 Chiyo Tonomura, letter to the editor, *New Canadian*, 5 September 1942, 2.

49 "Slant on Sugar Beet Incomes," *New Canadian*, 29 July 1942, 2.

50 The author examined "labour transfer" of Japanese evacuees in a different essay. Some reports indicated that several Japanese moved between farms for better jobs, without any permission. See Fujiwara, "Japanese-Canadian Internally Displaced Persons."

51 LAC, RG27, vol. 170, Placement of certain Japanese Families in the Province of Alberta. Phil Baker, who came to southern Alberta in 1919 from Utah, was the

president of the Alberta Sugar Beet Growers Association during the Second World War. He was the chief negotiator representing the Growers when the district accepted the Japanese evacuees as farm labourers.

52 "Survey Aims at Placing Family Units to Meet Farm Shortages," *New Canadian*, 12 August 1942, 1.

53 LAC, RG27, vol. 170, Placement of certain Japanese Families in the Province of Alberta, George Collins, Japanese Sugar-Beet Workers, Lethbridge, Alberta, 12 May 1943.

54 Ibid.

55 Ibid.

56 Ibid., W. Andrews, letter to Austin C. Taylor, 23 May 1942.

57 Ibid., George Collins, Japanese – Province of Alberta, 29 October 1943.

CHAPTER 10

Destroying the Myth of Quietism: Strikes, Riots, Protest, and Resistance in Japanese Internment

MIKHAIL BJORGE

There is a received wisdom concerning Japanese internment in schoolbook Canadian history that goes something like this. Following Pearl Harbor, Japanese Canadians were rounded up for deportation to the interior. They were stripped of their property, concentrated, and removed. Following quiet train rides, they spent their war years in camps, ghost towns, and farms, often subjected to forced labour. Later, their confiscated property was sold at fire-sale prices, and eventually they were released. As the *Canadian Encyclopedia* clearly states, "the Japanese did not resist the internment."[1] Some fifty-odd years later, they received redress from the Canadian state. The moral quandary was resolved, and all was right within capitalist, liberal, multicultural Canada.

Unfortunately, this schoolbook narrative is overly simplistic, and quite frankly wrong. Such a telling offers a far too neat correlation between history, myth, and memory. Given the prevalence of wildcat and illegal strikes throughout Canada during the Second World War—actions often punctuated by multifaceted and legally proscribed tactics—it is hard to believe that the exceptionally violent act of throwing masses of humans into camps (many of whom had experience in unions, community organizing, and political formations) and the confiscation of property—all encompassed within lives lived inside of the deeply racist province of British Columbia and the intrinsically racist Canadian state—could have precipitated no self-activity.[2]

A more careful analysis of the actual removal and carceral operation shows not resignation, but intense self-activity and confrontation—including strikes, protests, riots, and mass non-compliance. When examining the collection/concentration of Japanese for evacuation, we find not quietism, but riot and resistance. Later, in the work camps, there were extensive strikes of many different flavours and articulations.[3] Indeed, in treating the Japanese Canadians as workers, rather than a disarmed racial totality, the idea of evacuation/internment shifts to a dialectic of negotiated discipline and active resistance, much the same as with other Canadian workers, albeit under exceptionally difficult and dangerous circumstances.

This chapter focuses on the resistance to the government's original concentration and removal operations, and the ubiquitous strikes, riots, and protests of 1942 and 1943 in the work and concentration camps. As will be made clear, these actions involved thousands of people, with women and children playing prominent roles throughout. The protestors and strikers consciously leveraged their social and labour power for significant gains both in material conditions and in regard to the recognition of fundamental dignity.[4] Although petitions and legal arguments were extant, they exerted power and won concessions through direct action, not pleading. By articulating these workers' activities in this fashion, this chapter will examine the self-activity of the evacuees, the internal logic of capitalist democracy and racism, and the politics of education and redress—even as it challenges some of the historiographical understandings that surround the Japanese experience during the Second World War.[5] In particular, the idea that Japanese Canadians were a "model minority" who dealt with extreme violence and racist injustice with a quiet resilience will be shown to be false. This trope needs to be replaced with the actual story of remarkable pushback both during the removal operations and within the detention centres and labour camps. Moreover, it needs to be made clear that in this latter struggle, the Japanese had much in common with workers on the other side of the fence.

As was the case for the remainder of the Canadian workers, the state only had armed men available to put down strikes and protests in the most extreme cases, true even in armed camps. Although the government had gifted itself "extraordinary powers unprecedented in Britain or the United States," to control strikes and domestic resistance, it had little ability to actually *use* these broad legislative powers.[6] In this dance of activity and marginal disciplinary powers, the Japanese were able to make impressive gains through direct action, no matter how dire, grotesque, and fundamentally unjust their situation.

There has been no lack of writing on the plight of Japanese Canadians during the Second World War. Indeed, before the removal operation had even finished, Forrest La Violette penned a short monograph on the Japanese wartime experience.[7] The shameful tale is now well-known: "In February 1942 the federal Cabinet ordered the expulsion of 22,000 Japanese Canadians residing within one hundred miles of the Pacific coast. That order marked the beginning of a process that saw Canada's Japanese minority uprooted from their homes, confined in detention camps, stripped of their property, and forcibly dispersed across Canada or shipped to a starving Japan."[8] This core narrative has been relatively well fleshed out by historians since.

Attention to strikes and resistance, however, has been a notable lacuna within the historiography of wartime Japanese displacement and incarceration. The difficult nature of activist history, in this case providing the strongest foundations for the case for redress, meant that some narratives within the story have been minimized. This is unfortunate but not uncommon, as Kassandra Luciuk notes in her piece in this volume on First World War internment, and as Franca Iacovetta's essay does similarly for the Italian Canadian community. The histories of Japanese mass incarceration have not had the same opportunistic and historically questionable quality that imbues the work on other internment operations.[9] However, the nature of pushing for redress elevated and focused some ideas and histories over others.[10] The stoic "survivors' narrative" or the spirit of resignation ("shi-kata-ga-nai") is far more compelling, and sympathetic to a liberal audience, than those of the sit-down striker, the rioter, the protestor. There are notable exceptions, of course; namely Ann Gomer Sunahara and Pamela Sugiman, the latter who noted that "much of the publicized literature on the internment has promoted the idea that Japanese Canadians generally, and Japanese Canadian women especially, have been a passive and acquiescent lot."[11] But much of the literature, if it mentions self-activity at all, speaks of "passive resistance," or of the state "fearing sit-down strikes," instead of actual resistance and real sit-down strikes.[12] Moreover, much of the recent historiography focuses on the legal/liberal tropes of "citizenship" and "rights." Apart from decentring the Japanese themselves, these attempts at analysis produce a line of argumentation that requires a tremendous amount of diagnostic and theoretical gymnastics to force a narrative onto a trajectory where it does not really fit.[13] A more evidentially rigorous and theoretically informed examination rooted in understandings of power relations, of the instrumentalization of institutionalized racism by the state and capital, of the intrinsic problems of the "democratic" capitalist state, would be much more illuminating.

It needs to be said that this is not an argument about "agency." Agency is one of the theoretical-historical tropes that often manifests in deeply troubling ways, and often swerves into intellectually bankrupt territory. Although certainly a corrective to the shoddy history that ignores people who build societies and keep them running, or simply writes them out of the story, this trope strains credibility. Ham-fisted notions of agency are often predicated on the dubious foundation that regular people are generally an inactive and uncomplicated lot, prone to submission and simplicity, and that finding people acting otherwise is somehow anomalous rather than the norm. Any tropes of "an uncomplicated proletariat," of course, do not stand up to rigorous inquiry; this is particularly accurate following the institutionalization and concretion of capitalist social relations. Moreover, the obsession with agency has significantly occluded the power of organization, to the effect that ineffective "deviations" or minor cultural "subversions" are elevated to the level of, or even above, effective or organized activity, with the latter ignored. This is liberal nonsense that celebrates and elevates amorphous notions of discourse and the action of the individual, no matter how ineffective, rather than of concerted class activity. Such arguments dull the violence, exploitation, and deterritorialization being resisted and agitated against, positing false equivalency of liberal actors in its stead. For all of these reasons this essay's core argument is not one pertaining to agency, but to action, activity, and organization, all of which are found in significant diversity and quantity within the story.

Official removal of Japanese Canadians began in March of 1942, and immediately there was organized resistance from the community. In early 1942 former Progressive MP Ian Mackenzie organized the British Columbia Security Commission (BCSC) to oversee the forced removal of all peoples of Japanese descent in Canada. Officially, the BCSC had little power and was only to serve in an advisory role to the Department of Labour and the Cabinet Committee on Japanese Questions.[14] In practice, control over the operation was often muddy and deeply inexact. In March 1942, RCMP officer C.H. Hill sent a lengthy letter to the head of the BCSC, Major Austin Taylor, suggesting a five-point plan on how "to overcome the trouble which we are now having with the Nisei."[15] The five points suggested were necessitated due to "the resistance being shown" to removal operations. Japanese Canadians actively evaded removal from the one-hundred-mile exclusion zone created by PC 365 (16 January 1942) and the forced removal order PC 1486 (24 February 1942).

To pressure the Japanese into acquiescence, the commission decided that it would "under no circumstances interview or desire to contact delegations [from] the Japanese." Hill further suggested enacting a full ban on Japanese meetings and ensuring that "any persons convening such meetings will be subject to prosecution." Moreover, "delinquents" who did not report to the 7 March train, one of the first removal operations sending men to work in Ontario, "should report to the RCMP," and "failure to comply with this order will mean that all Japanese will be confined to their houses or quarters until further notice."[16] Hill continued, "There is no doubt whatever" that "unless drastic action is now taken, organized resistance will continue, and the situation will fast deteriorate." He closed by arguing that it was his "considered opinion that these suggestions be given immediate and careful attention, and that they be considered in the way of urgent priority over all others." Hill was correct; the resistance was organized.

Two days later, about 100 "British subjects" were to board a train to go from Vancouver to Schreiber, Ontario. Of the roughly 100 men ordered to board the train, eighty-five refused. BCSC officials were unable to coax the men onto the train, and ended up incarcerating them in an "Immigration Shed."[17] These same officials told the imprisoned men that if they did not "divulge the names of the instigators" of the action they would be hauled before the courts, but no one was willing to inform on their compatriots. RCMP Commissioner S.T. Wood then asked for a blanket Order of Internment that would allow him to formally arrest and incarcerate the men.[18] When a push failed, a shove would apparently do. These men would go on to become some of the first of what would eventually amount to over 800 Japanese Canadians who were interned for defying the forced labour and evacuation regime.[19] Hill later sent a list of "problem" Japanese who were to be sent to Ontario, instead of the BC interior, where he believed that they would cause trouble. His list included all those held concurrently by military authorities in Vancouver.[20]

Clearly, not all went quietly onto the trains. Apart from individual acts of resistance, like stealing "I Am Chinese" buttons or simply going underground and moving at night, some Japanese started collective action against the state during the removal operation.[21] On "the evening of April 7th, 1942 . . . 25 Canadian-born Japanese who were to have left Vancouver for work camps in Ontario . . . refused to go and were placed in the Immigration Building at Vancouver." While incarcerated, "they held a meeting from 10:30 to 1:30, they objected to leaving Vancouver without their families. Their spokesman and leader was Kojiro Ebisuzaec [*sic*], Canadian-born Japanese, a store keeper at Vancouver," who helped write demands. They quickly issued leaflets authored by the "Nisei Mass Evacuation Group, which "were posted on walls and distributed among the Japanese."[22]

Concomitantly, Assistant Commander C.H. Hill noted that "175 Canadian-born delinquents" were still at large. Although sizable numbers of evacuees had already been moved, many were still actively resisting their forced removal. Hill believed resistance was growing and that if "drastic action" was not taken, the "situation would deteriorate, and possibly get completely out of hand."[23] His specific concern was that the "Canadian-born Japanese are not [as] amenable to discipline as the Japanese Nationals, with whom [he] had experienced very little difficulty. When [they] fail to report for entraining, they naturally go into hiding . . . their attitude is changing, and they will resist the evacuation procedure as much as possible." Perhaps even more to the point, the "Canadian-born subjects feel that their status entitled them to preferential treatment." The nearly 75 percent of Japanese Canadians who were natural (or naturalized) subjects had little faith in British "fair play" or their "rights" to habeas corpus. Rightfully so, it turns out, as their position was legally murky (at best) within Canadian law, and most legally akin to psychiatric detention. Hill complained that although these Canadians were in fact receiving "preferential treatment," they were "unwilling to realize it." It must have been difficult indeed to see much in the way of preferential treatment, given the position in which the Canadian Japanese found themselves. Utilizing the hoary old trope of the oppressor regarding the insidiousness of those attempting to protect themselves, Hill claimed that the resistance was originally born of a "small group" of agitators, but that this "insubordination is now widespread."

The most telling evidence of this insubordination, apart from the mass resistance and protest, was a public meeting of 1,700 persons. Government officials were nice enough to attend and take notes for posterity. Hill's report from his spies noted that although an Issei speaker had "urged cooperation with the BCSC and the police" his comments elicited "a very lukewarm reception" from the attendees. A "Canadian-born" man spoke next. He stated that he had "lost his radio, his camera, his boat, his automobile and property, and was obliged to leave [his home] under the same conditions as almost any alien." This speaker "urged the gathering to resist," which unlike the conciliatory response, "was acclaimed in a most hysterical manner."[24]

Perceptively, Hill noted that the attempt by the RCMP and BCSC to divide and conquer the Japanese had largely failed. The collaborators who had been recruited by the state were now totally discredited in the eyes of the community. Furthermore, the attempt to recruit *funktionshäftling* had merely "divided the community into hostile camps," with collaborators in the minority.

Despite the difficulties of the RCMP in concentration and removal, Hill's greatest concern was that these "open violations of constituted authority" would cause "police prestige [to] suffer and the task of enforcing the regulations made increasingly difficult." Hill had good reason to worry, for fully "two-thirds" of those who were "slated to go to work camps on April 7th had failed to appear."

On 25 April, about sixty Japanese Canadians held a protest at the Immigration Detention Building. Following the protest, a leaflet demanding better treatment was circulated. Hill believed it was printed at the office of the *Continental Daily News* (Tairiku Nippō), the Vancouver-based Japanese Canadian newspaper. Rather than searching for evidence that might support his suspicion, which he believed would take a significant amount of time, he merely dictated that "in the best interest" of law and order, the newspaper and "all other printing establishments operated by Japanese [be] closed immediately." Hill was concerned with the "grave possibility" that if the Japanese were not quickly removed, and that "if there was any open demonstration against evacuation," that the public in BC "may be again aroused."[25]

By the end of April, the RCMP was aware that "evidence of organized resistance to the scheme continues in hand." Hill believed that the resistance, while widely popular, was organized by a small group of "Nisei and naturalized Canadians" who called themselves the "Nisei Mass Evacuation Group."[26] While Hill thought that the group "appears to be reasonable," their "whole movement" was "definitely aimed at hindering" the mass evacuation. Treading road-worn tropes of the "waylaid proletariat," Hill argued that the group's "sinister operations" had no more interest than merely "creating trouble and arousing dissension."[27] For Hill, the group's activities had hampered "the main issue, namely the speedy evacuation of all members of Japanese racial origin from the protected area," a task "necessary for the safety of the state."[28] Hill counselled a harder approach. He thought that "the troubles" manifesting during the evacuation were due to "a lack of firmness in handling the whole question."[29] However, repression breeds feedback, and the escalation had repercussions.

Indicative of the resentment that was developing towards the evacuation orders, on 13 May, a sizable group of evacuees rioted. A description of what happened appeared in the *Vancouver News Herald* of May 14th, and deserves to be quoted at length:

> Apparently incensed because friends and relatives were not allowed to approach close enough to carry on conversation, a number of

> Japanese men held in the Immigration Building rioted Wednesday afternoon and evening, causing extensive damage to the building and contents. Late in the afternoon the rioters were subdued when additional military guards were called out. During the evening, city police were asked to send a supply of tear gas when it appeared the rioters were still recalcitrant. The disturbance started soon after noon, and followed two days of sullen behavior on the part of the Japanese in the building. Until recently many fellow-Japanese were allowed to approach close to the building and talk with inmates at the barred windows.
>
> Soon after this the inmates started throwing objects out of the windows—including toilet paper, which fell in long streamers down the building. Then there came the crash of glass, as the first window crashed outward and then various objects, including bed springs, chairs and plaster from the walls fell from upper stories of the building to the roadway and railway tracks below. As guards moved forward to lend a hand in subduing the rioters, a fire hose, directed by the Japanese from an upper floor window, doused them with water. Various objects seized in the detention quarters also hurtled close to the guards. Throughout the disturbance the inmates shouted "Banzai," the cheer being echoed by Japanese sympathizers...
>
> Several times during the afternoon crowds gathered at the foot of Burrard Street and on the wharves to watch the disturbance. The crowds included many Japanese, the latter number being swollen shortly before CPR trains for the east left just after 7 p.m. These 125 young Canadian-born Japanese were interned as a result of their behavior.[30]

The riot in Vancouver coincided with early camp organizing, particularly in Ontario, where some "volunteers" and internees had already been sent.[31] By April, Dave Watanabe had already "established himself as spokesman."[32] At a meeting with Graham Pipher, a BCSC apparatchik, Watanabe demanded the workers' "rights as Canadian citizens," mainly regarding access to the nearby town of Schreiber.[33] The evacuees stated that their "volunteering" to work in Ontario should have earned them these promised minor freedoms.[34] Although not described as a job action, Pipher noted that sixty people attended this "meeting" to discuss grievances when they should have been working. Building on an earlier slowdown campaign, when the workers got word that the state was to restrict their movement, they brought their working pace to a crawl and threatened to strike.[35]

Pipher commented that any restriction "on free movement etc." would cause unrest to become "accentuated" and that he would lose control of the camp. The central administration pondered the imposition of stricter discipline, but the notion was junked well before implementation. From the start, the camps were not jail-cum-work-camps, and the incarcerated workers had much more latitude than the authorities had intended. As the camp was "small" and lacking in guards the Japanese enjoyed relatively free mobility. The "Japs at this camp [quickly] found favour with the majority of the citizens of Schreiber," and before long they were patronizing "local's stores and places of amusement," without "any adverse criticism" from the townsfolk.[36] It was of concern to T.S. Mills, the chief engineer on the project, that the men had access to the town and the telegraph office, and had the audacity to send uncensored messages directly to their families in British Columbia.

Mills related the story of a local railroad man's daughter, who inquired of her father whether it was acceptable to dance with the Japanese. The railroader told his daughter that "as long as the Jap was sober and conducted himself properly, he would sooner she dance with a Jap than a Dago."[37] The railroader's comment sheds some light on the process of racialization that was unfolding, solidifying, and mutating during the Second World War, and how the hierarchies of "race" were subject to significant gradation and shift. Although following the war there would be an "elevation" of some "peoples" to "white" status, the war period was still riven by the hierarchies of preference and stratification within the racial-taxonomic realm.[38] Be that as it may, Mills "saw problems arising" and predicted there "will be cases of too much intimacy between those young, well-mannered and conducted Japs and local girls." Despite the reservations of Pipher and the BCSC (let alone the state) about free movement, Mills noted that "too stringent regulations at this time will cause an unfavorable condition," and that "policies and regulations" need to be determined by need and on a local basis.[39] Although there certainly was martial rule in the camps, and many of the people in the camps were officially interned and under much stricter control, the reality was that spaces were consistently mediated and negotiated via direct action.

The BCSC thought it impossible to restrict free movement at Schreiber camp. They believed they had a responsible partner in Watanabe as a leader, and as Watanabe had the camp's "full support" they assumed that they could maintain rule by proxy.[40] Nearby Jackfish Camp had a beer parlour, and the BCSC wondered if adding a pub could be enough to keep the Japanese from wandering to the local dance halls. In the end, the BCSC decided against imposing their plan of a blanket movement ban. Interestingly, the state also gave up on censoring the mail of these specific workers, unless they were sending it abroad, as the mail "could not contain information of much value to the enemy"—a freedom not extended to interned antifascist Canadians.[41] Although Pipher wanted to move Wanatabe to another camp to "break" the impromptu organization, the BCSC thought better of it, noting that "should he be moved, he would cause trouble elsewhere." Preferring to contain the trouble rather than turning local agitators into travelling organizers, Dave Wanatabe was left alone.

Although those workers had won the right to send and receive uncensored mail, the letters did not go unwatched. The state was good enough to keep some of the mail from evacuees on file, and these provide some insight into evacuees' mindsets in 1942. In one intercepted letter, T. Sekine (working at a camp near Malakwa, BC) shared a common concern with his wife Y. Sekine that "it is tough, many things promised by the Security Commission doesn't seem to be here or in town." Alluding to the difficult position his wife was in, he noted that "if they are not going to look after our women folk the men will start another strike," insinuating that an upcoming job action was not the first of its kind. He continued on to say that all of the "married ones worry about the welfare of their wives. Guess it is just a racket, now they [the BCSC] bit off more than they can chew. I hope they choke."[42]

Mr. Sekine was an astute observer: the BCSC was indeed overwhelmed. By 1942 the Canadian state was dealing with a strike wave unprecedented since the workers' revolt of 1919, and the state lacked the manpower to crush major urban strikes, let alone those in rural areas or in far-flung work camps. Mrs. Sekine expressed apprehension that her husband would be interned if he was too militant, but he responded that he did not fear internment as he and his comrades lacked "privileges" in the work camps, and "on top of that work in this hot weather . . . refusing us compensation in case of accidents . . . the interned ones are treated better." The state had few methods of discipline to deal with the men in work camps when the punishment was seen as potentially preferable to the current situation. Sekine argued that he and his compatriots were "Canadian born and naturalised men" and presciently believed that "the way things are running here now, there's going to be trouble soon."[43]

Another letter in the censor's file confirmed growing unrest. As one man wrote, presumably to his wife, "This camp was considered the quietest along this route, but it seems that some of the straw bosses are getting a little swell headed so it won't be quiet here for long. It's getting stifling, as if something is going to burst."[44] His use of labour vernacular hints at experience with unions.[45]

The worker went on to relate to his wife how "the boys" stole the "camp truck" to go play baseball against another local team. He anticipated repercussions, but as the foreman was "drunk every weekend, and even some week days," he was not terribly concerned.[46] Baseball was an important part of the Japanese Canadian experience, and particularly so in the isolated work camps.[47] Apart from entertainment, it provided one of the few opportunities for the men to travel and fraternize. Workers in the road camps quickly set up "highly competitive, intercamp baseball games" soon after arrival.[48] Alongside baths and gardens, camp workers generally constructed baseball diamonds first, even while living in tents, prioritizing quality leisure, intercamp sport, and socializing. The man noted in his letter that he had heard that some of the camp "agitators" had won recourse to leave, and were allowed to roam free. As he had yet to be on strike, he thought that rewarding militancy with freedom was "no British way of fair play!"[49] Work camps may have been under martial law, but it was not martially enforced. If even in this "quiet" camp the workers were regularly striking via baseball, unrest would have been extensive and routine even during the very early days.

In the same months that Sekine and the other evacuees were writing their letters, neighbouring BC and Alberta construction crews at the Decoigne and Geikie camps on the Yellowhead Road undertook direct action of their own.[50] In June and July RCMP Constable A.P. Ridley was regularly in contact with the Decoigne camp, as workers there were constantly on strike.[51] On 11 July 1942 Ridley was sent to investigate some rumours about an upcoming strike in the Decoigne camp. He found that in June, Inspector Radcliffe of the Edmonton detachment of the RCMP had been sent "to remove some agitators" from Camp Geikie.[52] This was deemed necessary as a man named M. Inouye had allegedly assaulted a teamster during an earlier strike, and the RCMP had decided to prosecute him.[53] This decision precipitated another strike.[54] While Ridley was investigating the situation, Mr. Burpee, the engineer of both camps, recommended removing five specific workers from nearby Decoigne camp. Although these workers were unconnected to the ongoing strike or even to any form of "agitation," Burpee insisted on their removal, as he believed that they "were not good workers." Wary of further provocations

Figure 10.1. Group Portrait of a Baseball Team, Tashme, BC, c. 1942. Takahashi Family collection, Nikkei National Museum.

against an already agitated group, Ridley opposed the move. The removal was undertaken anyway, against the better judgement of all involved. Before this extraction, Ridley noted, "Decoigne was a very peaceful camp. There was never a strike nor a breath of trouble."[55]

This changed when the five men were removed. Suddenly the "Japanese were indignant and demanded to know why they were being taken away." When "no explanation was offered," the camp ignited—with Ridley eminently sympathetic. He opined that the Japanese "realized that they had a good camp and had behaved themselves, and could not understand why the police had invaded their tranquility." The men in the Decoigne camp struck that evening, and refused to work until either their comrades were returned or "the foreman discharged," and preferably both. The workers correctly accused the foreman of precipitating the removal of the five men despite his denials.[56] The original strike at Geikie was quashed, but now the Decoigne camp was in upheaval. The workers at Decoigne penned a letter full of demands to J.H. Mitchell.[57] They wrote that the five men who were removed had no "attitude," that they were working "peacefully," and "were very popular gentlemen." The same could not be said for their foremen, who did not "understand our situation" or "Japanese psychology," and was "unable to handle our men in a peaceable manner." The letter was signed "Yours faithfully, All the Japanese in Work Camp 3A, Jasper Route."[58] Mitchell responded that "your going on strike does not meet with my approval, and as a friend who is always trying to better your condition . . .

a strike is only an injury to yourselves."[59] Mitchell, however, was mistaken, as eventually the men went back to work on the basis of promises of a quick return to their wives; and in the end, the foreman was "transferred to another camp."

The sheer number of job actions garnered increasing attention. Superintendent of Jasper National Park J.A. Wood was concerned that "the Japanese are pretty much out of hand" and "do practically what they want." Offended by the lack of discipline and control, Wood deemed it important to inform the RCMP that "the local VVR [Veterans Volunteer Reserve], believing that trouble may start, have armed themselves with borrowed rifles and will be available if required." Needless to say, armed veterans of the Great War were not needed in quelling labour disturbances in the camps, much to their chagrin.[60]

Constable J.W. Faulkner agreed with Wood.[61] He argued that "while these Guards do the duties required of them, it was found at Gosnell that they were inadequate when faced with a show of resistance on the part of the Japs."[62] Furthermore, the Japanese "take it upon themselves to run the camps." Faulkner continued that the Japanese were using "these meetings, strikes, and labour disputes to feel out the Police and ascertain just how far they can go and what they can get away with."[63] In this regard, the Japanese mirrored the rest of the Canadian workforce, who were engaged in a decidedly similar set of exercises. And indeed, during this time there were further strikes by Japanese workers in Rainbow and Grant Brook camps.[64] Faulkner saw sedition and sabotage where others saw fellow humans attempting to make their lives better through the only, and best, means available—organization and the strike. Moral suasion was off the table once forced labour and relocation was on it. Faulkner was concerned with the "considerable number of strikes and labour disputes since the camps have been established in the district" because "as they continue, they become more intensified." In Faulkner's estimation, "in the event of a strike developing into a riot, the police would be absolutely helpless."[65] Far less sympathetic to the Japanese than other RCMP officers, he advocated that "more rigid measures be taken, and taken immediately, otherwise the seriousness of the camp disputes will grow." Faulkner did not say where he would procure the troops or guards to enforce such subjugation.

Sometimes the strikes manifested in comedic fashion. Mila Fry wrote a letter to her MP, which caused the local RCMP a significant amount of trouble. She bragged about how she had caused "the First Jap Retreat" on Canadian soil after "the Japs went on the rampage at Gosnell."[66] Constable Ridley added some context and reality to allay his superiors' potential fantasies of out-of-control Japanese men attacking the RCMP. He wrote that:

> After Constable S.M. Slinn had arrested a Japanese for being impertinent to a peace officer, he proceeded with his prisoner to the railway tracks. . . . There is a river separating the camp from the tracks and Slinn stationed two Special Constables at this bridge to stop the rest of the camp from coming to the track while he boarded a train. The Japanese felt that Slinn had arrested the wrong man and broke through the S/Csts. and proceeded to the tracks in a mob. Here they crossed the tracks and milled around Slinn and demanded that he release his prisoner which he finally did.
>
> When the Japanese had proceeded back to the camp, Miss Fry, who lives on the other side of the tracks from the camp and about 100 yards back in the bush, came to Slinn and told him that she had seen everything and had had him covered with her rifle. But until that time when she came out and spoke to Slinn, he was unaware of her presence. She was not visible from the tracks and so the Japanese were also unaware of her position in the bush. The Japanese had demanded the release of Constable Slinn's prisoner and when this was done they returned to their camp in an orderly fashion.[67]

Seeing little to object to in a crowd of Japanese workers "un-arresting" a comrade by force from an RCMP officer, Ridley considered the matter closed. Indeed, Constable Slinn penned his own report, and considered "further investigation unwarranted."[68] Slinn's telling of the tale is only moderately different, and gives some insight into how the RCMP dealt with strikes in work camps.

Slinn noted that "approximately 100 Japanese in the camp had been on a sit down strike since 2/6/42. . . . The cause of the strike [was] simply that the camp foreman was unsympathetic towards the Japs in these trying times." Slinn held a meeting with the camp and "explained to the Japs that they were being placed on two meals per day, would not be paid, and certain other privileges curtailed, while they continued to strike." Not without a carrot, he said that "they would be paid and [their] privileges restored if they returned to work." The workers mulled their options, and one "Kawaguchi" advised the agents of the state "that the Japs had decided to continue striking." The next day, Slinn arrested Kawaguchi, and a near riot ensued. Following the arrest "the remaining Japs broke through 5 Special Constables, crossed the narrow bridge over the Gosnell River at the camp, and some of the Japs tried to pull Kawaguchi back to the camp."[69]

The strikers continued to escalate their actions. "Several incidents happened in the next half hour including one Jap baring his chest at the point of a rifle held by s/Cst. Carmichael." Then "45 Japs [broke] through a second line formed by 5 special Constables and myself, and then proceeding to the CNR track where I had sent S/Cst Forbes and prisoner Kawaguchi." Following this "the Japs requested the return of Kawaguchi, saying that they had not sufficient time to think over the latest decision of the Government."[70] Officer Slinn "advised the Japs that Kawaguchi would be released provided they returned to work under the camp Foreman."[71] He continued that he "would report their action to Headquarters, and that [he] could not tell them what action would be taken by the Force. They all agreed to return to work, and Kawaguchi was released." Very direct action carried the day. For his part, Faulkner believed that "there was no cause for a strike at this camp," and he thought that "*the apparent reason for the strike was that Gosnell was the only camp that had not been on strike*."[72] Of note regarding the "Fry Incident" is that seemingly the only reason any paperwork was done at all was because an MP noticed it and demanded a report. Indeed, the amount of labour unrest within the camps is intrinsically difficult to ascertain, because a sit-down strike and near riot only received formal notice when provoked by an outside query. Moreover, that the workers knew that theirs was the only camp that had not been on strike, and attempted to rectify that situation, lends credence to the RCMP's complaints that job action was widespread and ubiquitous, if not broadly organized.[73] It also supports the argument that strike action was both widespread and routine.

As summer turned to fall in 1942 in British Columbia and Alberta, very little actual work was being done in the work or concentration camps. Both were in a constant state of strike and unrest. On 18 June 1942, workers from the Grantbrook camp struck and formed a grievance committee. Sufficiently organized, the men massed and marched towards Red Pass, picking up workers from the Rainbow camp along the way. Once the Rainbow men joined their strike, their host contained over 200 strikers.[74] They had three demands: an end to the delay in payments to dependants; an end to restrictions on movement (for socializing, travel, and baseball); and free access to the towns of Jasper, Red Pass, and Blue River. Having no other options save a terror regime, the RCMP acceded. Another strike at the nearby Albreda camp was successful in getting a hated supervisor fired.[75] Infuriated, the BCSC complained.[76] Lacking in instruments of terror, starvation, or violence as an incentive, getting good work out of forced labour is a difficult task indeed. For those who were not working in the labour camps and stuck in concentration centres, the BCSC and police had similar difficulties.

Slocan City was the largest of the centres. Slocan was also the site of a general strike that emerged out of a dispute by truck drivers from 19 August 1942 through the end of the month.[77] As late summer turned to fall there were continuing strikes and protests in and around Slocan City. A strike led by women and "girls" was launched on October 26th, at the Orchard camp, a smaller settlement on the east side of Slocan Lake. The strike was called because their water was piped in from a nearby lake, and the young women detested the task of procuring and hauling water and the quarter-mile hike each way in addition to their working duties.[78] Although the workers were supposed to show up daily at 07:30, they rarely showed up on time (generally around 09:00), and on that day, not at all.[79] At 09:00, the foreman "cut off the payroll" and sent the few workers who had arrived home.[80] The foreman cut off the food supply, leaving only cooking utensils and plates.[81] The Japanese simply purchased food, and continued the strike. The workers wanted the RCMP and BCSC to pipe in drinking water from town. Although the BCSC originally stated that nothing could be done, the strike ended when the BCSC agreed to pipe in the local town's water. The women of the camp, saddled with the dual task of procuring water and working, were able to cease the latter to alleviate the former.

In another case of unrest at Slocan, fourteen young men were being forced by the BCSC to relocate to work camps.[82] On 30 October, a special bus showed up in Slocan City to take these men to another transit station to be deployed. Instead of showing up for relocation, the men hid with their families and friends. When pressed, Frank Kawaguchi, the Japanese liaison, stated that he had no idea where the absconded men might be. The RCMP fanned out over the area, and found two fugitives. Later that evening, nine of the party showed up at RCMP headquarters. The men said that they merely had to pack their bags and would leave the next day. After releasing them to pack their bags with their families, "a large crowd gathered outside protesting the bus leaving with the boys." RCMP officers were surrounded and forced to retreat to their headquarters by a group largely "composed of women and children." The crowd sabotaged the bus, immobilizing it. Mr. Hartley, the BCSC commandant, beat a hasty retreat. A well-aimed rock was thrown through his retreating car's window. Due to the large crowd and the talent depth in the bullpen, it "could not be discerned who had thrown it."[83] Panicked, the RCMP sent for

Figure 10.2. Slocan City Arrival, Slocan City, BC, 1942. Canadian Centennial Project fonds, Nikkei National Museum. Slocan was depopulated after the mining rush of the late nineteenth century. The architecture that marked the period is clearly visible behind the bags from recently arrived sitting on dirt road. In the uppper left there is an RCMP officer overseeing the operation.

reinforcements and the crowd eventually dispersed.[84] Of the fourteen "boys" slated for forced labour, only nine eventually decamped.[85]

As the centres intensified their organizing and actions, so too did the workers in the camps. On 1 June 1943, Constable Ridley went to the hamlet of Blue River to investigate a strike at the nearby Thunder River work camp.[86] This strike is of note as it occasioned the first meeting between Mr. Bernard of the Spanish Consulate and A.W. Brereton of Mines and Resources. Following the declaration of war, staff from the Spanish embassy were charged with looking after the affairs of the Japanese Canadians. As Spain was fascist, but technically "neutral," their diplomats and attachés became Japan's diplomatic eyes and ears in Canada. When the constable and consular officer arrived, they found the workers on strike, or as they said, "loafing around."[87] By 1943, being on strike was routinized, with rations cut to two meals a day. The strikers had refused to return to work until the Spanish consul heard their plea. After Bernard met with a strike leader privately, the strikers convened a meeting with the agents of the Canadian state. The main concern of the Japanese was that their food was poor (and served in such small portions), and that "meatless Tuesdays" were an affront to human decency. Before the RCMP or government representative could intervene, the Spanish consul "broke down" the argument, and produced receipts that showed the caloric intake of the workers was higher than that of the "average Canadian," and their food was "certainly much better than he himself can afford in Vancouver." Bernard was livid, stating "while the Spanish Consulate is the protecting power" of the Japanese, "he did not propose to waste his time investigating accusations that have no foundation." Bernard told the men that they were well treated, and if they failed to call off their strike, he would not object to their being interned. The workers quickly held a vote and "unanimously" agreed to go back to work. Even from the standpoint of the RCMP, "the Japanese were very disappointed in Bernard's attitude and his talk had a salutary effect."[88]

By 1943, the strike situation in Japanese work camps was reflecting the new Canadian norm of constant and sustained unrest. Much like other government officials, RCMP superintendent Fowell was worried that he had lost control of his camps and workers.[89] Lacking the number of guards necessary to quell unrest through the old truncheon method, he asked Hill for some crowd control aid. By the fall of 1942, strikes and "meetings" in the Japanese camps had become normalized. Evacuees were protesting everything from the decidedly illiberal seizure of their property, to bad housing, low pay, and bad food.[90] Again, forced labourers reflected wider proletarian trends within the wartime Dominion. Without the hyperbole so common to security officials, Superintendent Fuller noted that "a short time ago we had a small disturbance at Slocan city," and "a considerable crowd gathered." He argued that he "might have had trouble in dispersing" crowds in the future if such actions continued or escalated. Indeed, a handful of aging RCMP and Great War veterans would not fare well against the "over four thousand" Japanese "concentrated at Slocan City." With the mood and spirit of the protestors, he was worried that more "unforeseen trouble might develop." To aid this task of "handling a large gathering" he lusted after "a tear gas gun, ammunition," and "gas bombs" as the "effective" party in crowd control.[91]

The RCMP was neither in the mood nor prepared for blanket repression. Hill responded that "regarding the above mentioned subject, I do not consider that tear gas should be supplied to you[r] headquarters as a means of dispersing Japanese in the event of any anticipated troubles." Hill was certainly wary of escalating the strike situation, but was also at pains to convey that "you must fully realize that with the present international situation as it is, it would not be, in my opinion a good policy for us to use gas under any consideration. If gas was used it might have far-reaching effects."[92] Indeed, "Canadian Government Gases Japanese in Concentration Camp" would not be a great headline in any year, let alone 1942. The tear gas was never sent. Men of fighting age were fighting, not policing workers and internees. And although there was always the possibility of uncomplicated mass internment or incarceration, the state lacked the guards, prison space, internment camps, and prisons to enforce disciplinary actions on a mass scale.[93] "If gaol sentences for vagrancy were handed out," Hill opined, it "would only mean a few days in gaol" and then back to agitation. If the RCMP started simply locking men up "many other Japanese would follow in sympathy" and would overcrowd the jails, a tactic the Industrial Workers of the World had used extensively in Western Canada.[94] Hill perceived a real possibility for serious problems on the horizon as "the whole situation c[ould] develop disagreeably unless considerable diplomacy is used."[95] Escalation was not an option.

The constant job action in the work camps provoked a conference in Ottawa between the Department of Mines and Resources, the RCMP, and the Department of Labour early in 1943. Tired of ubiquitous and relatively successful strikes, the state decided to take action in a very Canadian way—having meetings of bureaucrats in a city thousands of miles away from the problem, in a different language than the "problem" population spoke, and with little to no input from anyone involved. Conference attendees were very concerned that the Japanese slowed down and refused work "to such an extent that they did not earn their board."[96] Judgments on work ethic aside, the bureaucrats decided on a particularly light-handed approach to the problem. They decided to allow "troublemakers" to leave the camps "one or two at a time" with the local RCMP acting as hiring agents. Troublemakers would "be given lists of job opportunities" by the government to find other employment. Japanese malcontents were to be given three options:

1) Going into private employment at a designated point at prevailing wages.
2) Hanging around town with nothing to do until he is hungry.
3) Going back to the road camp on the agreement that he would work properly.

The conference attendees were all too clever. If the malingerers took option 1, then they would be provided free train tickets, and they would "scatter the trouble makers as widely as possible to various places of employment."[97] Failing to learn from the climate in the work camps over the past year, let alone the current labour climate of hundreds of illegal and wildcat strikes, conference attendees assured themselves that "with a few trouble-makers removed from each road project by this means, the others will surely settle down to work." The bureaucrats, happy with their technocratic solution, applauded their work in Ottawa and reminded the implementers that they wished to be informed of how "successfully it operates." What the conference had done, in fact, was hand victory to workers who fought back. Organizers won free movement, a literal train ticket, better job prospects, increased pay, and the possibility of proximity to family. Mass strikes had been effective, and the conference was little more than an official bureaucratic gloss on a rearguard action.

From the very beginning of the removal operations there was significant and effective resistance from the evacuees, and this continued and intensified throughout. None of this, however, should overshadow the violence of the involuntary removal program, the pain and humiliation of forced labour, full internment for resistance, or the hardship created by the state in the confiscation and eventual sale of property. No amount of stealing work trucks to go and play baseball against a neighbouring camp can make up for the fundamental injustice of the racist operations directed against people of Japanese descent living in Canada. No direct confrontation with the state could have stymied the "diminished aspirations, lost opportunities, troubled relationships, generational conflict, a yearning for privacy, boredom to tears, deportation, work-related injuries, attempted rape, suicide, and death due to inadequate medical care" that haunted the entirety of the operation.[98]

However, the strikes, riots, and protests in camps and transfer centres were of note not merely for their existence, but their effectiveness. Workers won material gains and basic dignity through strike action in the worst of circumstances. It is true that not all strikes were successful, but many were, particularly when viewed in aggregate. By 1943, "troublemakers" were given wide leave to work where they wanted, and many used this to reunite with their families. But it was not only the men in work camps. One of Sugiman's interview subjects may have noted that she was "too young to fight," but we have at least two clear and successful examples of women, old and young, fighting back against the authorities to better their lives. Some *did* fight back, and their battles were remarkably effective. If nothing else, their struggles, protests, strikes, and other organized resistance should be remembered and celebrated. These people may not have gotten their entire lives, dignity, time, and property back, but they won something in the face of tremendous adversity. People of Japanese heritage took direct action to better their lives, all while living under grotesquely tragic circumstances engineered through systemic racism. That was a victory, and one not to be ignored or obfuscated—let alone forgotten.

Notes

1 James Marsh, "Japanese Canadian Internment: Prisoners in Their Own Country," in *The Canadian Encyclopedia*, http://www.thecanadianencyclopedia.ca/en/article/japanese-internment-banished-and-beyond-tears-feature/. Since the publication of this chapter the *Encyclopedia* has completely changed their analysis of Japanese incarceration operations, de-emphasizing complacency and putting in examples of resistance where none had been before.

2 There is no space to go into the historically necessary nature of racism in the construction of the Canadian state, or the particular strain found in British Columbia, but an excellent place to start is Cole Harris, *Making Native Space: Colonialism, Resistance, and Reserves in British Columbia* (Vancouver: UBC Press, 2002); David Goutor, *Guarding the Gates: The Canadian Labour Movement and Immigration, 1872–1934* (Vancouver: UBC Press, 2007). For a more capacious view of racism in Canada, see Donald Avery, *Dangerous Foreigners: European Immigrant Workers and Labour Radicalism, 1896–1932* (Toronto: McClelland and Stewart, 1979).

3 Outlining the continuance of the carceral state, Japanese Canadian work camps were often reconstituted Depression-era forced labour camps. For more on the quality of work camps before they were abandoned, see Lorne Brown, *When Freedom Was Lost: The Unemployed, the Agitator, and the State* (Montreal: Black Rose Books, 1987); *Bill Waiser, All Hell Can't Stop Us: The On-to-Ottawa Trek and the Regina Riot* (Calgary: Fifth House, 2003).

4 I often refer to the evacuees in camps as "workers," and indeed, they were. One evacuee noted that under Second World War internment, "nobody [was] rich or poor or educated. We were all the same." Their immediate proletarianization levelled all to *relatively* similar circumstances. Pamela Sugiman, "Passing Time, Moving Memories: Interpreting Wartime Narratives of Japanese Canadian Women," *Histoire Sociale/Social History* 36, no. 73 (2004): 73.

5 The nomenclature of "evacuees" stands, as that was the government's proposition at the time. As roughly 75 percent of the evacuees were naturalized Canadians, they could not be legally interned as a group. Eventually around 800 Japanese Canadians were fully interned, generally for work-related agitation. Although the term is taxonomically and ideologically problematic, it has some measure of legitimacy—no matter how politically obfuscatory and explanatorily shoddy. Euphemisms were cheap shields to the violence of the removal operations, and remain so, but the constant use of the term in juxtaposition to "internees" makes for muddy historical investigation.

6 Judy Fudge and Eric Tucker, *Labour before the Law: The Regulation of Workers' Collective Action in Canada, 1900–1948* (Toronto: University of Toronto Press), 229.

7 Forrest E. La Violette, *The Canadian Japanese in World War II* (Toronto: University of Toronto Press, 1948).

8 Ann Gomer Sunahara, *The Politics of Racism: The Uprooting of Japanese Canadians during the Second World War* (Toronto: James Lorimer, 1981), introduction. Sunahara's monograph, now available online, remains the standard (and excellent) treatment of the Japanese experience of the Second World War. Among others, see also Ken Adachi, *The Enemy That Never Was: A History of the Japanese Canadians* (Toronto: McClelland and Stewart, 1976); Yuko Shibata, *The Forgotten History of the Japanese Canadians: Volume I* (Vancouver: New Sun Books, 1977); Peter Ward, *White Canada Forever: Popular Attitudes and Public Policy towards Orientals in British Columbia* (Montreal and Kingston: McGill-Queen's University Press, 1978).

9 The main understudied aspect of Slavic Austro-Hungarian internment during the Great War relates to its function as targeting the poor and destitute, political policing, union busting, and anti-leftism from the Canadian state. See Kassandra Luciuk's chapter in this collection for a more detailed analysis.

10 Japanese redress itself has seen investigation, notably by Roy Miki and Cassandra Kobayashi, *Justice in Our Time: The Japanese Canadian Redress Settlement* (Vancouver: Talon, 1991); Maryka Omatsu, *Bittersweet Passage: Redress and the Japanese Canadian Experience* (Toronto: Between the Lines, 1992); Roy Miki, *Redress: Inside the Japanese Canadian Call for Justice* (Vancouver: Raincoast, 2004). For a comparative interrogation, see Ian Radforth, "Ethnic Minorities and Wartime Injustices: Redress Campaigns and Historical Narratives in Late Twentieth-Century Canada," in *Settling and Unsettling Memories: Essays in Canadian Public History*, ed. Nicole Neatby and Peter Hodgins (Toronto: University of Toronto Press, 2012), 369–415.

11 Sugiman, "Passing Time," 51–79. Another useful source is Yon Shimizu, *The Exiles: An Archival History of the World War II Japanese Road Camps in British Columbia and Ontario* (Wallaceburg, ON: Shimizu Consulting, 1993).

12 Carmela Patrias, "Race, Employment Discrimination, and State Complicity in Wartime Canada, 1939–1945," *Labour/Le Travail* 59 (Spring 2007): 36. Patrias would later devote a paragraph to strikes in the work camps in *Jobs and Justice: Fighting Discrimination in Wartime Canada, 1939–1945* (Toronto: University of Toronto Press, 2012), 95.

13 Stephanie Bangarth, *Voices Raised in Protest: Defending North American Citizens of Japanese Ancestry, 1942–49* (Vancouver: UBC Press, 2008); Patricia Roy, *The Triumph of Citizenship: The Japanese and Chinese in Canada, 1941–67* (Vancouver: UBC Press, 2007).

14 "The British Columbia Security Commission was administered by three men: industrialist Austin C. Taylor, RCMP Assistant Commissioner Frederick J. Mead, and John Shirras, the Assistant Commissioner of the B.C. Provincial Police." Sunahara, *The Politics of Racism*, Chapter 4.

15 Library and Archives Canada, RG18, vol. 3568, C3129-1-7 [hereafter LAC, JSF] RCMP Report, 6 April 1942, C.H. Hill to Major Austin Taylor, BC Security Commission. Assistant Commissioner of RCMP "E" Division CH Hill was in charge of coordinating the RCMP with the British Columbia Security Commission and their removal efforts. The BCSC was hastily established 4 March 1942, to plan, supervise, and direct the expulsion of Japanese Canadians. It would be shown to be simultaneously cruel and incompetent.

16 LAC, JSF, RCMP Report, 6 April 1942, C.H. Hill to Major Austin Taylor, BC Security Commission.

17 LAC, JSF, Memo, 27 March 1942, RCMP Commissioner S.T. Wood to St. Laurent.

18 Stuart Wood was the ninth commissioner of the RCMP, an extreme reactionary, and a fascist sympathizer. He held the post from 1938 to 1951.

19 They were not the first Japanese men interned. The RCMP had incarcerated some members of the community deemed to be of particular risk in December.

20 LAC, JSF, RCMP Report, 25 March 1942, C.H. Hill to Commissioner.

21 Sunahara, *The Politics of Racism*, Chapter 3.

22 "The leaders in this movement are, F. TANAKA, a Canadian-born Japanese and graduate of the University of British Columbia, BOB SHIMODA, and a grocer on Denman Street, Vancouver, whose name has not been ascertained." LAC, JSF, RCMP Memo, 9 April 1942 CH Hill to RCMP Commissioner. Shimoda would later recount his experiences in helping organize resistance in Miki, *Redress*, 65–69.

23 LAC, JSF, RCMP Memo, 9 April 1942 C.H. Hill to RCMP Commissioner.

24 Ibid.

25 LAC, JSF, RCMP Memo, 28 April 1942, C.H. Hill to RCMP Commissioner.

26 Ibid.

27 The trope of the "waylaid proletariat" or the "outside agitator thesis" is exceptionally common in labour history. It emerges when an employer, the state, or the police argue that workers would not have taken action if it was not for an outside agitator, brainwashing, foreign agitation, Moscow Gold, and on and on. It is a way to transpose the manifestation of direct action or outrage into something other than social and economic realities.

28 This quote is doubly telling in regard to later protestations that the Japanese were removed for "their safety" and that this operation was most emphatically about the state.

29 LAC, JSF, RCMP Memo, 28 April 1942, C.H. Hill to RCMP Commissioner.

30 LAC, JSF, Japanese Activities in British Columbia, *Most Secret Report*. No Date, Clipping in Appendix 7.

31 By the beginning of 1943 1,850 people had been relocated to Ontario and Quebec, usually to work in road or forestry camps. These were generally male and usually full internees, "volunteers" who were "voluntold," or alternatively the "troublemakers." There were 12,114 persons in the interior detention camps, mostly families. 4,390 persons were located elsewhere in BC, mostly men engaged in road construction. 3,925 had been moved to the prairies, often (but not exclusively) as family units to work as agricultural labour. A further 42 were "exchanged" with Japan. Canada, Department of Labour, *Report on the Re-establishment of Japanese in Canada, 1944–1946* (Ottawa: King's Printer), 26–27.

32 For more on Dave Watanabe, see Shimizu, *The Exiles*, 595.

33 LAC, JSF, Report: April 1942, T.S. Mills, Chief Engineer/Graham Pipher (BCSC), to Intelligence Section.

34 A promise made by MacNamara, the deputy minister of labour.

35 LAC, JSF, Report, April 1942, T.S. Mills, Chief Engineer/Graham Pipher (BCSC), to Intelligence Section.

36 Ibid.

37 Ibid.

38 For more on the creation/institutionalization of racism and the production of whiteness, see Theodore W. Allen, *The Invention of the White Race, Vol. 1: Racial*

Oppression and Social Control (New York: Verso, 2012); David Roediger, *The Wages of Whiteness: Race and the Making of the American Working Class* (New York: Verso, 1999); Karen Brodkin, *How Jews Became White Folks and What that Says About Race in America* (New Brunswick, NJ: Rutgers, 1998); David Theo Goldberg, *The Racial State* (Hong Kong: Blackwell, 2002).

39 LAC, JSF, Report: April 1942, T.S. Mills, Chief Engineer/Graham Pipher (BCSC), to Intelligence Section.

40 LAC, JSF, 23 April 1942 BCSC to Asst. Commissioner Mead.

41 Ibid.; see also William Repka and Kathleen Repka, *Dangerous Patriots: Canada's Unknown Prisoners of War* (Vancouver: New Star Books, 1982).

42 LAC, JSF, Canadian Postal Censorship, Vancouver Branch. T. Sekine to Y, Sekine, 5 July 1942.

43 Ibid.

44 This letter was in the same file, but lacks an exact date or names.

45 LAC, JSF, Canadian Postal Censorship, file 5677, 1942. The BCSC referred to its workers as the "rank and file." LAC, JSF, J.H. Mitchell to T.S. Mills, 16 June 1942.

46 The men were constantly irritated by the heavy drinking of their foremen; for another example see LAC, JSF, C.P. Ridley report on "Investigation of damage in Japanese camp, Pyramid, BC," 15 November 1942.

47 For more information on baseball and the Japanese Canadian experience, see Ron Hotchkiss, *Diamond Gods of the Morning Sun: The Vancouver Asahi Baseball Story* (Victoria: Friesen Press, 2013).

48 Bill Waiser, *Park Prisoners: The Untold Story of Western Canada's National Parks, 1915–1946* (Calgary: Fifth House, 1995), 198–99.

49 LAC, JSF, Canadian Postal Censorship, file 5677, 1942.

50 A summation can be found in Waiser, *Park Prisoners*, 175–216.

51 Alan Ridley was the RCMP constable in charge of the Red Pass detachment in BC. Ridley was often tasked with policing the road work camps and seems to have detested the work.

52 LAC, JSF, RCMP, Red Pass Detachment, 14 July 1942, "Conditions at Decoigne Camp, Promise of Strike," A.P. Ridley.

53 After the job action, he was found guilty of common assault and given a $20 fine and thirty days in jail.

54 LAC, JSF, RCMP, Jasper Detachment, 30 June 1942, "Strike at Geikie & Decoigne Work Camps," J.W. Faulkner.

55 LAC, JSF, RCMP, Red Pass Detachment, 14 July 1942, "Conditions at Decoigne Camp, Promise of Strike," A.P. Ridley.

56 Ibid.

57 J.H. Mitchell was the engineer heading the road construction projects in the mountains from his headquarters in Jasper. Mount Mitchell in Alberta was named for him.

58 LAC, JSF, Letter, Camp 3A, 26 June 1942, to J.H. Mitchell, Red Pass, BC.

59 LAC, JSF, J.H. Mitchell, 29 June 1942, Red Pass BC, to Japanese Workers, Work Camp 3A, Decoigne AB.

60 LAC, JSF, A. Wood, 24 June 1942, Jasper, Alberta, Department of Mines and Resources – Lands, Parks, and Forests Branch. The VVR were the Veterans

Volunteer Reserve, a pseudo-military outfit made up of veterans from the First World War and hangers-on.

61 J.W. Faulkner was the head constable for the RCMP at Jasper, Alberta.

62 LAC, JSF, RCMP, J.W. Faulkner, 22 June, 1942, "Japanese Work Camps: Jasper to Blue River, Guarding Of."

63 Waiser, *Park Prisoners*, 191–94.

64 LAC, JSF, J.M. Wardle, 25 June 1942, Director, Department of Mines and Resources to MacNamara.

65 LAC, JSF, RCMP, J.W. Faulkner, 22 June 1942, "Japanese Work Camps: Jasper to Blue River, Guarding Of."

66 LAC, JSF, A. MacNamara, Deputy Minister of Labour, to C.H. Hill, 23 June 1942.

67 LAC, JSF, RCMP Report, 9 July 1942, Red Pass Detachment, "Strike at Japanese Work Camp – Gosnell," A.P. Ridley.

68 LAC, JSF, RCMP Report, 6 July 1942, Taber Detachment, "Strike at Gosnell Work Camp, BC," S.M. Slinn.

69 LAC, JSF, 9 July 1942, Red Pass Detachment, Strike at Japanese Work Camp – Gosnell, A.P. Ridley.

70 Ibid.

71 LAC, JSF, RCMP Report, 6 July 1942, Taber Detachment, "Strike at Gosnell Work Camp, BC," S.M. Slinn.

72 LAC, JSF, RCMP Report, Jasper Detachment, 17 June 1942, "Strike at Gosnell Work Camp," J.W. Faulkner. Emphasis added.

73 The RCMP correctly believed that the camps were organized by roving organizers and through baseball teams.

74 LAC, JSF, Telegram, 18 June 1942, J.H. Mitchell to T.S. Mills.

75 LAC, JSF, RCMP Intelligence Section, 13 August 1942, Sit Down Strike, Albreda, BC, Constable G. Upton to C.H. Hill.

76 LAC, JSF, Memo, 19 June 1942, J.W. Walker to the Department of Labour, memo regarding Yellowhead–Blue River Project.

77 LAC, JSF, 27 September 1942 – Conditions at Albreda Camp, AP Ridley to C.H. Hill.

78 LAC, JSF, 1 November 1942, Strike at New Denver, Strike/Disturbance – Slocan.

79 LAC, JSF, RCMP Report, Japanese Workers' Strike, 29 October 1942, H.M. Fowell to C.H. Hill.

80 LAC, JSF, RCMP Report, Japanese Workers' Strike, 29 October 1942, H.M. Fowell to C.H. Hill.

81 LAC, JSF, 5 November 1942, Strike in New Denver W.R. Cooper and Fuller.

82 LAC, JSF, RCMP Report, Refusal of Japanese Party to Leave for Labour Camps as Scheduled, Disturbance at Slocan City, Constable D.A. Deeks.

83 The rock thrower and bus-saboteur(s) remain at large.

84 That 75 families were still living in tents in the Canadian fall could not have helped their disposition.

85 LAC, JSF, RCMP Report, November 1942 – Strike at New Denver, Strike/Disturbance – Slocan.

86 LAC, JSF, 18 June 1943, RCMP Telegram, "A telegram report concerning a strike among Japanese workers at the Thunder River Camp," F.J. Mead to MacNamara, DM Department of Labour.

87 LAC, JSF, 9 June 1943, RCMP Report, A.P. Ridley.

88 Ibid.

89 LAC, JSF, RCMP Report, C.H. Hill, 12 November, 1942 – Tear Gas and Gas Gun for New Denver Sub-Division.

90 LAC, JSF, 6 November 1942, Supt. Fuller, RCMP to Hill.

91 Ibid. On 23 January 1943, the government empowered the Custodian of Enemy Alien Property to liquidate the property of the evacuees. "All the Japanese complained" that the "Custodian's office had charged them amounts equal to or exceeding the price realized on the sale" of their goods. This was particularly galling in the case of automobiles. In one striker's opinion, his car had been worth at least $200, but received a cheque for only $7.50. LAC, JSF, 6 April 1943, RCMP: C.H. Hill to F.J. Mead.

92 LAC, JSF, RCMP Report, C.H. Hill, 12 November 1942 – Tear Gas and Gas Gun for New Denver Sub-Division.

93 This was very similar to the rest of Canada, where thousands of illegal strikes shook both the state and capital.

94 Mark Leier, "Solidarity on Occasion: The Vancouver Free Speech Fights of 1909 and 1912," *Labour/Le Travail* 23 (Spring 1989): 39–66.

95 LAC, JSF, 18 March 1943, C.H. Hill to RCMP Commissioner and F.J. Mead to Hill (No date, attached, on or around 18 March 1943).

96 LAC, JSF, Memo, 24 February 1943, A. MacNamara to F.J. Mead.

97 Ibid.

98 Sugiman, "Passing Time," 78.

PART VI

PERSONAL REFLECTIONS AND DOCUMENTS OF THE INTERNMENT EXPERIENCE

CHAPTER 11

Japanese Canadian Internment: A Personal Account

GRACE EIKO THOMSON

My name is Grace (née Eiko Nishikihama) Thomson. I was born at the Japanese Fishermen's Hospital, in Steveston, British Columbia, to Japanese immigrant parents.

The following is a personal account of the Japanese Canadian internment (1942–49). It is therefore limited to my own experiences of internment, and its effects on my life. I include some of my mother's memories of these years (taken from her memoir, written within the last five years of her life, which she left with me to translate for family members). My research into this subject tells me that each individual's stories of the internment and dispersal years vary according to the age at which the speaker experienced these events. I was in grade two and attending Lord Strathcona Elementary School, in East Vancouver, at the time our lives were disrupted. My own and my family's experiences of these years dictated how we lived then, and continues to direct how I live even now.

I had no option to attend university after graduating high school, as my parents struggled to resettle in the city of Winnipeg, after restrictions on the movement of Japanese Canadians were lifted 1 April 1949. And so I attended Success Business College evening classes and began working as a stenographer, then as a legal secretary, to assist my parents in the purchase of a home that we could finally call our own.

In the late 1960s, as issues of identity continued to fester inside of me, and still not able to shake off the memories of internment, I began, with some trepidation, to study. Beginning in 1970, at University of Winnipeg, I began taking evening classes focused particularly on history and political studies, and as my sons grew older I registered full time at University of Manitoba School of Art (BFA, honours, 1973–77); then at the University of British Columbia (1980–82) I entered a graduate studies program in Asian art history to investigate my Asian/Japanese cultural roots.

My professional career began in 1983 when I was hired as assistant director/curator of University of Manitoba School of Art Gallery where for seven years I curated exhibitions focused mainly on Manitoba artists. During this time, however, I was offered an eye-opening experience that forced me to face reality, beyond my own life as a Canadian. I was asked to act as an advisor to Inuit printmakers of the Sanavik Co-operative, at Baker Lake, Northwest Territories. In this role I would fly 1,500 miles due north of Winnipeg, about three times a year, spending a few days each time advising on image choices for the co-op's annual production, and meeting with the Canadian Eskimo Arts Council, which juried the annual collection. In meeting the Inuit artists and their families, I realized that while a major industry of Inuit art was already flourishing in the south, the northern artists and their families were living in relative poverty.

In 1990, with the Redress (1988) compensation in hand, I took a sabbatical from the University of Manitoba. To update my education particularly in cultural studies, I registered in a social history of art program (MA), to study under renowned feminist scholar Dr. Griselda Pollock at University of Leeds, UK. Returning, I moved to Prince Albert, Saskatchewan, in 1992 in order to serve as director curator of Little Gallery as well as teaching a course at the University of Saskatchewan. Here, I was for the first time introduced to Aboriginal artists who were not yet included in this gallery's program. With support from local artists, and working with the late Bob Boyer, an artist and professor at Saskatchewan Indian Federated College, we produced a travelling exhibition of works by leading contemporary Saskatchewan Aboriginal artists titled *Identities: Sharing Worlds.*

In 1994, hired by Burnaby Art Gallery, I moved to Vancouver, where I curated a series of exhibitions, cross-cultural in theme, under the title *Tracing Cultures*, and also one of art and stories by immigrant students, *Tracing Cultures, Arts Alive '97*, with the local school district and teachers.

In 1998, after some fifteen years of focusing on intercultural artistic practices, largely centred on post-colonial issues of selective exclusions, I moved to an in-depth examination of Japanese Canadian history, as I was invited to serve as a developmental consultant, and then as the founding executive-director/curator of the Japanese Canadian National Museum.

The museum opened on 22 September 2000 with the exhibition *Reshaping Memory, Owning History, through the Lens of Japanese Canadian Redress.* After leaving the museum in 2002, I curated two further exhibitions: *Shashin: Japanese Canadian Studio Photography to 1942* (partnering with University of Victoria), which opened first at the Royal BC Museum in Victoria and then at the Japanese Canadian National Museum in Burnaby; and *Levelling the Playing Field: Legacy of Vancouver's Asahi Baseball Team,* which opened respectively at the Japanese Canadian National Museum and at Vancouver Museum.

Background

My father came to Canada, at the age of nineteen, in 1921, from the Village of Mio (now Mihama city), in Wakayama Prefecture, Japan, soon after he finished his schooling. His wish was to join his father and two older brothers who were already fishing on the West Coast of British Columbia. Instead of following in their footsteps, he was directed to take another path. So, after picking up basics as a house boy, he travelled, working on railway passenger cars as well as in railway hotels, as far east as Winnipeg, focusing on learning English.

According to family documents, he was registered as a naturalized Canadian in December of 1929. The following year he returned to Japan to marry (as arranged by his parents). Upon his return he and his bride lived in Steveston for a while, then moved to Vancouver in the mid-1930s. He had obtained a job as a buyer at the recently formed Codfish Cooperative Sales Society, established by Caucasian, Japanese immigrant, and Aboriginal fishermen, in East Vancouver. The family resided in an area often referred to as "Japantown," first on Powell Street, then on Alexander Street, as the family grew in size.

I might insert here that names like "Japantown," "Little Tokyo," and "Chinatown" used by media were not names given by the residents themselves, most of whom were emigrants struggling with English, but by the larger community, which regarded these areas as "foreign," not "Canadian," as means of discrimination. These settlements originated as places of support and security for the residents, and the Japanese immigrants called this area of settlement, located around Powell Street, *Paueru Gai* (Powell town).

When the Government of Canada issued Order-in-Council PC 365, which designated an area one hundred miles inland from the West Coast as a "protected area," and Order-in-Council PC 1486 (24 February 1942), which authorized removal of all "persons of Japanese racial origin" and gave the RCMP power to search without warrant, to enforce a dusk-to-dawn curfew,

Figure 11.1. Family portrait, 1938, taken on the day before Kikuko left to visit with Grandmother in Japan. Collection of the author.

and to confiscate cars, radios, cameras, and guns, my parents were expecting their fifth child. Beyond this, their first-born daughter, my older sister, was just then away from Canada, visiting our grandmother in Japan. She would not return to us until February 1951 when we became settled in Winnipeg.

Paueru Gai, a thriving community with its own infrastructures and amenities, had existed for more than four decades from the turn of the twentieth century, and with the abrupt removal of its residents, the place was a ghost town, described as follows in the 17 June 1942 edition of *The New Canadian* (a second-generation newspaper, which was published in English): "The Life Blood is Drained from the Heart of the Community . . . Powell Street was early adopted by the Japanese and under their care it just grew up. Now the Japanese are leaving and the street is beginning to look like a neglected orphan."

Internment

My parents and some 22,000 other Japanese Canadians of all ages were expelled from their homes along the West Coast of British Columbia in 1942. Since my mother was expecting, we moved first to Steveston where my father's older brother, Konosuke, was living (without his family, who at this time were in Japan). Here she gave birth to my sister at the Japanese Fishermen's Hospital (founded at the turn of the twentieth century by a Japanese immigrant benevolent society and sometimes described as the first instance of a health care system in Canada, as families paid yearly fees and medical care was provided to everyone in need, not only Japanese Canadian).

Rather than going to one of the sugar beet farms, or to government internment camps, the decision was made by my uncle that we would move with some of his fishermen friends and their families, to what was called a "self-supporting" site, which meant that internees paid for their own moving costs and housing.

In fact, in the end, all internees paid for their own confinement. All personal properties—for many, this included homes, fishing boats, cars, farmlands, and businesses—were understood to be under "protective custody" and left in trust with the Custodian of Enemy Alien Property, to be returned to them at the end of the war. However, as early as in January 1943, through Order-in-Council PC 469, most of these properties were liquidated by the government, without consent of the owners, and the proceeds used to defray the costs of internment.

The place we were moving to was in the interior of British Columbia, the former gold mining town of Minto Mines. My mother, Sawae Nishikihama, offers the following:

> We took with us rice, as much as we could carry, canned foods, other groceries, tea, minimum number of dishes, pots and pans, and left in early April, forty days after my giving birth, taking a Union Shipping Company boat from where Bayshore Inn is located today, arriving in Squamish some four hours later. . .
>
> We then took a train which chugged through the valleys and along a river, for a hundred miles or more, and remember arriving after six hours in Bridge River late at night. Mr. Naokichi Nishihama, who had earlier been sent to Bridge River, welcomed us, bringing us tea. We spent the night on the train and then a truck came for us early the next morning. We sat with the children, myself carrying the newborn baby, on a long wooden bench on the

Figure 11.2. Family portrait, 1943, in Minto. Torasaburo and Sawae Nishikihama, and four of their children, Eiko, Toyoaki, Kenji, and Keiko (missing: Kikuko, in Japan). Collection of the author.

> back of the truck, and were driven up the high Mission Mountain on curved roads, for about two hours, when we came to the peak.[1]

As each internee was allowed a very limited amount of belongings, only those things absolutely necessary were taken. For my uncle, what he could not part with was his Japanese *ofuro* (wooden bath tub heated from within), which he paid to take, but which gave our family and our immediate neighbour (distantly related to us) great comfort each evening.

I have memories of helping my mother carefully pack her "treasures" of potteries and dishes (for each season), ornaments, such as special sets of Japanese dolls celebrating the annual Boys' and Girls' Festivals, some kimono which she brought from Japan, books she treasured, etc., into wooden boxes which she had specially made. She carefully placed these boxes in a locked shed behind my uncle's home.

These possessions were soon taken or vandalized, some objects being sold at auctions, we were told. Few items were ever returned to the Japanese community. Many families lost their photo albums, too heavy to take with them, but no doubt everyone expected that they would be returning to their homes at the end of the war.

Only seven years of age, I had little understanding about what was happening to us. My mother was looking and acting stressed, though telling us we would be returning to Vancouver again so not to worry about what we were leaving behind. I thought then that she was upset because she was leaving behind a new kitchen stove that she had just recently bought that she had been so happy about. I wonder now if she really thought we would be returning. In leaving Vancouver, I had said goodbye to my grade two classmates at Lord Strathcona Elementary School in Vancouver. I remember only such mundane things as that I wore a red plaid skirt and a rose-colour knitted blouse on my last day of school, made by my mother, which I wore proudly. (As was the case of most Japanese immigrant mothers in those days, Mother was an excellent seamstress, and all our clothes, except my father's, were made by her. Suits that my father wore to work in Vancouver soon became clothes for my two brothers.)

Living in the internment site of Minto, located in the Bridge River Valley, idyllically surrounded by mountains and a river, my memories are those of a child, playing each day with friends and going to school, where lessons were taught by educated persons from our own community. The Japanese Canadian population in Minto is recorded as 322. Parents and community members worked hard to provide a peaceful environment and various community activities for their children, even as they spoke to each other in hushed tones away from the children, worrying about what would happen to them after the war, especially after learning that everything left behind had been confiscated and

Figure 11.3. Students attending school in Minto, BC (1944–45). The government did not provide teachers, and so classes were taught by thiose deemed to be qualified among the interned. Collection of the author.

sold by the government not long after they had left the West Coast. What would they be returning to?

Families helped each other and produced fenced-in vegetable gardens in spaces between houses and the produce was stored in the "basement"—often just a hole dug under the house—for winter use. Father was able to get a job at a nearby sawmill, the workers picked up each morning to be returned in the evening, which helped to pay for the rent and groceries, even though the wages were meagre. I remember my mother's happy face, when, in opening Father's lunch pail to wash at the end of the day, she would find *matsutake* (pine mushroom) that he had picked during his lunch hour.

Mother, in the meantime, together with other women, particularly *obasan* (elder) next door, learned to make *tofu, miso*, and *shoyu*. Many evenings were spent by us children, after bath, listening to *obasan*'s Japanese ghost stories, eating buns Mother had made filled with sweet bean paste (called *anpan).*

Since this was an abandoned gold-mining town, there were only a few former residents remaining, such as the mayor of the town, a rancher who treated the new residents respectfully. This may be due to the fact that shortly upon arrival and settling of Japanese Canadian families, the mayor experienced a fire at his home, and his new neighbours quickly went to help douse the fire with buckets of water. Throughout the time we lived in Minto, Mayor Davidson, when he went hunting and brought home his prey, often distributed pieces of moose meat to the residents. Also, my brother and his friends hung out at his ranch, watching activities around horses, a new experience. As my mother used to say, there are always some good people, despite what was happening to us.

The town consisted of a hotel, where single men and elders rented rooms, a post office, and one grocery store. I remember being given money from my uncle once, after losing a game of Chinese checkers to him, and going to the store to buy a cake—a rare treat in those days. Uncle Konosuke, who spoke little English, went daily to the hotel lobby to listen to the shortwave radio news from Japan, which he then summarized and offered in the evenings to the Issei (first-generation immigrants.)

> During the gold rush, our house had been used by the miners. Since the outside walls were only tar-papered, during the winter snow blew in through the cracks. . . . The first winter was a cold one . . . snow fell on Minto's mountains and young people enjoyed skiing . . . in the evenings, Mr. Etaro Shoji played the *shakuhachi* (bamboo clarinet) and the quiet melody resonated throughout Minto.

> These were truly peaceful moments . . . in this way, the harsh and nightmarish year ended.
>
> (Sawae Nishikihama)

There was little lacking in terms of basic everyday needs for us children. But for our parents, they were undoubtedly living in limbo.

Dispersal and Repatriation

It was not until the order came from the government to move again that I, now a little older, became interested and aware of our dire situation. I was now ten years of age, turning eleven in the fall.

In August 1944, Prime Minister Mackenzie King had declared, "the sound policy and the best policy for the Japanese Canadians themselves is to distribute their numbers as widely as possible throughout the country *where they will not create feelings of racial hostility* [my italics]." Thus began the policy of dispersal. But even worse was still to come, for as the war drew to a close a series of orders-in-council and then the passage of the National Emergency Transitional Powers Act made it clear that the Canadian government had only two policies concerning Japanese Canadians, one of "dispersal" and the other of "repatriation." There was no third option of returning to British Columbia, and refusal to comply with the two options offered would be taken as evidence of disloyalty to Canada. *Repatriation* was the term used by the government for forced exile to Japan, but those born in Canada could not be repatriated, for how could one "return" to a country they had never known?

My parents, especially my mother, at first actually considered going to Japan. As she explained in her memoir,

> Because we have an elderly mother and a daughter in Japan, we signed up . . . we pondered over what the best thing to do was, and ended up withdrawing our application. . . . We then decided to go to Manitoba. . . . My husband had lived in Winnipeg at one time in his past before we were married and was familiar with the City.
>
> (Sawae Nishikihama)

My father, who had been living and working in Canada since the age of nineteen (before his marriage he had lived briefly in Winnipeg, where he did not experience the West Coast's overt racism), had no desire or intention of living anywhere but in Canada, which he still believed would eventually adopt him and his family as full citizens. And so the decision was made to move to

Manitoba. However, among many Japanese Canadians who chose to move east of the Rockies instead of accepting deportation, there was an understandable fear of the unknown. As author Ken Adachi points out, "most people outside of British Columbia, in fact, had never seen a Japanese before—except as sinister characters in the movies. . . Indeed, during the entire relocation programme, the federal government did little to correct the impression."[2]

First Move to Middlechurch, Manitoba

> Arriving at this eastern point, I thought we would be more free, however . . . the RCMP and the Security Commission were there to meet us, and we were taken outside of Winnipeg to a vegetable farm in Middlechurch, where the house we were given turned out to be a barn.
>
> A stove and beds were brought in but the building, located in the middle of a farm, had a high ceiling and the walls inside were covered with tin sheets. Manure clinging on straw hung stuck to these walls. A bare light bulb hung from the high ceiling. I stood in the middle of this barn, which was to be home to our family of six, and couldn't hold back the tears. But remembering our situation, I knew there was no choice but that this is how it is and will be for some time yet.
>
> (Sawae Nishikihama)

And so, Mother began washing down the walls of our new home. Here is where my parents (who had never worked on a farm before) were to work at $2.00 per day. I remember my mother saying how embarrassed she felt when, at the end of each day, the farm owner came to hand out their pay, "but with each day I got used to the routine." They worked together with German prisoners of war, each wearing a shirt with a (target) red circle on the back.

> On August 15, 1945, the war had ended. We were picking raspberries in the field when we were informed that Japan had surrendered and there were great celebrations taking place in the City of Winnipeg. . . When we were living in Minto, we had listened to the radio so kept up somewhat about the war situation but here, on this farm, to hear about an unconditional surrender, and thinking about the Japanese people, mother, daughter, and relatives, we were for a time speechless.
>
> (Sawae Nishikihama)

In the meantime, my brothers and I played around the barn while our parents and our baby sister went to work each day on the farm. I was taught and given responsibility to prepare sandwiches, as they returned home for lunch each day, while in the evening, my eight-year-old brother went down to the river with our father to fill buckets of water for our daily use.

Manitoba winters are too severe to live in an open barn. And so we were moved into a nearby house, occupied earlier by a Mennonite family whose son we later learned was jailed as a conscientious objector.

We spent about a year in Middlechurch before my father found a job near Whitemouth, about 100 miles to the east. With no work on rainy days on the farm, the wages were not enough to sustain our family.

However, it was here in Middlechurch that for the first time I came to realize who I was beyond my family, and that I was not regarded as adequate here in Canada, where I was born. On rainy days, when there was no farm work, my mother and I would sometimes take the bus into Winnipeg, which was not too far away. (At this time, we were not allowed to live in the city.) On one such day, as I happily got on the bus with my mother, looking forward to shopping at Eaton's, a boy not older than myself pointed at us and shouted to his mother, loud enough for the entire bus to hear, "Look, Mom, there's a Jap!"

At twelve, I was old enough then to understand what was happening, but too young to understand its implications for the future. The feelings of humiliation I experienced at that moment remained with me into my adult life, as I began to deal with identity issues related to being Canadian; that is, born in Canada, yet not accepted, but also not belonging to, or having ever seen, the country of my ancestry, Japan. This was my first experience of "racism," an English language word I had not yet heard used or had to grapple with. Some years later, I would read a more eloquent but equally heartbreaking telling of such an incident, written by Frantz Fanon from his own experience.[3]

I had spent my life up to this point at an internment site, feeling secure in a community of Japanese Canadians, who felt and looked like relatives. And before that, at Lord Strathcona Elementary School, located on the east side of Vancouver, where my classmates were mostly immigrant children, largely from China and Japan, but also from Italy. As children, we were unaware of anything but play in the school grounds. I have no memory of maltreatment from either teachers or students. In those days, I knew nothing about Japanese immigrants and their children (mostly naturalized Canadians, or born in Canada), how they were being treated, or that they were struggling with discriminatory abuses in their everyday lives, at work and at play.

The school we attended was a quarter of a mile away from our farmhouse in the small town of Middlechurch, and my brothers and I walked to and from school every day. We were often picked up on the highway by passing cars (incredible when I think about this today). The younger of my two brothers had just started grade one (without having had opportunity of a kindergarten experience). It was the first time that we experienced the cold of a Manitoba winter (and my mother had sewn a parka for each of us to wear). And so we were grateful for the lifts we received on the highway.

But it was also the first time we attended a school entirely of European Canadian children. While the students were not unfriendly, certainly we were looked upon with curiosity, and living so far away from the townsite, and on a farm, there were no opportunities to become acquainted or to interact with students outside of the classroom.

It was here that I made my first attempt toward acculturation, not in the best of ways. My first name, Eiko, was mispronounced everyday by my classroom teacher, Mr. B—. He did not even bother to try to learn it and stumbled over it whenever he spoke to me, much to my embarrassment. I came home after each incident feeling mortified. It was bad enough that I looked different from other students, and was an object of curiosity, but to also call attention to my name as another sign of inadequacy was just too much. As I complained to my mother almost daily about this, she, who spoke no English, remembered two English names of Japanese Canadian women she had known in Vancouver—women she admired as having been quite accomplished. So she suggested that from the next term onward, I should become either Lily or Grace. We agreed I was no lily, so in 1946, I became *Grace*, to overcome the "stigma" of a "foreign" name. Today, when I speak to young people, I say to them, quoting Shakespeare, "To thine own self be true," regretting that I had at one time, in a moment of weakness, submitted to the wishes of others even to the point of changing my name, albeit to a good name that has served me well.

As I mentioned, I did not make friends with anyone in Middlechurch; that is, except for one girl who lived nearby. Of her own volition, she came across the highway and visited me and my family at our home. She was a classmate, named Mary Sarna, and I remember her name to this day as that of my first friend outside of internment. She had the courage (supported by her family) to come to visit us. I did not have such courage to approach my classmates as friends. More, I regret that I was too young to think about how my brothers were faring. My brother, two and a half years younger, had a very difficult name to pronounce, Toyoaki (Toyo aki), and I recall him being called "Tayo wacky," and seeing him often in fights.

Second Move to Whitemouth, Manitoba

My life and outlook changed somewhat when we moved to Whitemouth. This was a town larger than Middlechurch, and though surrounded by farmland, we lived in town. My father began commuting to Dryden, Ontario, returning home every other weekend, in order to work at a paper mill.

My brothers and I registered at the local school and I remember only a few days later, as we were lining up outside when the school bell rang, my ten-year-old brother already being reprimanded by a teacher, Mr. W—, who was my homeroom teacher. Without thinking, I found myself running over and intervening, saying this is my brother and he is new to the school and needs help, not scolding. To his credit, the teacher let my brother go and didn't say anything more. (In fact, he soon became my favourite teacher, as he encouraged me to study.) From this point, my brother's name had also changed . . . to Tom. What I couldn't do for my brother in Middlechurch, I was able to do successfully here in Whitemouth.

But this was how it was in Whitemouth. It was a small town in an area where there was a mixture of various ethnic families: German, Mennonite, Ukrainians, and others. My father was able to rent the upper floor of a house owned by a middle-aged Ukrainian immigrant couple.

While I think there was a bit of strangeness between us at the beginning, no doubt there was some sympathy toward us; indeed, in this town we were treated respectfully. Certainly, these communities were well aware of our situation. While Japanese Canadians were expelled from their homes on the West Coast (as security risks) and restricted in terms of movement, German and Italian Canadian community members were not.

When my parents decided the second-floor suite they had first rented was too small for our family and we learned that the service station owner at the edge of town had a suite behind his garage office for rent, we moved there. It turned out it was not much larger than the other. But it was on the ground floor, with private backdoor access. In fact, it had only one bedroom where my parents slept, a kitchen with a wood stove, and a very large room—part of which became the bedroom for us four children, as well as our living room. My mother installed a makeshift Ping-Pong table, as much for her own use as for us children. This was something she enjoyed (in her limited free time) when she was not doing household chores, or sewing. And, of course we had an outdoor "biffy."

In those days we did not have real furniture, only hastily built or found wooden chairs or benches and a kitchen table. No fridge, but an ice box, no sofas, or rugs on the floor. But I did not even think about such things since this was, as my mother would say, how it was for now. Soon after we moved here, the elderly couple who rented this space to us, owners of the gas station, seeing how little of anything we owned, offered Mother a washing machine which they had replaced for a newer model. This was accepted with great appreciation, as my mother was still doing our washing in an aluminum tub, with a scrub board, using, as I recall, Sunlight bar soap.

Although "dispersed," and living far away from what used to be our home on the West Coast, here in Manitoba we were still under restrictions and watched over by the RCMP. But in this town of Whitemouth, we (together with about five or six Japanese Canadian families who had moved here during the dispersal years) were able to live our everyday lives to the full, as we were largely welcomed by this community. My brother Tom was being invited to classmates' farm homes, to enjoy the animals and to join in farm chores.

The town had a hotel, bank, churches, hardware store, cafe, grocery and clothing store, and a train station where there was a grain elevator, and a town hall where musicians came and dances were held. The daughter of the station master, who had returned home after living in the city, offered me both stylish and practical clothes she had worn in her youth, which I gratefully and happily wore on special days. Possibly this was the first time I had worn store-bought clothes. I was soon invited to join the CGIT (Canadian Girls in Training), at the local United Church, and a couple of years later, hired as a part-time waiter at the café owned by the wife of a local attorney. I was taken under the wings of a student minister (later to become moderator of United Church of Canada), Rev. Lois Freeman, who motorbiked to Whitemouth to give the weekly sermons. She persuaded the local board chair, Mrs. Wardrop, to send me as representative to attend a United Church conference in Winnipeg, and very kindly invited me to stay at her father's (dean of theology, United College) manse for a few days. This was my first real visit to the city, outside of the few shopping trips to Eaton's with my mother from Middlechurch. Further, when Ms. Freeman was getting married, she brought her wedding gown to my mother for alteration.

So it was that life became closer to normal, as I learned to skate, and to cheer at local hockey games, and later joined a curling team. I even began to babysit for our next-door neighbours, overall doing what all teenagers normally do.

Undoubtedly, all of this was new to me but felt very comfortable as I became friends with girls from my class. At the same time some local mothers began bringing fabrics to my mother to ask her to sew dresses and clothing for their children.

All memories of this period except for one were of positive events that helped me to feel I was becoming a part of Canadian society for the first time, even as I knew I did not belong, that is, *really* belong, as always some part of me felt I was not quite adequate in the eyes of others. Of course, it is to be remembered that my family—living behind a garage office, without proper furnishings, and my father working in Dryden, coming home biweekly, and myself always at my mother's side interpreting for her as she went grocery shopping, or to pay the monthly rent to the owner of our "home," or to visit the school on behalf of my brothers—was different. This was not how "ordinary" families lived.

One particular event marred the otherwise happy memories of new friends and a kind community. Within the first year that we moved to Whitemouth I had learned that a music teacher came weekly to the town hall, to teach piano lessons using the piano installed there. I began bothering my mother for permission to take lessons, especially since the piano was available to students for practice.

Of course, at this time, my parents were struggling to put some money together, not knowing what their next order from the government might be, for even though the war had ended we were still not free of government control. For a family who had been uprooted from their home in Vancouver, moved several times, and was now living in a makeshift home, there was never any feeling of security in our lives. But my mother, an educated woman—who had come to Canada with my father with big dreams of a great life in this new world and instead found herself incarcerated and reduced to living behind a service station with her children in a small town where she had only one other Japanese-speaking family nearby to visit—decided that I should at least be allowed this opportunity of taking the piano lessons, and so obliged me.

However, within two months of beginning my classes, and happily practising every day at the town hall, on one such day, as I was leaving, some sixty- or more-year-old town clerk grabbed me and kissed me on my mouth. I was thirteen years of age at that time, with little experience about men. I had been living a very sheltered life in this respect, always living close to family and not yet familiar with the surrounding culture's social environment, particularly in dealing with adults. I escaped his grasp, and ran out. I immediately quit my lessons. I did not tell my parents why, and was scolded by mother who was very disappointed in me for quitting without seriously trying.

I was old enough at that time to know that speaking the truth of what happened was not wise. We were, for the first time in a while, feeling welcomed and supported. In fact, we were strangers to this town (uninvited guests). Without intimate friends or relatives, who could help us? To whom could we go? I could not tell, as this was the (perhaps respected) town clerk. Had I told my mother, in the absence of my father (working in Dryden and coming home only every other weekend), it would have distressed her, especially since she could not speak English adequately to act on her own, or to protect her daughter, and had Mother told Father, what could he have done? Would he have reported this to the RCMP, under whose jurisdiction we were still being held? And what would have been the outcome? We were living in a vulnerable state, entirely powerless.

I have learned in more recent years that such occurrences were not rare during the internment and dispersal years, when Japanese Canadians were living in situations without security.

End of Restrictions, Move to Winnipeg

Asian Canadians received the right to vote federally in June 1948, and provincially in March 1949. However, for Japanese Canadians the end of restrictions on civil liberties didn't come into effect until 1 April 1949, close to four years after the end of the war (which confirms for me that the internment was not about "security risks," but rather stemmed from a racist society and was perpetuated and directed by the government itself).

We were told that we were now free to return to the West Coast. But there was nothing to return "home" to. For parents like mine, who were still young and just beginning their lives in Vancouver when they were uprooted from their homes and my father from his job, it was a huge struggle to begin a new life anywhere with four children still of school age, and one still in Japan, so we stayed in Manitoba and moved into Winnipeg.

There was already the Manitoba Japanese Canadian Citizens' Association (MJCCA, formed March 1946) in Winnipeg, which offered newcomers some help to settle. Beyond this, Japanese Canadians were receiving active help and support from the Jewish community in Winnipeg. And so my family was able to rent a house from a Jewish landlord. And my father was hired by Stirling Fur Company, a tannery, and Mother by a sewing factory where she was soon doing piecework, and working overtime, earning extra money.

> On the first morning of work, I was amazed at the large traffic of people going to work which gave me strength. . . .
>
> On one winter day, after working overtime, until seven, I was taking the bus to go to Daniel McIntyre High School, where I was taking an English language course. . . . Once I returned home, we would speak in Japanese, and I continued to depend on my children's support. I think this was my biggest mistake in life that I did not take myself more seriously.
>
> (Sawae Nishikihama)

I remember her beginning this journey with great expectations. I believe it was not that she was "too old to learn," as she had told us, or that she did not take herself seriously, but more likely was too tired. Her daily life was too stressful. But for the first time in years, I felt that my parents seemed happy, as they settled into a life together, focused first on getting their oldest child back from Japan, and second on buying a home, which I believe represented for them a new resolution in their lives that had been destroyed in 1942.

In the meantime, I was quickly introduced to a high school in the North End of Winnipeg, St. John's Technical High School, as it was called then. Here most of the students were of Jewish, Scandinavian, Ukrainian, and Polish descent. It was a traumatic experience to get used to a city school, particularly class discussion procedures that intimidated me. I had heretofore been taught in classrooms that often had two or three grades, with one teacher teaching all subjects. Since the school was a fair distance away, over the Salter Bridge, to avoid the daily cost of a bus fare, a bicycle was bought for me, the first in my life. My younger siblings were in schools near home, the youngest now in grade two, and I was in charge of ensuring they returned home from school safely each day and to begin making dinner before our parents returned home from their work.

1950 was the year of Winnipeg's Red River flood. Mother learned that young Japanese Canadians were volunteering to help with the sandbagging, and encouraged me to join them. I began to participate in this already active community, which held annual concerts at the Ukrainian Labour Temple Hall, where, after receiving lessons from older members of our community, I soon learned to sing and dance and to perform. After turning sixteen, I joined a young people's club formed at the YWCA. A Christmas Ball, sponsored by MJCCA, was held annually in a local hotel, and as I grew older, since many young men came from Ontario and Quebec, registering particularly in the engineering and architecture departments at the University of Manitoba (one of the earliest universities to open its doors to Japanese Canadian students), I was to experience invitations to university proms, wearing beautiful gowns designed and sewn by my mother, and to be introduced to the idea of a university education heretofore not within my reach.

As well, I joined the young people's group at Knox United Church, and also sang in the choir. This is where, in 1959, I was to marry.

Soon after graduating high school, with training in typing and shorthand, I was hired as a stenographer in an insurance company, where I was treated very kindly by both the bosses and the employees, as their first Japanese Canadian staff member. On hearing about an office job open at a cast iron foundry (the Anthes-Imperial Co. Ltd.), where many Japanese Canadian men were hired, I applied and was hired and within a year was promoted as secretary to the vice-president. Incredibly, he and his wife soon began inviting me to go with them to Winnipeg Symphony Orchestra concerts, and even to Blue Bomber football games. He is remembered to this day as someone who helped me to develop self-confidence in the early years when I had great doubts.

It was around this time that, as I did my weekly walk through the aisles of books at the Winnipeg Public Library on William Avenue, I came across a title which startled me: *The Canadian Japanese and World War II: A Sociological and Psychological Account*, written by the sociologist Forrest La Violette in 1948. I took it home and read it thoroughly.

Naively, I felt I had to share this information with others, as though the content was not known to my friends, which was likely true, as not one of my friends took an interest in this past. They were all dressed stylishly and looking forward in their lives, as I too was trying to do. But I remember writing a couple of articles which the editor of the Manitoba JCCA's monthly bulletin, *Outlook*, very kindly published.

And some years later, as I watched my two young sons grow and saw that they were seen by others as having a "different" mother, I began to examine what my own position was, and especially thought back to my two younger brothers, who must have had difficult experiences with little guidance or support. So the idea of university study began to move closer to reality as means to reach full potential in the lives begun with our immigrant parents, not only for myself but for my siblings, and my parents.

In 1951, my older sister had returned to us. She had, as a seven-year-old child, in 1938, been sent with relatives to visit our grandmother in Japan; our family had planned to visit Grandmother the following year and to bring her back with us. However, due to the conditions of war between Japan and China, followed by Japan's attack on Pearl Harbor, the plan did not work out. My mother's memoir contains the following account of our family's reunification:

> February 11, 1951, our daughter, Kikuko, now 19 years plus 3 months . . . at long last . . . was returning home to Canada. . . . In those days, when airplanes were not accessible, my second daughter, Eiko, went to Vancouver by train to meet her.
>
> We went to Winnipeg's train station to greet her.
>
> Since this child left, I wondered why I had allowed this to happen. Why I let her go . . . and cried every night. In my dreams of her she is as at the time of departure only eight years of age, and although I had thought I would hold her tightly when she returned, of course the person who came off the train was a young woman. She came to me to be embraced by me, but I hesitated for a moment. I have come to realize more recently that the coldness she had shown toward me throughout her life was a result of this moment of hesitation on my part, and I forever regretted that I could not turn the clock back, to replay this moment.
>
> (Sawae Nishikihama)

My sister subsequently married a second-generation Japanese Canadian, had two sons and a daughter, and was actively involved in the Japanese Canadian community (teaching Japanese at the Manitoba Buddhist Church) while maintaining close connection with her friends in Japan, even contributing to the City of Winnipeg gaining a sister affiliation with a Japanese city, Setagaya (1970). However, there is no doubt that she had lived a stressful life. She passed away at the age of fifty-four, in 1986, of cancer, and during the last months of her life, our mother, now living in Vancouver and having lost her husband just a few months before, stayed by her bedside in Winnipeg until she passed away.

My parents' move to Vancouver in August of 1963 is described as follows by my mother:

> We have become seniors now and in Winnipeg the people who gather together as members of the Jodo Shinshu (Buddhist) sect are all very warm and kind and are all like family to us. While we worked hard for some seventeen years in Manitoba after the war, today, our children are each getting married, and we are now blessed with grandchildren. However, in view of the severely cold

> winter that has no end, we decided to move back to the gentler climate of British Columbia. . . .
>
> We boarded a train and headed for Vancouver. . . . We had lived in a prairie province for a long time so as we approached Vancouver, we felt great nostalgia in seeing once again the mountains and the sea. Whether the smell of the seashore, or the fragrance of the sea, it was like returning to one's *furusato* (hometown). . . . The haze hanging on the mountains . . . the ships from all over the world. . .the ebb and flow of the tide.
>
> (Sawae Nishikihama)

They had made the choice of moving to Vancouver, not because it was the place where they had begun their married life, or because of the climate, but more importantly, their two sons were settled there with their own families.

The younger of the two sons, my brother, Kenji, in his mid-teens had been caught with a friend breaking into a warehouse in Winnipeg, and after a trial at which he was represented by a distinguished legal counsel (who I was working for as his secretary at that time), was released by the judge, who sympathetically saw the predicament in which my parents lived, and allowed for my brother to be sent to Vancouver to live with relatives, where he could begin a new life. And so he did, resolving his past successfully, living to the full, as a kind and generous man.

The older of my two younger brothers, Tom (Toyoaki), soon after graduating high school, made his own plans and moved to the West Coast and got himself a job at a logging camp in Port Alberni. He then attended Vancouver Institute of Technology, where he trained as an arc welder, and after a few years of work experience with international and local companies, was teaching at this institute. He was a talented young man and showed great promise; however, he had problems. He carried a lot of anger and frustrations, as I recall, even in his childhood, when he was often in fights at school, and he was unable to release this anger in his young adulthood. When he lost his beloved wife, within months he followed her to an early death in 1983, not able to cope, leaving behind a very dear teenaged son.

These were incredibly difficult years for the family. I attribute the early deaths in our family to the disruptive and anxiety-filled lives each of us had individually experienced, moving from place to place, days and years lived as a hated minority, lives unfulfilled.

While I remained very close to my mother, there is no doubt that we had grown up with little connection to our father. Father (affectionately called "Papa" in those days) worked away from home throughout my teen years, and I and my younger siblings hardly knew him, as he had little time to spend with us. I remember my brothers being scolded at times, but did Papa ever sit down to talk about their future, or dreams? There was no such space or time. In fact, we had no future to dream about . . . only the present to survive.

These would have been preteen to early teen years for my brothers, developmental years, not understanding but dealing with daily discriminatory remarks, and looks, moving from one school to another, from one makeshift home to another, with no lasting friendships.

While I remember my mother as strict, and often expressing anger and frustration over small incidents, but always near us doing her best to look after our needs, I remember Papa as a quiet man, but kind and generous, with a big smile for us, whenever he returned to us every other weekend, during the dispersal years. But soon after moving into the house bought in Winnipeg in 1953, Father, who had off and on complained about stomach problems, was finally diagnosed as suffering from a duodenal ulcer and underwent surgery. During recuperation, he enrolled in a cooking school and found employment first at the Marlborough Hotel, then later at Misericordia Hospital.

Father had always enjoyed cooking, perhaps from the days of his youth when he worked at the railway hotels. And so unlike most immigrant families, who ate food prepared in the Japanese style, our family was used to Western (perhaps British) food, such as tapioca pudding, marmalade, pound cake, shepherd's pie, rare roast beef served with horseradish, etc. One fond memory is that of waking up on a Sunday morning smelling pancakes he would be making for us, eaten in those days with corn—not maple—syrup.

My younger brothers, did they have such fond memories of their father and childhood? I believe not.

Within the year before her own death, Mother lost her second son, who had been her sole caregiver before I moved back to Vancouver in the mid-1990s. He had phoned her each morning, ensuring she was well, offering her the daily weather forecast. With his passing she told me she would no longer take the prescribed high blood pressure pills. I did not argue. She said with a smile that she hoped she would die in her sleep. And so she did. She ends her memoir as follows:

> My elder son's wife in July, then my son himself in October 1983, leaving his one dear son behind, passed away from this world. Then, in February 1985, my husband, who had never caught a cold . . . died of lung cancer and, in the following year in March, my first daughter, who lived in Winnipeg, passed away. I was at a loss to explain to myself what was happening to our lives, and when I came to my senses, I realized that I was still alive. . . . Is this fate? I came to feel that it was through generosity and love of our daughters, sons, and friends that we live, and every night I chant the *sutra* . . . and remember the *haiku* of the famous Ryokan *san*:
>
> *Chiru sakura* (falling *sakura* [cherry blossoms]
> *Nokoru sakura mo* those remaining are also
> *Chiru sakura* falling *sakura*)
>
> Obeying the law of the universe, one day, the remaining *sakura* will also fall to the ground.
>
> (Sawae Nishikihama)

I will close here. And in closing, I want to share that I had in the past couple of years been privileged to take part in (*Gwawaneuk* First Nation) Dr. Chief Robert Joseph's *Reconciliation Canada*, as one of the ambassadors, honoured as an elder, and in the process attended workshops and even produced a circle, and through the process realize that reconciliation must begin first within oneself. Just as my mother had reconciled within herself by the end of her memoir, I too can say, as I near my mother's age when she began writing her memoir, that I am truly blessed.

I thank my two sons, Michael and David, their father, and my five beautiful grandchildren and their mothers, together with my remaining sibling, Keiko, and her husband, and nieces and nephews, and many friends, for giving me support and sharing their lives with me to this day.

Notes

1 Sawae Nishikihama, memoir (unpublished), written in Japanese, during some five years before her passing, translated by her daughter, Grace Eiko (Nishikihama) Thomson.

2 Ken Adachi, *The Enemy That Never Was: A History of Japanese Canadians* (Toronto: McClelland and Stewart, 1977), 279–80.

3 Frantz Fanon, *Black Skins, White Masks* (1952; repr. New York: Grove Press, 2008).

CHAPTER 12

Anecdote and Document: The Internment Experience of Rolf Schultze and Dorothy Caine

CLEMENCE SCHULTZE

To a child, the time that older people can remember has a special attraction. Not quite "history"—for that is the Romans, or King Henry VIII—it nevertheless constitutes an area both fascinating and exasperating. These elders possess a perpetual advantage, with their "oh, that was before you were born" or "when *I* was a little girl." This epoch, this liminal space of memory between the past that belongs to the long-dead and the living present, allures while it annoys—not to be experienced, yet lying so close. For me, born in 1950, the defining marker was the Second World War. "Before the war . . ." or "during the war . . ." were phrases that adults often used, and with which one could never argue and never compete. One was merely *told*, only later recognizing how ritualized was the telling and how censored the content.

My father, Rolf Schultze, arrived in the United Kingdom as a German political refugee in 1938, and early in 1939 he met my mother Dorothy Caine; they married only in 1949. Rolf was interned as an enemy alien from June 1940 to March 1941. The experience of internment (shared by thousands of Germans and Austrians, the majority of them either anti-Nazi in politics or Jewish) must have had an unnerving effect.[1] Neither the justice of the process as a whole nor that of the particular procedures was beyond dispute. To the physical dangers of wartime profound insecurities were superadded. One identity had been lost or renounced; a new identity was not yet securely gained, and perhaps never would be.

Like many who served and suffered in the war, my parents kept virtually silent about all this. The events and their impact were encapsulated in a very few striking anecdotes: in their case, just four. How my father, when first interned, was not allowed to send my mother a letter but was permitted to post the key of his house to her, tied to a postcard by a piece of string. How a German prince, responding to a question about relatives in the United Kingdom, named King George VI. How my father grew a beard in the Canadian internment camp, but was made to shave it off before his return. And how at an intercamp football match he located a friend in the other camp by walking through the crowd shouting out his name. That was the sum total of the tales they told.

But they kept documents that fill in the gaps and answer some of the questions. From Rolf Schultze there survive letters, envelopes, camp ephemera such as songs and poems, book lists (he was camp librarian), notes of lectures and courses done in the camp "university," pictures, and various lists. He recorded all the letters he wrote, often summarizing their content, and noted the dates of letters and parcels received. So I have both the typed letters that reached Rolf from my mother Dorothy Caine and also her preliminary pencil drafts, as well as a manuscript journal into which she stuck newspaper clippings. This is written in exercise books, and takes the form of a continuous letter to Rolf; it contains material that she could not include in her actual letters. In addition, there is some correspondence with official bodies and private people whom she thought likely to help get him released. And naturally she kept every one of the letters she received from Rolf.[2]

Rolf wrote (in English), using the special forms supplied to the internees. With his neat, clear handwriting he did not require the whole sheet for the permitted maximum of twenty-four lines. Two outgoing letters a week were allowed; this included any on business matters, e.g., to employers or to the Inland Revenue about taxation. There was no limit on the number of letters internees might receive, but postal delays and movements from one camp to another meant that there was no regularity at either end of the exchange. Both wrote in the knowledge that all post would be read by censors; they apparently were effective at self-censorship, since none of the surviving letters has any passages blacked out.

Selecting from these masses of material, the present essay tries to convey what it was like to communicate over a vast distance at long intervals, with uncertainties as to location, the arrival of letters, and even, at times, whether the addressees were still alive.

Background

Rolf Schultze (1902–1967) was born in Peine near the north German city of Braunschweig, the eldest son of Rudolf Schultze, classics teacher in the local Gymnasium and his wife Asta, née Fastenrath. Rolf studied science at Hannover Technische Hochschule and Frankfurt University, and gained his doctorate in physical chemistry in 1930. He remained in Frankfurt, working at the Deutsche Glastechnische Gesellschaft (a research institution for glass technology) as scientific librarian and editor. His academic-professional life brought him into contact with various scholars, notably Professor W.E.S. Turner of Sheffield, founder in 1916 of the Society of Glass Technology. In 1938 he applied for the post of research librarian with Kodak Ltd., at their research laboratory located at Wealdstone, near Harrow in Middlesex (about twenty-five kilometres northwest of London), and arrived in England on 4 November 1938.

Dorothy Caine (1908–2003) was the sixth child and youngest daughter of Elizabeth Caine (née Metcalfe) and Charles Robert Caine, an engineer who worked on contract for the firm of Mather and Platt, going abroad while his family stayed at home. She was born in Morecambe (Lancashire) on 11 October 1908 but when she was eight the family moved to west London, finally settling in the outer London suburb of Hillingdon. Here she and her two elder sisters lived with their (now widowed) mother, running the family's two adjacent shops: an ironmonger's, and one selling haberdashery and clothing. Because of wartime rationing, the shops had very little stock, and so Dorothy could sometimes write in the intervals between customers.

Dorothy had known Wilhelm Schultze (Rolf's brother) since about 1933, and in October or November 1938, he let Dorothy know of Rolf's move to England. Rolf spent Christmas 1938 in Paris, and the two first met in January 1939.

1940: Internment in England

When war broke out in September 1939, an Enemy Aliens Tribunal declared Rolf Schultze "category C" (i.e., the least suspect grade of enemy alien) and so he might continue working for Kodak. But because aliens were not allowed to live within a certain distance of Bomber Command HQ in Stanmore he had to leave his recently bought cottage at Wealdstone and move to lodgings elsewhere in Harrow. Then in early June 1940 when France fell and British forces were evacuated from Dunkirk, the government decided to intern even the "category C" aliens. On 26 June Rolf was interned, first at Kempton Park racecourse in west London, then two days later he was in 149 Pennard Avenue, Huyton, Liverpool. Huyton Camp had been improvised on a newly built housing estate, and contemporary sources report that conditions were fairly primitive. At that point, Dorothy had no idea where Rolf was.

On 2 July 1940 the liner *Arandora Star*, taking internees and POWs to Canada, was sunk by a German torpedo, with huge losses. British papers reported the event on 4 July, and the next day Dorothy's journal reads: "This afternoon longing for you completely overcame me so that I had no strength and had to sink down on my knees by my bed & rest my head on my arms until things straightened themselves out and I came back to reason again."

A letter dated and postmarked 2 July from Huyton will have given Dorothy reason to hope that Rolf had not been on the *Arandora Star*. Her journal describes its arrival on 9 July:

> A letter from YOU! . . . Not until I found myself grinning like 90 honigkuchenpferden [i.e. the German equivalent of "grinning all over one's face"] all at once at nothing at all & feeling warm & happy inside me, which used to be a natural state with me, did I realise I [*sic*] how tight & dried up with misery I have been since you went away. I have written you a long letter this evening & now I am very tired but very happy, at the end of my letter I sent "love from the family" because of the censor but here it is goodnight DEAR heart.

But her "long letter" says nothing of this, instead listing letters received from friends and various practicalities to do with Rolf's cottage, storage of possessions, and laundry. It ends almost casually: "Nice to hear from you at last, I shall be writing you again soon. The family send their love."

The first entry in Rolf's list of letters sent (compiled later, because it is written in a Canadian exercise book) reads "Huyton, 1 July 1940, Dorothy, Schlüssel [key]." But whereas the legendary tale was simply of the postcard's arrival with the cottage key tied on it, Dorothy's journal and letters reveal more. First, that she evidently had a key already and had started preparing the house for a prospective tenant; and second, that when the key arrived on 12 July, she couldn't actually guess what it was for:

> We laughed very much when the key came yesterday afternoon, simply can't imagine what it is for, if it is Oakley St [Rolf's earlier lodgings in Chelsea, London], why not send it there? the same applies if it is for 81 [his Harrow lodgings]. We were all overcome

> with admiration at the ingenious method of sending it, absolutely practical and sensible but completely german [*sic*]. Then I had a brilliant idea, of course it must be the key of your new lodgings, 149. JOKE. This will save a lot of bother because I had planned to rescue you in the good old fashioned method namely sitting on the prison wall and letting down my beautiful golden hair for you to climb up.

1940–1941: Internment in Canada

By this time Rolf was actually on board the SS *Ettrick*, which sailed on 3 July. A much later letter (19 January 1941) mentions how unsystematically the men were picked for embarkation: "I did not go to Canada voluntarily; at Huyton we have been selected rather at random, mostly non-married men." Extremely poor administration meant that the *Ettrick* was transporting a mixture of Nazi sympathizers and anti-Nazis, including many Jews. Not one word of the circumstances of that voyage, notorious for the ill-treatment suffered by the passengers, comes in the immediate correspondence. But a letter of 8 March 1941, written from the Isle of Man after Rolf's return crossing on MV *Georgic*, describes good treatment then, contrasted with "our very bad experience on the voyage to Canada aboard the 'Ettrick' (I assume you have read about it in the Parliament debates) . . . treated as a kind of convicts, or Nazis in disguise." And in a letter of 20 August he mentions that his beard started to grow on board ship "and here when we had no access to our suitcases and toilet outfits."

The SS *Ettrick* docked at Quebec on 13 July. Rolf's letter list describes a document as "'Ettrick' 8.7. Home Office (posted from Q, about 20.8). Applic. for release." The draft of this survives, written in ink and pencil on a sheet and a half of lavatory paper (the fine tough paper of that epoch, almost like tracing paper, which must have been the only paper available). A date "21/8/40 (3 copies)" may indicate when he submitted the formal version, posting it from Camp Q (at Monteith, Ontario; later known as Camp 23) which served as a transfer centre. As Internee 53825, he lists his education, qualifications, employment, referees, publications, professional memberships, and languages. The tale of the "German prince" who cited King George VI as a relative may belong to this period of formal application for release. He was Friedrich of Prussia (1911–1966), who had been studying at Cambridge under the name Count von Lingen and was later in Camp A (Farnham). There is no indication that Rolf met him, so the tale could be hearsay about a well-known character.

Rolf sent several letters and cards to various friends during August, including one to his parents in Germany, because internees' mail, like that of prisoners of war, could be sent to hostile territories via the Red Cross. Dorothy (who by 11 August had learnt from the British authorities that Rolf was in Canada) wrote frequently to him. Some news came on 25 September when a friend had a letter from him, but Dorothy received nothing directly until his 20 August letter finally reached her on 15 October. He is worrying how she and her family are and "whether you may have suffered from aerial attacks of which we read in newspapers." Much of it specifies clothing and other items he wants her to send: "My money being confiscated I cannot buy anything in the canteen." He ends "As I cannot write often enough, please tell my friends of my life here. . . . Pray that my applications for release will have success." It would be eight more months until he was free.

His next letter (9 September) provides a few details of life in Camp Q: "We have received a prisoners' suit (blue with a big red stripe and a red circle on the back) and woollen underwear. . . . We are still sleeping in tents, but wooden barracks are nearly finished. It is autumn now; once, a fortnight ago, the temperature was below freezing point."

Her reaction to these first two letters is dated 16 October:

> Yesterday morning, coming in from my daily torture—feeding the chickens before breakfast—went to collect the post and found a letter from you. I danced upstairs on air, so happy, threw the rest of the post to my sister in the kitchenette and went into my own room,—I simply had to be alone to read it,— read it very quickly, but found it inexpressibly sad and by the time I got to the end of it I was crying. All the rest of the day I was alternately happy to have heard from you and unhappy for you. This letter was dated August 20th. Today I feel much better about you because this morning another letter arrived from you dated September 9th. you [*sic*] sound more cheerful in this, but it is a horrid business and I hate the word interned. Do you notice I try not to use it, prefering [*sic*] to say, "since you went away" or something similar?

On 8 October Rolf wrote:

> It is a pity we can only write so few and short letters, and we are not allowed to give details on our life here. But on the whole you may rest assured that I am doing much better in internment than I had expected. Time is going on very quickly, and up to now I have

> not experienced boredom, mostly because of the agricultural work and of interesting co-internees. As to the long winter months, I hope to get books from my American friends. . . . We are allowed to subscribe to Canadian newspapers now and to draw from the accounts of the money taken from us when we were interned; so I can take advantage of the canteen now. Food is always very good. I hope you have not been affected by the bombings.

Between 14 and 21 October he was transferred to Camp A at Farnham, Quebec (later known as Camp 40), and wrote on 31 October: "You will have seen from Paul [Klepper]'s letter . . . that we are together now, in a new camp; we are well, and I am camp librarian again. . . . Your letter of Sep. 25 was the first answer from England for four months and therefore especially welcome. Kodak Ltd wrote me that they are trying to get me released or to transfer me to Rochester [NY, Kodak's HQ]; I hope they will succeed in the first move."

Being camp librarian put him in charge (by the end of 1940) of about 500 books donated by charitable organizations, plus a list of another 500 privately owned books which apparently their owners were willing to share. Among the papers there are book lists and notes of lectures or classes on various subjects, including quantum mechanics, English literature, and Spanish, which explains the allusion to "mental (school) work" in this letter of 17 November: "I am still well, although we have no work to do (apart from cleansing [*sic*] etc.) in the new camp. Paul showed me the Connell's [*sic*] letter quoting that "Rolf is having a nice time" which is somewhat exaggerated. I am sorry not to be allowed to write much more about our life here, so that my letters will look rather monotonous. We are doing quite a lot of mental (school) work, playing cards, chess etc. I always am longing for being allowed to do scientific work again, may it be in England or Canada or the U.S.A."

The imbalance between the number of letters sometimes exasperated Dorothy. She wrote on average twice a week but by 3 December had received only one letter per month, and complains of feeling "cross, irritable, ill humoured, bad tempered, with a frowning scowling face and a black shrivelled heart!!" Two days later, however, she is overjoyed at public developments:

> Such splendid news! 15,500 aliens are to be released. You will surely be among them. Mr A. Patterson [error for Paterson] has gone to Canada to select candidates for the Pioneer Corps for release under stated categories and for visas for the U.S.A. Also to secure release from the Pioneer Corps into civilian industry of men who have

> peculiar qualifications which the nation requires. I am so happy for you. . . . Oh Rolf! There could'nt [*sic*] be any better news in all the world for you, could there? Hand on my heart, I am rejoicing with you, even if it means you go to America, I will try and not go black with envy, but I fear I am doomed to a very dark green. Just imagine, by the time this reaches you you might already be free. FREE is'nt [*sic*] it a lovely word?

On 8 December, in her journal, she expresses her fears: "Free and perhaps returning to England, a little frightening, perhaps you will be a stranger, not the Rolf [I] knew."

A letter from Rolf on 4 December responds to a batch of hers written in late October:

> I was so glad to learn that Kodak Ltd. are still trying to get me released. There is a possibility now for the "C cases" in Canadian camps to be transferred to English camps, although it is not certain (even for the favoured categories) that we shall be released. I think I shall take the risks connected with this transfer because I would like to be nearer the British authorities (they alone, not the Canadians, deal with the release of internees), in order to have my release speeded up, if possible. I hope you will agree with my coming back, in spite of submarines, bombs and possibly not so good food as over here. . . . Thank you also for getting in touch with Prof. Turner, F.R.S. [of Sheffield University, an acquaintance from Rolf's time working in glass technology]. If Kodak Ltd. alone cannot get my release, I think I could apply, through him, to the Royal Society (Advisory Committee for Interned Scientists).

After Christmas (29 December) he mentions a camp "cabaret (by professionals and amateurs) which could scarcely have been better in London." But the main news is of the first batch of releases: "Some of my camp-mates have been released, and I hope one or the other will be able to tell you about my life here more than I can write. I do not know whether or when I shall be transferred back to an English camp."

1941: Isle of Man, and Release

Three weeks later (19 January 1941) Rolf anticipates "my release, which is not far, I hope, according to the newspapers. I understand I shall be transferred to an English camp after my release." That is the last letter to Dorothy from

Canada; and a note in the letter list records "22.II. Abreise nach England [i.e., departure for England]." The next item is from Hutchinson Camp, Isle of Man: "Benachricht.[igung]-Karte [i.e., notification postcard] an Davies, Kodak" on 6 March 1941, followed on 8 March by a card and a letter to Dorothy:

> I am glad to be able to write to you from English (or rather Manx) soil again. Just after receiving the five letters written by you between January 1 & 15, a number of internees who had volunteered for the Pioneer Corps or who (like me) had been considered by a Home Office representative visiting us, as eligible for release, were sent back to England. We travelled by rail more than 30 hours and embarked on a big passenger boat where we were treated as third class passengers. . . . We were allowed to don mufti . . . the guards on board and later the English officers and soldiers were very friendly. After a night in a drill-hut "somewhere in England" we were transferred to this Manx camp, two or three days ago. A block of houses surrounding a square amidst the town of Douglas has been fenced off with barbed wire. 20 to 40 internees forming a cooking and housing unit, live in each of the houses. We "Canadians" feel rather uncomfortable owing to the wet cold weather which is worse than the 20 degrees below zero dry cold over there, and many of us, like me, caught colds at once. One room in each house is heated, and there is one bathroom, lavatory and W.C. (in some houses even several). Food is not so plentiful as in Canada but quite good . . . our release may take a very long time, even months.

Just as Rolf was about to sail from Canada, Dorothy wrote on 21 February with the good news that Dr. Roy of Kodak was being allowed by the firm's management to deal personally with the government officials who could authorize Rolf's release: "one man with enthusiasm will no doubt be able to do more than a committee." On 3 March she tells him that "Dr. Roy has handed your case over to the people in Cambridge, The Institute of Scientific something or other—U [friend working at Kodak] did not know the name—anyway they are the people who handled Dr. Bergs case. [This might be the Society for the Protection of Science and Learning.] Dr. Roy saw the London police (I suppose the Chelsea branch, I do not know) and they said they had nothing in their papers against you."

Meanwhile, Dorothy had received a letter (postmarked 7 March) from Wolfgang Ziemsen, who had already been released:

> Dear Miss Caine, This note brings you Rolf's messages from Canada. Greetings, thoughts, thanks, love, dreams. Tried to convey all these various emotions at once by telephone. But there was no response—a dead end. Left him about a month ago on Febr. 4th after we peacefully worked, played and slept together for the last 7 months. If a bit stubborn Rolf—professor we called him much to his liking—is a dear and very very fond of you. His eyes sparkled with delight when he got a letter of yours, he giggled and chuckled when he read them . . . perhaps he is on his way by now. Who knows—
>
> Sincerely yours, Wolfgang Ziemsen

Dorothy replied gratefully, and bombarded him with a "questionnaire" about the details of release, to which he responded fully, though his own experience (not having been held in the Isle of Man on his return) differed from Rolf's. On 17 March she received both the card and the letter sent by Rolf on 8 March on arrival in the Isle of Man, and, although she continued to write until his release (eight further letters), she closed her journal with these words: "You are half way back but I can't write anything here, I want you & real life. This I think concludes the entries here. I hope the rest of the story will be acted not written. FINIS. With love from ME to YOU."

A final note adds: "RELEASED APRIL 15th 1941."

On 13 March Rolf reported that his cold was getting better, and mentioned the legendary beard: "Did I write you that I had to cut off my beard but kept a sketch of how I looked with it?" By 29 March he has heard from Kodak: "My boss wrote me a very nice letter, and I hope they will succeed soon in obtaining my release and permission to live in Harrow Weald [i.e., in his own cottage, currently let to a tenant]." On 11 April he describes the timings of actual travel, presumably from hearing about other releases: morning boat to Fleetwood (Lancashire), "some police dealings," then likely to be free to travel onward by the early afternoon. This letter also mentions meeting friend Paul Klepper (by then in Mooragh Camp, Isle of Man) at the intercamp football match—though without the orally narrated detail about walking through the crowd shouting out Paul's name.

That is his last letter. The next item is a telegram, dated [Tuesday] 15 April 1941: "PRIORITY CAINE 311 LONG LANE HILLINGDON

MIDDX RELEASED ARRIVING TUESDAY NIGHT PROCEEDING WEALDSTONE ROLF."

Conclusion

The common feature of the four anecdotes in which Rolf's internment experience was encapsulated for me, his daughter, is their upbeat and amusing character. They became set stories, even though unimportant in themselves; they were simple enough to retell with a warm smile. When retold, they changed, as the key-on-postcard story shows, for at the time the key's identity was not even recognized. Or other details were added, as in the football match story. Or the story may have been just a bit of hearsay, as that of the Prussian prince citing the King of England, or simply *ben trovato*: "this is the sort of thing that should have happened." Predictably, the documents are far more sombre than the stories, even though self-censoring suppresses almost all mention of public and community suffering. Running through them is the anxiety of separation and fear for the future, however divertingly Dorothy writes in the effort to keep Rolf's spirits up, and however reassuringly he responds about his well-being. Despite the fact that her journal was addressed to him like an ongoing letter, it discloses concern as to whether they will have a future: did she in fact show it to him, make him read it? Did he perceive pressure inherent in her imaginings of what they will do together? Even these relatively simple documents reveal layers of redaction—lists consolidated later, drafts and redrafts of letters, summaries, annotations and suppressions—and raise as many questions as they answer. What is documented is not necessarily without obscurities, and even this modest story has its ambiguous aspects.

Notes

1 Paula Draper and Christine Whitehouse, in their respective contributions to this collection, explore aspects of these Jewish refugees' internment experiences and their responses to the circumstances in which they found themselves once shipped to Canada.

2 This is not unlike prisoners in other internment contexts; Rhonda Hinther and Myron Momryk's articles in this collection describe the material and documentary culture useful in piecing together the experiences of Second World War left internees and their kin.

CHAPTER 13

Ukrainian Internment during the Second World War: The Case of the Ukrainian Labour Farmer Temple Association and Peter Prokopchak

MYRON MOMRYK

With the outbreak of the Second World War in September 1939, the Canadian federal government was faced with an unknown future in Canada and a modern war in Europe. The government was also challenged by the lingering effects of the Depression that had sharpened the social and economic divisions in the country. In this context, any effort to hinder or impede the war effort was perceived by the government as a danger to national security, and the Royal Canadian Mounted Police (RCMP) was made responsible for enforcing the Defence of Canada Regulations (DOCR) throughout Canada.[1]

During the turbulent years of the Depression, the RCMP had already compiled lists of potential left-wing "subversives" involved in strikes and labour actions. These lists included the names of labour leaders and activists, especially the leadership of the Communist Party of Canada (CPC) and the Ukrainian Labor Farmer Temple Association (ULFTA), organizations that were suspected as possibly disrupting the war effort.[2] The Molotov–Ribbentrop Pact of 23 August 1939 heightened the federal government's suspicion regarding the loyalty to Canada of the members of the Communist Party of Canada. According to the federal government, one method to control any potential disruptive actions that might negatively influence the war effort was interning the "left-wing" subversives and limiting their contacts with "illegal and subversive" organizations under the Defence of Canada Regulations (DOCR). Hinther and Mochoruk, in their introduction to this volume and their respective chapters, document aspects of this history. Hinther does so by examining incarcerated women activists; Mochoruk looks at the effects this repression had on the ULFTA-founded People's Co-op, several of whose leaders were interned. My chapter examines some of the ways that the internees, in their efforts to continue their pre-war contacts with the labour movement, coped with and contested the internment operations, especially the attempts to control and limit their communications with their families and friends in the ULFTA and the CPC.

The reasons for the internment of the CPC leadership including Peter Prokop have their roots in the national and especially international politics of the 1930s. Regarding the federal government policy towards the CPC, Ernest Lapointe, the minister of justice, was a strong anti-Communist and his views were shaped by the attitudes of the Roman Catholic Church in Quebec and the leading politicians in Quebec.[3] He was also strongly influenced by the RCMP who recommended stricter measures to ensure internal security during the war. Concerning the international political and military situation, events in Europe demanded that the Canadian federal government take "some action" about "internal enemies." Anti-Soviet attitudes were increasingly popular especially after the Soviet Union invaded Finland in November 1939. The CPC was perceived by law enforcement agencies as "loyal" followers of the Soviet Union and continued to be suspected as a "Fifth Column." The fall of France profoundly affected Ernest Lapointe.[4] France, with a large and modern military, collapsed relatively quickly before the onslaught of the Germany Army. Paris fell on 14 June and two days later the French government capitulated.

In the chaos of this collapse, various rumours and myths were circulated and attention centred on the role of the French Communist Party in demoralizing and weakening the French Army. The role of the French Communist Party was attributed to the Soviet–German Pact of August 1939, and this pact was interpreted as an alliance between the two powers. The fear of this alliance was extended to the activities of the Communist Party in Canada. From the outbreak of the Second World War in September, members of the CPC were arrested for spreading antiwar literature in various cities across Canada. Some of these CPC members were later interned.[5]

In any event, as Nazi Germany conquered more countries in Europe during 1939–40, fear of internal "enemies" spread in Canada, and the RCMP updated its list of potential subversives. By July 1940, the growing list of potential subversives included the name of Peter Prokopchak[6] and other members of the leadership of the ULFTA and its affiliated organizations. Around that time, ULFTA leaders were informed by a sympathetic newspaper reporter from the

Winnipeg Free Press that their organizations were going to be banned by the federal government. Suspecting that they might also be arrested, some of the senior leaders went underground while others like Peter kept a low profile.[7] This was to no avail; Peter was arrested by members of the RCMP on 6 July 1940 at his apartment in Winnipeg in the presence of his wife, Mary. This fate was shared that morning by several other men with ties to the ULFTA. All were arrested under Section 21 of the Defence of Canada Regulations. Peter was taken to the RCMP headquarters and then to the Headingley provincial jail. He and the other apprehended men were interrogated and fingerprinted. The next day, they were taken to the Canadian Pacific Railway (CPR) station in Winnipeg and placed on the train bound for Kananaskis, Alberta. Authorities informed them that they were incarcerated because of their membership in the CPC, which had been declared a subversive and illegal organization.[8] With the entry of fascist Italy in the war, members of Italian fascist organizations in Canada were also arrested and interned.

While Peter was being arrested, Mary was questioned by the RCMP about her friends and acquaintances but she pleaded ignorance. The apartment was searched and some books and other published material were taken but later returned.[9] Not knowing what had happened to her husband, Mary phoned the police that evening and was told that her husband was in Headingley jail. Through a lawyer, the families were told that the men had been interned and taken to Alberta.

Peter's arrest and internment began a traumatic and unpredictable period in the couple's lives. Despite censorship, correspondence between Peter and Mary was the central means by which they maintained their relationship. For Peter, gaining knowledge about events in Canada and the conduct of the war was equally important. Peter also attempted to make sense of his arrest and internment, and to identify his "enemies" who were responsible for the delays in his release. These two issues are documented in the couple's correspondence, notebooks, and individual memoirs on which this study relies.[10]

By 1940, Peter Prokopchak was one of the national leaders of the Ukrainian left-wing community in Canada. He was born to a peasant family on 12 November 1903 in the village of Wapenne in the Lemko region in the former Austro-Hungarian Empire (now in Poland). As a youth, he was active in local political activities. In 1926, he immigrated to Canada and worked in coal mining in Diamond City and Coalhurst, Alberta. He joined the Ukrainian Labour Farmer Temple Association (ULFTA),[11] miners' union and the CPC in 1926. In 1930, he attended the ULFTA's six-month higher education course in Winnipeg, an initiative to train organizers, journalists, and teachers to serve in the ULFTA. He continued his education in Kharkiv, Ukrainian Soviet Socialist Republic, at the Ukrainian Institute of Marxism and Leninism and completed three years of study. When Peter returned to Canada in 1933, he was appointed editor of the ULFTA newspaper for women, *Robitnytsia*. He was later the editor of *Narodna Hazeta* (People's Gazette) and in 1935, he was elected recording secretary of the Executive Committee of the ULFTA, and served as the recording secretary of the National Bureau of the CPC Fraction for Ukrainian left-wing organizations. In 1936–37, he was responsible for ULFTA courses for adults and put in charge of the political school in 1938.

Mary Prokopchak (née Michalchuk) was born in Slava, Alberta, on 7 August 1914, in a Ukrainian pioneer family. She completed grade nine and, from her earliest years, was an active member of the ULFTA. Mary was also active in the labour movement of the 1930s. She worked for the Farmers Unity League (FUL) and the Workers Unity League (WUL) in Edmonton. She then worked in Calgary and in Winnipeg for the CPC. In 1936, Mary attended the six-month ULFTA higher educational course in Parkdale, Manitoba, where she and Peter had the chance to become better acquainted. In January 1937, the two were married. When her husband was interned in July 1940, Mary became active in lobbying for his release.

Soon after their husbands were interned, the wives of the internees contacted each other and began to take stock of their uncertain social and financial situation. Mothers with children were in a particularly difficult financial situation. Although Mary worked outside the home, she had to move to another apartment and live with friends. But their main concern was the fate of their husbands and the unknown future. Mary did not wait to receive a letter from Peter and wrote to him on 10 July 1940. News was soon received from Peter by a letter that he wrote on 9 July. These first letters informed Mary that Peter was in a "concentration camp" in Kananaskis in the Rocky Mountains. However, the news that Peter was alive and in Canada was seen as relatively good news for Mary had feared the worst fate possible for her husband.[12] Anything was possible at this stage in the war.

Peter and the other internees were quartered among German internees and prisoners of war in several barracks. There were only a few "labour" internees among the Germans in each hut so it was the Germans who were the spokesmen in any dealings with the camp authorities.[13] Because the number of internees from the CPC was small in comparison to the German prisoners of war, they avoided any provocations that may have led to conflict with the

Germans. With time, other "labour" internees moved into one hut (although it still housed German internees), and they were able to exchange news and hold political discussions.[14] It was only in April 1941 that the internees received news that they would be quartered in barracks separate from the Germans.[15]

For the period of internment, communication between Mary and Peter Prokop was by letter and postcards. Sending and receiving letters became an important part of the lives of the prisoners in the camp and their families at home. Peter also received letters from his sister-in-law, brother, and friends and acquaintances. The prisoners could write three letters and four postcards per month.[16] The correspondence had to be numbered by the internees for control purposes by the censors.[17] Only family matters were allowed to be discussed in the correspondence. In some cases, the privilege to write letters was withdrawn for a certain period as a punishment for internees who broke camp rules.[18] The first letters from Peter contained requests for clothing since he had no time to take anything with him when he was arrested. The letters were sent free without stamps in brown envelopes, but included the statement "Prisoner of War Mail" in large black type at the top of the envelope. This information on the envelopes made it obvious to the mailman and neighbours about the "prisoner of war" status of the recipient's spouse.[19]

Complicating communication was the role of the censors, shadowy figures who monitored the contents of incoming and outgoing internee correspondence. Peter explained to Mary that he could write three letters and four postcards per month but there was to be no mention of politics and no criticism of authorities. He also told her that letters written in Ukrainian were sent to Ottawa to a Ukrainian-language translator; however, letters written in English were censored at Kananaskis.[20] Although his knowledge of the language was limited, he suggested that they write in English to reduce their letters' travel time. From January 1941, Peter first drafted his letters in a notebook that were corrected by fellow internees, an exercise that was also an opportunity to improve his English-language skills. This chapter is also based on the information in the notebooks, and it is not certain that all the drafts were sent as letters to Mary. Even though both took care with what they wrote, Mary claimed that, at times, practically all incoming and outgoing mail was destroyed by the censor. This mail was cut up and blacked out while other letters were rejected by the censor.[21]

In his letters, Peter described life in the internment camp. Some of the camp buildings were still being built when he arrived and considerable work had to be done to clear the surrounding forest. Peter and the other internees were assigned various jobs, and he worked outdoors sawing wood with a circular saw. He was paid twenty cents per day for this work and, with this money, he was able to purchase some food and other items at the camp canteen, which was of particular importance to Peter, as he was a vegetarian and appreciated the additional fruits and vegetables. For entertainment, the men were allowed to play cards and see three movies per week for twenty-five cents. In December 1940, Peter worked on various camp crafts and made a small jewelry box and a cigarette case as gifts.[22]

In his notebook, where he could write without fear of censorship, Peter noted that the Department of Justice at Ottawa had claimed that "it would appear that you are disloyal to Canada." He added, "My disloyalty to Canada is claimed on the ground that I belonged to a working-class organization, Communist Party of Canada. So officially I'm punished for what legally existed till June 5th, 1940."[23] But Peter did not let himself be demoralized. He concluded, "I know that barbed wire cannot stop progress from marching on and to be victorious over the dark forces of past."[24]

In August 1940, Chief Justice James D. Hyndman held hearings for some of the internees. A lawyer, Sol Greenberg, arrived from Winnipeg to assist the internees during the hearings. But this was a one-man commission with an RCMP constable serving as an assistant. Peter felt that the lawyer did not assist him in any meaningful fashion during his appearance before the judge and sat during the hearings mainly as a witness. Peter was hampered during the hearing by his limited knowledge of English. He was described by the judge at his hearing as "disloyal to Canada" and an "unworthy foreigner who came to Canada to make trouble."[25] Peter commented in his notebook that he had also been made to feel as a "foreigner" when he was a youth in Poland because of his Ukrainian ancestry and now he was receiving the same treatment in Canada. On 7 October 1940, Peter received a letter from the Advisory Committee on Orders of Restriction and Detention that informed him that his detention would be continued.[26] In a letter to his brother, Peter wrote that he was considered a "prisoner of war" and "it is a war and war has its own logic."[27] To Mary, Peter wrote that despite this setback, "I am keeping my chin up."[28]

Peter was convinced that his internment was instigated by some of his political enemies in the Ukrainian community in Winnipeg. In a postcard written on 4 February 1941, Peter wrote that "there are 'some people' (if they can be called that) who would like to keep me and others like me the whole life isolated from the outside world."[29] He later wrote that "there are many 'bed bugs' among Ukrainians who are interested that I should be here."[30]

Peter was referring to the leadership of the Ukrainian nationalist community in Winnipeg who were perceived as sworn enemies of the pro-Communist organizations. In any case, Peter remained optimistic about his situation and wrote "but I am sure that nicer days, bright days will come. . . . Yes, I am keeping my chin up."[31]

Meanwhile, back home in Winnipeg, the wives of the internees and their supporters had already formed two committees: the Committee for the Release of Labor Prisoners and an aid committee to assist the families of the internees. A conference was held in Winnipeg and plans were made to hold a similar conference in Ottawa. So perhaps there was some reason for optimism.

Peter and the other internees were especially interested in receiving news about local political events in Winnipeg and also world events. Mary managed to slip some news past the censors. On 25 November 1940, municipal elections were held in Winnipeg; Joe Forkin ran for the position as alderman and Rose Penner ran for the school board. Mary worked on their election campaigns. Although neither was elected, it was perceived as a significant victory because both received a substantial number of votes. In her attempt to pass this news to Peter without the censor's intervention, Mary wrote that "Joe and Rose didn't get into the city on November 25 as they were celebrating because their aunt left $3,012 for Joe and $3,200 for Rose. They were her first choices."[32] The sums of money were the number of votes each received.[33]

In some cases, the internees who had access to the camp guards and their locations within the camp "borrowed" newspapers and other publications that were left unattended. These were also circulated in secret among the internees and provided information about events in the outside world.[34] Jimmy Wilson was one of the friendly camp guards at Kananaskis. He was a former volunteer in the International Brigades in the Spanish Civil War and known to some of the internees,[35] including two who had also served in the International Brigades. Other friendly camp guards secretly brought illegal literature to the internees.[36]

It is clear that Peter spent much of his free time while interned reading and improving his language skills. In October and November 1940, Peter asked to receive the *Illustrated London News* and the magazine *Science Digest*. The internees could read local newspapers from Alberta, and Peter availed himself of this opportunity, but these were not enough to satiate his thirst for more in-depth reading. Thus, in a letter dated 26 January 1941, he requested that Mary send him the *History of Ukraine* by Dmytro Doroshenko in English and also by Mykhailo Hrushevsky in Ukrainian. Then, on 5 February 1941, Peter asked for an English dictionary and, also, an English–Russian dictionary. He further mentioned that he liked to read historical books and novels by authors such as Mikhail Sholokhov, Maxim Gorky, Leo Tolstoy, Sinclair Lewis, Henri Barbusse, and Romain Rolland. He also read *The Grapes of Wrath*. He acknowledged the receipt of two books by Knut Hamsun but noted that other books were with the censor.[37] Peter likewise mentioned that he was learning "practical English conversation." Although Peter appreciated the books he received by mail, he expressed concern about the cost of postage of the parcels sent to him.

Books received by Peter and the other internees formed an internees' library of several hundred books. The librarians were fellow internees, Peter Krawchuk and Bill Digby.[38] The internees also organized lectures on various political and economic subjects and discussions were held on the early history of the labour movement in Canada including the Winnipeg General Strike.[39] Classes in English conducted by the internees were held in the camp, and Peter was a regular student.

Mail, letters, and parcels such as those containing books were clearly important to Peter. Soon after news of their internment had spread throughout the Ukrainian left-wing community, Peter and the other internees began to receive mail and parcels. Peter was pleased that he received many greeting cards over the Christmas holidays.[40] He mentioned that one internee received a parcel with "kowbasa" (Ukrainian sausage) that was appreciated by the other Ukrainian internees. There were no limits on the number of parcels the internees could receive. In some cases, items in the parcels were wrapped in various Canadian newspapers including the CPC newspaper, *The Canadian Tribune*. The parcels were inspected before the internees received them and some camp officers discarded the newspapers while others ignored the pages. These pages provided information on events in the labour movement across Canada including campaigns to obtain the internees release.[41] News that the labour movement was still active gave the internees hope and boosted their morale.[42]

On 31 March 1941, a delegation of wives and family members reached Ottawa from Winnipeg and joined delegates and wives of other internees from other centres. Mary was listed as among the delegates. They lobbied the Canadian federal government and eventually were allowed to plead their case with Ernest Lapointe, the minister of justice, and the Advisory Parliamentary Committee on the DOCR.[43] A petition was prepared and presented to the federal government.[44] Among other requests, the petition sought to have Section 21 repealed and "extended writing and visiting privileges and uncensored mail."

The Toronto Star published extracts from this petition on 31 March 1941,[45] and the story of the internees became better known among the Canadian population. However, the delegates were accused of being "Communists" and supporters of the policies of the Soviet Union. Perhaps even more tellingly, they were informed that other delegations[46] were lobbying for a stricter application of the DOCR. Despite the implied threat, the delegation returned to Winnipeg on 5 April 1941 and continued their lobbying and political activities at the local and provincial levels.[47]

Mary wrote to Peter about the petition and the enclosed demands and sent him a letter with a copy of this petition. Peter replied that he was informed by the censor, Lt. Gibson, that the letter was forwarded but that the petition was retained because Mary had "cursed in it" and contained "much abuse and curses against Mr. [Ernest] Lapointe, so we burnt it."[48]

Censorship continued to be a major issue for the couple. In a letter to Mary on 20 April 1941, Peter inquired about the Manitoba elections. On 28 April 1941, the censor wrote, "Please take note that political matters are forbidden. You will advise the writer so as to save returning correspondence to sender. This is a warning."[49] Had he received a report on the political situation that he requested, Peter would have been quite pleased, for in Winnipeg William A. Kardash was elected to the provincial legislature on 22 April 1941 while Joe Forkin was elected to Winnipeg City Council as an alderman in a special by-election. Meanwhile, Dorise Nielsen was being particularly active in Ottawa on the internees' behalf as a member of Parliament. In effect, the movement for the release of the internees gained considerable momentum. But Peter and his fellow inmates would have to wait for some time to hear this news, as any reports about the war or about the campaign to release the internees was usually cut out or completely blacked out by ink.[50] On 4 May 1941, Peter wrote to Mary that "3 lines of your letter were 'blackened out.' I guess that the censor didn't understand what was written so he scratched it out." Letters to friends were also censored. Peter was informed that "half his letter to John [Kitzman] was 'blacked out.'" Peter had written about his internment.[51] Much of the correspondence with Mary during these months dealt with the interventions by the censor and what parts of letters were "blackened out." In July 1941, Peter was again chastised by the censor and informed that he should "tell the writer to confine herself to personal matters."[52]

Undaunted, Mary continued to send letters with coded information on activities in Winnipeg. When meetings were held at the Ukrainian Labour Temple, Mary wrote that friends and relatives gathered at Aunt Tereza's place.

The Ukrainian Labour Temple was mortgaged to the Workers Benevolent Association of Canada (WBA) and the WBA was not declared illegal. Peter could easily understand that the name "Tereza" meant R.Z.T. (Robitnyche zapomohove tovarystvo), the Ukrainian initials for WBA. In other cases, names and places were translated from English into Ukrainian or written in such a manner that the censor could not understand the message. Mary referred to some people by their physical appearance or by their nicknames.[53] In such ways, Peter and the other internees were able to receive news of events in Winnipeg.[54]

Peter was informed about the Nazi invasion of the Soviet Union on 22 June 1941 by a prison guard, and the news quickly spread to the other inmates.[55] According to Peter, this was "the greatest battle in the history of mankind." This news became the main focus of their discussions in the camp. The guards adopted a more relaxed attitude toward the CPC internees and informed them about the progress of the war. The Soviet–German War gave the internees hope that they might be released. Again, the question of Peter's release was discussed in his correspondence. Peter felt that he was interned because of his legal pre-war activities and his membership in the labour movement. He wrote that "if I belonged to the Ukrainian fascists movement, I would be out of here [internment camp]."[56] But he remained optimistic, for by now he knew about the recent political developments in Winnipeg and the work of Dorise Nielsen and others on behalf of the internees. Still, despite this change in the world situation, whereby the Soviet Union was fighting on the same side as England and Canada, the camp commandant informed the internees that their status remained the same.[57]

This news was a great disappointment to the internees and they blamed their various "enemies" for their situation. In a draft letter in his notebook dated 15 July 1941, Peter referred to "our Canadian Petains."[58] In other instances, he mentioned "Ukrainian fascists"[59] and "Ukrainian Nazis" in Canada.[60] According to Peter, there were individuals within the Canadian federal government that were sympathetic to fascism. The disbandment of the "progressive" organizations and the arrest and internment of the leadership of the labour movement "shows clearly that the Canadian bourgeoisie follows the fascist road."[61]

Reviewing his situation, Peter explained his predicament in his notebook, observing that "our opinions in regard to the Soviet Union make us allies of the Nazis and disloyal to Canada . . . the existence of a pact between Germany and the USSR at a time when Canada and Great Britain were at war with Germany justified the use of extraordinary powers involved in Section 21 on the grounds that wartime necessity required the adoption of precautionary measures against persons who might be considered as active or potential allies of the Nazis."[62] However, the international situation changed dramatically with the German invasion of the Soviet Union, and this pact no longer existed. There was hope that the internees would be released but, as matters turned out, their situation did not change for quite some time.

What did change, however, was this: many of the German prisoners of war began to boast about what they predicted would be Germany's swift victory over the Soviets. The potential for conflict between the Germans and the "labour" internees became a real possibility. It was perhaps as a result of this tension that only a month after the outbreak of the Soviet–German War, the CPC internees were transported by train to Petawawa.[63] The internees from Winnipeg travelled through Winnipeg on 22 July and were able to see some of their friends working in the train yard.

Finding themselves once again interned with fascists—but augmented in numbers by the eastern Canadian leftists who were already at Petawawa—the internees staged a protest and demanded to be immediately separated from the German and Italian prisoners and to be treated as political prisoners. The internees threatened to march out of the camp through the barbed wire.[64] The camp commandant consulted with Ottawa and the internees were transferred from Petawawa to the newly built Hull jail just across the river from Ottawa on 20 August 1941.

Once ensconced in this new internment camp, little seemed to change. The letters between Peter and Mary continued to deal with the lobbying efforts for his release, requests for reading material, especially newspapers, the censorship of their letters, packages received and lost. In summary, he found life in the Hull jail "monotonous."[65] The routine for the internees in the Hull jail remained mostly the same. Peter mentions in his letters that "I live as I lived before—eat, sleep, work a little, and read books and newspapers."[66] He was especially interested in receiving news about the Ukrainian Canadian contribution to the war effort. In another letter, he wrote, "I deeply regret that I cannot take my part in helping to win these battles against fascist hordes."[67]

Among the other subjects that Peter discussed with his wife was her health. In August 1941, Mary, entered the St. Boniface Hospital for two weeks. Correspondence for the next few months focused on inquiries about Mary's health.[68] However, Mary's health did not improve, and Peter learned that she suffered from an ulcer and was living on a minimum allowance of $7.60 a month. Mary received some assistance from friends and family.[69] Peter was clearly concerned by all of this and deeply regretted that he could not be more forthcoming in his letters to her. He wrote, "I hope you understand that I am in the Concentration Camp and consequently I am living under certain rules and regulations."[70] While in Petawawa, Peter had been informed that he was not to write about his days and feelings in the camp.[71]

Peter mentioned that he would like to continue to improve his English but proper facilities at the Hull jail were lacking.[72] During this period, he received correspondence from family, friends, and acquaintances across Canada. Following the harvest season, he also received large parcels of vegetables, jars, and containers of fresh fruit.[73] Among the parcels received by the internees was a pail of cottage cheese from the People's Co-op in Winnipeg, and in it was hidden a small crystal radio set with an earphone wrapped in wax paper. Two internees, Dr. Howard Lowrie and Jim Murphy, were able to assemble this set and, after an outside antenna was secretly erected, they were able to listen to radio news broadcasts.[74]

In his correspondence, Peter continued to express his growing frustration. He mentioned that Great Britain and the USSR were allies but he was still interned.[75] He continued to feel that his internment was unjust because of his membership in the CPC and the ULFTA when they were legal organizations prior to June 1940. He had signed many petitions to various politicians in Parliament and swore an affidavit reaffirming his loyalty to Canada.[76]

Perhaps not too surprisingly, after the German invasion of the Soviet Union in June 1941, Ernest Lapointe, as minister of justice, received many requests from a variety of individuals and organizations to release the CPC internees. The advisory committee on the DOCR also advised the release of specific individuals but Lapointe overruled this committee.[77] Lapointe sought the advice of the RCMP, which recommended that the internees remain incarcerated in almost every case. It was only after the death of Ernest Lapointe on 26 November 1941 that the federal government adopted a more lenient attitude towards the CPC internees. With the Soviet Union an effective ally in the war against Nazi Germany, the CPC was perceived as less of a threat to the Canadian war effort.

By the end of 1941, this leniency became evident when the federal government granted permission to the wives to visit their husbands in the Hull jail. The camp commandant informed the internees in November that visits from wives were to be allowed once a month for thirty minutes.[78] But to the wives in Winnipeg, this proved to be an expensive privilege, as most could not afford to travel to Ottawa;[79] indeed, Peter advised Mary not to come.[80] Undaunted, Mary had submitted a request to the Canadian federal government for free transportation to Ottawa to visit her husband, but the request was denied.[81]

Peter remained politically interested and motivated. In his draft letter of 10 December 1941, Peter mentions the Japanese attack against the United States and describes the Japanese as "imperialistic, fascist and . . . gangsters."[82] He was deeply interested in the Ukrainian Canadian contribution to the war effort and was glad to receive news about it, although he felt that the Ukrainian community was not fully mobilized for the war effort.[83] He was informed about the UNF (Ukrainian National Federation of Canada) acquiring the ULFTA printing press and was particularly concerned about the influence of the UNF among the Ukrainian Canadians that he described as "Ukrainian fascists." Peter mentioned a rumour that had spread among the Ukrainian Canadian left wing that the UNF had sent a gold watch to Hitler prior to the war.[84]

On 18 February 1942, Peter was surprised to receive the news that Mary was planning to visit Ottawa.[85] On 22 and 23 February 1942, a national conference was organized in Ottawa by the National Council for Democratic Rights. Mary was a member of a delegation from Winnipeg and, during this conference, lobbied for the release of the internees, but especially her husband.[86] During this conference, Mary visited Peter at the Hull jail.[87] Peter also informed Mary in a letter dated 28 February 1942 that he was scheduled to have a second hearing before the commission (advisory committee).[88] However, the commission hearings continued to be postponed and began during the first days of March.

An advisory committee of three judges was established and conducted hearings at the Hull jail. This time, the internees had J.L. Cohen, a well-known labour lawyer, to plead their cases. Peter was brought before this advisory committee. At these hearings, an RCMP officer supplied the judges with information from files kept on individual internees. In this file were documents, circulars, and newspaper articles. In addition, the judges asked a series of questions about Peter's activities in the ULFTA. Peter had been the recording secretary of the Central Executive Committee of the ULFTA. He had conducted educational courses, and the committee was interested in the textbooks he had used.[89] Peter was asked to admit that he wrote these documents and to explain their meaning. Although Peter did write many of these documents, they were issued under the names of various committees and were not personally signed. The committee was particularly interested in antiwar propaganda encouraging Canadians not to enlist in the Canadian military. Peter denied this accusation. However, several other internees later admitted that, when they were arrested, they had antiwar literature in their possession.[90] Peter later claimed that his documents were lost when he gave two suitcases of important documents to an acquaintance to hide but when he was released from internment, these documents had disappeared.[91]

According to Peter, the committee tried to have him admit that he was actively involved in the "Communist movement" and this movement supported various strikes and demonstrations and petitions against the Padlock Law. Much time was spent by the committee accusing the ULFTA of advocating the use of force and violence but after a whole day on this question, the committee could not prove that Peter advocated the overthrow of the Canadian government by force and violence.[92] The committee tried another approach to prove that Peter and the ULFTA supported the use of violence to promote political change. The committee suggested that since the Soviet Union was the result of a violent revolution and the ULFTA supported the Soviet Union, then they too supported revolutionary methods. Peter was fortunate that the lawyer, J.L. Cohen, intervened on his behalf. Peter also lamented that his limited knowledge of English prevented him from debating their interpretation of Soviet history. Cohen suggested that the committee's knowledge of history was deficient, and he was asked to withdraw his remarks.[93] The commission continued to consider their decision and there was no further news on Peter's case for quite some time. However, some of the other "labour" internees were gradually released.

Peter clearly felt that the leadership of the Ukrainian nationalist community was responsible for his continued internment. He wrote "that Ukrainian fascists and pro-fascist leaders and also renegades were working for my internment and their voice is still powerful."[94] However, in a subsequent letter, Peter denied that he described all the leaders of the Ukrainian nationalist organizations as fascists or pro-fascists, although he did suggest that the leaders spread "fascist ideas of conquest, race hatred, anti-semitism etc.," and that Hitler and German fascists were friends of these Ukrainians.[95]

In the meantime, Mary continued her work in the Ukrainian left-wing community. With other Ukrainians, she was a member of the committee that supported the plebiscite to authorize the federal government to introduce compulsory overseas military service that the federal government had promised not to introduce in 1940. This plebiscite was held on 27 April 1942 and approved with 66 percent of the vote. To the disappointment of many Canadians supporting a total-war policy, votes against overseas conscription were concentrated in the province of Quebec and also among some constituencies in Western Canada, with a large percentage of Ukrainian voters.

For Peter and the other internees, conditions in the Hull jail improved to a certain extent. The role of the Soviet Union in the war against Nazi Germany was increasingly appreciated by the federal government and the Western allies, and this attitude was reflected in the treatment of the pro-Soviet individuals and organizations in Canada. Peter was able to receive a wider selection of books, magazines, and newspapers including *The Canadian Tribune*[96] and the Ukrainian-language left-wing *Narodna Hazeta* (The People's Gazette).[97] The *Narodna Hazeta* was established by former members of the ULFTA in an attempt to renew contacts among the left-wing Ukrainians and support the war effort. Friends and acquaintances continued to send the "labour" internees, letters, greeting cards, and packages and in one case, some *pyrohy* (dumplings) from friends in Ottawa.[98]

Still, censorship continued to be a problem in Peter and Mary's letters, so much so that it grew to become a frequent subject of discussion in their correspondence. Peter wrote, "Was my letter of April 8 censored, that you could not understand it? Or perhaps my sentences in English are not properly built so you cannot understand them?"[99] Letters from Mary were also heavily censored. Peter wrote on 8 June 1942, "Your last letter of May 31 was mutilated to such a[n] extent that I hardly get an idea how are you getting along." Peter wrote to Louis St. Laurent, minister of justice, complaining about the couple's treatment at the hands of the censor, indicating that some of his letters were not received by his wife or arrived heavily redacted. Ironically, the censor rejected the complaint letter, commenting that "letters must not contain any references to operations of war nor economic or political situation."[100]

Nonetheless, the couple persevered in their correspondence. Peter wrote mostly about the commission hearings and the delay in receiving a decision for his release. Peter wrote, "Now I do not know what I can write. I am confused as never before."[101] He had written earlier that "to write 'what is personal and what is political'; I cannot solve this problem."[102] Peter lamented that 4 July 1942 was the second anniversary of his internment. He was waiting for a reply from the commission about his release. On 29 July 1942, Peter was still waiting for a decision from the commission, and this continued to be his main preoccupation.[103] A month later, on 31 August 1942, Peter wrote that there was nothing new.[104]

Finally, Mary was informed on 1 September 1942 that Peter, among the last of the leftist internees still in custody, was to be released.[105] Peter arrived in Toronto on 5 September 1942. Mary travelled from Winnipeg a few days later. As a condition of his release, Peter had to report to the RCMP twice a month and could not leave Toronto without permission. The Hull jail was closed by the end of September 1942.

After his release, Peter joined the editorial staff of the newspaper *Ukrainske Zhyttia* (Ukrainian Life) in Toronto. A new organization was established, the Association of Ukrainian Canadians (AUC), which campaigned through newspapers and meetings for a total-war effort and the opening of a second front to aid the Soviet Union. Peter and Mary also continued the campaign for the legalization of the CPC and the return of the ULFTA property and publishing company. Mary went to work in the war industry making components for the Bren gun. She also became involved in union activities and became chief steward and a member of the Labour-Management Committee at the John Inglis plant. The ban on the ULFTA was finally removed on 25 January 1945. Most of the ULFTA property was restored and compensation paid for what was not by April 1946.

Peter visited the Ukrainian SSR for four months in 1946 and went on a speaking tour of Canada after he returned. In January 1946, he was elected secretary on the National Executive Committee of the newly formed Association of United Ukrainian Canadians (AUUC)[106] and held this position until 1972 when he retired from full-time work. In May 1978, he was elected honorary president for life of the AUUC. Peter was also a founding member of the Canadian Peace Congress. After the death of Ivan Naviziwsky in 1954, he became the leader of the Ukrainian left-wing movement in Canada and was a member of CPC National Committee in 1950s. In later years, he was president of Kobzar Publishing Company, member of the Board of Directors of the Workers Benevolent Association, and director of the T.H. Shevchenko Museum at Palermo (Oakville). He was a member of the CPC for over fifty-five years and was elected several times to the Central Committee of the CPC and was, for many years, a member of the Political Bureau. Peter died on 31 October 1981 in Toronto.

After the war, Mary continued to be active in the Women's Branch of the AUUC and contributed to the press. She was a member of the Board of Directors for the Taras Shevchenko Museum, Toronto. She was a leading member of the AUUC and active in women's and workers' rights movements along with the world peace movement. She was a member of the CPC until 1991. Mary died on 27 February 2011.

Conclusion

In reviewing the Peter and Mary Prokopchak (Prokop) Family Fonds at the Canadian Museum of History, especially Peter Prokop's notebook in which he wrote summaries of his correspondence with his wife, Mary, and also Mary's memoirs about the period of Peter's internment, two main issues have been identified. The main problem was communications between Peter and Mary. From the first weeks of Peter's internment in Kananaskis, Peter was able to send letters and postcards to Mary. Despite the limited number of letters and postcards, and the interventions of the censor, Peter was able to receive news about Mary and her personal problems, and also about political events in Winnipeg and Canada. This "Aesopian" correspondence[107] continued until Peter's release from internment in September 1942. In addition, the other "labour" internees also received letters and postcards and they shared this information with the other internees. Newspapers, both legal and illegal, were obtained by the internees and were another source of information on events in the outside world. In the Hull jail, they were able to obtain a small illegal radio and receive news broadcasts from outside. Of particular interest was the campaign for their release, the survival of the "labour movement," and the Soviet–German War. In this correspondence, any information regarding the survival of the labour movement and the Soviet–German War was appreciated. The number of individuals and committees advocating for them—along with the National Council for Democratic Rights, which was composed of non-CPC members—gave the internees hope that their release was not impossible. After the internees were sent to the Hull jail, they were able to better maintain group solidarity and morale. They viewed themselves as victims of the Canadian federal government because of their political views, membership in the CPC, and activism in the labour movement. They felt that they were prevented by the Canadian government from participating in the war against fascism and as a result, questioned the political loyalties of the Canadian politicians. Despite the conditions in the Hull jail, Peter remained optimistic that he was with the "progressive movement" of history. After he was released, Peter continued his active leadership in the AUUC and the CPC along with his wife Mary and son, Larry Prokop.

Although Peter was arrested and interned as a member of the CPC, he blamed his arrest on the RCMP and especially on the Ukrainian "fascists" and "Nazis," the usual CPC terminology for the Ukrainian nationalists in Canada. He did not deny during his interrogations while interned that he supported the Soviet Union but he also declared his loyalty to Canada. This became more insistent after June 1941 when the Soviet Union was invaded by Nazi Germany. His letters contained statements that he wanted to be released so he could contribute to the Canadian struggle against fascism.

The internment of Peter and the trials and tribulations experienced by Mary were not quickly forgotten. Mary later wrote that "I still have a keen recollection of them because I was so profoundly affected."[108] Her participation in the campaign to release the internees was, for Mary, an education in dealing with the Canadian federal government and engaging with committees and organizations, and it was "not only school but university."[109] Both for Peter and Mary, it was perceived as a test of their loyalty to the Ukrainian "progressive" movement, and they remembered their experiences in detail. The internment confirmed Peter's status as a leader within the AUUC and the CPC and among the respected veterans of the Canadian "progressive" movement.

Notes

1 On 3 September 1939, a week before Canada officially entered the Second World War, the Defence of Canada Regulations (DOCR) were implemented under the War Measures Act. The DOCR introduced security measures that included the waiving of habeas corpus and the right to trial, internment, and bans on certain political groups.

2 See the attitude towards the CPC in the article by Commissioner S.T. Wood, RCMP, entitled "Tools for Treachery," in *The Canadian Spokesman, The Magazine on National Affairs* 1, no. 2 (February 1941). See also Gregory S. Kealey and Reginald Whitaker, eds., *RCMP Security Bulletins: The Depression Years,* vol. 1–5, 1933–39 (St. John's, NL: Canadian Committee on Labour History). There is an enormous amount of documentation on many members of the CPC and related organizations compiled by the RCMP during the Depression now preserved in the Library and Archives Canada.

3 Lita-Rose Betcherman, *Ernest Lapointe: Mackenzie King's Quebec Lieutenant* (Toronto: University of Toronto Press, 2002), 297–300.

4 Ibid., 312–13.

5 "Ben Swankey" and "Louis Binder," in William Repka and Kathleen Repka, *Dangerous Patriots: Canada's Unknown Prisoners of War* (Vancouver: New Star Books, 1982), 63, 140.

6 Although "Prokopchak" was Peter's surname, he used the surname "Prokop" when he applied for Canadian citizenship. In various records, the two names were used at the same time. The RCMP used the surname "Prokopchak" when he was arrested and interned and in this essay, I use the surname "Prokopchak."

7 "Peter Prokop," in Repka and Repka, *Dangerous Patriots*, 83–84.

8 Ibid., 91. The Communist Party of Canada and the Ukrainian Labour-Farmer Temple Association were declared illegal by Order-in Council PC 2363 on 4 June

1940. See also Chapter 4 in Rhonda L. Hinther, *Perogies and Politics: Canada's Ukrainian Left, 1891–1991* (Toronto: University of Toronto Press, 2017).

9 "Mary Prokop," in Repka and Repka, *Dangerous Patriots*, 97.

10 The Prokop Family Fonds is preserved in the Archives of the Canadian Museum of History in Gatineau, Quebec. The author prepared the finding aid to this collection. See: Prokop (Prokopchak) Family Fonds, http://collections.historymuseum.ca/public/objects/common/webmedia.php?irn=5410815 (accessed 30 June 2016).

11 The Ukrainian Labour Farmer Temple Association (ULFTA) was established in Winnipeg in 1918 as an association of cultural societies and community halls. Many of the leadership were members of the Ukrainian Social Democratic Party of Canada (USDPC) and later the Communist Party of Canada (CPC). By 1939, the ULFTA had branches in most Ukrainian urban and rural communities across Canada. The leadership of the ULFTA maintained close contacts with the Ukrainian SSR and also the Soviet Union.

12 "Mary Prokop," in Repka and Repka, *Dangerous Patriots*, 100.

13 "Peter Prokop," in Repka and Repka, *Dangerous Patriots,* 89.

14 Ibid., 91.

15 Peter Krawchuk, *Interned Without Cause, The Internment of Canadian Antifascists during World War Two* (Toronto: Kobza Publishing, 1985), 72.

16 Canadian Museum of History, Archives, Prokop Family Fonds, file 1-23, notebook, January 4, 1941. Peter kept copies of his outgoing letters in a notebook. In his memoirs, written in Ukrainian, he mentions that the internees were allowed 7 letters and 4 postcards per month. (Prokop Family Fonds, file 1-31). This limited number of letters was based on the similar number that British internees were allowed in Nazi Germany.

17 Prokop Family Fonds, file 1-27, 13 May 1942.

18 Prokop Family Fonds, file 1-31, Memoirs by Peter Prokop [in Ukrainian].

19 Prokop Family Fonds, file 7-12, 9 July 1940. In a petition submitted to the federal government in March 1941, family members complained that receipt of letters marked in this manner resulted in "callous and cruel discrimination" and left a "stigma." *Toronto Star*, 31 March 1941.

20 Prokop Family Fonds, file 1-31.

21 Prokop Family Fonds, file 4-14.

22 Prokop Family Fonds, file 1-23, 24 December 1940.

23 Prokop Family Fonds, file 1-26, 2 April 1941.

24 Ibid.

25 Prokop Family Fonds, file 1-23, 2 March 1941.

26 Prokop Family Fonds, file 1-23, 7 October 1940; "Mary Prokop," in Repka and Repka, *Dangerous Patriots*, 104.

27 Prokop Family Fonds, file 1-23, 10 October 1940.

28 Prokop Family Fonds, file 1-23, 2 March 1941.

29 Prokop Family Fonds, file 1-23, 5 February 1941.

30 Prokop Family Fonds, file 1-23, 2 March 1941.

31 Ibid.

32 "Mary Prokop," in Repka and Repka, *Dangerous Patriots*, 107; Prokop Family Fonds, file 7-12.

33 Prokop Family Fonds, file 7-12.
34 Krawchuk, *Interned Without Cause,* 71.
35 Prokop Family Fonds, file 1-31, p. 16.
36 Krawchuk, *Interned Without Cause,* 69.
37 Prokop Family Fonds, file 1-23, 16 March 1941.
38 Krawchuk, *Interned Without Cause,* 71.
39 Ibid., 72.
40 Prokop Family Fonds, file 1-23, 24 December 1940.
41 Krawchuk, *Interned Without Cause,* 68.
42 Ibid., 70.
43 Ross Lambertson, *Repression and Resistance: Canadian Human Rights Activists, 1930–1960* (Toronto: University of Toronto Press, 2005), 101.
44 Library and Archives Canada (LAC), RG14, vol. 2481, file 5, Brief submitted by the wives of interned labour leaders (2 April 1941). Mrs. P. Prokopchak is listed among the "Delegates on Behalf of Wives of Interned Labour Leaders."
45 *Toronto Star*, 31 March 1941.
46 The composition of these delegations was not indicated but probably included anti-Communists. The RCMP also advised stricter application of the DOCR.
47 "Mary Prokop," in Repka and Repka, *Dangerous Patriots*, 110–11.
48 Prokop Family Fonds, file 4-13, 11 May 1941.
49 Prokop Family Fonds, file 1-23, 20, 28 April 1941.
50 "Peter Prokop," in Repka and Repka, *Dangerous Patriots,* 93; Prokop Family Fonds, file 1-23, 13, 17 September 1941.
51 Prokop Family Fonds, file 1-26, 4 May 1941.
52 Prokop Family Fonds, file 1-26, 6 July 1941.
53 Krawchuk, *Interned Without Cause*, 70.
54 "Peter Prokop," in Repka and Repka, *Dangerous Patriots,* 93.
55 Prokop Family Fonds, file 1-31, Peter Prokop, Memoirs, p. 55.
56 Prokop Family Fonds, file 1-26, 10 September 1941.
57 Prokop Family Fonds, file 1-26, 3, 15 July 1941.
58 Prokop Family Fonds, file 1-26, 15 July 1941.
59 Prokop Family Fonds, file 1-26, 3, 6 September 1941.
60 Prokop Family Fonds, file 1-26, 27 September 1941.
61 Prokop Family Fonds, file 1-25, n.d.
62 Prokop Family Fonds, file 1-26, 15 July 1941.
63 Family members of the internees, in a petition submitted to the federal government in March 1941, complained that the "labour" internees were held in the same internment camp as the Germans. *Toronto Star*, 31 March 1941.
64 "Peter Prokop," in Repka and Repka, *Dangerous Patriots,* 160–61.
65 Prokop Family Fonds, file 1-26, 1 November 1941.
66 Prokop Family Fonds, file 1-27, 3 December 1941.
67 Prokop Family Fonds, file 1-27, 26 November 1941.
68 Prokop Family Fonds, file 1-26, 15, 25 August; 10, 13, 17 September; 1 October 1941.
69 Prokop Family Fonds, file 1-27, 18 April 1942.

70 Prokop Family Fonds, file 1-26, 5 November 1941.
71 Prokop Family Fonds, file 1-26, 11 August 1941.
72 Prokop Family Fonds, file 1-26, 27 September 1941.
73 Prokop Family Fonds, file 1-26, 22, 27 October; 8 December 1941.
74 "Dr. Howard Lowrie," in Repka and Repka, *Dangerous Patriots*, 216.
75 Prokop Family Fonds, file 1-27, 21 January 1942.
76 Prokop Family Fonds, file 1-26, 29 October 1941.
77 Prokop Family Fonds, file 4-13 (Mary Prokop – Notes).
78 Prokop Family Fonds, file 1-27, 10 November 1941.
79 "Mary Prokop," in Repka and Repka, *Dangerous Patriots*, 114.
80 Prokop Family Fonds, file 1-27, January 10, 1942.
81 Prokop Family Fonds, file 1-27, February 2, 1942.
82 Prokop Family Fonds, file 1-27, December 10, 1941.
83 Prokop Family Fonds, file 1-27, December 17, 1941.
84 Prokop Family Fonds, file 1-27, December 10, 31, 1941.
85 Prokop Family Fonds, file 1-27, February 14, 1942.
86 "Mary Prokop," in Repka and Repka, *Dangerous Patriots*, 115.
87 The topics of their discussions during their meeting were not recorded.
88 Prokop Family Fonds, file 1-27, 28 February 1942.
89 The document in question was Lessons in Political Education, (LAC, RG14, vol. 2482, file 36, Appendix A: Lessons in Political Education written by A. Mankowsky, edited by P. Prokopchak, and preface by P. Prokopchak).
90 "Ben Swankey" and "Louis Binder," in Repka and Repka, *Dangerous Patriots*, 63, 140.
91 "Peter Prokop," in Repka and Repka, *Dangerous Patriots,* 242.
92 Ibid., 243.
93 Ibid., 244.
94 Prokop Family Fonds, file 1-27, 6 May 1942.
95 Prokop Family Fonds, file 1-27, 13 May 1942.
96 Prokop Family Fonds, file 1-31, p. 51
97 Prokop Family Fonds, file 1-27, 1, 8 April 1942.
98 Prokop Family Fonds, file 1-26, 31 December 1941; 24 January 1942.
99 Prokop Family Fonds, file 1-27, 2 May 1942.
100 Prokop Family Fonds, file 1-29, 10, 17 June 1942.
101 Prokop Family Fonds, file 1-29, 6 June 1942.
102 Prokop Family Fonds, file 1-27, 18 February 1942.
103 Prokop Family Fonds, file 1-29, 4, 29 July 1942.
104 Prokop Family Fonds, file 1-29, 31 August 1942.
105 Prokop Family Fonds, file 4-18.
106 The Association of United Ukrainian Canadians (AUUC), founded in 1946, is a successor organization to the Association of Canadian Ukrainians (ACU). The ACU was originally called the Ukrainian Society for Aid to the Motherland (USAM) that was established on 26 July 1941. The primary goal of USAM was the support of the Soviet Union after the Nazi German attack on 22 June 1941. Former members of the ULFTA composed the new membership of USAM. The name of

USAM was changed to the Association of Canadian Ukrainians (ACU) in June 1942 and continued the work of the ULFTA. By the 1950s, the AUUC had branches in most Ukrainian communities across Canada and the national headquarters were located in Toronto. (Source: Finding Aid MSS2179 to the Association of United Ukrainian Canadians Fonds (AUUC) [MG28-V154] at the Library and Archives Canada. Prepared by the author.)

107 Aesopian language is communications that convey an innocent meaning to outsiders, in this case, the censor, but holds a concealed meaning to an informed correspondent.

108 "Mary Prokop," in Repka and Repka, *Dangerous Patriots*, 96.

109 Prokop Family Fonds, file 4-18, Mary Prokop, Memoirs – Internment 1940–42 (1958) [in Ukrainian].

PART VII

COMMEMORATING INTERNMENT: MUSEUMS, MEMORY, AND THE POLITICS OF PUBLIC HISTORY

CHAPTER 14

The New Brunswick Internment Camp Museum: Preserving the History of Internment Camp B-70

ED CAISSIE AND TODD CAISSIE

The United States and Canada operated a combined fifty internment camps during the Second World War. This internment of massive numbers of innocent civilians is a permanent stain on the historical memories of both countries. Over the course of the war Canada incarcerated an estimated 40,000 dissenters and British transfers[1] and more than 22,000 Japanese Canadians.[2] Of the British transfers, 2,284 were "camp boys," refugees from Nazism, some of whose experiences Paula Draper and Christine Whitehouse explore in their articles in this volume. Close to 5,000 were British subjects of Italian descent, among others. The Canadian government aggressively pursued German Canadians, antiwar protestors, communists, and possible Fascist and Nazi sympathizers. As for Japanese Canadians, in the aftermath of the attack on Pearl Harbor, Ian MacKenzie, the federal cabinet minister from British Columbia during the Second World War, was quite blunt. As he put it, "It is the government's plan to get these people out of BC as fast as possible"—and he was true to his word.[3] In their articles in this collection, Art Miki, Grace Eiko Thomson, Mikhail Bjorge, and Aya Fujiwara outline the impact and legacy of the "evacuation" of Japanese Canadians during this difficult period of Canadian history.

Many simultaneous events unfolded very quickly during the early stages of hostilities, including the formation of twenty-six internment camps throughout Canada. Camp populations included Canadian citizens, captured enemy soldiers, merchant seamen from enemy nations, and Jews who had fled Nazi Germany to England in the late 1930s, but who now, in the eyes of the British government, were possible spies.[4] Camp B-70, one of these twenty-six internment camps, is the focus of this chapter.

This essay will provide a brief historical overview of internment camp B-70, the only one located in the Maritime provinces, and shed light on the current preservation efforts of the New Brunswick Internment Camp Museum located in Minto, New Brunswick. This is one of only two museums in Canada dedicated exclusively to Second World War internment camps.

A broad range of historic events falls under the auspices of what is referred to as "negative cultural heritage." Examples include slavery, genocide, incarceration, terrorism, super viruses, Native American persecution, and nuclear incidents, to name just a few. Negative cultural heritage sites, described as places that may be interpreted by a group as commemorating conflict, trauma, and disaster, are certainly receiving more public attention.[5] Second World War internment camps are such places of negative heritage, and any museum dealing with the topic must be acutely aware of the contested narratives involved in places of incarceration.

Moreover, memorial museums, which are dedicated to historic events that commemorate suffering, are also becoming more popular and play an integral role in negative cultural heritage narratives.[6] Two examples that illustrate this point through tourism volume are the Nanjing Massacre Memorial, which has reportedly welcomed over 10 million visitors,[7] and the Robben Island Museum in Cape Town, which receives roughly 400,000 visitors a year.[8] In the most simplistic sense, these museums can provide, among other things, objects whose existence makes the reality of the event in question less easily dismissed. Memorial museums can effectively provide social responses to tragic events that can be as basic as offering a place to mourn.[9] The New Brunswick Internment Camp Museum visitor numbers pale in comparison to the sites mentioned above, but best efforts are still made to ensure the museum offers multiple narratives and handles the contested memories of internment in a balanced manner.

Camp B-70,[10] operated by the Department of Defence, was located in Ripples, New Brunswick, and covered 58 acres (23 hectares), including a 15-acre (6.07 hectares) fenced-in prison compound.[11] The camp had two phases of activity. The first ran from 1940 to 1941 and the second from 1941 to 1945, the year it was closed. Phase I involved the holding of 711 prisoners, mostly German and Austrian Jews who had fled Nazi Germany to England before British authorities arranged for them to be transported to Canada for incarceration. Phase II witnessed the incarceration of 1,200 Italian and

Figure 14.1. Wall mural in the New Brunswick Internment Camp Museum depicting internee uniforms, completed in the spring of 1997. Artist: Eugene Vautour. Photo by Griffin Mountan.

German merchant marines, along with many Canadians who had spoken out against the war and some who were deemed to be Fascist or Nazi sympathizers.

Camp Prisoners

Between 1940 and 1941, 711 POWs (517 Jews, 105 Protestants, 63 Roman Catholics, and 23 others) were incarcerated in Camp B-70 in Ripples, New Brunswick.[12] On the surface, life in the camp had all the trappings of prison. The camp consisted of five rows of barbed wire and six machine gun towers encircling fifty-two buildings.[13] The POWs wore uniforms that consisted of a jacket, pants, and hat, all made of denim. The jacket had a large solid red circle on the back. There was also a small red patch on top of the hat and a red stripe down the right pant leg (Figure 14.1).[14] Interestingly, the red circle on the back and the red stipe on the pant leg could not be removed without creating a large hole in the material as a deterrent against escape. According to one source, the prisoners resented wearing these uniforms even more than using outdoor latrines.[15]

Internees were required to make these uniforms as part of their work detail. Prisoners at Camp B-70 worked five and a half days a week with Saturday afternoons and Sundays off. The bulk of this work consisted of cutting 2,500 cords of wood a year to feed the camp's 100 large wood-burning stoves. The Phase I prisoners, who were Jewish internees (many highly educated) ranging from sixteen to sixty years of age, filled their time after work by setting up classes covering a variety of subjects.[16] Through these and other activities the prisoners displayed amazing creativity, ingenuity, and resourcefulness, often creating arts and crafts out of recycled items.

During Phase I, the Jewish internees did not try to escape. This is believed to be in part because they had nowhere else to go. Israel was yet to exist, and they certainly could not return to their German or German-occupied European homelands upon pain of incarceration and most likely death. The prisoners' biggest worry was the safety and well-being of their families back in Europe.

After eleven months, Phase I of Camp B-70's existence came to an abrupt end. The Jewish internees were to be relocated and replaced in the camp by German and Italian merchant seamen. The specific reason for the change in occupants is uncertain. In 1941 a small number of these Jews were returned to England. This event coincided with the demand for additional space to house this new influx of German and Italian prisoners. It is possible the government did not wish to risk potential prisoner disturbances by mixing enemy soldiers with the existing Jewish contingent of the camp and therefore relocated the entire B-70 population.[17] The Jewish internees faced an uncertain future: some would remain in North America after securing sponsorship from groups or individuals; others would choose to join the war effort in some capacity; and still others were transferred to other internment camps across Canada. Several prisoners from Phase I of Camp B-70 later went on to achieve considerable fame. Frederick (Fritz) Bender, inventor of waterproof plywood, was one such success story. Upon hearing what Bender had been working on in Europe, the Canadian government agreed to remove him from the camp to contribute to the development of an aircraft made from waterproof plywood called the Mosquito Bomber.[18] This plane proved to be a vital aircraft for the Allied forces during the war. Fred Kaufman was one of several other Camp B-70 internees who made a lasting contribution to Canadian society, eventually becoming a Quebec supreme court judge.[19]

The second phase of the camp's existence, 1941–45, was markedly different from the first. The new population who replaced the Jewish internees were primarily German and Italian merchant mariners, and transfers from other camps, thus creating a vastly different prison population. Their presence sharply altered the attitude and mood of the camp. Some of these prisoners were part of Hitler's regime and therefore at times planned escapes, usually by tunnelling. Four Phase II internees did manage to escape, but were all recaptured within a week. It is estimated that a total of 300 prisoners attempted to escape from Canadian camps, but only one (not from Camp B-70) ever made it back to Germany.[20] A well-known prisoner from Phase II was Montreal mayor Camillien Houde. Houde was interned for four years after being publicly associated with certain pro-fascist ideas and was eventually arrested for sedition for urging the Quebecois not to participate in the 1940 national registration.[21] However, some Canadians were interned for much more innocuous reasons. One such person was Rudolph Friedrich Soltendieck. A German citizen living in Canada, Soltendieck was imprisoned in Camp B-70 simply because he owned an insurance policy from Germany.[22] The New Brunswick Internment Camp Museum has more artifacts connected to this phase of the camp's life largely because Phase II prisoners remained interned for longer periods of time; indeed, some people were interned for the entire four years of the Phase II operation.

Internee Labour

In all of Canada's Second World War internment camps, craft workshops and work details were seen as important to the functioning of the camps, the maintenance of discipline, and the mental health of the internees. All internee labour during the Second World War was conducted according to the 1929 Geneva Convention, whether or not the convention applied to the internees and, when appropriate, was paid for at the rate of twenty cents per day.[23]

The internees at Camp B-70 even produced made-to-order wooden furniture pieces and other works of art for the reconstruction of Port Royal and the Fortress of Louisbourg National Historic Sites.[24] According to Byron Wile, a former overseer at the Acadia Forest Experimental Station, the internees of Camp B-70 carved signs and some of the furniture for the guest cabin as well as some of the furnishings for the Port Royal Habitation.[25] Katharine McLennan, honorary curator of the Fortress of Louisbourg Museum during the war years, had an oak plaque carved by Camp B-70 internee Rudolf Soltendiek, with a relief design depicting buildings and figures, and the caption "View of Part of the Town of Louisbourg Showing the Quay and Citadel from the North, 1745." The reproductions at Port Royal were made during the second phase of internment.[26]

Figure 14.2. Museum curator Ed Caissie (left) and Christian Soltendieck (right) hold the Fortress of Louisbourg plaque carved by Soltendieck's father and internee, Rudolf. *The Daily Gleaner*, 21 September 1995.

The New Brunswick Internment Camp Museum

The Port Royal story brings us to the New Brunswick Internment Camp Museum, which houses the above-mentioned plaque (Figure 14.2) and information on its origins. In 1993, Ed Caissie was developing alternate programs for at-risk students at Minto Elementary Junior High School. As part of his responsibilities, he mentored twelve at-risk students in his office on an individual basis. In an attempt to determine whether these students could work together on projects, he designed an assignment focused on the local internment camp site. This project, among other things, required the students to construct a scale model of the original internment camp (Figure 14.3) and dig for artifacts at the site.

Excavated artifacts were placed in display cases at the school, and the feeling at the time was that this display would constitute the end of the project. However, a number of parents and other visitors to the school who saw the display indicated that they also had artifacts from the camp and were willing to lend or gift them to the collection. Before long, they had accumulated so many objects that the display case capacity was far exceeded. During this

Figure 14.3. Scale model of the original camp. Model created by Ed Caissie's students. Photo by Griffin Mountan.

time, the project received some media attention, which resulted in even more acquisitions. Having reached a tipping point, Caissie sought out a group of people to form a non-profit organization that eventually led to the creation of the New Brunswick Internment Camp Museum in June 1997.

The museum is not located on the site of the original camp; rather it occupies a 2,000-square-foot space in the Minto town hall building. Minto is the closest town to the original site. The museum's collection includes over 600 artifacts and objects associated with the original camp. Through photographs, artifacts, oral histories, and interactive exhibits, museum visitors experience life through the eyes of the internees. Special emphasis is given to the experience of incarceration, constitutional issues, violations of civil liberties and civil rights, as well as the broader issues of race and social justice.

The museum's collection can be divided into three main categories: objects made by camp internees, internees' personal effects, and items found at the site. However, the museum has also collated a large number of oral history interviews from former prisoners that it plans to digitize and add to the collection.

Prisoner Art

Prisoner art constitutes the museum's most extensive collection of items and includes, model boats, ships in bottles, furniture, paintings, jewellery, and a cribbage board made of moose antler, to name a few. The museum also houses fifty of former prisoner Oscar Bendle's laser prints and one original painting, which were donated by his son, Lou Patrick Bendle. Largely because one of Bendle's five children died while he was imprisoned, he remained bitter about his imprisonment until his death. However, two of his children did attend the opening of the museum in 1997.

As a matter of practicality and limited resources, prisoners often recycled materials to make items and often gravitated toward easily duplicated methods in order to create multiples. This situation was common in other Canadian internment camps (Emily Cuggy and Kathleen Ogilvie's article in this volume, for example, describes their research on a violin made from a bed leg and chair seat by a First World War–era Brandon, Manitoba, internee). An excellent example of recycling at Ripples is a pair of dice in the museum collection (Figure

Figure 14.4. Game die (one of a pair). Wood and electrical fuses. These dice were made by a prisoner at the New Brunswick Internment Camp and given to David Middleton, a camp guard. The dice use fuses for dots. A close examination reveals pictures of the Middleton family on the fuses. New Brunswick Internment Camp Museum Collection. Photo by Griffin Mountan.

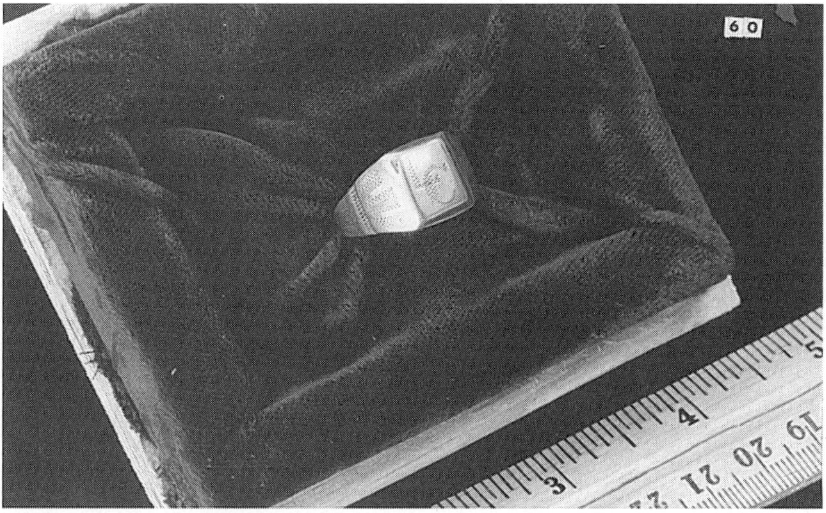

Figure 14.5. Ring made out of recycled dimes. New Brunswick Internment Camp Museum Collection. Photo by Ed Caissie.

14.4). The cube of each die is made of wood while the numbered dots are made of burnt-out electrical fuses. Ingeniously embedded in each fuse is a picture of a family member of one of the camp's guards. The museum also displays a ring made out of recycled dimes (Figure 14.5). The majority of the collection of prisoner art stems from Phase II, but there are a number of interesting pieces Phase I Jewish internees created. A cigarette case made from a recycled uniform and lined with birchbark is one interesting example (Figure 14.6).

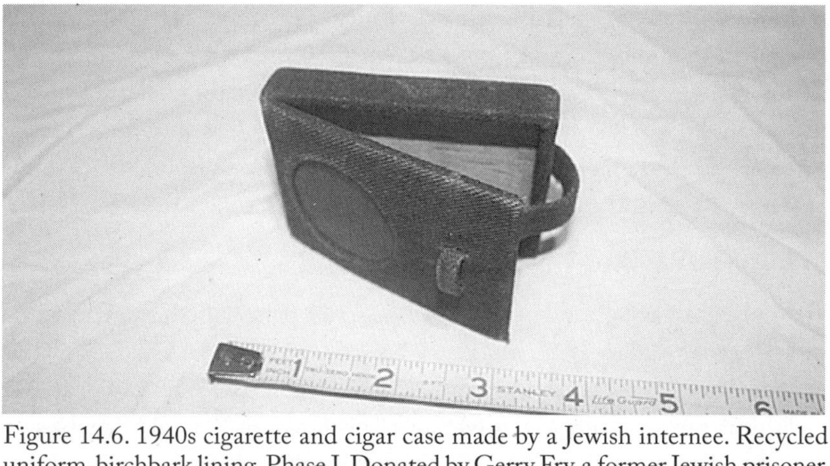

Figure 14.6. 1940s cigarette and cigar case made by a Jewish internee. Recycled uniform, birchbark lining. Phase I. Donated by Gerry Fry, a former Jewish prisoner.

Figure 14.7. Prisoner-made model ship, 32 x 5 x 17 inches. Portholes made of boot eyelets. New Brunswick Internment Camp Museum Collection. Photo by Ed Caissie.

The prisoners were allowed to sell their wares to the guards or trade for cigarettes and were even allowed to organize craft shows. The European internees often incorporated local birchbark and visual representations of Canadian Aboriginal lifeways in their crafts. Unfortunately, only a handful are signed, dated, or otherwise identified.

One of the museum's newest acquisitions is a large prisoner-made model ship (Figure 14.7). The thirty-two-inch-long vessel was originally gifted to Charles Collins, a camp guard. His daughter-in-law eventually donated the ship to the museum in 2014. The originality and complexity of the ship is evident in the more than 152 portholes made from boot eyelets. There was also a light which was originally inserted inside the boat through a hole in the bottom in order to illuminate the porthole windows from within. There is even a pool with a slide on one of the decks. This model ship is a wonderful example of the technical skill and ingenuity of some of the prisoners in Camp B-70.

Personal Effects

The museum has a limited number of prisoner personal effects. One item, rosary beads (Figure 14.8), illustrates how the memory and history of this camp still permeate the community. During Phase II of the camp, a local guard was prone to show off a picture of his fourteen-year-old daughter to the internees. One Italian POW was particularly taken with the girl and said

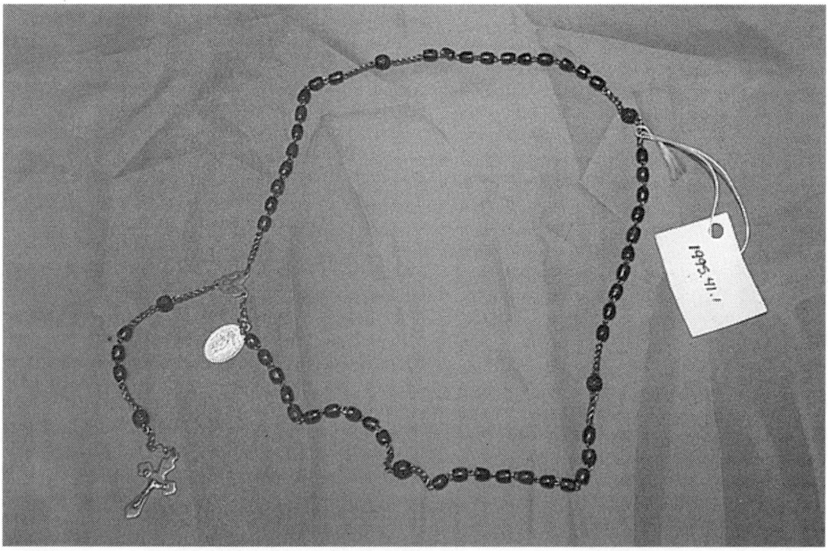

Figure 14.8. Rosary beads. New Brunswick Internment Camp Museum Collection.

he would someday return to marry the guard's daughter when she came of age and when the war was over. As a token of this promise the Italian gave the guard his rosary beads to give to his daughter. The Italian prisoner never did return, but when that fourteen-year-old girl grew up, she became one of the museum's very first committee members. This is a wonderful example of how the camp still exists in the narratives of lives of this community.

Artifacts

Excavated artifacts, for the most part, were discovered about three feet below the surface at the original prison site. The finds consisted mostly of enamel pots, pans, pails, plates, cups, and many bottles (including liquor and ink bottles), a mouth organ, a worker's pass, clay water pipes, part of a washing machine, and an assortment of other items including barbed wire. All the kitchen items discovered exhibited axe or pick damage. These holes were intentionally made by the Canadian military during the dismantling of the camp in order to make the items unusable to local residents (Figure 14.9). The military was acutely aware of the adverse effect such a large number of free salvageable items could have on the local economy.

The New Brunswick Internment Camp Heritage Committee, which oversees the museum, has also developed a historical walking trail at the original site. Fortunately, the camp and surrounding area are part of a large

Figure 14.9. Pot excavated from original camp site. The holes were intentionally made. New Brunswick Internment Camp Museum Collection.

game reserve and, as such, cannot be developed. Signage on the trail (Figure 14.10) now educates visitors on visible glimpses of the original camp such as the base of the water tower (Figure 14.11), a road inside the POW compound, two manhole covers, a cement foundation for the mess stoves, two fire hydrant pipes, and large stones that formed the base of the former grandstand.

Another unusual part of the museum's collection is a group of five large wooden crosses. Seven oak crosses were made by the German prisoners in Camp B-70 to mark the graves at the Hermitage Cemetery in Fredericton, NB, of their POW countrymen who died during incarceration in the camp. In 1966, local woodcarver Robert Kerton was commissioned to create new pine crosses to replace the originals, which had suffered serious deterioration.[27] On each cross (Figure 14.12) is a carved eagle, under which is a symbol indicating the man's profession, his name, the village and province of his birth, the year of birth and death, and "Gest. in GEFANGENSCHAFT," which translates as "died in captivity."

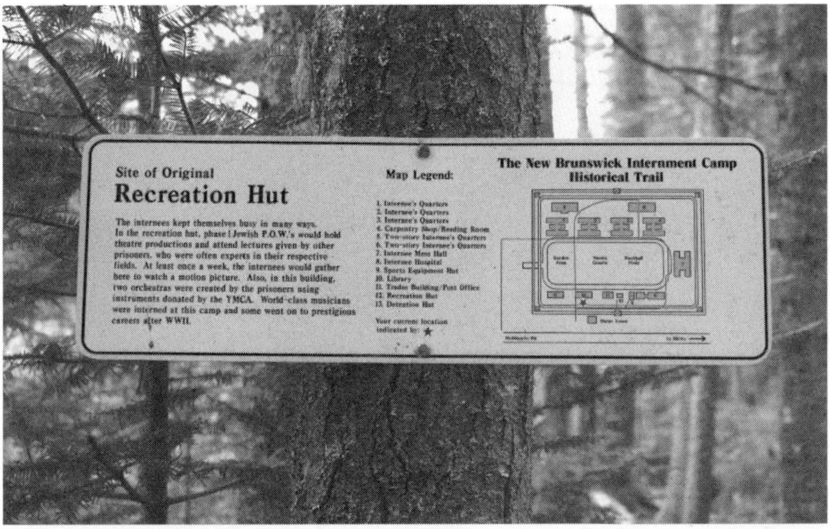

Figure 14.10. Signage on the historical trail. New Brunswick Internment Camp Museum Collection.

Figure 14.11. Base of the original water tower. New Brunswick Internment Camp B-70 Site. New Brunswick Internment Camp Museum Collection. Photo by Ed Caissie.

Figure 14.12. Five Wooden Crosses crafted by Robert Kerton in 1966. New Brunswick Internment Camp Museum Collection.

Conclusion

Heritage preservation activities, even negative heritage, serve to educate and enrich the collective memory of Canadians. The retention of memories of past events and personal narratives has an important influence on our culture's present and future. Negative heritage sites help people come to terms with disturbing aspects of the past, providing a safe zone to grieve and confront cultural difference through mediation and education. Other examples of material commemoration and physical marking of contested events that have been mobilized for positive purposes include memorials at Auschwitz, Hiroshima, and the World Trade Center. Negative cultural heritage preservation also helps avert the potential for collective amnesia about such events and places. This chapter provides only a glimpse of the history of internment and the fascinating collection at the New Brunswick Internment Camp Museum, but we encourage every Canadian to become more aware of the historical significance internment played in this country and how this narrative impacts the perceptions and actions of future generations. There is a paucity of internment camp site museums and interpretive centres in this country, and we hope this museum, in its own small way, keeps the dialogue alive.

Notes

1 Ted Jones, *Both Sides of the Wire*, vol. 1 (Fredericton, NB: New Ireland Press, 1988), ii.

2 Rob Mickleburgh, "Trio of Cabins Marks Japanese Internment Camp," 21 July 2013, *Globe and Mail*, https://www.theglobeandmail.com/news/british-columbia/trio-of-cabins-marks-japanese-internment-camp/article13337889/.

3 "Fighting from the Home Front: Japanese Internment," CBC, http://www.cbc.ca/history/EPISCONTENTSE1EP14CH3PA3LE.html.

4 Jones, *Both Sides of the Wire*, 1:1.

5 Trinidad Rico, "Negative Heritage: The Place of Conflict in Negative Heritage," *Conservation and Management of Archaeological Sites* 10, no. 4 (November 2008): 344.

6 Paul Harvey Williams, *Memorial Museums: The Global Gold Rush to Commemorate Atrocities* (Oxford, UK: Berg, 2007), 8.

7 Qian Fengqi, "Let the Dead Be Remembered: Interpretation of the Nanjing Massacre Memorial," in *Places of Pain and Shame: Dealing with "Difficult Heritage,"* ed. William Logan and Keir Reeves (New York: Routledge, 2009), 17.

8 Williams, *Memorial Museums*, 16. This is the site of Nelson Mandela's incarceration.

9 Ibid., 22.

10 Multiple names have been used to identify the camp, but for the purposes of continuity in this essay B-70 is used: Jones, *Both Sides of the Wire*, 1:27.

11 New Brunswick Internment Camp website, http://nbinternmentcampmuseum.ca.

12 Jones, *Both Sides of the Wire*, 1:25.

13 New Brunswick Internment Camp website, http://nbinternmentcampmuseum.ca.

14 After the war, prisoner jackets were often worn in the fields by local potato pickers.

15 Jones, *Both Sides of the Wire*, 1:84.

16 Ibid., 155.

17 Ibid., 270–71. 62 internees returned to England in June 1941.

18 Jones, *Both Sides of the Wire*, 1:183.

19 Fred Kaufman. *Searching for Justice: An Autobiography* (Toronto: Osgood Society, 2005), ix. Other former prisoners of Camp B-70 of note include: Helmut (Max) Kallmann, who rose to become head of the music division at the National Library of Canada and published Canada's first encyclopedia of music; Dr. Joseph Weininger, whose scientific career in North America was capped by his appointment as chief of research for General Electric; Dr. Henry Knepler, who was consultant to UNESCO and one-time chairman of the Department of Humanities at the Illinois Institute of Technology; Philipp Veit, who served in the Department of Modern Languages and Literature at the State University of New York, Buffalo; Dr. Gregory Baum, who for many years was a professor of religious studies at University of Toronto and then at McGill University, where he became renowned as one of Canada's leading theologians and advocates for social justice; Dr. Carl Amberg, a long-time member and eventually chair of the Department of Chemistry at Carleton University; and John Newmark, who became an accomplished pianist and musician, was made an officer of the Order of Canada in 1973, and received the Canadian Music Council Medal in 1979.

20 His name was Franz von Werra and he was subsequently killed in action within the year. *Homeland Stories: Enemy Within*, Reading and Remembrance Project 2010, http://www.readingandremembrance.ca/2010.html.

21 Jones, *Both Sides of the Wire*, 2:331–33. He later went on to be re-elected the mayor of Montreal.

22 Letter to the New Brunswick Internment Camp Museum from Soltendieck's wife. Archived at the New Brunswick Internment Camp Museum.

23 Jones, *Both Sides of the Wire*, 1:43.

24 Anne Marie Lane Jonah, Research Note, *Port Royal Reproductions Made at the Acadian Forest Internment Camp, 1942–1943*, 2.

25 Ibid., 5.

26 Ibid., 2.

27 There are only seven extant crosses. Five are in possession of the New Brunswick Internment Camp Museum while two are in the Fredericton Regional Museum.

CHAPTER 15

Exhibiting Contentious Topics: Finding a Place for the Internment Violin in the Canadian History Hall

EMILY CUGGY AND KATHLEEN OGILVIE

"This violin was made of the seat of a chair and the neck was made out of a leg of a bed by John Melnick #457 P.O.W." John Melnick was one of over 8,000 people classified and interned as "enemy aliens" during the First World War. Melnick crafted this violin during his internment at the Brandon, Manitoba, internment camp; however, both the violin and its maker have proved untraceable until 1982 when, according to a slip of paper found inside the instrument, it was purchased at an auction in Dunnville, Ontario. The violin later returned to Brandon after it was donated to the Daly House Museum. Through this object, the story of an individual becomes the story of a community and of a nation. Often forgotten due to its controversial nature and its frequent overshadowing by the war overseas, First World War internment involves many complex themes: Canada at war, both overseas and at home; a young country grappling with identity during a period of fear and uncertainty; and an immigrant community that faced exclusion and discrimination based on narrow notions of belonging. This story offers multiple layers of narrative, and serves as a reminder that Canada was not always the welcoming and diverse country that it is generally perceived to be today. At its most minute, it is the story of the journey of the violin itself from its beginnings as scrap wood from a bed leg and the seat of a chair, to a means of accessing much larger narratives about the Ukrainian Canadian community and a largely unknown part of Canada's history. The violin gives us access to a story about the Ukrainian Canadian community and its resilience in the face of adversity.

Figure 15.1. The internment violin. Photograph by Kathleen Ogilvie, 2017.

At the heart of the story of the internment violin is an individual. The information available about John Melnick is indeed sparse. Who he was before his internment is unknown, and we can only speculate on how he acquired the technical knowledge necessary to build the violin—whether he had previous experience in carpentry or making instruments, or whether he picked up this skill from other internees. A note found inside the violin reveals his name, prisoner number, and his role as its manufacturer; however, tracing Melnick's name and prisoner number results in a dead end, especially after his release or relocation from the Brandon camp when it closed in 1916. Without the violin, John Melnick would simply be a name and a prisoner number among thousands of others. Perhaps we would not know of him at all; internment records are incomplete, and we were unable to identify any other sources in which this John Melnick appears.[1] The violin thus tells the story of an individual who is otherwise untraceable, offering a means of commemorating and remembering a small portion of his life.

John Melnick and his violin represent a lesser-known aspect in the history of internment operations: the making of handicrafts within many camps. Other examples of this are evident in several essays in the collection, including those written by Sharon Reilly and by Ed and Todd Caissie. Making handicrafts originally began as a form of employment for internees. Director of Internment Operations Major-General Sir William Otter wrote in his 1921 report: "A further mode of employment was permitted to prisoners in the manufacture and sale of various articles, by the many clever artisans among them, the proceeds of which were placed at their credit, though the results were not very extensive or lucrative."[2] This form of employment was especially common at the Brandon camp because its location in the middle of an urban centre did not lend itself to the hard manual labour that was occurring elsewhere.[3] Internees fashioned a wide variety of items using scrap materials and supplies likely purchased at or distributed by the camp.[4] Items included picture frames, small model boats, and boxes carved out of wood, as well as decorative chains and gloves woven from scrap thread or animal hair.[5] Wooden handicrafts appear to have been most common, as internees could use scrap wood from boxes, boards, and furniture to carve their creations. Without proper tools, internees carved using ordinary penknives and even kitchen knives.[6] Internees made a variety of models pertaining to warfare, such as aeroplanes, dreadnoughts, and zeppelins. Oil paintings and other types of artwork were also produced, and—at least in Brandon—items might be displayed and sold at markets and fairs, with money going back to internees.[7]

Perhaps the most impressive objects were a reported fifty violins made by internees in Brandon. Made from wooden boards or, in the case of the violin discussed here, a bed leg and the seat of a chair, these violins were quite attractive and had great playing value.[8] While it is possible that the violins were being sold alongside other handicrafts, newspaper reports indicate that internees were in fact playing the violins.[9] We can only speculate on what they were playing; perhaps traditional music from their home country, or music learned after arriving in Canada.[10] Music remained an essential cultural practice for Ukrainian immigrants to Canada, although the specific ballads and themes that were performed changed and were adapted by each wave of immigration.[11]

Victoria Shevchenko argues that the different conditions and experiences faced by each wave of immigration—the first wave of which came before the First World War and was the group of Ukrainian immigrants affected by internment operations—influenced the cultural practices of each group in terms of the themes that they explored and related to in their musical and artistic expression.[12] In her interviews with members of the Ukrainian community in Canada, Shevchenko found that "folk ballads continue[d] to be performed among immigrants . . . the dominance of certain ballad topics that were identified during the participant interviews, reflected the likes and dislikes, concerns, attitudes, interests and experiences of the performers of each wave. As a result, every immigration wave developed a distinctive ballad tradition."[13] While the music enjoyed by Ukrainian immigrants changed over time to speak to the experiences of the community, Shevchenko's study indicates that the folk music tradition remained an essential part of maintaining and expressing their cultural identity. The making and playing of violins within the camps, while a tale not often heard in the history of internment, reflects this, tied as it is to the personal experiences of internees as they discovered ways to find solace in the face of discrimination.[14]

More broadly, the violin acts as a tangible point of access to the story of internment in Canada. In situating the violin within its historical context, multiple narratives emerge. First is the experience of Ukrainian Canadians, shaped by their arrival and experience in Canada, and the ways in which the First World War impacted their community both socially and politically. From this comes the narrative of the internee experience within the camps, which, as the violin indicates, is complex and varied. In tandem with this is the perspective of the Canadian government and its decision to intern "enemy aliens" in response to the early events of the war. The contemporary Ukrainian Canadian perspective has been generally unsympathetic towards the government's decision, insisting that it was unnecessary and emphasizing the false nature of the "alien" threat, the mistreatment of internees, and the need for redress. The complexity of these multiple and layered narratives demands that any honest representation of First World War internment be approached in a critical and balanced manner.

We had the opportunity to tell these stories in the fall of 2014 when our graduate seminar on museums, national identity, and public memory at Carleton University collaborated with the Canadian Museum of History (CMH) to create exhibit proposals to be considered for inclusion in the museum's new Canadian History Hall.[15] Each group of students worked in a small team with a curator and other museum staff in the development of our proposals, and had opportunities to attend design and planning meetings for the new hall. We presented our proposed exhibits to museum staff and curators at the conclusion of the project. Traditionally, museums have been assigned the responsibility to inform, educate, and engage visitors; presently, however, there are more tasks being added to the museum's list of responsibilities.[16] While supplying empirical data and accurate physical representations of the past is indeed important, the responsibility of the museum goes beyond empiricism. Conveying information is not as significant as what visitors do with this information and how they perceive it, for it is awareness that fuels thought and spurs action. Museums must therefore supply the context and information required for visitors to form opinions or engage in debate, while themselves maintaining an impartial and factually accurate stance.

When discussing the roles and responsibilities of the museum, Susan Ashley argues that "in the public mind, the museum is where history is kept; we agree that these public institutions represent us and can speak for us in matters of history and national identity. The very act of representing history in a building like a museum assigns significance to these events—an historical occurrence is raised from a first order meaning to a mythic meaning signification when it is depicted in a museum."[17] Given the significance that a museum can endow upon events and thus transmit to visitors, we needed to exercise caution when preparing our exhibit proposal in order to ensure that the meaning we were attaching to the violin and to the story of internment was an honest and balanced one. For many visitors, our exhibit might well be their first introduction to First World War internment, as the subject has yet to gain greater weight in the public imagination when compared with, for example, Second World War internment operations. Museums should provide a safe environment in which to explore and debate sensitive topics such as internment.[18] We therefore had a responsibility to propose an exhibit that would be informative, engaging, and evocative.

The CMH's status as a national museum confronted us with a new set of challenges in the creation of our exhibit proposal. Not only did we need to consider the responsibilities of the museum in general, but we also needed to contemplate those more specific to a national museum. Historically, national museums have played an important role in the consolidation of national identity.[19] Indeed, national museums have the ability—and often the expectation—to create a unifying national identity that facilitates social cohesion and stimulates national pride. The issue then became how to disrupt a generally patriotic national narrative without attacking it or displaying bias. The messaging and objectives that the CMH set out for the new hall encouraged an honest and critical approach to the national narrative, one that would include both the moments of pride and the moments of shame in our history. As the Exhibit Hall's conceptual document put it, "Canada's stories have great power: to shock and excite and reveal. It is our mission to collect and share them—whole, unadorned, uncensored, in respect of memories and points of view. They are sources of great pride, and deep humility."[20] This concept statement governed the ways in which we developed our proposal for an exhibit that highlighted a controversial period in Canadian history for a national museum, that is to say, without softening the story or proposing anything other than what the historical documents indicated about the event. Instead, we sought to equip visitors with enough information for them to walk away with their own opinions.[21]

One of our greatest challenges was dealing with the topic of internment itself. How we approached the project was greatly complicated by the fact that ours was a contentious topic that might elicit a varied response. Susan Ashley argues that "the museum must be open to ways that will temper the authoritative agency and certainty; remove homogeneity and single points of view, reject exclusion, encourage complexity and pluralism, and ensure conversation, dialogue, and true cohesion."[22] These are responsibilities with which we agreed and strove to meet in the creation of our exhibit. The CMH as a whole is striving towards these ideals and working to meet these responsibilities, and we wanted our exhibit to be a part of this process.[23] The difficulty of curating a contentious topic such as internment, however, is that it may potentially jeopardize the patriotic messages typically associated with a national museum. The CMH was open to challenging narratives, however, and after meetings with museum curators, we agreed that museums have a responsibility to present controversial topics, albeit in a particularly sensitive manner. As evidenced in past examples such as the Royal Ontario Museum's *Into the Heart of Africa* exhibit, the Canadian War Museum's exhibit on the Bomber Command, and the representation of the Enola Gay Affair at Washington's National Air and Space Museum, when presenting contentious topics there is a strong risk that an exhibit will spark controversy.[24] To avoid this, we recognized the necessity of presenting the internment story in a way that was sensitive to multiple points of view but did not shy away from its negative aspects.

One of the issues that arose from these controversies was that of representation. What authority does a white Canadian anthropologist have to tell the story of culture and colonialism in Africa in the *Into the Heart of Africa* exhibit, and what gave Canadian War Museum curators working on the Bomber Command exhibit the authority to relay experiences that only veterans lived through? Indeed, representation was an issue we struggled to address. As historians, we had the skills to research, interpret, and represent histories, and thus had a kind of professional authority. We did not feel, however, that we had any authority to speak for the experiences of the people we were representing, given that we had no claims to the community or its history, and knew little about it before beginning this project. We could not change this set of factors; we could only change how we addressed them by recognizing our separation from the events and people that we were representing. While we sought to challenge the status quo and design an exhibit that would contribute to the democratization of the museum, we were increasingly cautious about ensuring that we were providing a fair representation of a group to which we did not belong. One of the greatest challenges in creating the exhibit was to demonstrate cultural persistence without avoiding or denying the very negative realities that confronted internees. The aim was not to revise history by portraying this new side to internment; rather, it was to incorporate a lesser-known perspective into a story that is itself not widely known or discussed. In order to successfully address the problem of representation, we endeavoured to incorporate multiple perspectives to create an interpretation of events that would be respectful and impartial to all sides.

Examples such as the Royal Ontario Museum's *Into the Heart of Africa* exhibit, which demonstrated a lack of collaboration with the community that the exhibit sought to represent, and which flushed out the trauma and hurt caused by misrepresentation, or misinterpretation by visitors, caused us to be increasingly wary of the very real consequences, both positive and negative, that can come from a museum exhibit. Such examples shifted our approach to the project to focus on the different museum visitors who might encounter the exhibit. Some may not have known that internment camps existed in Canada, and be distressed or angered by the information presented to them. Others could be very young children, veterans' descendants or relatives, or, most significantly, members of the Ukrainian Canadian community. We wanted our exhibit to be accessible and informative to all of these groups. This project brought to the forefront the reality of presenting an historical topic in a museum, and put faces to what can sometimes seem like a body of imaginary visitors.

Our proposed idea for the design of this exhibit had two possibilities. Our first suggestion was to use lighting and shadows in order to visually contextualize the violin. For this, we proposed casting light to appear like barbed wire. This could be done either on the violin itself, or cast on the floor around the violin. This would indicate that this is not just the story of a musical instrument, and that there are much more complex, and perhaps shocking, circumstances under which the violin was made and used. The second design involved a greater use of space, but allowed for more material to be used and for increased visitor interaction, while seeking to communicate the same sense of foreboding as the first idea. We envisaged an alcove, designed to look like fence or barbed wire, with a gap in the front, through which the violin could be seen by visitors. The outside walls of this alcove would have text, photographs, and other documents, such as the publication of the War Measures Act in newspapers, which explore the perspective of the Canadian government on enacting internment operations. Visitors would then be able to enter the alcove, the inside of which would also contain photographs, documents, and text that contextualize and visualize the experience of internment by the Ukrainian community, and the circumstances under which the violin was created and used.

A digital storyboard could feature in both versions of the exhibit. For this, we envisaged an interactive board that could feature several primary documents such as acts, newspaper articles, and letters, as well as photographs and stories of other individual internees to complement and contrast the central story of John Melnick. This would also be an ideal way of interacting with young adults, teenagers, and older children, prompting them to engage with historical content and materials more directly.

We wanted to create a reflective experience so that visitors could form their own conclusions about internment and its legacy.[25] While we hoped that visitors would realize that internment was a dark moment in Canadian history, we did not want to impose any particular interpretation upon them. It was our hope that our exhibit would be informative but not imposing, so that visitors could gain knowledge, from which they could form their own ideas about what they saw.

Looking back on this process, we hope that our exhibit proposal effectively dealt with the issues that we were confronted with throughout the term. Forced to constantly re-evaluate ideas about both content and design, we learned that museum theory and museum practice are often difficult to connect; what is on the page does not always translate into viable or appropriate practice. Confronting these varied issues reinforced our certainty that, rather than shying away from difficult topics, museums must confront them directly with sensitivity and transparency. John Melnick's violin does appear in the Canadian History Hall, and in the summer of 2017 we had the opportunity to see it for the first time. We were hopeful that in this new setting the violin would help to secure a greater space for First World War internment and the many stories it involves in a way that was both challenging and complex. Space was indeed made for internment within the First World War exhibit, which serves as the beginning of the Modern Canada gallery. Titled *Subjects of Enemy Countries*, the exhibit displays the violin alongside two other items made by internees: a crucifix fashioned from barbed wire, and a shovel used in an escape attempt made by a prisoner in Fernie. Above the display case, there is an enlarged photograph of internees at the Castle Mountain camp in Alberta, staring out

Figure 15.2. The *Subjects of Enemy Countries* exhibit within the First World War section of the Canadian Museum of History's Canadian History Hall. Photograph by Emily Cuggy, 2017.

through the barbed wire fence—and through the photograph—at the visitor. The accompanying text consists of a single text panel, and a short description of each artifact. The text is brief, offering only basic details on internment. In line with the idea that museums act as mediators rather than as suppliers of information,[26] the internment exhibit relies primarily on objects and images to communicate. Using the same artifact that we ourselves utilized in our curation of internment, visitors are entrusted to confront this contentious topic and decide for themselves how the violin and the story of internment fits within a complex and diverse national narrative.

Notes

1 Although we did locate sources that include the name John Melnick, this was a very common name and we found no convincing evidence that any of these individuals were the John Melnick we were seeking.

2 William Otter, *Report on Internment Operations: Canada, 1914–1920* (Ottawa: Thomas Mulvey, 1921), reproduced in Lubomyr Luciuk, *In Fear of the Barbed Wire Fence: Canada's First National Internment Operations and the Ukrainian Canadians, 1914–1920* (Kingston: Kashtan Press, 2001), 134.

3 Although *Brandon Daily Sun* records indicate that there was talk of having internees construct a road between Brandon and Carberry ("To Consider Employing Aliens on Sewell Road," *Brandon Daily Sun*, 9 March 1916), we have found no other records proving whether or not this idea came to fruition. In contrast, prisoners interned in more isolated camps were made to work on projects such as road building, land clearing, wood chopping, and railway construction. In some cases, they were even forced to build or expand the internment camps they were held in. Internees further west, for example in Banff, were involved in the construction of national parks, while internees in Ontario and Quebec cleared land for experimental farms. It is estimated that the labour costs being performed by internees amounted to $1.5 million per year (see Luciuk, *In Fear of the Barbed Wire Fence*, 14, 159).

4 Otter, *Report on Internment Operations*, 135–36.

5 *Robochyi Narod*, 25 November 1915.

6 Ibid.

7 "Inter-Provincial Fair to be Great Success," *Brandon Daily Sun*, 19 July 1915, http://manitobia.ca/content/en/newspapers/BDS/1915/07/19/articles/14.pdf/iarchives.

8 *Robochyi Narod*, 25 November 1915.

9 Ibid.

10 In email correspondence, filmmaker Yurij Luhovy discussed different possibilities with us regarding what music internees may have been playing. If they were playing traditional Ukrainian music, Luhovy speculates that these would have been tangos, foxtrots, and waltzes. In the winter, Ukrainian Koladas may have been played.

11 Victoria Shevchenko, "Ukrainian Canadians: The Manifestation of Cultural Identity through Folk Ballads" (MA thesis, University of Alberta, 2012), 3.

12 Ibid.

13 Ibid.

14 For more on music traditions in the Ukrainian community in Canada, see: Marcia Ostashewski, "Performing Heritage: Ukrainian Festival, Dance, and Music in Vegreville, Alberta" (PhD diss., York University, 2009).

15 This project, part of a seminar taught by Dr. David Dean at Carleton University, was intended for us to gain valuable experience in museum curatorship and

collaboration. The scope of the project was limited to a proposal of our ideas, and we were not required to create a physical exhibit. The proposals submitted by our class are property of the Canadian Museum of History and may be altered at their discretion. Not all exhibits proposed by the class appear in the Canadian History Hall; however, the internment violin has been included.

16 As Fiona Cameron notes, museums should be thought of as "mediators and advocates for knowledge rather than suppliers of information, and to provide tools for visitors to explore their own ideas and to reach their own conclusions." Fiona Cameron, "Beyond Surface Representations: Museums, 'Edgy' Topics, Civic Responsibilities, and Modes of Engagement," *Open Museum Journal* 8 (2006): 22.

17 Susan Ashley, "State Authority and the Public Sphere: Ideas on the Changing Role of the Museum as a Canadian Social Institution," *Museum and Society* 3, no. 1 (March 2005): 6.

18 Cameron, "Beyond Surface Representations," 23.

19 Flora Edouwaye S. Kaplan, "Making and Remaking National Identities," in *A Companion to Museum Studies,* ed. Sharon Macdonald (Malden, MA: Blackwell, 2006), 165.

20 Canadian Museum of History, *Canadian History Hall Exhibition Concept* (Ottawa: May 2014), 7.

21 Cameron, "Beyond Surface Representations," 23.

22 Ashley, "State Authority and the Public Sphere," 15.

23 Canadian Museum of History, *Canadian History Hall Exhibition Concept,* 9–10.

24 For detailed examinations of these controversies, see Shelley Ruth Butler, *Contested Representations: Revisiting* Into the Heart of Africa (Peterborough, ON: Broadview, 2008); David Dean, "Museums as Conflict Zones: The Canadian War Museum and Bomber Command," *Museum and Society* 7, no. 1: 1–15; and Vera L. Zomberg, "Museums as Contested Sites of Remembrance: The Enola Gay Affair," in *Theorizing Museums,* ed. Sharon Macdonald and Gordon Fyfe (Oxford, UK: Blackwell, 1996), 69–82.

25 Our goal aligned with Fiona Cameron's finding that museum visitors want to be able to form their own opinions: "Ideally scholarly information ought to be presented in a way that empowers people to engage in critical thinking, stimulates or prompts debate, assists audiences to weigh up information to inform their own decision making and to draw their own conclusions." Cameron, "Beyond Surface Representations," 18.

26 Cameron, "Beyond Surface Representations," 22.

CHAPTER16

Civilian Internment and the Impact of War: Legacy and Public History

SHARON REILLY

This chapter explains how the history of civilian internment in Canada during wartime came to be included within the Parklands/Mixed-Woods Gallery of the Manitoba Museum in Winnipeg. It describes two exhibits in the Social History portion of the gallery that focus on wartime and explains how these displays interpret this history.

The first war-related exhibit focuses on the experiences of Japanese Canadians who arrived in Manitoba during the Second World War. Labelled "enemy aliens" and evicted from their homes in British Columbia, these families provided cheap labour working on sugar beet farms in southern Manitoba. Their history is a complex one, as essays in this collection by Art Miki and Grace Eiko Thomson demonstrate. Both of these authors came to Manitoba as part of this coerced migrant cohort.

A wide view can enable the emergence of a breadth of thematic content, as Jodi Giesbrecht underscores in her contribution to this collection on curating internment histories at the Canadian Museum for Human Rights. This can allow for a richer exhibition experience even in the face of limited word counts and minimal physical space. This is certainly true of the Manitoba Museum's second exhibit, which examines the impact of war from a much broader perspective. It includes the First and Second World Wars, and both the military and civilian experience. The exhibit tells many different stories, including the internment of pacifists, conscientious objectors, and those labelled "enemy aliens" because their countries of origin were at war with Canada. Integrating the history of civilian internment within the larger theme of the impact of war made it possible to include this subject in the gallery and, in doing so, resulted in a much richer interpretation of Manitoba's history.

The Manitoba Museum is the largest heritage and science centre in the province. The museum and its adjoining planetarium opened in their current location, on north Main Street across from City Hall, in 1970. The museum was mandated to explore the human and natural history of the province. Over time, it opened nine permanent galleries that interpret Manitoba, its history, and its environment to visitors by exploring the various biomes, or regions, of the province.

The Parklands/Mixed-Woods Gallery, which opened in 2003, was the last of these galleries completed and is the largest single gallery at the Manitoba Museum. Often referred to as the Parklands Gallery, this multi-levelled, 10,000-square-foot exhibition focuses on the transitional zone that links the boreal forest, to the north, and the more southerly grasslands. Rolling valleys, lakes, rivers, marshlands, mixed woods, and poorly drained, rocky land characterize the region.

The Parklands includes the area surrounding "The Forks," or meeting place, of the Red and Assiniboine Rivers. This region was home to, and traversed by, many different Indigenous groups for thousands of years before Europeans first arrived in the early 1700s. Settlers began to make their way to southern Manitoba a century later. In the late nineteenth and early twentieth centuries, tens of thousands of homesteaders of British, European, and other origins arrived here in search of free farmland. New communities sprang up, linked by developing railway and road networks, and providing industrial, commercial, financial, and social services to the surrounding farmlands. By the mid- to late twentieth century, however, this growth slowed and then reversed. Rural populations declined in all but a few centres in the face of ongoing social, economic, and environmental change. The Parklands/Mixed-Woods Gallery aimed to portray this region in all its diversity, from both a human and natural history perspective.

Planning for the Parklands/Mixed-Woods Gallery involved a team of curators, designers, interpreters, and other staff who met to discuss a multitude of questions ranging from the physical and interpretive flow of the gallery to the allocation of space for exhibits, programs, and storage. The group discussed the major dioramas and dozens of smaller exhibits proposed by the curatorial team. Curators from archaeology, ethnology, social history, and the various natural sciences were tasked with conducting research and identifying artifacts, images, and other assets for possible inclusion in the agreed-upon exhibits.

Figure 16.1. Ukrainian Rye Farm Diorama, Parklands/Mixed-Woods Gallery, the Manitoba Museum. Rob Barrow, TMM, 2003. This lifelike exhibit portrays a farm family at work in southeastern Manitoba in the 1920s. Elsewhere in the gallery, artifact-based exhibits explore many other aspects of life in the region. The internment of so-called "enemy aliens" is considered in two separate exhibits. One of these displays focuses on the impact of war on the people of the region; the other considers the experiences of Japanese Canadians.

Some twenty different exhibits fell into the category of "Social History" and the interpretation of the social, cultural, and economic experiences of newcomers to the region. These ranged from the bucolic rye farm diorama, pictured above, to a multidisciplinary digital map that included segments on changing population patterns and transportation networks. One exhibit used salvaged barn boards to recreate a facsimile of a barn, which featured early twentieth-century agricultural implements, enlarged archival photos, and interpretive text. Another display described summer leisure activities at Winnipeg Beach, using woollen bathing costumes, early soda bottles, and sand to tell the story of this popular resort and suggest a picnic at the lake. Other, more traditional exhibits presented artifacts, archival images, and interpretive text to explore various aspects of daily life. These displays ranged in theme from the role of fraternal groups, like the Odd Fellows and Rebekahs, to childhood, midwifery, and cultural practices. They examined the introduction of electricity to the region and the industrial fishery of the early to mid-twentieth century as well as industries like the Manitoba Glass Factory, Leary Brickworks, Garson quarries, and Mary Maxim woollen mills.

Preliminary plans, which dated to the 1970s, called for some mention of the impact of war in the Parklands region. Although no part of Manitoba remained unaffected by war, the once densely populated Parklands region felt this experience deeply. Many of the Manitobans who enlisted in the armed forces during both the First and Second World Wars came from the small towns and farmlands of the region. Virtually every small town today remembers the lives that were lost in these conflicts with its own war memorial. The museum's longstanding collections reflected this history. They included military uniforms and badges; firearms and other equipment; and service medals, mementos, and photographs of the individuals who once owned these items.

One anticipated focus of an exhibit on the impact of war on the Parklands was the story of the British Commonwealth Air Training Plan, which built and operated some twenty-one training sites across southern Manitoba during the Second World War. The air training plan had a huge impact on social and economic life in the region and affected the lives of thousands of civilians as well as military personnel. The landing strips used to train pilots from Australia, New Zealand, England, and Canada during the war remained one of the distinctive features of the built environment well into the late 1900s. As these sites faded, interest grew in preserving the legacy of this history.[1]

Another story in the original plans for an exhibit on war was that of the Winnipeg Grenadiers. Recruited from across southern Manitoba, members of the Grenadiers became prisoners of war in Hong Kong in 1941 when stationed there to protect the British colony from possible invasion by Japanese troops. Regimental Sergeant Major John Robert Osborn, who lost his life in the Battle of Hong Kong, received the Victoria Cross posthumously for his selfless efforts to save his men. The soldiers taken prisoner suffered brutal treatment for the duration of the war, and many did not survive. The "Hong Kong Vets" and their experiences became an integral part of Manitoba's identity in the years after the war. In the early 1970s, museum staff conducted a research project focused on these stories, collecting oral history interviews, photographs, artifacts, and personal diaries. This collection provided a rich resource for exhibition.[2]

As research into the broad social history of the region progressed, it became clear that the British Commonwealth Air Training Plan and the Winnipeg Grenadiers in Hong Kong were but two of many important themes that connected the Parklands and war.

Deciding which additional stories to include in an *Impact of War* exhibit meant thinking carefully about the objectives of the display. One important goal of the social history exhibits in general was to preserve stories that were in danger of being lost. Another goal was to include recent history, and to present stories that were relevant in a contemporary context. This meant including the experiences of women, children, and minority groups who often were not included in historical accounts. It also meant including difficult stories that discussed controversial and/or painful aspects of the region's past.

The experience of Japanese Canadians who arrived in the Parklands during the Second World War was one of the moist poignant of the region's difficult stories. In 1942, close to 21,000 Japanese Canadians who were living along the coast of British Columbia were forced to abandon their homes, jobs, and businesses when authorities claimed they posed a threat to national security. Most of these individuals were sent to the interior of British Columbia. Women, children, and elderly men were placed in internment camps, while the remaining men were sent to work camps and assigned to logging or road building. Some families, about 3,600 individuals, managed to stay together by agreeing to work on sugar beet farms in Alberta and Manitoba. About a third of these detainees came to Manitoba and were placed on sugar beet farms located in rural areas south, west, and sometimes east of Winnipeg.[3]

Life on the farms was harsh, and both government supervision and controls upon the movements of Japanese Canadians remained in place until well after the war, when authorities acknowledged that Japanese Canadians never, in fact, posed a risk to Canada. It took many years for those who survived this social and economic upheaval to begin to recover from this experience, and for the community to re-establish itself and raise public awareness of these injustices. An official apology came in 1988 with a redress settlement signed by Canada's prime minister.

The importance of this story resulted in the agreement of the gallery team to include a small, but distinct, exhibit that focused solely on the experiences of Japanese Canadians who arrived in the Parklands region during wartime. Not surprisingly, this exhibit contrasted sharply with the surrounding displays on immigration to the region and rural life. Planned in consultation with members of the community, it included wartime images of Japanese Canadians, from toddlers to aged grandparents, at work on Manitoba's vast sugar beet farms. The photos also showed the simple tarpaper shacks these people lived in throughout the long, cold winters.

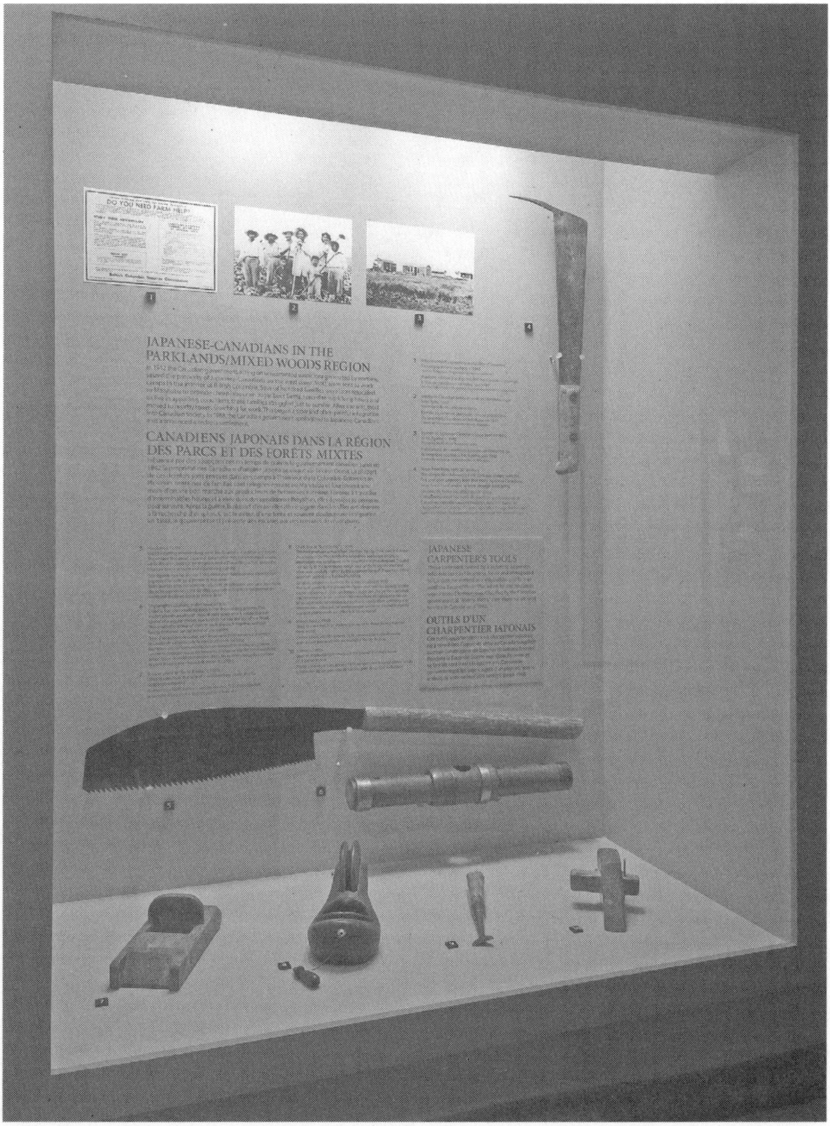

Figure 16.2: *Japanese-Canadians* exhibit, Parklands/Mixed-Woods Gallery, the Manitoba Museum. Rob Barrow, TMM, 2003. This display contrasted life before and after internment with a selection of intricate carpenter's tools, owned by a Japanese Canadian ship builder in British Columbia, and a simple sugar beet knife used by Japanese Canadians in Manitoba.

Figure 16.3. Japanese Canadians on a sugar beet farm near St. Agathe, Manitoba, c. 1942. Japanese Cultural Association of Manitoba. This photo was included in the display to show that entire families, including the very young and the very old, did heavy manual labour on the sugar beet farms. The photo also hints at the fight for justice that came after the war ended. It shows a young Art Miki (child at bottom right), who grew up to become a leader in the fight for redress. Miki served as president of the National Association of Japanese Canadians. On 22 September 1988, he and Prime Minister Brian Mulroney signed the Japanese Canadian Redress Agreement.

The exhibit presented a replica poster that showed the province's role in these actions. Distributed by the British Columbia Security Commission, it advertised the availability of Japanese Canadians to assist sugar beet farmers during the wartime labour shortage.

The exhibit highlighted the impact of internment on one Japanese Canadian man by contrasting the workplace tools he used before and after he became a detainee. It displayed a simple sugar beet knife, contrasted with a collection of intricate, high-precision carpenter's tools. Born in Hiroshima, Japan, this man apprenticed as a master carpenter before moving to British Columbia, where he earned his living building fishing boats and farming. Following internment, he and his family laboured on a sugar beet farm in Manitoba.

The *Impact of War* exhibit, originally planned to discuss war and the Parklands, stood nearby. This display included information about the Japanese

Figure 16.4. Japanese Canadians outside the flimsy tarpaper shacks where they lived and worked on a sugar beet farm in St. Agathe, Manitoba, June 1942. Japanese Cultural Association of Manitoba. This photo showed the terrible living conditions imposed upon Japanese Canadian families who lived on sugar beet farms in southern Manitoba during the Second World War.

Canadian fight for redress, but also aimed to show the many different ways in which war affected people's lives. Set into a small niche, it included text panels, a display case filled with artifacts, several pullout panels with archival photos, and a curatorial notebook located on a pedestal in the front of the main exhibit. The curatorial notebook—a "hands-on," interactive exhibit element—contained twenty laminated pages and an equal number of stories about the wartime experiences using images and text.

Representatives of the Japanese Canadian community; the Hong Kong Veterans Commemorative Association; the various military museums in Manitoba; the Ukrainian Labour Temple Association; and other community members assisted in providing guidance and content for this exhibit.

As originally planned, the *Impact of War* exhibit told the stories of the British Commonwealth Air Training Plan and the Winnipeg Grenadiers, who became prisoners of war in Hong Kong. It also included other important military themes: trench warfare training during the First World War at Camp Hughes, near Brandon, Manitoba; the fledgling role of women in the armed forces during both the First and Second World Wars; and the role

Figure 16.5. The *Impact of War* exhibit, Parklands/Mixed-Woods Gallery, the Manitoba Museum. Rob Barrow, TMM, 2003. This exhibit explored the impact of war from a wide range of perspectives, from civilians and military recruits to internees and prisoners of war. It included pullout panels with photos and text, a soundtrack with a group singing a wartime knitting song, and the curatorial notebook, shown below.

of Winnipeg's naval base—HMS *Chippewa*—during wartime. The display showed images of Victoria Cross and other war medals recipients from the Parklands, and displayed postcards sent home from the battlefields.

The exhibit diverged from the military aspects of war to discuss the war effort on the home front, including the contribution of workers at the Transcona cordite plant; the women who went to work at Bristol Aerospace; and those who gathered to knit socks and assemble care packages to send to loved ones overseas. A hidden speaker carried the voices of women singing a wartime knitting song. Archival photos showed the women, children, and elderly family members who worked on the farms in the absence of their menfolk.

The display also talked about Indigenous soldiers[4] and Indigenous workers who were drawn into the industrial and agricultural workforce by the wartime labour shortage. It showed little-known images of German prisoners of war interned at Riding Mountain National Park, discussed the scare tactics used to sell war bonds during the Second World War, and described the dramatic role played by returned soldiers in the 1919 Winnipeg General Strike.

Figure 16.6. Curatorial notebook for the *Impact of War* exhibit, Parklands/Mixed-Woods Gallery, the Manitoba Museum. Sharon Reilly, 2011. This binder, presented on a pedestal in front of the *Impact of War* exhibit case, included twenty laminated pages filled with archival images and interpretive text. The addition of the note-book made it possible to include many more stories in the exhibit than otherwise would have been possible.

The curatorial notebook also explains how, during wartime, Canadian authorities declared that Canadians of Ukrainian, German, Italian, and Japanese heritage were "enemy aliens" because Canada was at war with their countries of origin. It describes the actions of the RCMP, which monitored members of the labour movement and radical political organizations suspected of posing a threat to Canadian society. Many of these men lost their jobs and had to report regularly to government authorities. Authorities detained others in remote internment camps where they performed manual labour.

The internment of Japanese Canadians, conscientious objectors, and so-called "enemy aliens" was included in these pages using the archival photos shown above and below.

The story of civilian internment during wartime is told through the experiences of Matthew Shatulsky. A Canadian of Ukrainian descent, Shatulsky was among those arrested and imprisoned without trial for two years when the federal government banned the Ukrainian Labour Farmer Temple Association under the War Measures Act on 5 June 1940. Shatulsky was later cleared of all charges.

Figure 16.7. Envelope mailed from the Kananaskis Internment Camp, postmarked 11 July 1940; curatorial notebook, p. 18. This envelope contained the first letter sent home by Matthew Shatulsky from the Kananaskis Internment Camp to his wife, seamstress and union activist Kathleen (née Semeniuk) Shatulsky. Note the censors' validating stamp.

The notebook also told the story of families divided by war, like Mennonite brothers Ted and John Friesen. As a conscientious objector, Ted spent the Second World War in a remote work camp and later returned to his hometown of Altona. Like many other Canadian Mennonites, John Friesen chose to enlist, and flew bombing raids over Germany. Rejected by his community because of his actions, John never again lived in his hometown. This story, little known in the broader community, is the theme of the National Film Board (NFB) of Canada production *The Pacifist Who Went to War,* 2002.[5]

Through these two exhibits, then, the history of civilian internment in Canada during wartime is included along with many other stories about the impact of war in the Parklands/Mixed-Woods Gallery of the Manitoba Museum. Visitors to the museum have been able to view these exhibits since the gallery opened in 2003.

Museum visitors who spend time at the exhibits on Japanese Canadians and the impact of war in the Parklands Gallery will get a glimpse of this history and the story of civilian internment in Canada during wartime. They will have the opportunity to learn something of what war meant for different people and see that controversial parts of our history remain relevant today, in a time when racial profiling and intolerance persist.

Figure 16.8. Mennonite brothers Ted (left) and John (right) Friesen; curatorial notebook, p. 17; the *Impact of War* exhibit, Parklands/Mixed-Woods Gallery, the Manitoba Museum. Mennonite brothers Ted and John Friesen, found themselves divided by the issue of war in 1939.

Notes

1 The British Commonwealth Air Training Plan Museum opened in 1980 in Brandon, Manitoba, to commemorate this history and assisted the Manitoba Museum with this exhibit.

2 Winnipeg Grenadier member families founded the Hong Kong Veterans Commemorative Association beginning in 1993 to keep this history alive and assisted the Manitoba Museum with this exhibit. See http://www.hkvca.ca/aboutus/index.htm.

3 Shelly Ikebuchi Ketchell, "Carceral Ambivalence: Japanese Canadian 'Internment' and the Sugar Beet Programme during WWII," *Surveillance and Society* 7, no. 1 (2009).

4 The story of Tommy Prince, one of Canada's most decorated First Nations soldiers, appears in nearby section of the gallery that focuses on Indigenous life.

5 The NFB webpage describes the documentary as the story of two Mennonite brothers from Manitoba who took different positions on the matter of pacifism. "Ted became a conscientious objector while his brother went into military service. Fifty years later, the town of Winkler dedicates its first war memorial and John begins to share his war experiences with Ted." See https://www.nfb.ca/film/pacifist_who_went_to_war/.

PART VIII

INTERNATIONAL INTERNEES: CANADA AS "HOST"

CHAPTER 17

The Paradox of Survival: Jewish Refugees Interned in Canada, 1940–43

PAULA J. DRAPER

> *Our suffering was psychological: firstly, the painful, undeserved deprivation of freedom, and secondly, the mental anguish a Jew must feel to be locked up as a German and as a suspected Nazi sympathizer.*[1]

On 31 May 2015 Rabbi Erwin Schild celebrated his ninety-fifth birthday with his family, friends, and congregation in Toronto. After all the moving tributes, his own speech remarked on the astonishing trajectory of his life. Schild was a teenage rabbinical student in Germany when he was thrown into Dachau concentration camp, where he spent five terrifying weeks. After his release he was forced to leave his parents and siblings behind in order to escape to the United Kingdom. There, Schild was interned and shipped to Canada as an enemy alien. Upon regaining his freedom, Schild completed his studies and served forty-two years as the spiritual leader of a large Toronto synagogue. Rabbi Schild was awarded Germany's Order of Merit in 2000, and in 2001 became a member of the Order of Canada. He was honoured for "improving dialogue between the Christian and Jewish faiths, promoting harmony at home and abroad."[2] The ninety-five-year-old concluded his comments by emphasizing his love for Canada. Despite the painful years of internment he had "a true patriot's love for this precious country."

Between 1940 and 1944 a little-known episode of the Holocaust unfolded in Canadian internment camps. Rabbi Schild was one of 2,284 "camp boys" who escaped from Nazi terror to refuge in the UK, only to be confined, transported, and then dumped into the lap of Canada—a country that had kept its doors tightly closed against those fleeing Europe, particularly Jews. Nine hundred and sixty-six of the interned refugees were able to remain until the end of the war, though the number who settled is unclear; many found their way to the United States. Like Rabbi Schild, most of those who became Canadian had a profound love for and significant impact on the country. But they never forgot the circuitous routes that brought them here, nor the almost insurmountable obstacles placed in their way by the Canadian government.[3]

Perhaps the bittersweet nature of the tale of refugee survival in internment camps has limited scholarly focus on their stories. Unlike the unfortunate passengers on the *St. Louis*[4] the stories of refugees who were saved through internment by the British in Canada[5] and Australia[6] have been limited to articles in journals and to monographs. While in the United Kingdom the wide-scale internments prompted a number of memoirs and histories as early as 1940,[7] recent publications on Jewish refugees from Nazism barely mention the British internments.[8] Authors of volumes devoted to Canada and the Holocaust refer to my research[9] or include short sections on the topic.[10] An exhibit curated by the Vancouver Holocaust Centre[11] in 2012 reflected a renewed interest in the history of the Canadian refugee internment camps. Videotaped interviews with former internees are available in several depositories,[12] and postwar memoirs and biographies continue to be published some seventy years after the Holocaust.[13] Young scholars are approaching the internment with fresh perspectives, examining culture, interpersonal relations, and issues of memory as the field of Holocaust studies grows. In this volume, essays by Christine Whitehouse and Clemence Schultze help to further enrich our understanding of this internment episode.

The Canadian Government and the Interned Refugees

As the Second World War began, the government of William Lyon Mackenzie King pursued a policy of extreme caution regarding the internment of enemy aliens residing in Canada. The sheer numbers of German-born residents in Canada had prevented any mass internments during the First World War. Likewise, in 1939, the difficulties involved in rounding up and incarcerating all but the blatantly fascist, whether enemy aliens or Canadian citizens, proved financially and physically untenable to the Liberal government. Certainly there was no discussion in Canada of interning resident refugees from Nazism. Besides, only the barest handful had managed to squeeze through the cracks in Canada's stringent pre-war immigration policy. Frederick Charles Blair, the director of the Immigration Department, had seen to that.[14]

As Britain faced the possibility of imminent invasion in the spring of 1940, Canada hesitantly agreed to aid the war effort by incarcerating prisoners of war and "dangerous enemy aliens" interned in the United Kingdom. In order to release the armed forces guarding British camps to prepare for battle, the internees would be sent by ship to Canada (and Australia).[15] Once this was decided, the government faced the sticky question of where to put the new camps. The general view was that the majority should be located in New Brunswick, Quebec, and Ontario, rather than in the western provinces where the camps might provoke the large German population in Saskatchewan. To send some to Alberta and not to Saskatchewan might appear to be a reflection on the loyalty of the other province.[16] Ironically for the interned refugees, this was to prove a great advantage, as they were thereby placed in close proximity to the largest Jewish communities in Canada.

On 19 June 1940 Mackenzie King made the decision public. He explained the reasons for giving the internment of enemy aliens and prisoners of war priority over evacuee programs for children from Britain.[17] There was some grumbling in the House. As far as Parliament members and the Canadian public knew, only dangerous enemy aliens were on their way to Canada.

Information contradicting this assumption reached Canada just as the first ship landed on 28 June. Telegrams arrived from the UK high commissioner, Vincent Massey, outlining that most of the civilian internees were "friendly enemy aliens."[18] The British had created A, B, and C categories for enemy nationals and the refugees were labelled, with some unfortunate exceptions, as B's and C's. As yeshiva students with payot (sidelocks), hundreds of teenagers and other refugees trudged off the ships, government became even more puzzled. Few seemed to know what "B" and "C" categories meant. All that seemed crystal clear in late June 1940 was that Canada had to take what it got.

Letters demanding release soon poured into government from internees, their friends and relatives, concerned private organizations, and even public figures on two continents. Bad news, at least for the Canadian authorities, travelled fast. On 16 July, Charles Ritchie, then a diplomat in the Canadian embassy, recorded in his London diary: "I now hear that the ferocious internees whom the British Government begged us on bended knees to take to Canada to save this country from their nefarious activities are mostly entirely inoffensive anti-Nazi refugees who have been shovelled out to Canada at a moment's notice where they may have a disagreeable time."[19] Confirmation that these were indeed legitimate refugees was not long in coming. On 22 July, Massey wrote to the Dominions Office insisting that the Canadian government be told why it had received "innocent refugees" instead of the dangerous internees it had consented to accept. Massey cabled Canada: "Home Office state unofficially that a substantial number of anti-Nazi refugees have been transferred.... In addition it appears that a number of individuals were sent to Canada by mistake after their release had already been ordered."[20] The number of refugees among the internees soon grew from "some" to almost all. Officials responded that the problem of the interned refugees belonged to the British. Canada was keeping its promise—guarding those sent.

The British urged the Dominion governments to release their refugees rather than force them to risk the dangerous Atlantic crossing once again. Those who wished to join the British Pioneer Corps (a non-fighting unit) were soon able to return to Britain. Also released were scientists who had been working on top-secret military intelligence technology, and a few others who were needed for war work. The rest languished in Canadian camps. Eighteen when he was interned, aspiring writer Henry Kreisel kept a diary in the camps. He envied those who had the courage to return to Britain. He wrote: "A list comes out bearing the names of 61 men to be returned to England. Everyone longs to be on this list, everybody is sick of internment. We want freedom, even if there are bombs in England and none here. Internment bears heavy on my nerves, the barbed wire seems almost choking me. Freedom, freedom."[21]

After a decade of concerted efforts to keep the door firmly closed against Jewish immigration, the unexpected arrival of close to 2,500 largely Jewish refugees was greeted with great unease in many quarters of the Canadian government. As for the niceties of who was or was not dangerous, Canada chose to ignore the problem of differentiating among them as long and as stubbornly as possible. Whether government's initial motives were anti-immigrant, anti-refugee, or anti-Jewish is open to conjecture. In this early period, officials chose to plead ignorance. At first this seemed a legitimate approach; certainly the records were confused. But as time dragged on for the incarcerated, the validity of this strategy began to wear thin. The motives were increasingly clear: Canada had resisted all pressures in the past to grant admission to Jewish refugees, and they were determined not to let Jews gain entry through the back door of internment.

Camp Administrations

While officials at the highest level of government were well informed early on, the military in charge of the camps were not. The officers who ran Canadian internment camps had expected military prisoners; instead they were confronted with civilians brandishing petitions and orthodox Jews requesting kosher food. The refugees were bewildered by their reception. Mostly German and Austrian Jews, they had barely evaded the growing abyss of the Holocaust—a fate they comprehended better than anyone in Canada—only to find themselves victims once again. Leo Klag was a twenty-year-old student from Berlin. His father and brother had disappeared on Kristallnacht, and he had escaped to England in February 1939. "The morale was certainly low," Klag explained, "there was no getting away from it. It was low . . . because many of the people left families behind in Germany. There were young married people who left babies, young children. . . . The only thing that could boost their morale was the fact you said to yourself, after all, you're better off than in a deportation camp in Poland. That was the only way to look at it."[22]

The refugees were spread out in makeshift prisoner-of-war camps in New Brunswick, Quebec, and Ontario. While some commandants and guards displayed tolerance, if not sympathy for their prisoners, others combined anti-German and anti-Jewish attitudes when dealing with them. Major Ellwood, commandant of Camp N in Sherbrooke, Quebec, expressed this attitude in the camp's War Diary: "In spite of the fact that a certain percentage may be heartily anti-Nazi, it cannot be forgotten that they are German-born Jews. Jews still retain much of the same instinct they had 1,940 years ago, and these in particular are apt to try and take advantage of privileges which once given result in demands for more. The combination of this insidious instinct and the well-known characteristics of the German habit of breaking every pledge ever made is not a particularly easy one to handle except by maintaining strict discipline."[23]

The internees were hardly compliant. There was a united struggle to secure decent living conditions and release. Through democratically elected spokesmen, the refugees presented memoranda, petitions, and appeals to the administration and outside organizations. When camp conditions became intolerable, they resorted to strikes, disobedience, and general insubordination. Ellwood was likely responding to a petition from thirty-one of his prisoners, which complained: "In the eyes of most internees such conditions constitute a humiliation which does not increase their willingness to cooperate and to listen to reason." After seven months incarcerated in Canada, they protested that "the language with which they have been addressed . . . can only be described as abusive, insulting and very undignified, and their ways of treating internees is most humiliating. The use of such language together with threats of maltreatment have been held . . . to be indications . . . of hostility on the part of their custodians which . . . they cannot but resent."[24]

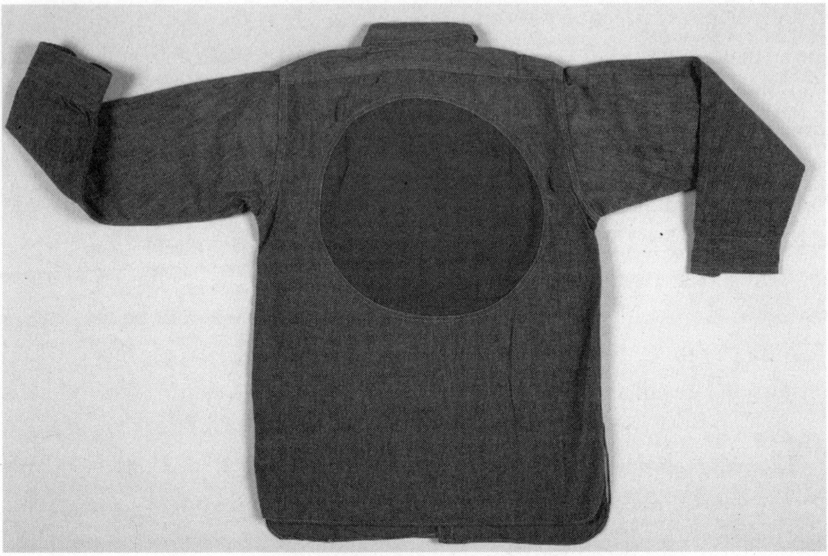

Figure 17.1. "The uniform an internee is required to wear is both degrading and unworthy of a civilization that believes in encouraging the individual, rather than treading on his soul. It was disturbing to find distinguished university professors dressed as clowns. The red circle, which is commonly supposed to be a target for the machine guns, is a shabby insult to men who are ready to wear the red cross."—Alexander Paterson, "Report on Civilian Internees Sent from the United Kingdom to Canada During the Unusually Fine Summer of 1940." Photo: Harry Seidler internment camp uniform, State Library of New South Wales.

For up to three and a half years the refugees languished in camps that had changing names (from "Prisoner of War" to "Refugee") and a wide range of administrative styles. Some were benevolent, some not so much. Colonel Campbell commanded Camp Q in Monteith, Ontario. Responding to internee complaints, he "pointed out to this leader that he must remember that there was a very serious war on and that their troubles were of comparative unimportance . . . in the meantime they must be patient and maintain proper discipline and decent standards of cleanliness."[25] Although this kind of response seemed reasonable, the recurring comments in War Diaries and correspondence about "cleanliness" were both a typical military obsession and a reference to underlying anti-Semitic attitudes toward the "dirty Jews." When Canada's first female Senator, Cairine Wilson—a tireless advocate for refugees—wrote a seasonal greeting to the internees, commending them for their "unusual form of sacrifice," Director of Internment Operations Colonel Hubert Stethem reiterated the military view: "The majority of persons in the camps," he wrote, "have no interest in the present life and death struggle in which we are engaged. They are self-centred and would not turn a hand to help along a British victory, and the claim that they are refugees from Nazi oppression has, they feel, placed them in a position where they can do or demand anything. Encouraging this feeling is extremely harmful to them as it prevents them from trying to help themselves."[26]

How could they "help themselves"? Camp administrators enforced the regulations very narrowly and saw little need or room for flexibility. This left the refugees at the mercy of the camp guards and officers. Privileges could be granted and withdrawn arbitrarily. On 25 June 1941, an order-in-council created a commissioner of Refugee Camps and removed jurisdiction of the three remaining camps from the Department of National Defence to the secretary of state. Yet the military refused to cede real control; orders were still to be obeyed, censorship of mail continued, and visitors were strictly controlled. Lieutenant-colonel Reginald Sydney Walter Fordham, a lawyer from Niagara Falls who had been a prisoner of war during the First World War, took Stethem's place. Constance Hayward worked with Senator Wilson. She remembered that there was little to celebrate. "He was a man of integrity; he was fair," she commented, "but he had a military background and he first saw these people as German. . . . When he started it was difficult to understand the mentality of the men in the camp. To him it was a military camp. Here was this group of nervous, excitable people who felt they were being mistreated and this was a psychology he didn't understand."[27]

All the refugees suffered the effects of years of persecution, flight, and fear for family caught in the Nazi web. Walter Igersheimer was a twenty-three-year-old medical student when he was interned. In his memoir, he described the despair many felt: "Here we are: rich men poor men, scientists and businessmen, artists, factory workers, and students, all thrown into the same pot. After sliding down into this pit of frustrated hopes, of degradation and misery, we all look alike. This decline has happened in just a few months. What will happen to us if we are interned for a whole year, or as long as seven years?"[28] Thirty-nine-year-old Leonard Spanier remembered: "I would wake up in the middle of the night. Then I would ask myself—am I dreaming it? Is it real? . . . You, who run away from Hitler. You are interned by the British?. . . . That happened to me very often."[29]

The basic problem of internment remained—the incarceration of innocent men. On this the government seemed immovable. The camp boys pressed

Figure 17.2. Camp L, Quebec City, 1940. Drawing by Harry Seidler (1923–2006). Harry moved to Australia in 1948 where he became a prominent architect. Courtesy of Penelope Seidler.

relentlessly for release. "We have been repeatedly promised that our cases—one humble word for the misery and tragedy of our present situation—would be reconsidered," one of them wrote in his camp's newspaper. "We have been promised this and that. . . . We have waited patiently for some concessions, some alterations with regard to our position as persons interned without even knowing why. A convict gets an idea of why he has to serve his sentence. The murderer knows why he is not free, but we do not know. What will be our fate?"[30] Policy-makers preferred to avoid the issues. Complaining about Canadian intransigence, one British official poked holes in their subterfuges. Authorities, he wrote, believed "the term refugee . . . so far from being held to denote an individual to whom sympathy is due, is regarded as equating with Jew, Communist, something we don't like and don't want. Prisoners of war could be understood, and could also possibly be used eventually in exchange for Canadian prisoners. Refugees are just a burden."[31]

Most of the refugees, frustrated as they were, tried to make the best of their situation. Erwin Schild found himself living with a large group of teenage yeshiva students like himself. Not only did they "continue their own studies but [they] set up study opportunities for others. There was religious worship daily, and joyous celebration of the festivals. Some students and also nonstudents studied, taught and followed the high standards of Jewish interpersonal ethics, and elevated what could have been a rough prison lifestyle by means of their gentle and unselfish deportment. While striving to refine their own conduct and hone the edge of their moral character through the quiet practice of a religious discipline, they set a high tone of the entire observant community."[32] Egon Kenton was in his twenties and had worked in his family's insurance company in Düsseldorf. He found internment made him "a much better person. All the experience. Because I was rather spoiled. I came from a wealthy home and . . . mixing with the working people and seeing their point of view. . . . They got a much bigger kick out of life than we did because they took it much easier. . . . And I learned to relax a little, which I never did before." But Kenton admitted it was not easy for everyone. He felt some "lost their guts to live. . . . You have to keep your morale up, this is the main thing I figured, and some people would become terribly sloppy. They wouldn't work, they would let everything go. And the group that I associated with, we made sure that we dressed neatly—our clothing was always clean . . . we would never let ourselves go. It keeps you going the right way. . . . Anything that would be demoralizing I would just stay away from. You don't want to talk about unpleasant things. You try to keep your morale up, to talk about the future, the pleasant things and you try to keep as busy as possible."[33]

Dale Brown represented the YMCA and often visited the internees. He reported on his observations about life in the Île aux Noix camp. "I went walking out on the river ice this morning," Brown wrote, "and caught the sharp, icy wind full in the face but that is simply what the fellows here experience every cold day, and there is no getting away from it for them. . . . I stepped into the hut where on one side of a partition the camouflage networkers were slowly weaving their nets . . . and on the other side men were trying to read and study in their small reading room; everything from Esquire to intricate Biochemical equations were absorbing their minds. . . . I played some ping pong with a couple of the chaps and was beaten both times; then another fellow showed me some of his favourite card tricks."[34] "I tried to kill my time," recalled Julius Pfeiffer, known as the camp joker, "in order to forget that I was in the camp, didn't know what to do with my life. I didn't know where my wife was, whether she was alive—my two children, my parents, so I made jokes." After the war he found his wife and children; they had survived Bergen-Belsen. His parents perished in Birkenau.[35]

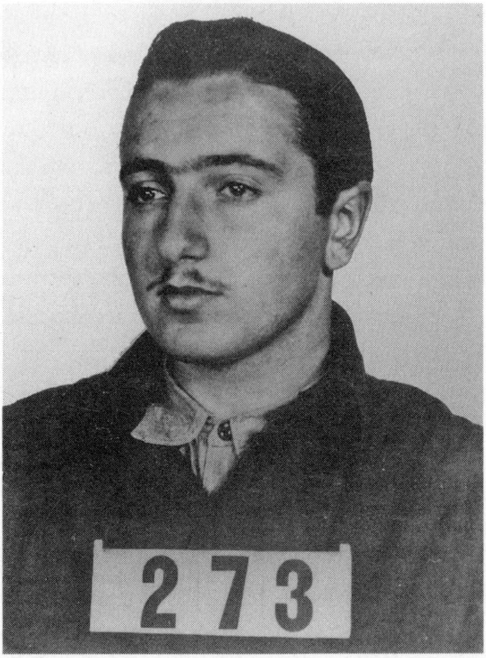

Figure 17.3. Canadian Internment Camp identification photo, 1940. Marcell Seidler (1919–1977) took a series of photos with a pinhole camera in Camp N, Sherbrooke, Quebec. He later moved to Australia and became a professional photographer. Courtesy of Penelope Seidler and Marcell Seidler family.

Saddled with refugees it did not want, the government maintained a policy of inertia regarding their welfare, their status, and their release. The alteration to Refugee Camps proved little more than cosmetic. Policy-makers preferred to avoid the issues. If continued internment was disagreeable to the internees, their presence in Canada was no pleasure to the government either.

Refugee Advocacy

While the interned refugees fought for their freedom from behind the barbed wire, they were not alone in their struggle. The Canadian Jewish community was represented in refugee matters by the United Jewish Refugee and War Relief Agencies (UJRA). An arm of the Canadian Jewish Congress (CJC), the UJRA was directed by an determined young Montreal lawyer, Saul Hayes.

What Canadian Jewish representatives felt they could or could not do for the internees was largely determined by their relationship with the government. The war against Germany added more fuel to the fire of a Canadian anti-immigration feeling grounded in economic recession, indifference to the problems of the outside world, and an anti-Semitism that was overt in Quebec and socially acceptable among Anglo-Canadians elsewhere. In a period when the term "refugee" meant "Jew," and Jews were seen as unassimilable immigrants, the CJC knew that release of the interned refugees would not be welcome. It was with the burden of past failures of rescue, and the community's priority of directing aid to the suffering Jews of Europe, that the UJRA gingerly approached government on their behalf. For almost a year the UJRA focused its efforts on getting the internees, many of whom held U.S. quota numbers, across the border. Only when that scheme failed did they address release in Canada. Meanwhile, they provided communication, kosher food, religious items, and a multitude of materials to the camps to ameliorate everyday life for the internees.

The perceived lack of tangible action by the organized Jewish community was a sore point among the camp boys. Julius Pfeiffer, who held a PhD in law and was well into his thirties by this time, wrote, "The help that did come from the CJC officials was in the form of a beautiful Chesterfield set for the reading room where from 30 to 40 daily, weekly and monthly papers were available. Unfortunately for our spirits they felt compelled to write to us, who were hoping to be released within weeks, that they had paid for those subscriptions for 'two years.'"[36] The refugees were feisty and it wasn't just the camp administrations that were frustrated with them. "I had many unpleasant dealings with the internees," Saul Hayes recalled, "and I don't blame them. What the hell, when you're cooped up like that. . . . They know they're innocent. They know they're victims. Try and convince them it's got to take time because the people who have the authority don't know what you know."[37]

But internees were grateful for the visits from various groups trying to help ease the insult of incarceration. Jewish communities and their rabbis in the cities neighbouring the camps provided support and tried to help fill the religious needs of the refugees. The Jewish Community Council of Montreal sent Passover goods to the camps, though the orthodox Jews in the New Brunswick camp were not satisfied and pooled their funds in order to obtain separate dishes and kitchen utensils for the holiday. Remarking on the visits of members of an orthodox Jewish youth group to his camp on the Île aux Noix, observant Jew Harry Loewy wrote: "It is also most gratifying to see that these visitors are prepared to do sacrifices just for the sake of seeing us—complete strangers from another continent. These are hard-working people who use their free Sunday afternoon to drive out here, a round trip of about 100 miles from

Montreal. This is really and truly something." Loewy exclaimed, "All these kind people have helped immensely to restore our faith in human kindness. We begin to realize that we are not alone after all. . . . We shall never forget this."[38]

Looking back at those difficult years, Saul Hayes admitted: "I don't think we did enough at the beginning for these people, because we knew they were safe in Canada and we were trying to rescue people who weren't safe. . . . The fact that we couldn't get them out only underlies what I'm saying. . . . We paid more attention to those who were still [in Europe] than we did to those who had three square meals a day and who were in a safe position."[39]

While the internees were physically safe, they often faced harassment from hostile guards and commandants. Their advocates faced a similar struggle. This was clear to Alexander Paterson, His Majesty's Commissioner of Prisons, who had been sent to Canada to work on the release of the refugees. He arranged return passage for those willing to join the Pioneer Corps in the United Kingdom. He then pushed Canada to allow entry to the remaining prisoners. Paterson was infuriated with the treatment accorded the internees who remained. When quiet diplomacy failed, he unleashed a volley of criticism at the Canadian government. Paterson's critique of Canadian policy began with an apology that the British had "most unhappily misled you as to their degree of danger." He then suggested that the camps for anti-Nazis be separated from those for prisoners of war and pro-Nazi civilians and less stringent conditions of incarceration be applied. Paterson recommended the removal of the interned refugees from military jurisdiction since army officers invariably treated their charges as soldiers. This was neither appropriate nor desirable. Especially since it seemed "that in many cases the better brains should be inside the wire."[40] Paterson's report identified Col. Stethem as a particular barrier to better treatment. "[Stethem unleashed] a tirade against refugees and Jews and Voluntary Agencies," wrote Paterson. Stethem insisted "upon the need for a maximum degree of security, to the exclusion of every other consideration. This manifested itself in many directions, and particularly in the bitter distrust of all voluntary agencies. . . . All voluntary workers were regarded as smugglers and traffickers, the inevitable enemies of security and peace."[41] On 2 May 1941, Paterson's proposal was approved by cabinet, and Lieutenant-colonel Fordham replaced Stethem. Yet the underlying attitudes remained.

Alexander Paterson accomplished a great deal—the derogatory labelling of internees as prisoners of war was erased and, even more critically, after emigration to the United States receded as a possibility, he lent his weight to a program of release in Canada. If interned refugees were hesitantly and reluctantly released in Canada, it was largely through the spade work of Alexander Paterson.[42]

Paterson worked closely with the advocacy groups and they were informed of struggles he had with Canadian officials. Aware of the attitudes of those who held the lives of the refugees in their hands, the UJRA knew it needed the cooperation of another organization. One which could provide a supportive non-Jewish profile and thereby simplify the public relations problem of Jews helping "enemy aliens." Hayes therefore approached the Canadian National Committee on Refugees (CNCR). It had been formed in 1938 to focus public attention on the plight of refugees. The CNCR was a pressure group, composed of prominent non-Jews who felt morally bound to aid victims of fascism and included church leaders and wives of senators. Senator Cairine Wilson was its chairperson. A staunch Liberal and friend of Mackenzie King, Wilson devoted a great deal of energy to lobbying on behalf of refugees. "[Senator Wilson had] a sense of responsibility to her values," Constance Hayward explained. "Probably there was no other single cause—and she had several—to which she gave so much of herself and which counted for so much as the refugee committee. She was compassionate; she was indefatigable."[43] On the issue of the internees, the CNCR became, in essence, a non-sectarian front for the UJRA. Its major impetus and funding were, for the most part, provided by the UJRA.

The internees were not aware of the hoops through which these organizations had to jump to gain any concessions on their behalf. Constance Hayward was the executive secretary of the CNCR. She found working with the camp boys just as exasperating as did Hayes. "The refugees were not the easiest people to deal with," Hayward recalled. "I remember one morning saying to Senator Wilson I wish these boys didn't have so much of what it takes to make a refugee. Because they were argumentative and they were resistant to regimentation in camp. Of course they were sending messages out to all their friends and relatives in order to get help."[44]After a few months' internment, Stethem complained to Wilson. "It is safe to say," he wrote, "that the greater part of our time is being taken up with questions connected with these B and C internees. The office is being flooded with correspondence from relatives, friends, legal advisors, and a very large number of Jewish societies and refugee organizations. . . . It is desirable that all the various associations concerned should follow the procedure adopted in Great Britain and organize a joint unofficial body to represent . . . those who are concerned with the welfare of the refugees. In England this is known as the Central Department for Interned Refugees."[45] Soon the informal cooperation between the CNCR and the

UJRA led to the formation of the Central Committee for Interned Refugees (CCIR). For the first half of 1941 the CCIR had a limited range of activity. The internees were granted refugee status in July 1941 and the beginnings of an organized release program were organized. Social work was begun. Files were compiled, originally to assist emigration to the United States, and later to facilitate release in Canada. The CCIR tried to work with the refugees and their supporters. Yet, when community representatives gained access to the camps they often found the military uncooperative. "The poor refugees were cowed and were afraid to speak," reported Ben Robinson, a Montreal lawyer who visited on behalf of the CCIR. "It was quite humiliating to find one of the officers at your shoulder, listening to the questions . . . and finding that instead of obtaining a frank answer from the refugee, the answer is, on occasion, given by the officer. Nor was it any less humiliating to have your conversation interrupted."[46]

Another young Montreal lawyer, Stanley Goldner, was appointed liaison officer and accorded access to the camps on behalf of the CCIR. Goldner became a lifeline between the refugees and the committee. He had to walk a fine line between the military and the internees. In one of his early reports, Goldner explained his approach:

> A visit by a member of our Committee to any of the camps is the signal for a good deal of excitement. Officers of various camps have told me that often for two days after my departure the tension is such that ordinary duties are thrown off schedule. As it is essential to my liaison work that I at all times retain the confidence and goodwill of the officers of the camps . . . my relations with them would be strained if they should come to feel that whenever I turn up at their camp I was immediately going to tattle behind their backs in Ottawa. This would render me persona non grata and jeopordize [*sic*] the work I am trying to do.[47]

Along with their direct dealings with government, the CCIR began a campaign to educate the public about the true nature of the interned refugees, and push at policy from the outside. They distributed material among the Canadian Jewish community, appealing for assistance with content like: "Refugees Interned: Alien born, thus interned, they are innocent victims of a double-edged sword. Jews, young and old, scientists and tradesmen, craftsmen and unskilled. . . . We cannot allow them to be 'twice forgotten souls.'"[48] Committee members felt that a multi-pronged approach toward government might work. Hayward explained: "Government didn't like to show that they were doing anything in recognition of a voluntary organization. Even if we pushed them to do something they would do it but they would never acknowledge that it was a result of our request."[49] The CCIR worked with Paterson pressuring government for an alteration of status from internee to refugee, and for eventual release into Canada.

There were other religious and non-sectarian groups trying to help the camp boys. Some were brought in by the UJRA to demonstrate to government that the internees were not solely a Jewish concern. Hayes told his committee: "We know that the internees are really refugees behind barbed wire, but the public at large still looks at them as prisoners of war, therefore the assistance that we are to give must be rendered with circumspection and care. [It was] felt that it was up to us to enlist the support of outside organizations such as the YMCA and American groups in order to bring help to the internees, even if we shared in the cost. The main point was that it was impolitic for us to prosecute our work vigorously and ostentatiously."[50]

The War Prisoners Aid Committee of the YMCA, chaired by Sir Ernest MacMillan, principal of the Toronto Conservatory of Music, worked with the CCIR on behalf of the interned refugees. The YMCA program began in August 1940, prompted by its British counterpart, which had worked with the internees before their deportations. YMCA activities covered all internment camps; Nazis, prisoners of war, and refugees were all treated alike. While MacMillan pressured government officials, YMCA representatives provided material relief for the refugees. The YMCA liaison, Dale Brown, often commented on the morale of the refugees. In June 1942, after many of the refugees had been released, he visited the Sherbrooke camp. He wrote that "the personal contacts which come from these long visits are worth ever so much. One marvels at the persistence with which fellows carry on, and yet they see nothing remarkable in it."[51] Deeply sympathetic, Brown declared, "the determination on the part of some of them to keep themselves occupied and interested in the community life of the camp was magnificent to behold. No self-respecting person is willing to live under these conditions indefinitely if there is no reason for it."[52] Working under the YMCA umbrella were representatives of the World Student Christian Federation and the European Student Relief Fund (ESRF). Recreational equipment, books, films, art supplies, musical instruments, and Christian religious items were provided. Funds for the programs often came from the UJRA.

Release

Kurt Swinton (Schwitzer) was a young radio engineer. His mother and two brothers had arrived in Canada in June 1939 under special permit, and his case reached cabinet on 24 January 1941. Thomas Crerar, the minister in charge of immigration, recommended that the "government agree, as a matter of policy, to admit to Canada internees whose release was permitted by the United Kingdom government, where such internee had first degree relatives resident in Canada." This policy was approved, and by 18 February 1941 the first eight interned refugees were released. They were advised that their admission was temporary and they were required to keep in touch with the nearest immigration officer. After four months, if their records were satisfactory, their permits would be extended—for the duration of the war.[53]

On 1 April 1941, the question of internee release, and their immigration, was breached in Parliament. One member asked: "What is the possibility of some of these people being permitted to make a contribution in Canada towards defeat of our common enemy?" Another considered it "desirable" to grant admission to those who "wanted to stay here," adding that "they would be an asset to our country as I am sure they are to Great Britain."[54] Public opinion was also turning in the internees' favour. The logic of keeping men in custody whose sympathies lay with the Allies, and whose abilities were daily wasted, started to come under pointed criticism.

Beginning in the early months of internment the question of utilizing the refugees to remedy wartime labour shortages was raised within government. The under secretary on manpower policy approached the prime minister, suggesting "we should not forget the small pocket of anti-Nazi refugees . . . who are not only doing little or no useful work themselves, but keeping several hundred men employed in guarding them. Under present conditions it might be worth reviewing the policy that has kept these men idle and useless, at public expense . . . with a view to determining whether they could not, subject to any appropriate safeguards, be incorporated into the working population of the country for the duration of the war."[55] These attempts were vigorously obstructed by Immigration Director Blair, who argued: "At least 80% of them have tried unsuccessfully to get into the United States and having failed are now endeavouring to secure their release in Canada by hook or by crook. I expressed the opinion that a good many of them are much more interested in getting release than doing war work . . . I remarked that these internees seem to have great facilities for changing their coat like a chamelion [*sic*] and they are able in short notice to establish that they are qualified to work in almost any industry." Besides, release would "interfere" with the free labour refugees provided behind the barbed wire.[56]

The bulk of the most highly skilled men, many plucked from top secret war laboratories, had already been hurried back to Britain. The Minister of Munitions and Supply, C.D. Howe, had been alerted that skilled workers needed by the Canadian economy were locked up in camps and he wanted those particular men out. The release of Anton Fleybeck, a roof prism expert, was requested by the government's Research Enterprises Limited.[57] Four days after the decision to release the first eight refugees, cabinet authorized the release of Fleybeck "upon being made fully aware of the exceptionally secret nature of the work in which it was proposed that he be employed." The day after Fleybeck's release was approved, Howe discussed the general issue of skilled internees with Blair. Howe "thought that we ought to get these people out of the internment camps and keep them in Canada if they are skilled workers and safe." Paterson met Howe, and a survey found fifty to sixty machinists, toolmakers, and other technicians whose skills could be put to immediate use in Canada's war industry.[58] Blair felt trapped; except for delaying the process a little, he could do nothing to stop their release. Blair's defences were crumbling, and he feared release was a prelude to immigration. In a time of war, the pro-refugee lobby argued all the more forcefully, 2,000 educated and skilled men could only be a boon to Canada.

Eventually, schemes were worked out whereby individuals could be released to study if sponsored by Canadian families, farmers could request internees to help them, and skilled workers could be released for war work. The process was slow. Blair had the final authority on every case, and he used his power to obstruct the process. Once out of the camps, the threat of re-internment was constant. Men found themselves detained because they complained publicly about their treatment, or refused to remain with their government-approved employers. The CCIR cautiously but persistently fought to widen the cracks in Blair's formidable barriers. Just as Blair often predicted, each release became a precedent for his "Jewish friends" to squeeze more refugees into Canada "by hook or by crook."

By November 1943, with the horrific fate of European Jewry plastered all over the news, Canada agreed to release the remaining interned refugees. The last refugee camp was closed and about fifty re-interned, mentally and physically ill, and otherwise "unreleasable" refugees were shipped back to Britain. Internment was over.

The 966 interned refugees who were eventually released into Canada remained accountable to various government departments and lived in a perpetual state of legal limbo. They held documents that had to be endorsed every month by local immigration officers and the RCMP. Changes of address and intercity travel had to be reported. Their status as temporary residents in Canada left the threat of postwar deportation hanging over their heads. Marriage was discouraged, and their new wives faced loss of citizenship. When thirty-five-year-old Ernst Neuburger, who had been released to a farm, became engaged to a Jewish woman in Hamilton, Ontario, he was forced by Blair to sign a statement undertaking "if permitted to remain outside the refugee camp, that I will remain with my employer and do my best to render satisfactory service and further that as I have no immigration status in Canada and may be returned to England . . . I will defer my marriage until my immigration status has been decided. I agree that failure to observe these two conditions will make me liable to immediate return to the refugee camp." It took two years for Saul Hayes to successfully intervene on Neuburger's behalf so he could proceed with his marriage.[59]

Alfred Bader was accepted at Queen's University in Kingston. Before he left the camp, he "had to sign a form renouncing all claims against H M Canadian government—a small price to pay for freedom. . . . I was also cautioned not to tell anyone where I had been, otherwise I would be sent back to the camp, and I had to report weekly to the local office of the RCMP."[60] Gerry Waldston remembered that "the only thing that was told to us . . . is behave well and be sure that we don't make any trouble . . . otherwise we'd be returned immediately. This fear was with us all the time. . . . So with that kind of attitude you don't mingle in politics, you don't join anything, you don't do anything wrong."[61]

Students, with the support of their sponsors, fared extremely well. Harry Seidler would become a renowned Australian architect. He was eighteen, attending the University of Manitoba, where he enjoyed the irony that "after being guarded by soldiers with machine guns, exactly one week following my release I was such a soldier taking COTC training. . . . I remember making a point of reporting to the mounted police, which I was required to do every week, wearing the King's uniform."[62]

It was harder for those released as workers, especially the older refugees. Permission was needed to change employers, and many complained of exploitation. "The Imperial Optical Company needed—what I will call slave labour," Egon Kenton recalled, "because we were grossly underpaid I think . . . anybody who knew anything about optical or lenses was asked to work at a certain wage and even if it had been for free I would have taken it because I wanted to get out of camp. . . . The pay was very low." Kenton's complaint was a common one. It was mirrored by the experiences of the survivors who came to Canada on various labour schemes after the war. "The thing is you don't expect it from a Jewish man somehow, because we had nothing, absolutely nothing. . . . We couldn't buy anything because we couldn't save," said Kenton.[63] The men sent to farms were particularly vulnerable. But five years of uncertainty finally ended on 25 October 1945 when cabinet passed an order-in-council allowing first immigrant status, then citizenship to refugees who were then living on temporary residential permits.[64] With all impediments gone, the camp boys were finally free to create their new lives.

Reflections on Internment

Speaking to a meeting of the CNCR in January 1941, Alexander Paterson told Senator Wilson and her committee that "over a period of years his work as His Majesty's Commissioner for Prisons had made him familiar with tragedy, but never, he said, had he seen such a degree of misery or heard such tragic stories, as he had encountered in the Internment Camps in Canada."[65] In the decades following the war, none of the refugees forgot those experiences under Nazism they had related to Paterson, nor their years in the Canadian camps. It marked their lives and determined the progress of their adjustment to the Canadian and Jewish communities.

Some internees found comfort in retaining their camp friends. They had already lost much, but the camaraderie of fellow internees allowed them to share common feelings. Every internee might ask: "Why was I protected? Who protected me? How was I chosen? How come the other ones all went to Dachau, Buchenwald and never came out? All my cousins are dead. They cleaned up all my friends. All my friends are dead."[66] Yet, as they recalled camp life, it was in the context of deep and abiding relationships. Gerry Waldston realized: "This was my family. These were the people I was closest to. These were the people I understood."[67] For most, marriage, schools, and jobs brought new contacts and eased adjustment. Some never overcame the despair of internment and buried the experience, refusing to socialize with other camp boys. "Every once in a while," a reluctant interviewee explained in 1979, "I speak to somebody about it and usually I don't sleep for three days, even now. So I'm very hesitant to talk about it. I never think about it. I have it in the back of my mind."[68] Others openly reflected on their internment experience, sometimes seeing it as part of the common adjustments all survivors of the

Holocaust endured. "Naturally you lost several years of your life," reflected Heinz Warschauer. "My whole life didn't develop the way I wanted it to. But these are romantic dreams. . . . You make things do."[69] "I think of it every day of my life," explained Gerhard Jacobson. "Till I die, I will never forget it. I can't."[70]

With time, and a perspective on the enormity of the Holocaust, most interned refugees eased into their places in the Canadian community. For some there was a realization that the internment experience, scarring as it was, saved their lives and opened new horizons. Indeed, many of the camp boys succeeded in Canada, and their achievements far exceeded anyone's expectations of them. For some this serves to magnify the irony of their internment and intensifies their pride in their achievements. According to several camp boys, internment and the resulting hardships created its own motivation to excel in all they did. Many proved their worth far beyond even their own wildest dreams: "We all received a drive—to make up for the lost years we had as kids. The totally useless two years. . . . We had to make up fast, quick and get somewhere and try and recreate the type of life that we remembered as children . . . it's because we had nobody to rely on. They had to make it on their own. . . . We just couldn't afford to fail. We had to succeed."[71]

The achievements of the interned refugees belied the arguments of the many government representatives and officials who opposed their final resettlement in Canada. Their story is a complex one, directly touching the governments of three countries, voluntary organizations on two continents, and the politics of the Second World War and the Holocaust. Refugee advocates developed strategies that aided them in battles to come. And Canada benefited immensely from the contributions of these "accidental immigrants." Their accomplishments became a beacon for the many refugees who followed, as Canada slowly opened its doors to the persecuted and oppressed.

Notes

1 Erwin Schild, *The Very Narrow Bridge. A Memoir of an Uncertain Passage* (Toronto: Adath Israel Congregation/Malcolm Lester, 2001), 222.

2 "Rabbi Emeritus of the Adath Israel Congregation, he has devoted many years to improving dialogue between the Christian and Jewish faiths, promoting harmony at home and abroad. An active member of the community, he is admired by his contemporaries for his leadership, generosity, commitment to multiculturalism and positive interfaith relations. He has travelled extensively throughout Germany as an invited lecturer. A Holocaust survivor, he is the author of *World Through My Window* and *The Very Narrow Bridge,* which emphasize the significance of tolerance, values and ethics in our daily lives." (Order of Canada Citation, 30 May 2001).

3 Research on the interned refugees was conducted for: Paula J. Draper, "The Accidental Immigrants: Canada and the Interned Refugees" (PhD diss., University of Toronto/OISE, 1983).

4 Gordon Thomas, *Voyage of the Damned* (New York: Stein and Day, 1974); John Mendelsohn, *Jewish Emigration: The SS* St. Louis *Affair and Other Cases* (New Jersey: The Lawbook Exchange, 2010).

5 Eric Koch, *Deemed Suspect: A Wartime Blunder* (Toronto: Methuen, 1980).

6 Benzion Patkin, *The Dunera Internees* (Berkeley: Benmir Books, 1979); Paul Bartrop and Gabrielle Eisen, *The Dunera Affair* (Sydney: Jewish Museum of Australia, 1990).

7 Francois Lafitte, *The Internment of Aliens* (London: Penguin Books, 1940); Chaim Raphael, *Memoirs of a Special Case* (London: Chatto and Windus, 1962); Peter and Leni Gillman, *Collar the Lot: How Britain Interned and Expelled Its Wartime Refugees* (London: Quartet Books, 1980).

8 Deborah Dwork and Robert Jan van Pelt, *Flight from the Reich: Refugee Jews, 1933–1946* (New York: W.W. Norton, 2009), 277.

9 Irving Abella and Harold Troper, *None Is Too Many: Canada and the Jews of Europe, 1933–1948* (Toronto: Lester and Orpen Dennys, 1982), 72n; Franklin Bialystok, *Delayed Impact. The Holocaust and the Canadian Jewish Community* (Montreal and Kingston: McGill-Queen's University Press, 2000), 27.

10 Gerald Tulchinsky, *Branching Out: The Transformation of the Canadian Jewish Community* (Toronto: Stoddart, 1998), 60. Gerhard Baessler, *Sanctuary Denied: Refugees from the Third Reich and Newfoundland Immigration Policy, 1906–1949* (St John's: Memorial University of Newfoundland, 1992).

11 See http://www.enemyaliens.ca/.

12 Along with interviews collected in Vancouver for the exhibit, videotaped interviews are available in the USC Shoah Foundation collection, including those collected in Montreal and Toronto by local community projects.

13 Along with several cited in this paper is Ernst Zimmerman, *The Little Third Reich on Lake Superior: A History of the Canadian Internment Camp R*, ed. Michel S. Beaulieu and David K. Ratz (Edmonton: University of Alberta, 2015); Jaleen Grove, *Oscar Cahen: His Life and Work* (Toronto: Art Institute of Canada, 2016).

14 See Irving Abella and Harold Troper, "The Line Must Be Drawn Somewhere: Canada and Jewish Refugees, 1933–39," *Canadian Historical Review* (June 1979) and *None Is Too Many*.

15 In the end Canada received 2,284 B and C internees. A further 2,075 went to the Australian desert.

16 Cabinet War Committee Minutes, 10, 14 June 1940, RG2, 7C, vol. 13, Library and Archives Canada (LAC); DEA to Massey, 10 June 1940, RG25, D1, vol. 824, f. 713, LAC.

17 Canada, Parliament, Parliamentary Debates (Commons) (19 June 1940), 911.

18 Massey to DEA, 29 June, 2 July 1940, RG24, vol. 6585, f. 421, also RG25, D1, vol. 824, f. 713, LAC.

19 Charles Ritchie, *The Siren Years: A Canadian Diplomat Abroad, 1937–45* (Toronto: Macmillan, 1974), 61.

20 Massey to Caldecote, 22 July 1940, D035/996/PW19/143, PRO, GB; Massey to DEA, 26 July 1940, CRF 621K40, pt. 1, DEA.

21 Henry Kreisel, "Diary of an Internment," *White Pelican* (Summer 1974): 24–25 (diary entry dated 14 June 1941). Kreisel became a prominent Canadian novelist, chair of English department and later vice-president of the University of Alberta. He was made an officer of the Order of Canada in 1988 ("his fiction has a universal quality and is a bridge between the worlds of Europe and Canada").

22 Interview with Leo Klag, Montreal, 10 September 1978.

23 RG24, C17, vol. 15, 399 no. 42 (War Diary, Camp N), folder 1, 22 February 1941, LAC.

24 War Diary, Camp N, folder 1, vol. 4, Appendix 2, 16 January 1941, LAC.

25 Department of National Defence, "Camp Q," 24 July 1940, RG24, C4, vol. 11253, f. 11223, LAC.

26 Cairine Wilson's "Christmas Letter," December 1940, R624, C4, vol. 6581, f. 333, LAC; Ibid. Stethem to Wilson, December 1940.

27 Interview with Constance Hayward, Toronto, 13, 14 June 1978.

28 Walter W. Igersheimer, *Blatant Injustice: The Story of a Jewish Refugee from Nazi Germany Imprisoned in Britain and Canada during WWII* (Montreal and Kingston: McGill-Queen's University Press, 2005), 76–77. Igersheimer became a professor of psychiatry at Yale and a pioneer in group therapy.

29 Interview with Leonard Spanier, Montreal, 24 July 1979.

30 "Goodbye Camp L," *Camp L Chronicle* #2, n.d.

31 Livingstone to Hoffman, 19 November 1941, CRF, 621AF40, part I, DEA.

32 Erwin Schild, "A Canadian Footnote to the Holocaust," *Canadian Jewish Historical Society Journal* 5, no. 1 (Spring 1981): 36.

33 Interview with Egon Kenton, Toronto, 30 January 1977.

34 Dale Brown, "Report of Educational Activities in Internment and Refugee Camps in Canada for December and January 1941–42," D. Brown private papers.

35 Interview with Dr. Julius Pfeiffer, Montreal, 7 September 1978.

36 Julius Pfeiffer, "From Amsterdam to Montreal for $1.25," *Jewish Life Magazine* (New York: Union of Orthodox Jewish Congregations of America, July 1973), 47.

37 Interview with Saul Hayes, Montreal, 11 September 1978.

38 Harry Loewy, "Days Behind Barbed Wire" (unpublished manuscript), Canadian Jewish Congress Archives, Montreal (CJC/M), 336.

39 Interview with Saul Hayes, Montreal, 11 September 1978.

40 *Report on Civilian Internees Sent from the United Kingdom to Canada during the Unusually Fine Summer of 1940*, Dominion Office 35/996/PW19/1/82, Public Record Office, Great Britain (Paterson Report).

41 *Paterson Report*, 2–6.

42 For a detailed account of the cooperation between the CCIR and the British representative, Alexander Paterson, and the successful strategy to gain release of students to educational institutions, see: Paula J. Draper, "'The Camp Boys': Refugees from Nazism Interned in Canada, 1940–1944," in *Enemies Within: Italian and Other Internees in Canada and Abroad*, ed. Franca Iacovetta, Roberto Perin, and Angelo Principe (Toronto: University of Toronto Press, 1999).

43 Interview with Constance Hayward, Toronto, 13, 14 June 1978.

44 Ibid.

45 Stethem to Wilson, 27 December 1940, General Files, CJC/M.

46 Robinson to Wilson, 4 September 1941, Minutes, UJRA Internment Operations Committee lists of Supplies sent to Camps by UJRA, 26 September 1941, General Files, CJC/M.

47 CCIR, Goldner Memorandum, 5 April 1941, General Files, CJC/M.

48 Flyer, UJRA 1941–1942 National Campaign, General Files, CJC/M.

49 Interview with Constance Hayward, Toronto, 13, 14 June 1978.

50 Minutes, UJRA, Meeting of Eastern Division, 21 October 1940, General Files, CJC/M.

51 Brown to Mackie, 5 June 1942, CRF 286640, DEA.

52 Dale Brown, Report of Educational Activities in Camps, 5 June 1942, p. 6, Dale Brown private papers.

53 Minutes, Cabinet War Committee, 24 January 1941, RG2, 7C, reel 1, LAC; RCMP Memorandum, District Superintendent to Christison, 15 February 1941, RG76, Internees, part 1, LAC. Kurt Swinton was one of the few internees permitted to enlist in the Canadian army where he became an officer.

54 Canada, Parliament, Parliamentary Debates (Commons) (1 April 1941), 2058–59.

55 Quoted in Pearson to Wrong, 15 December 1941, CRF 621AF40, part 1, DEA.

56 Blair Memorandum, 17 October 1941, RG76, Internees, part 2, LAC.

57 Sheils to Stethem, 13 January 1941, R676, Internees, pt. 1, LAC. The need for men with skills like Fleybeck's was underscored in the numerous requests for his release which persisted through April 1941. "The great importance of our obtaining the services of anyone who is skilled in the production of roof prisms renders it advisable that we pursue the matter of Fleybeck's release as relentlessly as we can. So far, despite frequent requests to England for a roof prism expert, we have not made much progress." Sheils to Stethem, 4 February 1941, R624, C4, vol. 6593, 5212, LAC.

58 Minutes, Cabinet War Committee Meeting, 29 January 1941, RG2, 7C, reel 1, LAC; Blair Memorandum for file, 30 January 1941, RG76, Internees, part 1, LAC; Ibid., Blair Memorandum for file, 12 March 1941.

59 Neuburger Statement, 2 December 1942, E. Neuburger file, CJC/M.

60 Alfred Bader, *Adventures of a Chemist Collector* (London: Weidenfeld and Nicolson, 1995), 33. Dr. Bader became a chemist, businessman, art collector, and philanthropist. Queen's University has been a large beneficiary. Bader received the CBE (Order of the British Empire).

61 Interview with Gerry Waldston, Toronto, 1 April 1979.

62 Letter from Harry Seidler to Paula Draper, 10 April 1978.

63 Interview with Egon Kenton, Toronto, 30 January 1977.

64 Abella and Troper, *None Is Too Many*, 202.

65 Minutes, CNCR Twelfth Executive Committee Meeting, 24 January 1941, MG28, V 43, vol. 6 f. 27, LAC.

66 Interview with Max Abusch, Toronto, 20 January 1977.

67 Interview with Gerry Waldston.

68 Interview with Dr. Kurt Hellman, Toronto, 15 March 1979. Dr. Hellman became an anaesthetist in Saskatchewan, then Vancouver.

69 Interview with Heinz Warschauer, Toronto, 14 January 1977. Warschauer became the director of education at Holy Blossom Temple in Toronto.

70 Interview with Gerhard Jacobson, Montreal, 10 September 1978.
71 Interview with Gerry Waldston.

CHAPTER 18

Narrating Internment, Narrating Canada: Wartime Experiences of German Merchant Seamen

JUDITH KESTLER

One of the least known examples of wartime civilian internment in Canada is the experience of German merchant seamen. Based on a larger study concerning the Canadian internment of German merchant seamen as a whole, this essay focuses on the making of the specific Canadian captivity narratives related to this experience.[1] Analyzing oral history interviews with former internees as well as autobiographical writings, the essay develops a cultural anthropological interpretation of these narratives. It aims at reconstructing the inner logic of these internment tales and at contextualizing the findings within the larger historical, cultural, and biographical framework. As the German merchant shipping crews are a relatively unknown group of internees and have seldom even been mentioned in studies about civilian internment, this chapter will also briefly examine both the composition of these crews and the circumstances that led to their capture.[2]

German merchant shipping crews brought together people of different generations, social backgrounds, and professions. Young men who were aiming to become captain of a ship hoped to lay the foundation for their nautical career; others, often very young boys, had already trained as mechanics and worked as assistant engineers on board of the ships. Apart from the few officers—mainly the captain, his nautical officers, and the engineers—there were other ranks who typically worked together on board of a merchant ship only for a short period of time. All of them were civilians. On average, the crews were rather young: in 1934, two-thirds of all German crew members were between fifteen and thirty-five years of age.[3] This was due to older seamen quitting seafaring altogether after a few years in order to seek land-based employment that would allow them to live with their families year-round.

It is difficult to make any reliable blanket statements concerning the political leanings of the German merchant shipping crews. From the beginning of National Socialism, merchant seamen were special objects of the Nazis' indoctrination efforts, because they travelled around the world and could, on the one hand, act as representatives of the new Germany as well as connect the German Reich to the many Germans living abroad.[4] On the other hand, they were also exposed to manifold experiences and ideas that could have lessened their commitment to National Socialism.[5] So the National Socialists undertook great efforts to shape the seamen into loyal followers. This was difficult because often the crews were too small to ensure regular political and ideological instruction, and moreover, on the high seas, Germany was far away. However, between 1933 and 1939, the number of German merchant seamen that were members of the NSDAP rose constantly.[6] But still this fact is not enough evidence as to the intensity of their Nazi conviction. It is safe to say that there was a mixture of ardent Nazis, Nazi sympathizers, communist, or otherwise antifascist resistance crew members, as well as politically indifferent seamen, on board these vessels. It is also safe to say that all of these men had to cooperate in their professional life on board the ships. After their capture and incarceration this cooperation became more difficult to maintain, as political positions shifted under the influence of the war and the long captivity exacerbated conflicts among the internees.

German merchant vessels played an important role in the strategic planning of the German Reich. For this reason Germany tried to get as many ships as possible back to German harbours in order to use them for the transportation of supplies, troops, and weapons after the outbreak of the war.[7] But this was no easy task as more than 400 German merchant ships were scattered around the world in September of 1939.[8] Even before the beginning of the war, the German Maritime Warfare Command sent official messages informing ships' captains of the imminent danger of war. The ships were to return to Germany, or, if this was not possible within a few days, go to neutral or Axis countries. For the crews, this latter option created a difficult and nerve-racking situation, because they did not know how long they would have to stay there. From the point of view of the German government, it was also rather expensive to have ships lying out of reach in overseas ports, largely because of the quayage and other costs.[9] For this reason, many German vessels received orders to return home during the first months of the war. So from the outset, the crossing was a dangerous undertaking which was best accomplished during long dark autumn and winter nights—preferably under the cover of fog.[10] Despite the numerous precautions, for a large part of the crews, the passage to Germany ended not with a return home, but with capture by a British warship.

The reason why civilian seamen were captured at all was that they were viewed—quite logically—as the reserves of the German Navy. So, according to the logic of naval warfare, Germany's enemies not only sought to reduce the number of German ships but also the number of men who were able to operate them. During hostilities, any encounter between a German merchant ship and an enemy warship was—at least in theory—regulated by the international laws of armed conflicts. In addition, the prevailing national prize law applied. The British prize law, for instance, governed the conditions under which a German ship could legally become a British prize. The German Maritime Warfare Command tried to avoid this by ordering the captains to scuttle their ship in case of encountering an enemy cruiser.[11] Today, historians regard these orders as part of the Nazi scorched earth policy that aimed at destroying as much infrastructure as possible.[12] There are some reports written by captains or engineers focusing on technical details of the scuttling, but very few written comments by other crew members survived.[13] In any case, for the crews the attempted scuttling of their vessel was the difficult commencement of their captivity experience, because they had to leave the ship hastily in lifeboats and were seldom able to bring along anything more than the clothes they wore. According to the maritime code of ethics, the shipwrecked crew was in most cases immediately taken aboard the British ship. The German seamen were then transported to the nearest port and from there to temporary camps. Eventually, they were brought from all over the world to England or Scotland and, after Canada had agreed to accommodate 4,000 internees and 3,000 prisoners of war, they were transported from England to Canada from summer 1940 onward.[14]

In the following years, the transportation of prisoners from England to Canada increased significantly, so that at the end of the Second World War, Canada held approximately 34,000 prisoners of war and internees.[15] In the early phase of the transportation of prisoners to Canada, the story of the German merchant seamen was closely connected to that of the German-Jewish refugees, a matter which has been studied by Paula Draper, elsewhere and in her essay in this collection, and Patrick Farges.[16] Christine Whitehouse also offers new insights on their experiences in her chapter in this volume. As the seamen were not mentioned as a distinct group in the official correspondence between authorities in Britain and Canada, they shared camps with the refugees, at least for a short time after their arrival in Canada, for instance in Camp Red Rock.[17] As Martin Auger has pointed out, "Canada was unprepared to accommodate this influx of prisoners and lacked enough proper detention facilities."[18] In the months and years following the initial agreement to house British detainees—and facing ever-growing numbers of prisoner arrivals—the Canadian government established several new camps. Due to their unique status—they were neither combatant prisoners of war nor civilian internees in the strictest sense—German merchant shipping crews were soon accommodated separately. They were housed in camps in Mimico, Monteith, Fort Henry in Kingston, Hull, Petawawa, Farnham, Sherbrooke, Sorel, Fredericton, Neys, Kananaskis, Red Rock, and Chatham.[19] After the expansion of Camp Monteith in 1941 and again in 1944, all the seamen were concentrated there by the end of the war.[20]

It is difficult to give exact numbers of the interned seamen. To begin with, the makeup of the crews often changed during their stays in overseas ports after the war had begun. Second, prisoners were frequently transported from one camp to another and in rather small groups, so that former crews did not always stay together. When reports about the interned seamen reached Germany, they were often already out of date, and keeping track of prisoner movements was difficult for German authorities.[21] The records kept by the insurance company for German seamen do include some information on the duration of internment for each crew member, but unfortunately, they are not accessible for scholarly purposes. Given these limitations, the best estimate possible suggests that there were at least 7,200 German seamen interned in countries all over the world, and that over 3,500 were held in Canada.[22] From 1943 on, more than 50 percent of all captured German merchant seamen lived in Canadian camps.[23]

Despite the generally positive conditions of internment in Canada in regard to living quarters, nutrition, hygiene, medical care, and the like, depending on the individual's state of body and mind, internment could bring about a sense of oppression and a crisis of identity. From internees' letters and other sources, we know that there were many depressing aspects of camp life: the separation from loved ones at home, the inevitable delays and censorship difficulties associated with wartime correspondence, worries for friends and relatives in Germany or at the front, uncertainties about how long the war (and their confinement) was going to last, pressing but unsolvable questions about their personal futures that were closely connected to the political future of Germany, the cramped conditions of life in an internment camp and the ensuing loss of privacy, the many causes of conflict everyday life in confinement brought about, the loss of freedom of movement, the restriction of self-determination, the dependence on financial support and humanitarian aid, the insecurities concerning career prospects, and many other concerns all weighed heavily on the minds of the internees.[24]

In spite of all this, the former merchant seamen's overall assessment of their internment in Canada during the Second World War is, retrospectively, startlingly positive. In oral history interviews and memoirs, these former internees present their experience in a rather favourable light.[25] This raises important questions about how to interpret and contextualize these narratives: First of all, how can one explain such positive assessments of captivity? What was the role of the specific conditions of internment in Canada? How does knowledge about the events of the Second World War influence these retrospective captivity narratives? What roles do individual biographical aspects play? What other aspects shape the presentation of the internment experience in the context of oral history interviews and genres of life writing?

German Merchant Shipping Crews in Canada: A Contact Zone

Although the internees spent most of their time in Canada in internment camps, they talk much more about their experiences on the other side of the barbed wire. This may have to do with suppressed negative emotions and feelings of monotony and boredom connected with camp life that are difficult to speak about.[26] But it is also the case that, during the last years of the war, many of the seamen worked outside the camps on farms and in lumber camps. Merchant seamen were among the first prisoners to be allowed to work outside, because, unlike the German soldiers also confined in Canada, they were regarded as less dangerous and thought to be more easily accepted by the general public.[27] Even before the internees left the camp for the first time, they had ample opportunity to fuel their imaginations regarding Canada. The internment of the merchant seamen must thus be regarded as much more than only their confinement. Movements from one camp to another and work assignments outside the camps formed the internees' perception of Canada. In many different ways, these experiences also shape the way they remember and tell about their internment.

Experiencing Canada: Internment and the Perception of Space

Once in the camps, internees had considerable time and occasions to think about their host country, for example by observing the differences in climate and thereby gradually forming an opinion of the character of this country. One ship's officer, Rudolf Becker, regularly included descriptions of weather phenomena when writing to his father in Germany and often indulged in comparisons of the two countries.[28] What most impressed the seamen were the long distances they had to cover by train when being moved from one camp to another.[29] Although in the beginning of their captivity in Canada, apart from urgent journeys to the hospital, the internees were not allowed to leave the camp, they had many opportunities to gradually get to know different aspects of Canadian life and the Canadian society.[30] Newspapers, radio, educational courses, consumer goods, and typical North American sports like hockey and horseshoe pitching were the most important points of contact.[31] Thanks to financial and organizational support from the Young Men's Christian Association, which helped them with subscriptions,[32] the seamen could read a wide variety of daily and weekly newspapers and magazines from Canada and the United States.[33] Through them the internees became acquainted with the Canadian point of view on the war and with other social and political questions discussed in the media. The radio was another important means of not only following the news, but also listening to popular music and improving language skills.[34] In Camp Sherbrooke, for example, the visiting Swiss consul noted that the radio was turned on every day from morning till the evening and that the internees liked to listen to CMB from Montreal and other local stations.[35] The YMCA cooperated with Twentieth Century Fox and other American movie distributors in order to regularly show movies.[36] After the internees had also watched several German movies, YMCA secretary Hermann Boeschenstein noted "that whatever the emotional appeal of these home products may be, a definite technical superiority is readily conceded to the American films."[37] For educational purposes, the seamen were also shown productions of the Canadian National Film Board.[38] In every camp, a library provided some reading material. Some camps even cooperated with local university libraries in order to expand the range of books available for the internees.[39] After the war, many internees showed an increased interest in information about Canada and other English-speaking countries. According to YMCA secretary Boeschenstein, they hoped "to get a closer view of everyday-life in Canada."[40] Martin Auger has described how the YMCA and the European Students' Relief Fund organized lectures about a variety of political and historical topics in several internment camps.[41] In all the camps the inmates established a course system with, among others, arts, sciences, vocational, and language classes. Boeschenstein thought this method of teaching English was particularly successful. Early in 1945, he stated: "If the number of English books requested by various camps is any indication, a reading knowledge of English has become quite prevalent. Progress along this line has been accompanied by the regret that familiarity with the spoken word remains slight for obvious reasons."[42]

Movements from one camp to another, which occurred frequently, were an opportunity for the internees to gain more and more impressions of Canada. Usually the seamen were transported by train. Particularly in 1945 and 1946, the number of movements increased, due to the rising number of working internees who had to be transported from camp to their places of employment. Rudolf Becker, already mentioned above, commented that he appreciated the change of scenery very much.[43]

"Associate with Members of the Public": Making Contacts

Work provided opportunities to get to know Canadian citizens and Canadian life apart from the guards and escorts the internees met in the camp (but technically were forbidden to talk to). When working on farms and in remote lumber camps, many of the internees got to know rural Canada, which was, especially for the seamen, a rather exotic setting. Only very few worked in the vicinity of bigger cities. The many new impressions contrasted with camp life and at the same time enabled the seamen to regain access to their own civilian, pre-internment identity, even though they were still prisoners. Some of the seamen worked alone with their farmers, without the company of their fellow internees who, until that moment, had been ever present. In the beginning of those work projects, the seamen returned to a work camp in the evening and only spent the workday at the farm.[44] Staying overnight out of camp had initially not been permitted for security reasons (and was only granted later from July 1943 onward).[45] Later on, most lived on the farms. Many things were new and strange to the men, including farming itself. They had to learn new skills; for example in Chatham, in May 1944, sixty internees got an introduction to thinning sugar beets.[46] In spite of the new tasks they were asked to perform, the internees' work was described by farmers and camp officials alike as "very satisfactory."[47] Those who worked as lumberjacks also entered a totally different and exotic world: working with horses and sleighs, making contact with experienced lumbermen, many of whom had a European background, and spending weeks and months in the bush in comparative freedom constituted some very interesting and trying conditions. In fact, many of the bush camps were so basic as regards the living quarters provided that the government recommended more comfortable furnishing and a generalized improvement of lodgings to the companies.[48]

For the seamen, the most interesting aspect of working outside the camp was meeting a lot of new people, not only the farmers and their wives and children, but also friends and acquaintances. Particularly attractive after the long stay in the exclusively male society of the camps was the possibility of encountering women. Sometimes, the internees had more contact than the authorities wished, as noted by the commandant of Camp Chatham: "Ps.O.W. have entered taverns, and other buildings frequented by the general public, and have been permitted to associate with members of the public. In some cases they have been permitted to send telegrams or telephone, and pictures have been taken."[49] In certain cases not only did the farmers act as accomplices to the internees, but so too did members of the guard escorting them. Being outside the camp entailed many new points of contact between guards and internees, not all of them in accordance with the official regulations. For instance, in September 1944, near Chatham, it became known that "members of the Guard and P/W personnel have been entering orchards and stripping trees of fruit."[50] The commandant threatened severe punishment should this happen again. But there were also cases of helpfulness between internees and guards as is described in the Chatham war diary of July 1945: "One party of five P/W with one guard. The guard collapsed and 2 P/W carried him (guard) and one P/W carried rifle to farm house, where another escort was sent after the farmer called in. Guard taken to Chatham Military Hospital."[51]

By working, the internees got to know a less severely controlled Canada, where at times they could live under the illusion of freedom, all the time knowing quite well that they still were prisoners. Working opened up new geographic and social spaces that rapidly and fundamentally changed their world view and expanded their personal horizons. Ship's officer Rudolf Becker wrote to his father: "Often, we work every day with another farmer. This provides me with a fairly good insight into the life on Canadian farms."[52] Apart from the work itself and the social contacts it involved, the internees appreciated the possibility of earning a little money and, still more important, spending it. In April 1946, when internees came back from their work projects and had been searched on entering the camp in Monteith, the commandant complained that they were "laden with everything but the family piano and the kitchen sink."[53] Time and again the seamen tried to smuggle forbidden items into the camp, in order to take these things back to Germany. After the war, coffee, tea, soap, and tobacco were particularly popular because many prisoners knew from their relatives that these consumer goods were scarce in postwar Germany. Buying as many provisions as possible while in Canada seemed to them a good way of preparing for the months to come.[54]

From the point of view of the YMCA and the Canadian government, the work projects also played an important role in re-educating the Germans. Some scholars share this opinion; Martin Auger, for instance, stresses that the internees experienced firsthand the many advantages of living in a democratic country.[55] Moreover, they were working outside the camps during the so-called "post-Depression boom,"[56] when "the war . . . elevated tens of thousands of families into the ranks of the middle class."[57] Already on their arrival in Canada, many of the German internees had been overwhelmed in the face of the good living conditions in the Canadian camps, as the following passage from an internee letter demonstrates: "We have now arrived into an actual Fairyland. In a few words, I may say that I am satisfied, and have no more wishes. Please refrain from sending parcels. That would be senseless, as everything can be had here."[58] Two years later, when working on the farms, many also witnessed the "dramatic increase in yields"[59] that Graham Broad describes in his analysis of Canadian consumer culture during the Second World War. The technical equipment on the farms also reflected this development: the number of tractors on farms in Ontario grew rapidly during and immediately after the war.[60]

Merchant Seamen's Canadian Internment Narratives

Oral history interviews with formerly interned merchant seamen show how profoundly working in Canada has influenced their internment narratives. In great detail, and often with much enthusiasm, these men told me about their experiences. In articulating their memories, they reconstruct social spaces that are relevant for their internment experiences and in which they position themselves.[61] There are several topics closely related to this kind of narrative mapping. The places they mention are mainly socially defined. The internment is the framework that connects all these single places. So, in the interviews, the narrators evoke fragments of the Canada they experienced,[62] disclosing spatial information only as far as it is necessary for me to understand their story.[63] Most of the former internees I spoke with travelled through three or more countries as a prisoner, due to their capture on the high seas or in foreign ports. When they told me about their internment, they followed the chronological order of these events. The most important step of this tour is the arrival in Canada. Often, the narrators contrast Canada to the other countries they knew (especially England and Germany) and mark it as an exceedingly positive experience, compared with places they had passed through before as prisoners. One important topic in this context is food. The former internee Hans Plähn stressed that in England they had not enough to eat and had expected the same when coming to Canada. But to their surprise, on the train from Halifax to their camp, they were handed a large package of food and were told that the next day they would get a proper lunch. Hans Plähn emphasized that this was so unimaginable that they just could not believe it and were really astounded when indeed the next day they were served a hot lunch.[64]

In other interviews as well, the arrival in Canada is presented as a kind of liminal situation that marked the beginning of a new era. Some former internees say that everything they had experienced before was then simply "forgotten."[65] Another typical topic mentioned was the accommodation in the camps, which, compared to the tents and barracks they had encountered in Africa and England, seemed to the seamen rather generous, warm, dry, and clean.[66] Many narrators tend to generalize single observations and to take them as evidence for their positive evaluation of the Canadian internment situation as a whole. Thus, the internment experience is closely linked to constructions of Canadianness and Canadian national identity. The assessment of Canada as a "fairy land," as quoted above, also appears in some of the interview texts and also in memoirs, even if this term is not always used explicitly. Many aspects of the country are labelled as "unbelievable" or "fantastic," for example the amount of snow in the winter,[67] or the fact that the seamen were allowed to use knives at dinnertime.[68] The latter can be interpreted as a symbol of civilian life; it represents the possibility of eating as one was used to before captivity, without being suspected of criminal intentions. Such remarks, found in several wartime sources, reflect the internees' awareness of their relatively privileged situation. Apart from food and accommodation, there is another topic which the narrators use to show the extraordinary quality of Canada: the physical nature of the country. Some former internees mentioned the northern lights, for example.[69]

Many seamen would have liked to stay in Canada after their internment ended, which was not possible at the time.[70] But this wish remains present in some of the interviews: Hans Plähn, for example, calls it his "dream of Canada."[71] This was a common motif mentioned in many German travelogues of the nineteenth century, as pointed out by Gisela Sigrist. According to her analysis, many authors wrote about Canada with great yearning, describing it as the object of their wanderlust. Sigrist therefore calls Canada a "Wunschraum,"[72] meaning that many Europeans longingly regarded it as an ideal, exotic world, because it represented the greatest possible contrast to the supposedly dull and boring life in their own respective countries. According to Sigrist, even well into the twentieth century, many Germans tend to seek in Canada things that can no longer be found in Germany, like huge, supposedly untouched forests with bears and wolves.[73] Apparently, this narrative of Canada as a kind of exotic wilderness was so strong that even being interned in this country did not destroy its fascination; one could even say that the internment itself was an opportunity for many seamen to form their own opinion of Canada and connect this personal empirical evidence of Canada's greatness with the cultural pattern of exoticism.

The Canadian immigration regulations of the postwar era were rather restrictive towards applications from Germans, unless they had been persecuted by the Nazis. This closed off Canada for the former internees, at least for some years. Disappointment, nostalgic transfiguration, a longing for the life they could have lived, and memories of their youth come together in those remembrances and imaginations of Canada as a land of promise. This impressionability can also be explained, at least in part, by many of the internees having been in their teenage years during the war, which would have made them very receptive to new impressions. Today, as older men, they look back on successful personal and professional lives. As mentioned above, working outside the camps was the key to getting to know the country. In the interviews, the most important settings mentioned in this context are lumber camps and farms. Where exactly the interviewees had worked often remains vague, for instance in the interview with Hans Plähn, who stated that he had worked "everywhere."[74] But exact geographic information does not matter and does not impede the narrative construction of social spaces in oral history interviews and memoirs of former internees. At the same time, the topic of work creates a narrative frame for the interpretation of Canada as a space of positive experience. One central aspect is that working seemingly increased the prisoners' status. Seen in retrospect, work transformed the internment experience, which otherwise would have been a rather gloomy chapter of their lives, transforming it into a valuable and emotionally enriching part of the men's lives.[75] The actual geographic distance between the work project and the camp was irrelevant for this interpretation; however, what was crucial was that the spaces opened up by work had, in the eyes of the former prisoners, a totally different quality in terms of subjective freedom, social contacts, belonging, and participation. Many narratives show a great amount of emotionality; in some interview passages, the former internees even use the present tense and thus make the related events seem particularly intense and close. The experience of and the ability to work enabled the former internees to narrate the spatial and cross-cultural aspect of their internment that had nothing to do with the barbed wire. In particular, they tend to narrate work-related episodes that have a special emotional quality. Therefore, in the narrative context, the quality of working in Canada consists of external impressions as well as inner reactions that can be communicated with the aid of specific episodes. One very common narrative technique in this context is the use of anecdotes.

The Lumber Camp as Iconic Canadian Setting

The positive Canadian experiences of the former internees interviewed seemed to intensify when they were talking about working in a lumber camp. Their descriptions of life in the bush camps show traces of the typical European fascination for the supposedly adventurous life in the North American wilderness. Their enthusiasm when talking about lumber camps reminds one of the exotic narratives that conjure up myths of unspoiled nature.[76] This may seem a bit of a paradox, for the seamen were used to clearing these supposedly untouched woods. But contradictions like these are common elements in narratives that stress the otherness of exotic settings.[77] The remote and isolated location of the lumber camps was a stark contrast to the former maritime habitat of the seamen. It built the framework for extraordinary experiences that appear, romantically intensified, in the interviews and memoirs. In these narratives, the fact that lumbering was unpopular and hard work and that the seamen were first and foremost easily available workers is often transformed into a privileged possibility of being very close to nature and of doing things that had been forbidden before or otherwise had been inconceivable.[78] Thus, in these internment narratives, the lumber camp is presented as a space of freedom, as Hans Plähn mentioned during the interview: "We could do everything there, including bear hunt."[79] Also in the memoirs of one ship's officer, Harald Wentzel, the freedom and creativity displayed in after-work activities play an important role. He describes vividly that the seamen laid out a flower garden and also built a boat with mast and sails in order to cruise about on the lake in the evenings.[80] Wentzel notes that the seamen combined their professional knowledge with that of the First Nations peoples and constructed boats that resembled canoes more than traditional European sailing boats. He mentions explicitly that the lumber camp brought together three different groups of people: German seamen, old-established Canadian lumberjacks, and, on a more temporary basis, First Nations people who occasionally visited. The lumber camp thus is presented as an important "contact zone"[81] that not only inspired creativity on the part of the seamen, but that to this day influences the way the former internees think and speak about Canada. Although the seamen knew forests and woods at home in Germany, the Canadian bush represented for them a different kind of nature, a "space of alterity."[82] In the narratives, the bush functions as a metaphor for many things that seemed strange and fascinating to the internees. The analysis has also to take into account that these narratives were articulated during oral history interviews. Therefore, they must be regarded as closely, if implicitly, linked to the narrators' present situation in life as retired captains or pilots. Both—the wartime internment in the permanent camps and their postwar professional lives—are radically different from living in a bush camp, making lumbering such an extraordinary experience and at the same time a narrative reservoir. This biographical singularity of lumbering is an important reason why it is presented in such an outstanding way. It is a unique episode in the seamen's lives that enables them to tell fascinating tales.

As mentioned above in connection with food, the positive aspects of lumbering in these narratives are closely connected to Canada in general. The former internees describe the bush camp as a strange and exotic setting representing Canadianness. The bush camp is characterized by its location, by a special quality of the surrounding landscape, iconic elements like a log cabin, and direct contact with certain animals like bears or moose. The fact that they mention these animals underlines the exotic character of the scenery. Not only can this be noticed in the oral history interviews, but also in some of the letters the internees wrote to their relatives during the war. For example, one seaman wrote to his wife in 1941: "Every evening, there is a big bear coming to the camp; once I saw him with two young."[83] In interviews and memoirs, the narrators make use of bears, wolves, and moose to vividly sketch the wilderness and at the same time stress their own privileged position in witnessing this. Moreover, they show their knowledge about this kind of life and about nature. One former internee explained in detail how he watched moose grazing and added an explanation about the dietary habits of moose.[84] So telling others, or, to be precise, telling a scholar about their internment experience can also provide a kind of social capital.[85] Moose are a narrative and visual commonplace in Canadian internment memories. Pictures of bush scenes with animals are common as substitutes for detailed descriptions in interviews. Some of the former internees I interviewed showed me ample photographic material;[86] some even made drawings or had a collection of drawings by other internees that played an important part during the interview. To show these pictures, to comment on them and to take them as starting points for smaller, associative narratives, is a kind of narrative technique one often finds in biographical interview settings. On one hand, the narrator shows the pictures to the interviewer, on the other hand, he himself can discover them afresh every time.

Canada as a Space of Personal Development and Growth

Another aspect that makes working in Canada so important for the former internees is the fact that retrospectively, they connect it with various opportunities of learning and personal growth. There are many passages in the interviews that show how trying out new occupations is connected with their positive opinion about Canada. In fact, during the whole time of their internment, the seamen could, and had to, adapt to new roles. Even before they were allowed to work outside the camp, they worked in various areas of camp maintenance and camp services. One former internee, for instance, worked as chair assistant for the camp dentist and thereby learned a lot about dentistry.[87] Others worked as cooks, bakers, or plumbers. They characterized these jobs as challenging and at the same time as providing a chance of proving themselves and proving what they had learned in a new social context. In retrospect, these changes of role are often connected with a narrative transformation of the whole internment period as an enriching and therefore meaningful life experience. One similar example is how the former internees talk about climatic conditions of Canada and present themselves as tough. Thereby they construct Canada as a space of intellectual, bodily, and social growth. Getting used to rough conditions is a major topic in these narratives which also has to be connected to normative discourses of masculinity. Mentioning climatic conditions enables the narrators to position themselves as tough guys without having to do so explicitly and directly. For example, one former internee told me that he often took a bath in Lake Superior, at a water temperature of 12° C.[88] Another mentioned that he quickly became accustomed to the 13° C of the outdoor swimming pool in the internment camp.[89] Other former internees also stressed that life in Canada required adaptation and that there was "much to be learned during the bitterly cold Canadian winter."[90]

Another important field of learning that appears in the interviews concerns the English language, as evidenced in particular in an interview with Bruno

Pichner. This former internee's use of the English language during the interview can be interpreted as a sign of his intense non-academic study of this language during his internment in Canada. He showed me little texts he had written since the 1980s and corresponding drawings that showed important scenes of his internment. Part of these writings included a vocabulary list he had learned during his stay in a lumber camp: corduroy road, lunchbox, smock, cord, hemlock, spruce, pine, tamarack, balsam tree, and poplar. In showing and explaining this vocabulary list he presented his language skills (and at the same time tested mine!) and took on the role of an expert at lumbering. The vocabulary list was a document of his educational gain linked to the lumber work, strengthening the close association between language learning and work. Another interesting aspect is that, seemingly, some of his experiences can only be told in English. This is also a sign for a strong identification with the country and social setting of his internment and, at the same time, a narrative means of reducing the temporal and spatial distance between today's self and his former self.

Apart from specific educational contents, some former internees present Canada as the space of extensive personality development. This is very evident in the autobiography of Hans Peter Jürgens. He states that Canada, in spite of the barbed wire surrounding the camp, widened his personal horizon, his knowledge, and his knowledge of human nature. In his opinion, the years he spent in Canada enabled him to learn skills and show abilities that otherwise probably would have remained hidden and unexplored. They furthered his thirst for knowledge and opened up the ideological limits of thinking that had shaped the education of his whole generation in Germany. He is convinced that his stay in Canada laid the foundations for an openness of mind and cosmopolitan attitude that he nowadays regards as an important part of his personality.[91] In this passage of his autobiography, Jürgens interprets his internment as a de-limitation of his personality. He does not name any specific persons associated with these developments; indeed, the single most important actor in this process is the country itself, which is simultaneously intangible and yet omnipresent. The terms he uses in this passage—home, open-mindedness, culture, knowledge—show that he judges his internment not so much as an experience of exclusion but as a privilege, the more so because he stresses the constant connection between the camp and the country—over and away from the barbed wire.

Spaces of Belonging and Participation

Tales of friendships between prisoners of war and workers of the host country are common elements in other captivity narratives. Even former German soldiers who were Russian prisoners of war and lived under very difficult conditions sometimes mention that they were on good terms with Russian civilians.[92] By telling about the people they met at work, the formerly interned merchant seamen also position themselves in social contexts that had opened up thanks to the opportunity to work. And—what may seem paradoxical—they tend to characterize these short temporary relationships that only emerged by chance as close, trustful, and long-lasting. Internee work is thus often narrated as an experience of inclusion; this can be interpreted as a biographical strategy of making sense of one's experiences to balance the internment as an extreme form of exclusion. In stressing the aspect of belonging, the narrators shape their own work experiences as a space for relationships and participation.

In the interviews with those who worked on farms, the unreserved acceptance by the family is a commonly stressed topic. To be once again part of a family was something they had missed since the beginning of captivity. At the same time, these narratives seamlessly fit into the greater narrative of Canada as a country that attracts a large number of immigrants. Often, they mention that their employers were not native Canadians, but Europeans who had migrated to Canada some years earlier. So, this common European background is presented as a connection between the internees and their employers. At the same time in those stories, the employers seem to play an important role as "cultural brokers"[93] who show the internees how a diverse society could work. Therefore in the episodes that reflect this kind of diversity, the ethnic and cultural background of the participants is particularly stressed and reminds one of the much-discussed thoughts on the Canadian mosaic by John Murray Gibbon.[94]

One example shows how a former internee discusses the opening up of new social spaces through work. In this case the interviewee was one of the few who worked neither on a farm nor in the bush. He worked in a tannery in New Toronto, together with fifty other seamen, standing at the tubs where the skins were tanned. During the interview, he stated that after a while, he knew more people in Toronto than at home in Bremen.[95] As an example he told me about a girl who worked as a summer employee in the tannery and with whom he still exchanged letters in the late 1940s. In general, he described his relationship to his colleagues and bosses as very close. For instance, he mentioned that the foremen chose particular internees with whom they liked to work so that some of the internees got "permanent jobs."[96] This may seem paradoxical, because the whole context of internee work was impermanence, subject as it was to frequent and often very sudden change. But in this narrative the mentioning of permanent jobs is a central element that shows how important social acceptance based on hard work and dependability is for the narrator. It is a story of personal success: he proudly noted that by the end of his time at the tannery, he had his own desk in the office of the sales manager and no longer had to do the hard work at the tubs. The desk, as a symbol of white-collar work and the fact that he shared the space with his Canadian boss, who, we may assume from the story, chose him particularly for this work, represent his professional and personal success in a foreign country.[97] His interpretation of work at the tannery stresses not only the experience of inclusion, but also the possibility of success and social advancement; the desk in this constellation is proof of social recognition.

Canada as Symbolic Space

In many internment narratives, Canada is presented as a space of friendship and positive social relationships between the German seamen and Canadian citizens. An important aspect of this topic is the easy way in which these relationships seem to emerge. The places that are connected to these relationships remain meaningful, well beyond the period of internment. One former internee related that in 1999, he travelled with his son to the former sites of his internment in Canada. In describing this journey, he presented Canada as a kind of topography of remembrance where not only every place but also every chance encounter evokes past experiences and enables him to tell about them.[98] One former internee told me that the place of his first work project was the small village of Sunshine. During the interview he said that for him, this was a good omen, because his whole stay in Canada was such a positive experience. The same former internee, Bruno Pichner, drew a symbolic line between his own surname and the name of the bush camp where he worked for some weeks, "Little Pic River." He told me that later on, during his career as a pilot, the abbreviation of his name used for radio communication was "Pic." This always reminded him of his stay in Canada and made those pleasant memories part of his daily work. He and his wife also nicknamed their first son, who was born after the war, "little Pic" and regarded this nickname as another symbolic connection to the Canadian internment experience. Bruno Pichner interpreted these reminiscences as symbols for the close and lasting connection of his wartime experience in a remote Canadian bush camp with everything that became important to him in his postwar life: his professional career and his family. Stressing these symbolic lines as part of his internment narrative is for him a means of closely and meaningfully integrating the internment experience into his biography and his daily life. Canada thus became a biographical topic to which he continually gave attention by writing small texts and making sketches and drawings.

These examples show how the possibility of working outside the camps not only created shared spaces between the internees and Canadian citizens, but continues to shape the way in which former internees present their internment during oral history interviews, in memoirs, and in other forms of autobiographical writing. They construct Canada as a space of emotionally intense experiences, as a space of freedom (even if they knew this was not actual freedom, but only the appearance of it), of personal growth and learning, as a space of belonging, as a space of various symbolic interpretations that stress the pleasant aspects of internment and therefore, on the whole, as a sphere of contrast which enabled the seamen to lead a good life in Canada. The fact that the internees were still under the control of guards when working, although in a different manner than before, does not appear in those work-related internment narratives. The space of alterity the former internees construct in their narratives is not at all hostile, but enables the narrators to place themselves in a variety of social contexts. Topographical aspects of Canada are only a part of these narratives where they can be connected with important personal experiences or social relationships. Implicitly, in many texts and interviews, the narrators evoke a specific Canadianness, the appraisal of which they base on their own experiences. This positive, specifically Canadian space of alterity represents the complete opposite of everything that is usually connected with internment. Retrospectively, the former internees associate their stay in Canada with physical and mental well-being, with nature, enrichment, inclusion, participation, and transnational social relationships. These merchant navy Canadian captivity narratives reflect the fact that many forms of wartime captivity can be seen as "contact zones" in which, as Mary Louise Pratt puts it, "subjects previously separated by geography and history are co-present."[99] This framing of captivity experiences as contact zones is not intended to equate colonial contexts (which had enduring effects on all societies involved) with the temporary constellation of wartime internment. Rather, this perspective helps to bring into focus the complex merger of relationships that evolved on different levels between many different actors: captors, internees, and humanitarian aid professionals, only to name a few. Pratt's concept can thus contribute to a more precise approach to the importance of everyday interactions and their lasting effects in the study of captivity and internment.[100]

Beyond the Internment: Contextualizing Merchant Seamen's Captivity Narratives

Of course, one must not conclude from the many positive reflections of captivity that the actual experiences during the work phase of internment were equally and universally positive. One also has to keep in mind that this rather small group of former internees represents the ones that were very young during the war. In the years following their repatriation they profited greatly from the postwar economic upswing in Germany. When remembering the internment in writing or during oral history interviews, on the whole they look back on a lifetime of success, professionally as well as personally, and therefore tend to shape this biographical episode so that it fits well with the whole picture they want to present of their personhood.

The fact that the former internees I could interview were rather young during the war is sometimes mentioned in the interviews; Bruno Pichner, for instance, said that because he was so young, everything was fun.[101] This is not unlike experiences of children and youth in other internment contexts; Grace Eiko Thomson touches on this in her contribution to this collection where she recalls her childhood spent in a Second World War Japanese Canadian camp. A close examination of Pichner's whole interview reveals several clues that show that the internment was first of all an unsettling and frightening experience.[102] But it also clarifies the meaning of "fun" in this context: Pichner hints at the fact that there was much time and little in the way of distraction so that the young seamen could concentrate on studying math and other subjects relevant to their professional fields. In this interpretation the lack of information and amusement is presented as an advantage that created a particularly intense atmosphere of learning and resulted in the feeling of fulfillment.

These narratives are closely connected to the assessment of the whole internment experience. Some of the former internees pointed out positive biographical effects of the internment that became visible in their life after the war. Often, internment is presented as a precondition for professional success because it was an opportunity to make up for missing formal education and provided them with knowledge and skills that later on proved useful in obtaining the master's certificate. In all the internment camps where merchant seamen were housed, they established navigation courses and classes on other aspects of the nautical and nautical engineering field. Captains and ship's officers instructed the younger men who aspired to become captains themselves one day. Because there was an agreement between the shipping companies and the German educational authorities,[103] young seamen like Bruno Pichner who attended these classes could skip one year of the naval college after the war. In consequence, they could go on the fast track to becoming a ship's captain. In the narratives of former internees, this is stated very clearly: internment was a privileged experience that enabled a small part of the seafaring community in Germany to start a successful career. This is also part of the specific merchant marine Canadian internment experience and narratives. Former internees like Bruno Pichner closely connect the internment with their professional career. Not only had internment enabled them to obtain academic qualifications, but the specific circumstances of the internment led to the discovery of talents not previously developed. The fact that many of them had only attended primary or junior high school before the war suddenly did not matter anymore. In this way, internment indeed levelled different social and educational backgrounds and opened up chances for social advancement.

Another factor which helps to explain the positive assessment of their internment in Canada is the fact that captivity in Canada ensured they would survive the war. In the interviews and in retrospective texts, this is often very clearly stated. As they learned after returning to Germany, many of their classmates, friends, colleagues, and relatives had not survived the war. Regarded from today's point of view, internment represents much more the continuity of their life history than, as might have been thought at the moment of capture, an interruption. Episodes where there was a risk of not surviving, like the sinking of the *Arandora Star*,[104] or violent incidents in temporary camps in Africa,[105] are described vividly, so that it becomes very evident how lucky the narrators themselves were in safely reaching Canada and spending the remainder of the war there. This is an important element that also links these to the narratives of other prisoners of war who state that the captivity was "the central experience of their lives."[106] Some Canadian scholars also stress the positive recollections of former internees and attribute them to the good living conditions in the Canadian camps.[107] There is no doubt about the excellent conditions in those camps, but, as I have tried to show, there is more to these positive assessments than good food and proper living conditions: in remembering their internment experiences, the former internees connect them to various biographical events, to their personal educational backgrounds and development, and to a broader knowledge about the impact of the war. What they tell in the interviews is only a snapshot of the process of remembering that always adapts the way such experiences are viewed in regard to today's life situation and many other factors, including the person to whom one tells these stories.[108] Clearly, how the experiences are presented changes over time. Temporal and spatial distance from the internment also is a major factor in shaping such narratives, a point made by German cultural anthropologist and former prisoner of war Hans Moser regarding his own captivity memories.[109]

Another important aspect to consider, as mentioned above, is the generational context. Letters the ship's officer Rudolf Becker, born in 1911, wrote in the late 1990s show that even at that late date, he judged the internment as illegal and compared the situation of the interned seamen to that of hostages. Becker was ten years older than the former internees whose points of view are described in detail above. Unlike them he had already started his career as a ship's officer when he was captured. During his time in Canada, he tried desperately to keep his mind engaged, but he felt the interruption of his career quite keenly. After the war, he was not able to resume his former career with the same vigour as before. So in general, the whole biography of a (former) internee (including the former social background and the momentary life situation) is the crucial backdrop for judging the internment experience. The fact that there are so many aspects of internment about which many former internees speak with pleasure shows that for them the internment is of major biographical meaning. All the positive effects which they ascribe to their internment are typical for contact zones: the close contact to colleagues from which they learned, and the contact with Canada and Canadians that proved to be mind opening. Internment must thus be regarded as an important resource for identity work.[110] For the former merchant seamen internees, remembering the internment is an opportunity of reconsidering former selves and making sense of their experiences. As the close examination of oral history interviews and memoirs by formerly interned German merchant seamen shows, the implications of wartime internment are diverse and reach far beyond the barbed wire. Discussing these interpretations not only in connection with the respective national historiographies of war but in a broader, transnational context of internment and captivity studies opens up further possibilities of better understanding internment as a complex cultural phenomenon.[111]

Notes

1 See Judith Kestler, *Gefangen in Kanada: Zur Internierung deutscher Handelsschiffsbesatzungen während des Zweiten Weltkriegs* (Bielefeld: transcript, 2017); and Judith Kestler, "Internierung und humanitäre Hilfe: Perspektiven auf eine kulturelle Praxis," *Zeitschrift für Volkskunde* 112, no. 2 (2016): 253–76.

2 My master's thesis is a case study of one merchant seaman's biography: Judith Kestler, "Kriegsgefangenschaft und Weltreise: Untersuchungen zur Biographie eines unfreiwilligen Teilnehmers am Zweiten Weltkrieg" (Bremen: Hauschild, 2010).

3 Wilhelm Prüsse, *Der Seemannsberuf und die Problematik seines Arbeitseinsatzes und der Nachwuchslenkung* (Rostock: Hinstorff, 1940), 115–16.

4 See A. Mackert, "Die Auslands-Organisation und die Seefahrt," *Jahrbuch der Auslands-Organisation der NSDAP für die Seeschiffahrt* 1 (1939): 55–59, 56.

5 Ernest Hamburger, "A Peculiar Pattern of the Fifth Column: The Organization of the German Seamen," *Social Research* 9, no. 4 (1942): 495–509, 496.

6 Peter Kuckuk, "Seefahrt unter dem 'Hungerhaken': Die Bemühungen der Nationalsozialisten um die politische Organisierung der deutschen Seeleute in den dreißiger Jahren," *Deutsches Schiffahrtsarchiv* 21 (1998): 101–21, 104.

7 In fact, Germany had tried to develop plans for this case since 1934. Part of the preparations was to supply the ships with orders for the emergency, the so-called "Sonderanweisung." See Ludwig Dinklage and Hans Jürgen Witthöft, *Die deutsche Handelsflotte 1939–1945: Handelsschiffe, Blockadebrecher, Hilfskriegsschiffe. 2 vols.* (Hamburg: Nikol, 2001), 1:17.

8 This can be gathered from the reports of the German Maritime Warfare Command who was constantly monitoring the situation of the German merchant fleet around the world. See: Lageberichte der Seekriegsleitung über die Handelsschiffahrt, August 1939 bis Dezember 1940. Federal Archives, Department Military Archives (Bundesarchiv-Militärarchiv, BArch-MA), RM 7/2557; Kriegstagebuch der Seekriegsleitung, Teil D. 27. August bis 31 Dezember 1939. BArch-MA, RM 7/310.

9 Lagebericht zur deutschen Handelsschiffahrt, 17 September 1939. BArch-MA, RM 7/310.

10 German maritime historian Stefan Kiekel points out that the best time for such passages to Germany were the first one and a half years of the war, until the end of 1940. For all ships sailing after that, the risk of seizure and capture was very high. See Stefan Kiekel, *Die deutsche Handelsschiffahrt im Nationalsozialismus: Unternehmerinitiative und staatliche Regulierung im Widerstreit 1933 bis 1940/41* (Bremen: Hauschild, 2010), 251.

11 See Sonderanweisung für die deutsche Handelsschiffahrt, C, 14. BArch-MA, RM 7/2501.

12 Markus Laugsch, "Das Ende: Die letzte Reise," in *Mit der Kamera in die Welt: Richard Fleischhut (1881–1951). Photograph. Katalog zur Ausstellung "Mit der Kamera in die Welt – Richard Fleischhut (1881–1951) Photograph" im Stadt-und Schiffahrtsmuseum Kiel vom 18. November 2005 bis 5. März 2006, Ostfriesisches Landesmuseum Emden vom 19. März bis 20. Mai 2006 und im Deutschen Technikmuseum Berlin 2006/2007*, ed. Hermann Haarmann and Ingrid Peckskamp-Lürßen (Bönen: Kettler, 2005), 275–285, 277.

13 See, for instance, the report of Officer K. Hirsch (Steamship *Adolf Woermann*). BArch-MA, RM 7/2559.

14 Annette Puckhaber, *Ein Privileg für wenige: Die deutschsprachige Migration nach Kanada im Schatten des Nationalsozialismus* (Münster: Lit, 2002), 196.

15 See Helmut Wolff, *Die deutschen Kriegsgefangenen in britischer Hand: Ein Überblick* (Bielefeld: Gieseking, 1974), 97.

16 Paula Jean Draper, "The Accidental Immigrants: Canada and the Interned Refugees, part 1," *Canadian Jewish Historical Society Journal* 2 (1978): 1–38, and Paula Jean Draper, "The Accidental Immigrants: Canada and the Interned Refugees, part 2," *Canadian Jewish Historical Society Journal* 3 (1978): 80–112; Paula Jean Draper, "The Camp Boys: Refugees from Nazism Interned in Canada, 1940–1944," in *Enemies Within: Italian and Other Internees in Canada and Abroad*, ed. Franca Iacovetta, Roberto Perin, and Angelo Principe (Toronto: University of Toronto Press, 2000), 171–93; Patrick Farges, "Nous les Camp Boys: Constructions de la masculinité dans les récits des réfugiés-internés au Canada," *Migrance* 27 (2006): 62–69. See also Paula Jean Draper's chapter in this collection.

17 Paula Jean Draper, "The Accidental Immigrants : Canada and the Interned Refugees" (PhD diss., University of Toronto, 1983), 53.

18 Martin F. Auger, *Prisoners of the Home Front: German POWs and "Enemy Aliens" in Southern Quebec, 1940–46* (Vancouver: UBC Press, 2005), 23.

19 Ibid., and "Summary Report respecting the Application of the Prisoners of War Convention in Canada (1939– 1945)." Federal Archives of Switzerland (Schweizerisches Bundesarchiv Bern, BAR), E2200.150-01#1000/219#2*.

20 David J. Carter, *POW – behind Canadian Barbed Wire: Alien, Refugee, and Prisoner of War Camps in Canada, 1914–1946* (Elkwater, AB: Eagle Butte Press, 1998), 248.

21 See note in the files of the German Foreign Office, June 1943: Political Archive of the German Foreign Office (Politisches Archiv des Auswärtigen Amtes, PA AA), R 127941.

22 See Archives du Comité International de la Croix-Rouge (ACICR), G 17/29; PA AA, R 127.882, R 127.951, R 127.941.

23 Ibid.

24 This is evident, for example, in many of the letters ship's officer Rudolf Becker exchanged with his father. The letters Rudolf Becker sent to his father during his captivity can be consulted in the Archives of the German Maritime Museum (DSM) in Bremerhaven. DSM, III A 3324.

25 See, for example, former internee Hans Peter Jürgens' memoir: *Sturmsee und Flauten: Logbuch eines Lebens* (Hamburg: Koehler, 1995). The question why internment—in itself an act of violence—is not labelled in this way in oral history interviews with former merchant seamen internees is further explored in Judith Kestler, "Internierung erzählen – Gewalt erzählen? Narrationsanalytische Perspektiven auf Interviews mit Besatzungsmitgliedern deutscher Handelsschiffe," in *Storylines and Blackboxes: Autobiografie und Zeugenschaft in der Nachgeschichte von Nationalsozialismus und Zweitem Weltkrieg*, ed. Johanna Gehmacher and Klara Löffler (Wien: nap, 2016), 63–83.

26 See Gabriele Rosenthal, *Erlebte und erzählte Lebensgeschichte: Gestalt und Struktur biographischer Selbstbeschreibungen* (Frankfurt am Main: Campus, 1995), 79.

27 Stefania Halyna Cepuch, "'Our guests are busy': The Internment and Labour of German Prisoners of War in Ontario, 1940–1946" (MA thesis, Queen's University at Kingston, 1993), 57; "Ottawa Plans Using Prisoners to Meet Farm Labor Shortage," *Globe and Mail,* 13 May 1943; "5,500 Nazi Prisoners at Work: Their NSS Rating Ranges from 'Indifferent' to 'Splendid,'" *Financial Post*, 26 May 1944.

28 DSM, III A 3324.

29 See, for example, the letter from Rudolf Becker to his father, 2 November 1941. DSM, III A 3324 b.

30 German historian Laura Hannemann has pointed out that German prisoners of war in the United States came into close contact with their host country. See Laura Hannemann, "Gesandte in Fesseln? Kulturtransfer in Kriegsgefangenenlagern des Zweiten Weltkriegs," *Comparativ* 16, no. 4 (2006): 179–99, 183.

31 See, for example, letter of thanks by the internees of Camp Fredericton to the YMCA for two horseshoe sets. 14 May 1942. LAC, RG 24, 6583, file 3-3-5, vol. 3.

32 See report by YMCA secretary Dr. Hermann Boeschenstein, July to September 1945. LAC, MG 28, I 95, 273, file 5.

33 For a detailed list see Auger, *Prisoners of the Home Front*, 120–21.

34 On the connection between internment and music as a means of getting to know the popular culture of the host country, see Judith Kestler, "Eislauf im Dreivierteltakt – Musik als Zugang zur Alltagskultur in kanadischen Internierungslagern, 1941–1946," in *Musik – Kontext – Wissenschaft. Musiques – contextes – savoirs. Interdisziplinäre Forschung zu Musik. Perspectives interdisciplinaires sur la musique*, ed. Talia Bachir-Loopuyt et al. (Frankfurt am Main: Peter Lang, 2012), 247–59.

35 Report about the Swiss consul's visit in Sherbrooke, 23 September 1943. PA AA, R 127.704.

36 Auger, *Prisoners of the Home Front*, 122.

37 Report by YMCA secretary Dr. Hermann Boeschenstein, October to December 1944. LAC, MG 28, I 95, 273, file 3.

38 Ibid.

39 For example, the library of Queen's University in Kingston temporarily lent books to the library of Fort Henry internment camp. See *War Diary Camp Fort Henry / Kingston*, vol. 42, November 1943. LAC, RG24, 15394.

40 Report by YMCA secretary Dr. Hermann Boeschenstein, July to September 1945. LAC, MG 28, I 95, 273, file 5.

41 Auger, *Prisoners of the Home Front*, 134–35.

42 Report by YMCA secretary Dr. Hermann Boeschenstein, January to March 1945. LAC, MG 28, I 95, 273, file 5.

43 Letter from Rudolf Becker to his father, 14 December 1941. DSM, III A 3324 b.

44 See Auger, *Prisoners of the Home Front*, 101.

45 Cepuch, "*'Our guests are busy,'*" 15.

46 War Diary Camp Chatham, folder 2, vol. 1, 28 May 1944. LAC, RG24, 15396.

47 War Diary Camp Chatham, folder 2, vol. 2, 15 June 1944. LAC, RG24, 15396.

48 Ian Radforth, *Bush Workers and Bosses: Logging in Northern Ontario, 1900–1980* (Toronto: University of Toronto Press, 1987), 105.

49 War Diary Camp Chatham, folder 2, vol. 1, 22 May 1944. LAC, RG24, 15396.

50 War Diary Camp Chatham, folder 2, vol. 5, 1 September 1944. LAC, RG24, 15396.

51 War Diary Camp Chatham, folder 2, vol. 10, 13 July 1945. LAC, RG24, 15396.

52 Letter from Rudolf Becker to his father, 25 August 1945. DSM, III A 3324 b.

53 War Diary Camp Monteith, folder 4, vol. 64, 24 April 1946. LAC, RG24, 15393.

54 War Diary Camp Monteith, folder 4, vol. 61, 24 January 1946. LAC, RG24, 15393.

55 Auger, *Prisoners of the Home Front*, 102.

56 Graham Broad, *A Small Price to Pay: Consumer Culture on the Canadian Home Front, 1939–1945* (Vancouver: UBC Press, 2013), 12.

57 Ibid., 21.

58 Quotation from a letter from an internee to his parents, included in the report by the commandant of Camp Kananaskis, June 1942. PA AA, Bern 4275.

59 Broad, *A Small Price to Pay*, 43.

60 G. Elmore Reaman, *A History of Agriculture in Ontario*, vol. 2 (Toronto: Saunders, 1970), 176.

61 Here, I follow the theoretical concept of "positioning" as elaborated by Michael Bamberg, "Positioning between Structure and Performance," *Journal of Narrative and Life History* 7 (1997): 335–42.

62 Teresa Bridgeman, "Time and Space," in *The Cambridge Companion to Narrative*, ed. David Herman (Cambridge, UK: Cambridge University Press, 2007), 52–65, 63.

63 According to Marie-Laure Ryan, this is the most common narrative "mapping strategy." See Marie-Laure Ryan, "Cognitive Maps and the Construction of Narrative Space," in *Narrative Theory and the Cognitive Sciences*, ed. David Herman (Stanford: CSLI, 2003), 214–42, 219.

64 Oral history interview Hans Plähn (Author's archives).

65 Harald Wentzel, "Chronologie zur Seefahrts-Legende (Original)" (Lilienthal [1986 / 1987]), 30. Unpublished typescript, collection Peter Kiehlmann, Pinneberg, Germany.

66 Oral history interview Bruno Pichner (Author's archives).

67 Wentzel, "Chronologie zur Seefahrts-Legende," 32.

68 Ibid., 30.

69 Oral history interview Bruno Pichner.

70 See Auger, *Prisoners of the Home Front*, 43; Chris M. Madsen and Robert J. Henderson, *German Prisoners of War in Canada and Their Artifacts, 1940–1948* (Regina: R.J. Henderson, 1993), 92.

71 Oral history interview Hans Plähn.

72 Gisela Sigrist, "Kanada – Wunschraum, Kanada – Wunschtraum," *Zeitschrift für Kulturaustausch* 45, no. 2 (1995): 208–18.

73 Ibid., 216.

74 Oral history interview Hans Plähn.

75 Oral history interview Bruno Pichner.

76 Gerhard Pickerodt, "Aufklärung und Exotismus," in *Die andere Welt: Studien zum Exotismus,* ed. Thomas Koebner and Gerhard Pickerodt (Frankfurt am Main: Athenäum, 1987), 121–36, 135.

77 See, for example, Thomas Koebner, "Geheimnisse der Wildnis. Zivilisationskritik und Naturexotik im Abenteuerroman," in *Die andere Welt: Studien zum Exotismus*, ed. Thomas Koebner and Gerhard Pickerodt (Frankfurt am Main: Athenäum, 1987), 240–266, 43.

78 This is not necessarily a phenomenon specific to Canada: German cultural anthropologist Klaus Schriewer has pointed out in his study of lumbering in Hesse that the lumbermen themselves tend to romanticize their hard work. See Klaus Schriewer, *Waldarbeiter in Hessen: Kulturwissenschaftliche Analyse eines Berufsstandes* (Marburg: AVK, 1995), 49–50.

79 Oral history interview Hans Plähn.

80 Wentzel, "Chronologie zur Seefahrts-Legende," 34.

81 See Mary Louise Pratt, *Imperial Eyes: Travel Writing and Transculturation*, 2nd ed. (London: Routledge, 2008), 8.

82 Monika Fludernik, "Identity/alterity," in *The Cambridge Companion to Narrative*, ed. David Herman (Cambridge, UK: Cambridge University Press, 2007), 260–273, 264.

83 Letter from an interned seaman to his wife, 24 October 1941. PA AA, R 127.705.

84 Oral history interview Bruno Pichner.

85 See Pierre Bourdieu, "Le capital social," *Actes de la recherche en sciences sociales* 31 (1980 Janvier): 2–3.

86 On the meaning of photograph collections for the process of remembering, see Judith Kestler, "'Travel only when you must': Remembering the Internment of German Merchant Seamen in Canada during World War II," in *Interpreting Canada: New Perspectives from Europe / Interpréter le Canada: Nouvelles Perspectives du côté de l'Europe*, ed. Luigi Bruti-Liberati (Brno: European Network for Canadian Studies in collaboration with Masaryk University, 2012), 97–111.

87 Oral history interview Franz Renner (Author's archives).

88 Ibid.

89 Oral history interview Hans Peter Jürgens (Author's archives).

90 Wentzel, "Chronologie zur Seefahrts-Legende," 32.

91 Jürgens, *Sturmsee und Flauten*, 53.

92 Albrecht Lehmann, *Gefangenschaft und Heimkehr: Deutsche Kriegsgefangene in der Sowjetunion* (München: Beck, 1986), 97.

93 See Bernard Bailyn and Philip D. Morgan, "Introduction," in *Strangers within the Realm: Cultural Margins of the First British Empire*, ed. Bernard Bailyn and Philip D. Morgan (Chapel Hill: University of North Carolina Press, 1991), 1–31, 21.

94 John Murray Gibbon, *Canadian Mosaic: The Making of a Northern Nation* (Toronto: McClelland and Stewart, 1938).

95 Oral history interview Franz Renner.

96 Ibid.

97 See Raimund Beck, "Arbeitsräume für Angestellte," in *Großstadtmenschen: Die Welt der Angestellten*, ed. Burkhart Lauterbach (Frankfurt am Main: Büchergilde Gutenberg, 1995), 152–65, 159.

98 On the question of how internment experiences and the respective narratives are passed on to children and grandchildren of former internees see Judith Kestler, "Opas Erzählungen? Kriegsgeschichten aus zweiter Hand," *Bayerische Blätter für Volkskunde* N.F. 8/9 (2006/07 [2008]): 88–97.

99 Pratt, *Imperial Eyes*, 8.

100 See also Judith Kestler, "Internment and Humanitarian Aid: Perspectives on a Cultural Practice," *Journal of European Ethnology and Cultural Analysis* 1, no. 2 (2016): 148–71.

101 Oral history interview Bruno Pichner.

102 See Kestler, "Internierung erzählen – Gewalt erzählen?"

103 Letter from the Reich Ministry of Science, Education and Culture (Reichsministerium für Wissenschaft, Erziehung und Volksbildung) to the Foreign Office, 1 July 1942. PA AA, R 127.957.

104 Oral history interview Franz Renner.

105 Oral history interview Bruno Pichner.

106 Lewis H. Carlson, *We Were Each Other's Prisoners: An Oral History of World War II American and German Prisoners of War* (New York: Basic Books, 1997), viii. Another example: historian Arnold Krammer mentions that "former prisoners held in the United States recall their experiences as 'the best time of their lives.'" See Arnold Krammer, *Prisoners of War: A Reference Handbook* (Westport, CT: Praeger, 2008), 23.

107 For instance, Madsen and Henderson, *German Prisoners of War*, 96.

108 John A. Robinson, "Perspective, Meaning, and Remembering," in *Remembering Our Past: Studies in Autobiographical Memory*, ed. David C. Rubin (Cambridge, UK: Cambridge University Press, 1999), 199–217, 202.

109 Hans Moser, "Gedanken zur heutigen Volkskunde," *Bayerisches Jahrbuch für Volkskunde* (1954): 208–34, 221.

110 Here, I refer to the concept of "narrative identity" as described by Garbiele Lucius-Hoene and Arnulf Deppermann, *Rekonstruktion narrativer Identität: Ein Arbeitsbuch zur Analyse narrativer Interviews,* 2nd ed. (Wiesbaden: VS Verlag, 2004).

111 Or, as suggested recently by Gilly Car and Harold Mytum, "POW cultural studies." See Gilly Carr and Harold Mytum, "The Importance of Creativity behind Barbed Wire: Setting a Research Agenda," in *Cultural Heritage and Prisoners of War: Creativity behind Barbed Wire,* ed. Gilly Carr and Harold Mytum (New York: Routledge, 2012), 1–15, 1.

PART IX

THE POLITICS OF REDRESS

CHAPTER 19

A Numbers Game?: Stories of Suffering in Italian Canadian Internment in the Second World War

FRANCA IACOVETTA

This chapter considers a central but under-analyzed theme in Italian Canadian internment during the Second World War: stories of suffering. It takes the form of a reply to a critic who once denounced *Enemies Within: Italian and Other Internees in Canada and Beyond*, the 2000 volume I co-edited with Roberto Perin and Angelo Principe,[1] for denying the trauma endured by people like herself—the granddaughter and grandniece of Italian Canadian brothers, both naturalized citizens, successful businessmen, and community leaders whose unjust internment for alleged association with fascism caused untold suffering for all involved. As my role in *Enemies Within* makes clear, I came to study internment initially because the historical narrative adopted in 1990 by the Italian Canadian internment redress campaign—which resonated emotionally with many Italian Canadians, including those with neither personal connection nor previous knowledge of the episode—offered a simplistic story that neglected fascism and antifascism in the immigrant communities. Noting that *Enemies Within* repeatedly asserts that "only 600 Italians were interned," my critic countered that by turning suffering into "a numbers game," we unfairly negated or minimized the suffering of Italian Canadians.[2]

A critical theme of this volume on civilian internment is the liberal state's misuse of its wartime powers, the demonization of minoritized groups, and the violation of human rights. Certainly, Italian Canadians suffered hardships and humiliations as a result of the Canadian government's wartime measures, which included: the designation of approximately 31,000 Italians, including naturalized and Canadian-born citizens, as enemy aliens required to register with the local RCMP or police office, the internment of about 600 of them, the freezing of assets, and the seizure by the Custodian of Enemy Property (CEP) of property and businesses. As editors of *Enemies Within*, we stressed instead the selective nature of Italian Canadian internment. We considered misplaced the equivalencies being drawn within certain Italian Canadian redress circles between the internment of a tiny percentage of the Italian Canadian population (0.44 percent) and the dispossession, forced removal, and internment of the Japanese Canadian population, and, in at least a few instances, between Italian Canadian internment and the Holocaust. In countering such claims, and reinserting the history of fascism and other understudied elements of the "story," did *Enemies Within* neglect the suffering of those who continue to remember and live with a traumatic past? My critic articulated it thus: "These stories are the sound-track of my life. These events were discussed in our living room over and over again as people tried to make sense of our world gone mad." While tinged with anger, the critique is a well-considered one, and it deserves a thoughtful response. My reply, which draws on recent projects on the subject, such as a digital archive that features oral histories conducted with the adult children and other relatives of the (now mostly deceased) internees, sheds light as well on key themes related to the politics of redress campaigns that demand an apology and compensation from the state for the past mistreatment of an aggrieved group. In particular, it considers the historian's role as public intellectual and the complex relationship between scholarly and popular versions of history. Or, put another way, what does a (an activist) scholar do when someone who lived through the past events being studied accuses you of writing bad history?

A Risky Business

As Ian Radforth observes in his study of redress campaigns related to wartime internments in Canada, historians who intervene in contemporary controversies over the past engage in "a risky business." Those who help to construct the community redress narrative risk having their professional status tarnished by journalists, politicians, and activists who might reshape their evidence to fit their own purposes as well as by colleagues who might present alternative evidence and interpretations. Those who criticize their community's version of events risk a backlash from its acknowledged leaders and their scholarly allies.[3] In her contribution to this collection, Kassandra Luciuk addresses the challenges of complicating the history and collective memory of Eastern European internment in Canada during the First World War, a body of knowledge in large part established by historians and community leaders concerned with supporting the redress movement. The Italian Canadian historians who publicly intervened in the Italian Canadian redress campaign acknowledged that political lobbies need to state their case boldly, but criticized the National Congress of Italo-Canadians (NCIC) for oversimplification. Initially, our efforts had little impact on the Italian Canadian or Canadian media, and while a few individuals expressed informally their displeasure with it, there was no public outcry. I attributed the silence to the fact that, as editors, we did not simply adopt the diametrically opposed position of justifying internment. Instead, we laid out our intentions of shedding more light and encouraging further research on the complex and contradictory history of internment without condoning the state's heavy-handed tactics and with sympathy for the falsely accused and the women and children affected. I thought, too, that we had provided useful comparative contexts for assessing the Italian Canadian case, accomplished largely through the contributions of scholars of the Canadian state and of other groups interned in Canada, and of Italians in other wartime countries. That we also brought together authors who did not necessarily agree with each other, and said as much in our introduction, precluded stark generalizations about the book, or so I thought.

The strongest rebuke I received came from the woman cited at the outset of this essay, who, between 2009 and 2012, sent me three letters. As neither of my co-editors, both men, received letters, she may have written me because she thought a woman might be more receptive to calls to emphasize the suffering involved. Or perhaps she assumed that as the first name among the editors, I was somehow more responsible for the book's contents. The first two critical letters—the third one was quite different—identified a number of what she called the book's "troubling" themes, beginning with its supposed denial or dismissal of "accounts of Italophobia." Citing as one (inexplicable) example Enrico Cumbo's chapter on Hamilton's Italians, she writes that *Enemies Within* neglects "the stories of Italian Canadians being beaten in public by the army, the regular RCMP 2 a.m. raids on Italian homes—ransacking homes and 'roughing up' the Italian owners, the relentless spying." Surely, she correctly adds in reference to our understandable but still regrettable bias in favour of big cities with the largest Italian populations, such events were not confined to her smaller city.

As for the related claim about our playing "a numbers game," she sarcastically admits to losing count of how many times we stated "that ***only 600*** Italians were interned," adding: "how did you determine how many people had to be interned before it was deemed as 'suffering'? Is there some sort of chart [or] graph that historians use to determine such things?" Arguing that the "greater suffering" of another "does not diminish someone else's pain," an important insight, she invokes an alternative yardstick for measuring suffering, saying that even one instance of an Italian family who had a member imprisoned without having committed a crime, its assets "taken (stolen)," and the wife and children "literally starving" is sufficient cause to cry foul. Yet, *Enemies Within,* she writes, does not really discuss dispossession until the final chapter, which I co-wrote with Robert Ventresca, and even then its acknowledgement that, in many cases, the enemy alien property seized by the government and sold off for the war effort was never returned to the owner is insufficient as it ignores the suffering of the many wives and children whose men lost jobs or customers because of anti–enemy-alien sentiment. With little interest in our efforts to bring together different assessments, my critic chides us as editors for including claims made for the general reliability of RCMP intelligence on Italians as well as the RCMP's use of some questionable Italian Canadian informants who "vented personal feelings against a fellow neighbor or (former) friend." Indeed, she says *Enemies Within* ignores the implications of repeated research findings that prominent fascists escaped untouched, while others with little activism were swept up—"that innocents were interned"—because "this seems to be of little concern to the authors." As for the "complicated question" of deciding "just who was a fascist," especially once war with Italy broke out, she argues that the Italian men who joined the Order Sons of Italy (OSI) and other organizations that came under fascist control—but which were legal entities until June 1940, when Italy and Canada became belligerents—paid too heavy a price for their homeland passions. This was so largely because membership in what were essentially social, fraternal, and cultural groups amounted to early multicultural practice and in no way negated these men's loyalty to Canada—though she acknowledges many OSI members fully supported Fascist Italy. No sympathy is extended to the antifascists or leftist internees. Citing a quotation in Radforth's chapter on the Communist internees, which conveys their viewpoint, she writes that the book's reference to "'the pretensions and privileges among the "rich" Italians who acted as bosses of work gangs,'" merely reflects the "feelings" of the same "resentful leftie sources" who no doubt enjoyed "the fabulous feasts" the former laid out.

Finally, my critic scolds us editors for not making the fact that "not one internee—NOT ONE—was *ever* charged or convicted of being a subversive" the recurring theme of *Enemies Within*. Decrying our supposed insistence on identifying the internees as fascists, she expresses her gratitude to anthropologist Sam Migliore and others for helping "to correct this imbalance," a reference to the three projects, one of them a volume of historical essays in which Migliore's critique of *Enemies Within* appears (see below), launched at the 2012 event where my critic and I met. Co-produced by the Toronto Columbus Centre and Association of Italian Canadian Writers (AICW), these projects, which also include a volume of fiction and the website detailed below, were funded through the federal government's Community Historical Recognition Program.[4] My critic also asks me to respect her comments, rather than dismiss them as the "misty-eyed" recollections of someone with "a fuzzy lens on their own sense of history" because, although not an academic, she has "first[-]hand experience and knowledge about this time."[5] Fair enough. Furthermore, her reference to stories of suffering constituting the "soundtrack" of her life offers a compelling metaphor that well captures something of the oral historian's theoretical understanding of memory, including of past trauma, as dynamic rather than static. As numerous studies have documented, people's memories inform their present just as the present may shape their memories.[6] In the interest of engaging in a respectful exchange with a thoughtful critic, and also of moving beyond our individual differences to address major debates over internment, I offer the following reply.

Overlapping or Clashing Narratives?

In critiquing *Enemies Within*, my critic offers a narrative that corresponds to that of the Italian Canadian redress campaign. That narrative maintains that the enemy-alien designation and internment was a travesty of justice, the result of a war against ethnicity carried out by a state that pandered to widespread xenophobia and used its excessive powers to violate the civil rights of a law-abiding people who came from all walks of life. Moreover, their love of Italy had not compromised their loyalty to Canada, as evidenced by the absence of any act of sabotage or other fifth-column activity. I do not know whether or how much the community memory of internment the redress campaign helped to shape, largely through the public airing of internees' stories in meetings across Canada and in the 1997 National Film Board documentary *Barbed Wire and Mandolins* (dir. Nicola Zavaglia) and other venues, but the overlap is significant. (The campaign also well illustrates how history can prove therapeutic for a group with a painful past.) What is clear is that her memories have been shaped in part by the stories told and retold by family members and friends, including years after the event.

My critic's complaints about *Enemies Within* reflect her overall assessment that the book denies or discounts the existence of anti-Italian prejudice and Italian Canadian suffering. This is not the case, though I appreciate that we might have provided readers with more extensive coverage of what is, after all, a well-documented phenomenon. Scholarly assessments of internment do differ among the authors in *Enemies Within,* and certain distinctions are drawn—for example, that Italians were victims of discrimination but not of its worst excesses, as were Asians and Jews. But the introduction and most authors acknowledge the existence of long-term Italophobia[7] as well as the heightened xenophobia unleashed by wartime developments, and suffering caused by the government's decision to apply so broadly the enemy alien classification, and the RCMP's internment of those falsely accused on the basis of information supplied by vindictive Italian rivals. Everyone agrees that the prejudice many Italians had long suffered at the hands of Canadian employers and others helps to explain the pride they took in Mussolini as "the modernizer of Italy," and that it was encouraged by Canadian officialdom, the press, and prominent persons until Italy's invasion of Ethiopia in 1935–36. A number of authors who assign blame stress that the *majority* of Italians suffered unfairly because of the actions of a very few: Mussolini's consular officials, who as diplomats escaped any punishment for implanting fascism in the communities, and the most activist, and increasingly marginalized, Italian Canadian fascist leaders.[8] Similarly, a number of authors reference the war's painful ironies by noting a particular family whose sons served in the Canadian armed forces while the parents and even grandparents reported to the local RCMP or police office. Even Luigi Bruti Liberati, who argues that the state, using mostly reliable intelligence, interned active fascists, many of them "middle-class" men who had been courted by the consular officials, nevertheless suggests that the case for a "witch-hunt" against Italians is best made through attention to the vengeful actions of Canadians (vandalism) and the vitriolic attacks published in the English-Canadian press.[9]

It is also important to clarify the mischaracterization of Cumbo's chapter, which focuses on Italophobia and suffering. Our critic's decision to quote only the first half of the following sentence—"*While no reports of property damage or physical violence against Italians were reported in Hamilton*, respondents recalled fearing for their safety"—distorts Cumbo's twofold argument. First, the frenzy of fear and hostility unleashed by the declaration of war with Italy and the June 1940 arrests drew on long-standing stereotypes of Italians as black-handers, conspiratorial, and vengeful. And second, the absence of official police reports notwithstanding, other sources document that an anti-Italian backlash occurred. Cumbo then documents the many indignities suffered, including job layoffs, language restrictions, boycotts against small businesses, and denial of provincial relief, and the enduring legacy of a divisive episode on the community.[10]

On Suffering

Notwithstanding my counter-claims, I fully appreciate that a reader seeking vindication of her own painful stories of internment would feel frustrated by *Enemies Within*'s emphasis on political developments and comparative contexts, though the book also broke new ground in writing about the social and gender history of internment. The distance between us cannot be dissolved by simply elaborating on the suffering, but I thank her for the powerful reminder of how suffering takes its toll on the affected long after the painful event is over. Moreover, recent projects like the Community Historical Recognition Program (CHRP)–funded *Italian Canadians as Enemy Aliens: Memories of World War II* (ICEA) allow me to revisit the subject. One of the Toronto Columbus Centre/AICW collaborative projects noted above, this digital archive contains photographs, archived documents, private correspondence, and 105 interviews ranging from thirty to ninety minutes long.[11] Conducted by a fairly disparate group of people, the interviews contain rich material but vary in quality.[12] My selection of a dozen of the videotaped and transcribed interviews reflects my effort to include representation from small and big cities and to highlight themes related to women and children, and allow me to consider clues indicated by body gesture as well as careful listening for recurring phrases, tone, and silences that convey meaning.

My sample reflects the dominant profile of the internees, the majority of whom came from business and professional backgrounds: the interned father, grandfather, uncle, or grand-uncle to whom the narrators are linked included several businessmen, a doctor, studio-owning photographer, highly ranked firefighter, newspaper editor, and a few shop-owning tradesmen who became community leaders. With two exceptions, one of them the son of artist Vincenzo Poggi, who speaks frankly and poignantly about the shock of learning of the possibility that his father was working alongside the Italian consul in Montreal, Giuseppe Brigidi, in an effort to create sympathetic press coverage for the regime in the city's French-language newspapers,[13] the narrators insist that all the groups to which their relative belonged were social or cultural clubs. This is the case even of the man who described his father as a lifelong fascist. Thus, memories belong to those who, like my critic, feel deeply aggrieved because no one ever committed a criminal act. For their part, the interviewers appear keen to document instances of trauma, but, with a few exceptions, I cannot tell if they are aware of the extensive oral history scholarship on memory and trauma, much of it on women.[14] Opportunities to gain greater insight into a narrator's reflections are sometimes missed as the interviewer jumps to the next question. The narrators vary in their knowledge or experience of the events they describe, but most have clearly told their story before. Indeed, as with my critic, these are not only eyewitness recollections but family and group memories.

The interviews deserve a more in-depth assessment, but I raise a few themes for consideration here. First, these wartime memories are childhood or teenage memories, and one recurring theme is that internment created a rupture in a happy childhood in cities big and small. While nostalgia is evident, these narrators' memories also reflect children's different experiences of the event or their protection from its worse effects.[15] Speaking in positive, even glowing, terms about their childhood, many of the narrators, usually with a smile or wistful look, stress that life revolved mainly around a loving family and supportive ethnic community but also that their most vivid memories are of playing with the ethnic mix of "kids" in their neighbourhood. This was particularly so of narrators who, like Beatrice, daughter of internee Emilio Galardo, a professional photographer and leader in Sudbury's Italian community, came from small cities where Italians were much outnumbered. The immigrant children she grew up with in Copper Cliff, she says, got along well with each other and with the French Canadians who dominated her neighbourhood.[16] Using a language of early multiculturalism, Sandra O'Grady, whose grandfather, the construction magnate Leo Mascioli, was interned in Camp Petawawa for alleged fascist sympathies when she was about three years old, also described her childhood in Timmins as "Huckleberry Finn days" when she and her Croatian, Serbian, and Romanian friends "played in the streets," "tromped through the bush," and "went sliding at the Gulch." She acknowledged tensions, even beatings, and "an ugly slang word for every nationality," but, like others, makes light of these "school yard" antics.[17] Echoing this theme, Eugene Guagneli, a teenager in Niagara Falls when his mother, Luisa, became one of four Italian Canadian women interned for alleged fascist associations, also uses the notion of early multiculturalism to discuss the neighbourhood where he played "on the streets" with the "Anglo-Saxon, Scottish origin or Irish," and "Czech boys" who lived nearby. Indeed, he says that his first encounter with Italophobia was watching the plainclothes RCMP officers arrest his mother and "ravage" his house looking for incriminating evidence. With a small shake of his head, he conveyed the resentment still felt at the RCMP for taking even his prize-winning school "bristol board project on Canada," which took years to get back, and the shock of witnessing an RCMP officer strike his mother as she tried to save a saint's statue from falling off the bedroom dresser he was rifling through. Mimicking the movement of the officer's fist, he said, "He hit her. . . . And, um, I remember that shocked me. I'd never seen anything like that before. Uh, and then, uh, she just left with them. And . . . everyone was very upset."[18]

Asked about the internment's impact on their mother, a number of the female narrators stress, as did my critic, that as difficult as it was for them, poorer women faced more desperate circumstances. Phyllis, the daughter of Luigi Mascia, a Hamilton liquor salesman, horse-owner, and prominent member of a local *fascio* (a branch of the Italian Fascist Party) typically responded with "well we survived" and "carried on as a family" thanks to "relatives, aunts, uncles" who helped each other, the local United Church they attended, and some (financial) support from her father's Toronto-based employer and other "English business contacts." The latter included a Jewish owner of a local soda company who "remembered" how her father had once supported him. Although clearly bitter about having to postpone her own marriage because of internment, she shifted attention to the poorer women without working husbands, saying they suffered the most. Like my critic, she used the word "starving" to underscore their plight and that of their children. In exhibiting their empathy for those worse off, she, like other narrators, were also drawing attention to the wider crisis in which their own stories took place.[19]

Both women's and men's narratives also provide us with evidence of how women from varying backgrounds proved resilient and resourceful in dealing with their financially reduced and anxiety-ridden circumstances. Phyllis herself speaks of women with several children surviving partly by pulling certain children out of school to work on nearby farms and elsewhere. One of the few working-class narratives in my sample is of factory worker Maria Zaffiro, wife of interned shoemaker husband Francesco, who had been provincial vice-president of the Ontario Order Sons of Italy and acting secretary of the Hamilton *fascio*. As recalled by her son Nicholas, age ten in 1940, Maria could support her children despite the loss of income from his father's shop largely because she was able to hold on to the job she already had in a clothing factory (as did some other Italian women). But her eldest daughter—who, according to Nicholas, was the most traumatized by the internment and still refuses to speak about it—also had to go out to work, forfeiting a high-school education. Nicholas helped out too, he says, with some wages from a part-time job at a fish-and-chips shop. "My mother," he adds, "was too proud to go for social assistance"—she would have been rejected had she tried—but speaks of getting much appreciated help from others, including some "English" and "Canadian" neighbours.[20]

As their daughters, sons, and others recall it, better-off women who owned homes responded to their financially reduced situation by renting out rooms, though some of them also benefited from other resources. The daughter of interned photographer Emilio Galardo of Sudbury, Beatrice remembered how her mother, with five children to raise, rented rooms, taking on the extra cooking and cleaning involved. Her son also secured permission from the Custodian of Enemy Property (CEP) to continue running their photography studio, which provided some additional income.[21] Largely because the family grocery store in Hamilton was allowed to remain open, Antonio Olivieri's internment, though very stressful, did not create a financial crisis for wife Anna and her two daughters mainly because, as daughter Toni McDermott recalls, Anna cooked and cleaned for the boarders and family while she and her sister "ran the store," though they did lose customers.[22] A few women were compelled to move in with parents. Emma Giradi did so in Vancouver, after her Canadian-born husband Bruno, a lifelong fascist, co-founder and editor of the Italian Canadian newspaper *L'Echo,* and member of the local Circolo Giulio Giordoni *fascio* and Sons of Italy, was interned in Camp Kananaskis. As some of these examples also suggest, contrary to conventional wisdom, the CEP sometimes allowed an internee's family to operate their business. Without denying the hardship and enormous anxiety and fear, these examples suggest, too, that one cannot easily measure suffering and that internment memories need a more nuanced analysis than that suggested by "starving" women and children.[23]

While most narrators agree that mothers both struggled and suffered, closer attention to their words and gestures reveals three main if also overlapping portraits: the stoic, heroic, and supported mother. The strongest wartime memory the daughters of Canadian-born Loretta Masciolo Sterling have of their mother is of her remarkable stoicism in the face of adversity. Loretta's

Italian-Canadian father, the Timmins-based industrialist Leo Masciolo, who rose spectacularly from humble immigrant miner to construction magnate, was interned at the same time that her Scottish Canadian–born husband, a recruiter and major with the region's Algonquin Regiment, was interned (for five years) in a German prisoner of war camp. Leo Mascioli had both his supporters and detractors, and both groups included some of Timmins' most prominent figures (his detractors also included unionized workers who resented the role he had played in a major 1912 mining strike), but it was his Canadian-born married daughter Loretta who felt most acutely the ironies of war. In addition to the dual internment of her Italian Canadian father at home and her Canadian military husband overseas, some of her Canadian husband's army recruits were behind a violent anti-Italian riot in Timmins' Little Italy (The Moneta). Speaking of her mother's capacity to handle this grim situation despite enormous anxiety, daughter Sandra smiles as she recalls her mother's remarkable ability "to keep a good face forward" in a crisis. According to her sister Joan, their mother insisted that "we're going to keep our heads down, making no waves." Still, the sisters, listening in on family conversations instead of going to bed, picked up bits of information about friendships and associations maintained and lost, the fact that the family had hired a lawyer (they could afford to do so immediately, in part because Loretta's brother convinced the CEP to let him manage some of his father's affairs), and details from the letters from Camp Petawawa. While both sisters attribute the relative normalcy of their lives during this period to their mother's heroic stoicism, and the support of family and friends, they also recall that, as Joan put it, her mother was also lonely, worried, and embarrassed that "everybody" knew the Canadian government thought her father a dangerous "subversive."[24]

The most vivid image of a heroic mother who met the challenges caused by internment emerges in the narrative of Vladimira, daughter of Montreal internee Angelo Delle Vedove, who was arrested on her tenth birthday. With obvious pride, she details her mother's exploits. They included holding down as many as three different jobs, including a full-time factory job, and borrowing money to get the house they had just started to build when her father was arrested into decent enough shape to move her grandparents and them into it. She laughs as she recalls how her father was stunned when he saw how his wife had created virtual rooms by covering "the two-by fours that divided the house" with beige-coloured tar paper. He was also shocked, she adds, that the local lumberyard owner would continue to extend credit to help finish the house to her mother, whom he clearly trusted to pay him back.[25]

Some of the men who spoke about mothers tended to highlight the support given them by their family, though this may reflect the women's stay-at-home status as well as their own paternalism. During his interview, Attilio, the son of Bruno Girardo, the lifelong Vancouver fascist, is visibly upset as he denounces the state's "unconscionable" decision to ignore its obligation to support the Canadian-born children of Canadian-born citizens like himself by disallowing assistance for the families of enemy aliens. "Thank God," he says, "that my mother had her mother and father here" in Kitsilano because "otherwise we would have starved or my mother would have had to do . . . I don't know what [to support us] because she was not educated." (Before marriage, she worked in her parents' shop.) Attilio stresses, too, that his father was acutely aware of his mother's difficulties, and that in his letters, he told them that, with food, sports, and chefs, he was far better off in camp than were women like Emma, who, it turns out, was denied medical attention by a doctor refusing to treat enemy aliens.[26] The son of an interned firefighter and a leader of Ottawa's Italian community, Sal Pantelone recalls the financial support he and his brothers offered their stay-at-home mother and younger siblings with the military salaries they (ironically) earned from jobs with the Canadian navy and army, respectively, but also recalled her effort to earn money from renting rooms upstairs and through the sale of a knitting machine, which fetched far less than she hoped.[27]

The ICEA narrators shed light on the uneven process of granting visits with the arrested or interned men and how visits are remembered. Women who speak of trying to visit men held in the horse stables at the CNE in Toronto (before being shipped to Camp Petawawa) are especially indignant about the "horrible" humiliation of their men being forced, "like animals," to march in the nude to the showers, which exposed them to outside bystanders.[28] The most striking memory of a camp visit comes from Vladimira, who, mimicking a disbelieving woman, recounts how her mother, upon seeing her husband looking well-fed, and with a scar earned from a soccer game, declared: "per la Madonna. . . . Here I am in three jobs, working, everything, and they're you know. . .," her silent nodding effectively completing the sentence (eating well and playing sports). The interviews also confirm observations made in *Enemies Within* about the varied responses to camp life: some of their adult children speak about fathers who expressed their fear and anxieties, while others recall fathers who, like Girardi, said they were fine and more concerned about their family. Some men revealed a wry sense of humour: Girardi recalled that his father loved the irony of potential saboteurs being trained (in Camp

Kananaskis) to use explosives for road building in Banff. Just as the narrators speak in detail about the circumstances surrounding the arrest of a father or grandfather (and one mother)—either because they witnessed it or family accounts have also become their memory, or a mix of both—they remember the return. Stories of the men's (surprise) arrival home contain a range of scenarios, from the father who offered his family a brisk hello to the one who, his dark hair now turned white, sat in a dark corner and sobbed.[29] As for longer-term observations, the dominant pattern to emerge was that the experience, however short, changed the men, mainly for the worse, though one said life turned "back to normal" relatively soon afterwards.[30] According to their daughters, granddaughters, and sons, even the men who rebuilt businesses and careers felt embittered and stigmatized by the episode. Some of the men were capable of a gallows humour, at least in the company of fellow internees, while others, scarred by their inability to resume their old jobs or otherwise feeling shunned, remained largely silent about the issue for many years.[31]

Antifascist Suffering?

A resounding silence in my sample of ICEA interviews concerns the suffering of Italian Canadian antifascists, suggesting that, like my critic, the children and grandchildren of the internees keen to demand a public stage for their painful memories are uninterested in the mistreatment meted out to Italian Canadians who, out of their commitment to liberal or radical ideals, spoke out against fascism. Speaking historically, this situation indicates in part the success with which pro-fascists were able to equate patriotism for Fascist Italy with loyalty to Canada, a major contention of *Enemies Within*. Speaking from today, one might argue that those keen to expose the mistreatment of Italian Canadians might devote some effort to pursuing the evidence presented in *Enemies Within* and other publications[32]—and now also on the ICEA website—indicating that antifascists faced recriminations for speaking out against fascism or censored themselves out of fear of reprisals on family members in Italy. Isn't just one case of such mistreatment enough to cry foul? Here are just two possible cases involving Montreal Italians that deserve closer study: restaurateur Primo Lorenzetti was reportedly beaten up by thugs after denouncing Italy's invasion of Ethiopia, and musician and band leader Giuseppe Agostino's career appears to have suffered (or at least he became less visible) following his refusal to play "Giovinezza" (a fascist marching song), at community events.[33] With a few significant exceptions,[34] the organizers of and participants in the recent spate of historical, literary, and media projects on internment, all useful additions to the debate, appear similarly uninterested in antifascist suffering. Have the descendants of the antifascists felt silenced by all of this? Indeed, it is time that Italian Canadians recognize the suffering endured by radical antifascists like the anarchist Attilio Bortolotti, who faced fascist denunciation, an RCMP raid, arrest, and imprisonment, and the threat of deportation (and likely death) for his antifascist activism.[35]

Being Heard

My critic and I met briefly, between the first and second letter, and shortly afterwards, she sent a third, much shorter, letter that effectively exonerated me. We met at the Columbus Centre in spring 2012 during the launch of the ICEA website and related internment book projects. On the previous evening, the centre's director had attended the launch of *The Italian Question*, a documentary funded by a grant that Gabriel Scardellato, author of an important photo essay in *Enemies Within*, and I secured from the CHRP program, and we were returning the courtesy.[36] In a curt exchange, my critic scolded me for lying about the internees and denying their families' suffering. I suggested she view the documentary, and then we ate lunch at separate tables. Shortly afterwards, I received her last letter. Having viewed *The Italian Question*, she applauded me for my balanced treatment of the internment episode and my masterful handling of this difficult and complex history.[37] Since the views I express in the documentary do not deviate from what I wrote in *Enemies Within* or delivered in lectures I wondered why, finally, the positive reply?

A few related factors probably mattered. A one-hour documentary focused exclusively on Italian Canadian internment that quickly draws the viewer into the story through a judicious mix of narration, personal recollections, and film footage, and that features historians and family members of internees whose differing interpretations include those like her own, resonated better with my critic than an edited collection that was more focused on critiquing the official redress narrative, among other things, and that included comparative case studies. She likely viewed the documentary as balanced because in giving her viewpoints a serious airing, it also validated the legitimacy of her perspective. Or, in other words, her stories of suffering had been heard. The documentary also asks viewers to think critically about the larger question of suspending civil liberties, especially in light of the current demonization of Muslims as terrorists.

Furthermore, the viewpoints that resonate with my critic are articulated not only by historians unassociated with *Enemies Within*, such as Bruno Ramirez and Joyce Pillarella, but also by those who, by virtue of our ties to the book, are assumed to be less sympathetic to the internees and their families, thereby also making our criticisms of the "official" narrative more palatable. Ramirez describes the pro-fascist activities as being of a ceremonial, not criminal, character, and says the government's decision to apply the enemy alien status so broadly adversely affected the entire minority group, psychologically and materially. An oral historian and granddaughter of a deeply committed fascist who saluted Mussolini as two RCMP officers escorted him from his Montreal home, Pillarella explains how she "switched sides" in her assessment of the internees as her MA research shifted from the archival documents, which included the formal oaths that men like her grandfather swore to Mussolini and Fascist Italy, to interviewing some of the Montreal internees, who convinced her of their loyalty to Canada. In addition to making divergent points, Perin and I also present viewpoints with which my critic agrees, in many cases reiterating what we wrote in *Enemies Within*, yet, within the context of the film, we perhaps convinced her that one can criticize the official narrative as overly simplistic without being apologists for state repression. Perin details the prejudices toward Italians and, readily agreeing that the RCMP arrests were "very frightening acts," he says they were intended as such by a state flexing its political muscle. He also attributes the contradictory nature of internment in part to the sly tactics of certain "guilty" parties—committed fascists who had benefited from their association with Mussolini's consular officials—who avoided internment by pointing a finger at other "guilty" parties, and the state that accommodated them. This third letter offers no criticism either of Sal Pantalone, the son of the interned Ottawa firefighter who, in the documentary, details the negative impact of internment on his father and family but also defends the Canadian government's actions as necessary precautions taken in wartime.

As with *Enemies Within*, my critic attributed the documentary's treatment of the subject mainly to me rather than to the mix of participants or to the filmmaker Sunny Yi, who, having researched the subject for her master's degree, chose the format, footage, and (unrehearsed) questions, wrote the female narrator's script, and edited our replies. (We were filmed separately and did know what others said.) But since my critic focused on me, I note that my contributions to the documentary were likely also affirming for her because, although I did not deviate from my position, my replies to the questions also addressed her concerns. Asked about fascism, I attributed the consular officials' success in planting fascism in the immigrant communities partly to the *prominenti* who benefited from the association, but also declared that even the most ideologically committed fascists had likely never contemplated sabotage. Like Perin and Ramirez, I criticized the enemy-alien designation for making an entire minority group vulnerable to harassment and violence.

While agreeing to answer Yi's questions, I also had my own priorities, including highlighting the antifascists. I used an exchange about the widespread support for Ottawa's wartime actions to speak about the small but vocal minority who opposed the suspension of civil liberties, adding that the decision to do so while sacrificing Canadian lives to fight totalitarian regimes was an ugly irony of war. Another priority was to focus attention on the women and shift the language of "suffering," with its passive connotations, to the women's active survival strategies, which I did all too briefly in my comments about working-class and poor women's capacity to cope with crisis. My final priority was to restate my main reasons for "going public" in the first place. Noting that scholarly and popular versions of past events often differ, I stressed the historian's responsibility to try to understand the messiness of the past in all of its complexity. And I insisted upon the inappropriateness of equating the selective internment of Italian Canadians with the evacuation, dispossession, and incarceration of the entire West Coast Japanese Canadian population, or with the Holocaust. Within the overall context of the documentary, I think, perhaps, that my critic finally heard me say that one can be critical of the official narrative without condoning state repression, and attach some blame for the internment on the few while opposing internment. Perhaps, she also revised her singular antipathy to our supposed "numbers' game approach to suffering" as she watched the footage of a Nazi crematorium that Yi chose to accompany my comments about parallels to the Holocaust being unacceptable, given "the scale, the horror" of the former, even as I think using the footage is problematic. Still, I do think that *Enemies Within* has rendered unacceptable the public articulation of such equivalencies within Italian Canadian circles. Even several narrators in the ICEA interviews refer to the greater mistreatment of the Japanese Canadians. As historians, we often encourage people to understand a particular racist, or sexist, act in the context of a broader spectrum of assumptions and viewpoints, but, sometimes, it is also important to draw distinctions.[38]

Ongoing Debate

In the time since my critic sent me her first letter, the study on Italian Canadian internment has expanded, thanks in large part to CHRP federal funds. If the response to *Enemies Within* took longer than anticipated, it is now clear that our volume has provoked further historical research, based on documentary and oral history sources, as well as debate, on the subject. Entitled *Beyond the Barbed Wire*, the (non-peer-reviewed) volume of research essays produced by the Columbus Centre/AICW collaboration funded by CHRP, reflects recent research and reflection dealing with regions outside Ontario and Quebec, namely British Columbia, particularly Vancouver, the prairies, and Atlantic Canada, particularly Cape Breton's Italians. The Ontario-based research in the volume includes John Potesio's chapter on Thunder Bay, while Adriana A. Davies's chapter on Alberta includes intriguing references to antifascist Alex Pico. There is detailed documentation of the shift in public opinion over fascism and the growing frenzy of fear that, as authors in *Enemies Within* argued, helps to explain the Canadian government's draconian measures.[39] Travis Tomchuk's research on the despicable August Bersani—the corrupt Protestant minister who used his position as a RCMP informant to exact revenge on former opponents—is an important contribution to the debate over the reliability of the RCMP intelligence information (his research on Bersani appears in this book as well, complementing commentary in James Mochoruk's essay here on the role prejudiced informants played in the internment of Ukrainian leftists). The mostly oral history research being carried out on the Italian Canadian internees and their families varies enormously in quality, but the chapters by Pillarrella for Montreal and Sam Migliore's on Cape Breton offer some compelling arguments about the internees' viewpoints. Drawing on public and private family archives, the new research presented on millionaire industrialist James Francischini challenges the portrayal of him in *Enemies Within* as moderately involved in fascism, and offers an intriguing counter-explanation. And if, as the volume's editors predict in their introduction, Italian Canadians sensitized to the critical issues through their critique of Italian Canadian internment become activists for the civil rights of Muslim and other victims of the post-9/11 war on terror, this will be an excellent thing indeed.[40]

On the negative side, I note that, as a left historian who has never justified the internment, I am disappointed that some researchers, including some contributors to *Beyond the Barbed Wire*, sloppily mischaracterize *Enemies Within* as justifying the internment. In that regard, the debate remains heavily polarized, one concerning aspect of which is a tendency among certain supporters of redress to perpetuate one-dimensional portraits of the internees as innocent of any fascist connections. A troubling example of this distortion appears in the work of Sam Migliore, the anthropologist whom my critic praised for supposedly correcting the anti-internee bias of *Enemies Within* (see above). Since Migliore's misplaced criticism also informs the description of a large set of internment camp photographs provided on the ICEA website, which, in turn, may influence many users of the site, it must be addressed at least briefly here. A revised version of a previously published article, Migliore's chapter in *Beyond the Barbed Wire* takes specific aim at the photo essay in *Enemies Within* written by Scardellato, which features photographs of internees displaying their illegal fascist regalia—the fez and a flag with the militant fascist phrase, "me ne frego" ("I don't give a damn"). In two of the group photographs, we can also see an individual man posed assertively, arms crossed, in a manner reminiscent of Mussolini's famous stance. In keeping with *Enemies Within*'s aim to complicate the simplified narrative of internment, Scardellato rightly asks whether such images should lead us to question whether the internees were as politically innocent or naive as the NCIC and other redress advocates have argued. In response, Migliore, a folklorist, simply asserts that such symbols might hold any number of meanings other than pro-fascist sentiment. While I agree with his premise that the meanings people attach to symbols can change depending upon time and context, I find deeply problematic Migliore's ahistorical, culturally relativist thesis that all symbols, fascist regalia included, are open to multiple interpretations. Surely, meanings are also historically contingent. Surely, he would not advise multiple interpretations of Nazi iconography? I could not agree more with his call to be vigilant about state repression today, but caution against adopting a postmodern any-interpretation-is-valid position. Such relativism is irresponsible when actual freedoms are at stake.[41]

Finally, while it is too early to see what kind of response *The Italian Question* documentary will generate beyond my critic, in light of the problematic categorization of *Enemies Within* as a pro-internment book I am glad that I again took the risk of intervening in a heated public debate. If it attracts an audience, it may prove more effective than *Enemies Within* in moving the debate beyond the dichotomies—"for" or "against" internment—that can obscure more than illuminate.

I thank Greg Kealey, Roberto Perin, Gabriele Scardellato, Ian Radforth, and Matthew Poggi for their feedback on earlier versions of this chapter.

Notes

1 Franca Iacovetta, Roberto Perin, Angelo Principe, eds., *Enemies Within: Italian and Other Internees in Canada and Beyond* (Toronto: University of Toronto Press, 2006).

2 Critic to Author, Private Letter, 23 March 2009.

3 Ian Radforth, "Ethnic Minorities and Wartime Injustices: Redress Campaigns and Historical Narratives in Late Twentieth-Century Canada" in *Settling and Unsettling Memories: Essays in Canadian Public History,* ed. Nicole Neatby and Peter Hodgins (Toronto: University of Toronto Press, 2012).

4 A product of what some have called the "culture of redress" in Canada (and elsewhere), CHRP devoted five of its twenty-five-million-dollar budget meant "to acknowledge and to educate Canadians about the historical experiences of ethno-cultural communities affected by wartime discriminatory measures and immigration restrictions applied in Canada" to projects related to Italian Canadian internment. On "culture of redress," Jennifer Henderson and Pauline Wakeham, eds., *Reconciling Canada: Critical Perspectives on the Culture of Redress* (Toronto: University of Toronto Press, 2013). See also Matt James's analysis of the Canadian government's management of historical redress through neo-liberal measures such as CHRP in Ibid., 39–41.

5 Private letters, 23 March 2009; 2 April 2012 plus attached note.

6 A tiny sample of this literature includes Luisa Passerini, "Memory," *History Workshop Journal*, 15, no. 1 (Spring 1983): 195–96; Alessandro Portelli, "The Peculiarities of Oral History," *History Workshop Journal* 12 (Autumn 1981): 96–107.

7 R.F. Harney coined the term in his "Italophobia: An English-Speaking Malady?," *Studi Emigrazione/Etudes Migrations* 22, no. 77 (1985): 6–43.

8 See the essays by Angelo Principe, Luigi Pennacchio, Roberto Perin, and Franca Iacovetta and Robert Ventresca in *Enemies Within.*

9 Essays by Enrico Cumbo and Luigi Bruti Liberati in *Enemies Within.*

10 Cumbo's essay in *Enemies Within.*

11 "Italian Canadians as Enemy Aliens: Memories of World War II," http://www.italiancanadianww2.ca/villa/home.

12 They include those with MAs and PhDs in history and folklore studies, journalists, and writers. Some Toronto members attended a training workshop at Concordia University's Centre for Oral History and Digital Storytelling. Conversation with Travis Tomchuk.

13 Maurice Poggi, interviewed by Melina De Guglielmo, Montreal, 29 November 2011.

14 Such as Luisa Passerini, "Memory and Totalitarianism," *International Yearbook of Oral History and Life Stories,* vol. 1 (London: Oxford University Press, 1992); Marlene Epp, "The Memory of Violence: Soviet and East European Mennonite Refugees and Rape in the Second World War," *Journal of Women's History* 9, no. 1 (1997): 58–87; and Sugiman below.

15 Pamela Sugiman, "Passing Time, Moving Memories: Interpreting Wartime Narratives of Japanese Canadian Women," *Histoire sociale/ Social History*, 36, no. 73 (May 2004).

16 Beatrice (Galardo) Ladyk, interviewed by Christine Sansalone, Sudbury, 25 May 2011.

17 Sandra O'Grady, interviewed by Travis Tomchuk, North Bay, 10 August 2011.

18 Eugene Guagneli, interviewed by Melina De Guglielmo, Grismby, 21 June 2011.

19 Phyllis Morreale and Rita Morreale, interviewed by Nadia Mior, Hamilton, 2 May 2011.

20 Nicholas Zaffiro, interviewed by Nadia Mior, Hamilton 10 May 2011.

21 Ladyk interview.

22 Antoinette McDermott, interviewed by Stephanie Petrilli, Toronto, 30 August 2012.

23 Attilio Girardi, interviewed by Raymond Culos, Coquitlam, 31 May 2011.

24 O'Grady interview; Joan McKinnon, interviewed by Louanne Aspillaga, Waterloo, 14 April 2011; Charlie Angus, *Mirrors of Stone: Fragments from the Porcupine Frontier* (Toronto: Between the Lines, 2001), ch. 9.

25 Vladimira Delle Vedove Tontini, interviewed by Joyce Pillarella, Montreal, 23 June 2011.

26 Attilio Girardi, interviewed by Raymond Culos, Coquitlam, 31 May 2011. That he does not mention the incident involving his mother's health in this interview suggests the importance of not interpreting interviews in total isolation. See Raymond Culos, *Injustice Served: The Story of British Columbia's Italian Enemy Aliens during World War II* (Montreal: Cusmano Books, 2012).

27 Sal Pantalone, interviewed by Francesca L'Orfano, Ottawa, 16 September 2011. On mothers, consult also Noreen (Gaggi) Alberico and Linda (Gaggi) Rosati, interviewed by Melina De Guglielmo, Toronto, 14 July 2011.

28 Morealle interview. On the failure to get a visit, Paula Mascioli, interviewed by Cristina Pietropaolo, Ottawa, 16 July 2011.

29 For example, Tontini and McDermot, and Pantalone interview, respectively.

30 Zaffiro interview.

31 Interviews with Tontini, Pantalone, McKinnon, O'Grady; Gloria Miron and Richard Ladyk, interviewed by Sansalone, Sudbury, 25 May 2011. Guagani said the same of his mother.

32 Such as Angelo Principe, *The Darkest Side of the Fascist Years* (Toronto: Guernica, 1999); the volumes of Gregory S. Kealey and Reg Whitaker, eds., *RCMP Security Bulletins: The War Series, Part 2, 1942–45* (St John's, NL: Canadian Committee on Labour History, 1993).

33 This information, which also hints at collusion between fascists in Italy and Canada, comes from the surveillance files of Italy's political police, which grew exponentially under Fascism, and which contain the reports of Italian consular officials in foreign countries, local police and security officials in Italy and abroad, and private letters exchanged by the "subversives" in question. See Archivio Centrale Dello Stato (Central State Archives), Rome, Italian Ministry of the Interior, Casellario Politico Centrale (Central Political Records Office/CPC), Primo Lorenzetti, Busta (file) 2838; Copy of CPC files contained in Archivio-Biblioteca Enrico Travaglini, Fano, Le Marche, Italy, File on Giuseppe Agostino. My thanks to Roberto Perin for sharing his archival research with me.

34 Travis Tomchuk, referenced below.

35 See, for example, https://www.katesharpleylibrary.net/8pk1h4 (accessed 8/28/2018); Theresa Moritz and Albert Moritz, *The World's Most Dangerous Woman: A New Biography of Emma Goldman* (Vancouver: Subway Books, 2001) Chapter 12.

36 *The Italian Question: Italian Canadians and the Second World War*, director Sun-Kyung Yi, Aysha Productions, 2012.

37 Private Letter, 12 April 2012.

38 For another example, Culos, *Injustice Served.*

39 See the essays by Raymond Culos, Adriana A. Davies, Guilia DeGasperi, Patrick Marsh, Sam Migliore, John Potestio, and Venera Fazio in Licia Canton, Dominic Cusmano, Michael Mirolla, Jim Zucchero, eds., *Beyond Barbed Wire: Essays on the Internment of Italian Canadians* (Toronto: Association of Italian Canadian Writers and Columbus Centre of Toronto, 2012). For a summary of related works, see Licia Canton and Joseph Pivato, "Writing the Silence," in Ibid.

40 See the chapters in Canton et al., *Beyond Barbed Wire* written by the authors named in this paragraph and those by Frank Giorno and James McCreath (Francischini); Culos, *Injustice Served.*

41 The photographs in question belonged to internee Osvaldo Giacomelli. Gabriele Scardellato, "Images of Internment," in *Enemies Within*; Sam Migliore "Painful Memories of a Forgotten Past," in *Beyond Barbed Wire*, 355–87. Scardellato has since published a rebuttal. See his "What's in a Photograph? Debating Images of Italian Canadian Internment," *Histoire sociale/Social History* 51:104 (November 2018) 253–373.

CHAPTER 20

The Internment of Japanese Canadians: A Human Rights Violation

ART MIKI

I was in kindergarten in Haney, British Columbia, when my family was forcibly uprooted from our homes in May 1942 and transported by train to the immigration centre in Winnipeg where sugar beet farmers would come to select families to work on their farms. So began my journey with what would come to be known as the internment and forced relocation of Japanese Canadians during the Second World War, a historic human rights violation. For me, and many of my generation, the road was an especially long one. Though the war ended in 1945, and all restrictions on Japanese Canadians were finally lifted in 1949, our attempts at making sense—and challenging a racist national narrative—of our experiences and those of our elders would culminate in an historic, path-breaking struggle for national redress and apology. I was honoured to play a key role in that fight. Here, I share my story.

Both of my parents were born in British Columbia and had established their home in Vancouver and later moved to Haney to live on my grandparents' berry and fruit farm. Both my grandparents came from Japan at the turn of the last century. On my mother's side, Tokusaburo and Yoshi Ooto came from Fukuoka in 1903 and journeyed to the Prince Rupert area to a fishing cannery in Port Ossington where they lived. As the children grew older, my grandparents decided to move into the Fraser Valley and in 1918 established a farm in Haney where they remained until their relocation to Manitoba. On my father's side, my grandparents, the Shintanis, came to Canada in 1892. However, an unexpected misfortune resulted as Grandmother became ill and went back to Japan, where she died. Subsequently, my grandfather married Kiyo Miki, took her name and returned to Vancouver through Hawaii in 1899.

My parents were married in 1935, and by the time we were forced to leave British Columbia, they had three children, myself, Kunio, and Joan. My parents and grandparents opted to come to Manitoba because they were assured that the families would remain together, unlike in the internment camps where families were often separated. Once on the farm the Japanese were not permitted to visit or travel without permission. The harsh winter conditions, the terrible non-insulated housing, the lack of water and electricity, and the short growing season made life difficult. We lived in a four-room house with three families consisting of seven adults and three children near the town of Ste. Agathe, approximately forty kilometres south of Winnipeg. I recall that in November 1942 my mother, who was pregnant, had to request special permission from the RCMP to travel to Winnipeg to have my brother, Roy. I began school in Ste. Agathe, a French-speaking community. Our family remained in Ste. Agathe for two years and then moved to North Kildonan, located on the outskirts of Winnipeg (Japanese could not reside within the boundaries of Winnipeg unless special permission was granted by the BC Securities Commission). My father Kazuo received special permission to work as a machinist at Monarch Machinery in Winnipeg to support the family. In 1948, we were allowed to move into Winnipeg.

The removal from the West Coast had a devastating effect on Grandfather Ooto, who was forced to do tedious and back-breaking work unlike life on a berry farm. He had lost everything—the farm that he built by himself—and was at an age where he should be enjoying the fruits of his labour. He passed away shortly after the move to North Kildonan. I felt that he died a broken man, having very little to give his family and grandchildren.

What were the circumstances that led us to Manitoba and supported the internment and forced relocation of 21,000 Japanese Canadians? Almost overnight, the lives and future of the Japanese in Canada were drastically altered following the bombing of Pearl Harbor in 1941 and the Canadian government's declaration of war on Japan on 8 December 1941. The pre-existing racist mentality was evident when Canada commenced a movement to use the state's wartime emergency powers to remove the human and civil rights of a portion of the Canadian population, namely Canadians of Japanese ancestry living on the West Coast of British Columbia. Under the guise of national security, the Canadian government used the powers granted under the War Measures Act and passed orders-in-council to remove the Japanese from the "protected area": 100 miles inland from the West Coast. The War Measures Act, passed on 22 August 1914, allowed the governor in council or the federal cabinet unlimited powers to govern if it perceived the existence of "war, invasion or insurrection, real or apprehended."[1] This act was first used against Ukrainian and other Eastern European civilians during the First World War.[2] During the Second World War, the powers given to cabinet led to the registration of Japanese Canadians with the Royal Canadian Mounted Police and the labelling of them as "enemy aliens." A curfew was imposed on the Japanese living in the protected area and restricted them from possessing motor vehicles, cameras, radios, firearms, ammunition, or explosives. The properties belonging to Japanese Canadians were confiscated and later sold without their permission. On 4 March 1942 the cabinet used the act to initially "detain" Japanese Canadians at Hastings Park—in the livestock buildings on the exhibition grounds—and then move them from the protected area to makeshift internment camps in the interior of British Columbia. Others were sent to sugar beet farms or prisoner of war camps.[3]

The government was extremely careful in the wording of its orders, noting "that Japanese Canadians were being detained at the pleasure of Minister of Justice, Louis St. Laurent" because under the Geneva Convention it was illegal to intern persons born in Canada who were Canadian citizens (the convention only permitted internment of aliens). In the eyes of the victims, the uprooting and dispossession were viewed as "internment," as movement was restricted and the internees were held under RCMP guards.[4] Some 800 men, community leaders, and persons of influence were sent to northern Ontario to prisoner of war camps surrounded by barbed wire and under armed guard. They were definitely interned. Some 4,000 people were sent to sugar beet farms in Alberta and Manitoba because of the shortage of labourers but regardless were under the strict control of the BC Security Commission and the RCMP.[5]

There was already an established bias against Japanese Canadians that manifested itself in anti-Japanese and anti-Asian sentiments amongst politicians and the white Anglo-Saxon population. The denial of human rights goes back to the very arrival of Japanese to Canada. The BC Provincial Elections Act of 1885 stated: "No Chinaman, Japanese or Indian shall have his name placed on the Register of Voters for an Electoral District or be entitled to vote at any election."[6] Besides being unable to vote, Japanese Canadians were prevented by this legislative sanction from entering certain professions. Even if a Japanese Canadian graduated successfully from university in medicine, pharmacy, engineering, or education, they were not allowed to practise because in order to be registered in these professions, you were required to be on the voters list. This exclusion from the professions or employment with either the federal or provincial governments was a clear message that Japanese were not deserving of equal treatment.

Tomekichi Homma was one of the foremost human rights activists in the Japanese community. To challenge the law that denied Asians the right to vote, Mr. Homma applied in 1900 to place his name on the voters list. When the returning officer denied his request, he appealed to the courts. The BC Supreme Court ruled in his favour and so did the Supreme Court of Canada. However, it was the Privy Council in Britain that overturned this decision in 1902. Finally in 1949 the British Columbia government passed a bill to grant Japanese Canadians the provincial vote.[7]

The history of our community in Canada reveals that Japanese Canadians consistently encountered discrimination from the larger population and from its own governments. In 1907, a mob of several hundred anti-Asian protestors, reacting against the increasing number of Asian immigrants, stormed Chinatown, vandalizing properties and then converging on Powell Street, the centre of Japanese Canadian business activities. There, the rioters were beaten back by waiting Japanese Canadians, armed and ready to fight. This insurrection was an early indication that Japanese and other Asians were not wanted or accepted in Canada.[8]

The BC government imposed legislative sanctions against Asians. Unlike the Chinese, who were prevented from immigrating to Canada with the Chinese Exclusion Act in 1923, the Japanese were allowed to migrate to Canada but quotas were imposed to restrict the numbers. Also, as Japanese became successful fishers, the numbers of fishing licences available to them were reduced through government legislation.[9]

Excluded from the professions, Japanese Canadians turned to resource-based industries such as fishing, lumbering, and farming. Towns such as Steveston, located at the mouth of the Fraser River, and smaller communities along the coast of British Columbia and Vancouver Island emerged as the result of the fishing and lumber industry. Lucrative berry farms and market gardens were established in the Fraser Valley. My grandfather, for example, owned a successful seven-acre berry farm in Haney, BC. In 1942 he lost his farm and everything that he had built up. With the denial of citizenship rights, Japanese Canadians were second-class citizens in their own country.

Sergeant Masumi Mitsui was a decorated veteran of the First World War and was awarded a military medal for "his conspicuous bravery and distinguished conduct." He, along with 200 other Japanese Canadians, volunteered to fight for Canada during the First World War even though they did not have full citizenship rights. In 1931 Japanese Canadian veterans were finally given the franchise after a long struggle. Yet in 1942, despite having fought for Canada, he was interned along with other Japanese Canadians. When he was summoned before the security commissioner after being forced off his property, Mitsui reached into his pocket, pulled out his First World War medals, and threw them on the floor. "What good are these!" he demanded in fury. In the eyes of the government Sergeant Mitsui was still an "enemy alien."[10]

In August 1944, Prime Minister Mackenzie King declared in the House of Commons: "It is a fact no person of Japanese race born in Canada has been charged with any act of sabotage or disloyalty during the years of war."[11] Meanwhile, with the end of the war, the cabinet in December 1945 issued orders-in-council to "repatriate" or expel Japanese Canadians to Japan from internment camps, prisoner of war camps and from sugar beet fields. If they were to remain in Canada they must live east of the Rockies and be dispersed to other provinces across Canada. Protest ensued, resulting in a mixed ruling by the Supreme Court, but this dispersal order was upheld by the Judicial Committee of the Privy Council. However, following the negative reactions from politicians and academics, the orders were revoked in 1947. By this time some 4,000 people had already been sent to Japan, half of whom were born in Canada. Although they were no longer a threat, Mackenzie King would not allow Japanese Canadians to return to the West Coast. It would take until 1 April 1949 until this final restriction was removed. By refusing Japanese Canadians the right to return to the West Coast after the war ended, the BC government was clearly seeking to erase Japanese from the coast. Politicians openly incited racism.[12]

Thomas Reid, a liberal member of Parliament from BC, said this of the Japanese in 1942, "Take them back to Japan. They do not belong here, and there is only one solution to the problem. They cannot be assimilated as Canadians, for no matter how long the Japanese remain in Canada, they will always be Japanese."[13] Even though many were born in Canada, citizenship rights were blatantly ignored.

Ian Mackenzie—an MP and the only member of the cabinet from British Columbia responsible for giving advice on the Japanese question—said this in his nomination speech in 1944, "Let our slogan be for British Columbia: 'No

Japs from the Rockies to the sea.'"[14] Needless to say, the policies perpetuated upon Japanese Canadians bore Ian Mackenzie's footprint. Even before the war there were cries that the Japanese were dominating the fishing and farming sectors and that "they were taking over."[15] Major General Ken Stuart, in advising the government with regard to their removal from the coast said, "From the army point of view, I cannot see that Japanese Canadians constitute the slightest menace to national security."[16] The National Association of Japanese Canadians (NAJC) has always felt that the decision to remove the Japanese from the coast was based more on economic and political reasons than any consideration of national security.

The day after Pearl Harbor, all Japanese-owned fishing boats were confiscated; most were dry docked and eventually sold to ensure that Japanese fishers would have nothing to come back to. Most of the market gardening and berry farms were sold or given to veterans returning from the war. The government strategically disposed of the properties rather than holding them in trust as was promised to Japanese Canadians as a way of ensuring that very few Japanese would return to the West Coast to start again.[17]

The initial redress movement began in 1946 when the government established the Bird Commission to reimburse people for losses resulting from sale of the confiscated properties during the war. However, the Bird Commission settlements were not satisfactory to Japanese Canadians, who received only 10 percent of the value of what they had lost. Many felt that something further needed to be done. Three decades later, the celebration of the Japanese Canadian centennial in 1977 gave cause for reflection on our past and aroused debate within the community on the issue of redress. By this time many of the documents related to the uprooting and the orders-in-council had become available for public scrutiny and research. By 1978 the NAJC established a reparations committee to explore the possibility and forms of redress.[18]

Several events at this time served to help raise the awareness of past injustices inflicted upon the Japanese community. On Wednesday, 26 November 1980, the NAJC president, Gordon Kadota, and other members of NAJC appeared before a special joint committee of the Senate and of the House of Commons on the constitution of Canada. In his presentation he emphasized, "Our [Japanese Canadians'] history in Canada is a legacy of racism made legitimate by our political institutions, and we must somehow ensure that no group of Canadians will be subjected to the whims of the political process as we were. We feel that this can only be done by entrenching a Charter of Rights in our constitution, unconditionally entrenching, beyond the reach of Parliament and beyond the reach of the provincial legislatures." His passionate comments brought attention to the wartime treatment of its citizens and explained how our rights were violated. The results of the hearing led to adoption of the Canadian Charter of Rights and Freedoms that Canadians enjoy today.[19]

In the United States the congressional Commission on Wartime Relocation and Internment of Civilians travelled across the country and talked to Japanese Americans about their experiences in concentration camps. Out of their deliberations came a report called *Personal Justice Denied*, which recommended that Japanese-Americans who had been relocated should be awarded individual compensation of $20,000.[20] This was important later for the Canadian redress movement when the discussion of individual compensation caused conflict within the community. I would suggest that this was the catalyst that stimulated movement in Canada toward the possibility of redress, giving notice to our media—and the nation at large—that the internment of Japanese Canadians was not forgotten.

In 1982 the Vancouver-based Japanese Canadian Centennial Project Redress Committee produced the first document that was used "to educate Japanese Canadians and other Canadians on the wartime injustices and to advocate for redress."[21] Their pamphlet was distributed across Canada and attracted the attention of the media. The group sponsored several community forums in Vancouver.

Initially, community consensus was not forthcoming. In 1982 in Toronto, Sodan-kai, a group made up of Nisei and Sansei,[22] formed out of a concern that the redress issue "was in danger of being resolved without grass-roots participation." Their purpose "was to contribute to the democratic process through open discussion, community meetings, educational activities, writing, and listening, hoping this process would lead to consensus and unity before any proposal was put to the Canadian government."[23] At the same time, there was a conflict developing between the NAJC and the NAJC Redress Committee members who were working independently of the parent organization. The redress committee in prior discussions with government officials had determined that the government would be favourable to an apology and redress in the form of group compensation. However, the NAJC council had no knowledge of this arrangement nor had it endorsed this position. The redress committee was given government funding to convene a national meeting with the idea that over a weekend meeting in September 1983 at which participants would deliver an agreement from our community to accept the apology as well as a group compensation package. The delegates, such as myself, attending the meeting and representing centres across Canada rejected the proposal because we felt that there had been no prior consultation with the Japanese communities. Further discussions were needed within the community and so no decision was made on the government's redress proposal.

As there was no clear agreement within the Japanese Canadian community, this would curtail our campaign for two years. In 1984, NAJC took the initiative to get the community involved and adopted a resolution to seek redress. The redress proposal called for the government to acknowledge that a wrong had been committed against Japanese Canadians during the 1940s, to provide compensation for losses to individuals and the community, and to make legislative changes to the War Measures Act to prevent similar treatment to other Canadians in the future.

When the redress movement began, many Japanese Canadians, especially the Issei, or the first-generation, felt apprehensive about stirring up the past. There is a saying in our community, "shikata ga nai," that means "it can't be helped." What it means is that we have no control over whatever happens. Therefore, accept it and move on, a core Buddhist belief.

There were fears within the Japanese Canadian community that there would be a backlash and renewed racism directed toward them. Many felt that seeking redress was a futile effort for a community of only 60,000 and that we wouldn't be heard by the government or have the political clout to win such a struggle. With the feeling that redress was not attainable, it was difficult for many Japanese Canadians to support NAJC's redress mandate. Some were reluctant to talk about a past that they were trying so hard to forget, especially the horrific wartime experiences that brought shame, humiliation, and embarrassment. The NAJC had to counteract these apprehensions to gain the support of the community.

Maryka Omatsu, a member of the NAJC strategy and negotiations team and author of *Bittersweet Passage,* describes the following event:

> Shortly after my father's death in 1981, I returned to his small sunlit bedroom in our family home in Hamilton to go through his personal effects. All his worldly and prized possessions fit into one drawer. Going through his wallet I found his plastic Canadian citizenship card, his Hamilton senior citizens transit card, and—tucked away in the back compartment and neatly

> folded—his worn World War II government-issued "enemy alien" card, complete with his photo and thumb print. During the war and for the time after, all Japanese Canadians were legally required to carry these numbered identification cards. They had to produce these upon request by police and government officials. Later at one of the community events I learned that my father had once been incarcerated for improper identification. My father had applied to the RCMP for a permit to travel to another town to look for work. The officer, unfamiliar with Japanese names, had misspelt his name and instead of writing "Omatsu" had written something approximating it. Later on, when officials asked my father to show his identification papers and found the wrong name, my father was thrown in jail, without trial, for "traveling without authority." My father, apparently shamed by this episode, went to his grave with this secret.[24]

In order to address the negative attitudes toward redress we held community meetings and had prominent community advocates share their perspectives on the importance of exploring our past so that we as a community could move forward. Because some Issei, and Nisei, were reluctant to talk about the past, much of the younger generation was completely oblivious to their parents' history or why they ended up where they were living. It was not something that was talked about in the home. In the early stages of the redress movement the NAJC's goal was to create an understanding of what redress represented. The NAJC organized house meetings where friends and relatives would gather and share stories of the past. It was through this process and community meetings that the Japanese Canadians became aware of what redress entailed. As the publicity grew through media coverage, more Japanese Canadians began to believe that Canadians were not as negative as they had perceived and were interested in our past experiences and supportive of NAJC's efforts. There was a growing feeling that seeking redress was important for our self-respect and identity and that past injustices should be revealed and acknowledged.

New voices emerged from within the community: confident, well-educated individuals who believed strongly in justice and fair play. These voices embraced the feelings of the past and carried these feelings to the present. These voices belonged to the Sansei. Together with the support and guidance of the Nisei, they raised public awareness about how their and their parents' citizenship rights had been violated. They felt that in a democratic society, citizens have the obligation as well as the right to pursue justice.

Nationally, a Special Committee on Participation on Visible Minorities in Canadian Society was established by Parliament and consisted of MPs who went across the country and interviewed many people from various visible minority groups. This committee produced a report, *Equality Now!*, that made references to the Japanese-Canadian experiences and the wartime mistreatment.[25] It recommended that the government should acknowledge the past injustices and consider some form of redress. This gave considerable legitimacy to the Japanese Canadian redress movement.

In 1984, the NAJC officially requested Prime Minister Pierre Elliott Trudeau to consider redress, but he dismissed this notion of trying to right past wrongs. He said rather that we should be looking toward the future. Brian Mulroney, leader of the opposition at the time, reacted to Trudeau's comments, saying that if the Conservatives were the governing party, they would certainly compensate Japanese Canadians.[26] His words became the commitment that the NAJC would continuously remind the prime minister to honour throughout his term in office. When the Conservatives were elected to government in 1984, they agreed publicly in a joint press release to negotiate a redress settlement.[27] Finally, we thought that justice would be achieved.

However, after several meetings with government officials, we realized that we were not involved in a negotiation process. The NAJC was offered an acknowledgement and a $6 million community fund that would be administered by the government, but the Mulroney administration was unwilling to consider individual recognition. In early 1985 Jack Murta, minister for multiculturalism, when questioned on national television by CBC anchor Barbara Frum regarding the government's commitment, indicated that the government had had no intention to negotiate, but rather to consult.[28]

Several times during the negotiation period the government attempted to impose a settlement through a motion in the House without the approval of NAJC. Each time we were able to lobby the opposition parties that were committed to a negotiated settlement as opposed to a motion in the House. The government attempted to divide and conquer by using people within the Japanese Canadian community to speak against the NAJC redress campaign. There were some people within the community who wanted to accept whatever the government was willing to offer. These people did not officially represent the community, but the government helped them organize press conferences to speak out against the NAJC. The media became aware of this tactic and supported the NAJC. Perhaps they saw us as the underdog being bullied by the government.

Jack Murta, during one of the discussions, raised an interesting question: "What did your community really lose?"[29] We had no idea, nor could we offer an educated guess on how much the community lost monetarily. We realized then that we needed to quantify the losses suffered by Japanese Canadians and undertook a campaign to raise funds for such a study. Price Waterhouse offered to conduct a study to determine the economic losses resulting from the internment. The study revealed that the losses to the Japanese Canadians amounted to $443 million in 1986 dollars.[30] This would become the benchmark for the negotiation process. The other issue that became apparent to us was the need to determine what forms of compensation that individuals in the Japanese Canadian community supported. The NAJC conducted a national survey and the results indicated that the majority would like the NAJC to seek individual compensation.[31] The second option was to seek both individual and group compensation. The feedback was invaluable to counteract the position taken by the government-backed opposition group, which claimed that Japanese Canadians did not want individual compensation. Using this information the NAJC developed a comprehensive redress proposal. The proposal called for an official acknowledgement, individual compensation of $25,000 each, a community fund of $50 million, the establishment of a human rights foundation, and amendments to the War Measures Act.[32]

There were a number of factors that eventually led to the final redress agreement. The media turned out to be a powerful ally. They generally portrayed Japanese Canadians as victims of the government's abusive and unchallenged powers during wartime. The media helped Japanese Canadians realize that other Canadians supported the cause.[33] Initially, the support for redress within the community was limited, but as public opinion changed, so did the attitudes within the Japanese Canadian community. Reassurances that we were not alone in this struggle helped enhance our collective self-esteem. The support of the media helped keep the redress campaign alive even when it appeared that there was very little or no progress. Canadians learned about the forced removal from the West Coast, the internment and dispersal, through media coverage, television documentaries, radio talk shows, print media, and other means of communications.

Politicians played an important role as well. To begin with, both opposition parties supported the principle that a meaningful settlement is one that is negotiated between the NAJC and the government. Sergio Marchi, Liberal, and Ernie Epp, NDP, the multiculturalism critics for their respective parties, were the two MPs with whom the NAJC had the most contact.

Other politicians from all parties also came forward to offer their support. I felt some of the key influences in favour of the NAJC were Dalton Camp, Prime Minister Mulroney's chief of staff, and Honourable John Fraser, the Speaker of the House.

The message that the NAJC emphasized to the public through the media was designed to gain both support and sympathy. We used language such as "negotiated settlement" rather than "financial or individual compensation." The focus was more on working out an agreement with the government rather than talking about specific amounts of compensation that we knew would generate opposing reactions from the public.

In statements to the press, we continually stressed that interned victims were Canadian citizens. Because of our visual appearance, most people perceived the Japanese to be immigrants, not realizing that most were born in Canada or were naturalized Canadians. Therefore, a strong emphasis was placed on being Canadian citizens, especially when detractors would make comments such as "go back where you came from."

One of our strengths turned out to be the simple power of saying "no." We said "no" to several proposals which did not reflect the gross injustices suffered by Japanese Canadians. The government used scare tactics to try and divide our community while pressuring us to abandon our position, especially on individual compensation. Each time we rejected the government's proposal, our movement gained strength. We said "no" to what Honourable David Crombie claimed was the government's final offer. He said by not accepting, the community would get nothing from the government and that the NAJC would be criticized by the community. Unless the principle of individual compensation, an important component of the redress proposal, was met, we had no qualms in rejecting Crombie's final proposal.

When negotiations terminated in July 1987 after the meeting with David Crombie, the NAJC strategy committee met in Vancouver with its legal advisors and decided that a different approach was needed. Up to now it had been the Japanese community (through NAJC) against the government. A decision was made to expand our scope and make redress a Canadian human rights issue. Thus, we devised a plan to create the National Coalition for Japanese Canadians Redress and solicit support from other Canadians. Chief Justice Tom Berger agreed to be the honorary chair for the coalition and David Murata was hired as the national coordinator to contact prominent individuals across the country and from a wide variety of national, provincial, and local organizations. Those who came on-board agreed to support a negotiated agreement between the NAJC and the government. This approach of involving other Canadians turned out to be a highly effective strategy. Coalition members sent letters of endorsement to the prime minister and politicians, and signed petitions and postcards urging the government to negotiate a just and meaningful settlement with the NAJC.

The government of Manitoba (my home province) under Premier Garry Filmon passed a resolution in support of the NAJC. A multicultural rally of ethnic organizations was held in Toronto in October 1987, where a resolution in support of Japanese Canadian Redress was endorsed. The resolution stated: "We, the undersigned national organizations representing Canadians of diverse ethnocultural heritage, hereby call upon the Prime Minister to intervene personally to resolve the basic human and civil rights issue. We urge the Prime Minister to act swiftly to heal this wound on our national psyche and, thereby, to reinforce for all Canadians their faith in accountability of parliamentary democracy."[34]

The support we received from other groups such as unions, religious organizations, civil liberties groups, and ethnic and Aboriginal organizations throughout Canada helped push the government to recognize that redress was nothing short of a Canadian human rights issue. Terms such as "justice" and "human rights," which the Canadian public could easily understand, were used repeatedly to emphasize that redress was more than just a Japanese Canadian issue.

The Ottawa Rally held on 14 April 1988 was the culmination of the coalition's activities. This event was unconventional for the Japanese Canadian community. We were warned by some community members that having elderly Japanese Canadians march on Parliament Hill would be embarrassing: "It is not in keeping with the character of the Japanese personality," we were told. We took a risk. The national media coverage put a human face to the stories of the elderly victims, and their memories of hardships and alienation. The rally had a positive impact on our community and on the Canadian public and forced the government to reconsider its position. The demonstration, conducted in a solemn and respectful manner, I thought was in keeping with the way Canadians express their frustration to the government. At the rally in the West Block, David Suzuki and speakers representing various organizations within the coalition spoke eloquently on the importance of righting past wrongs. Honourable Gerry Weiner, the fourth minister of multiculturalism to hold that portfolio since the redress campaign had commenced, spoke at the rally—despite advice from his staff not to attend—and his comments gave us hope.[35] This coalition had organized a postcard campaign. On the day of the rally Gerry Weiner along with some other rally participants carried the 15,000 signed postcards in large sacks to the prime minister's office.

After the rally was over there was a change in the government's attitude. I had a call from the minister's office saying that they would like to sit down with the national association to discuss redress. The first thing I mentioned was that if they were to put forward the same offer that the other ministers had proposed before, there was no point in meeting. However, if the government was open to discussing individual compensation, then we would meet. When we finally spoke in person, Mr. Weiner assured us that the prime minister was willing to put everything on the table.

The signing of the redress bill in the United States by President Ronald Reagan in August 1988, "providing for the payment of $20,000 to each surviving internee," was clearly a major factor in the government reversing its original position of no individual compensation.[36] In meetings with the three previous ministers of multiculturalism, individual compensation was not up for discussion, but the American bill became the precedent that NAJC needed to justify the importance of individual compensation and would become the cornerstone of the final agreement.

The timing could not have been better for our cause. There was a possibility of a fall election; the U.S. bill had been signed; individual compensation was now an established precedent in a case that was strikingly similar to that of the Japanese Canadians; the opinion polls across the country were very favourable to redress; and finally, some high-profile cabinet changes helped pave the way. In the latter case, I know of one minister in cabinet who was extremely powerful during the time that Mulroney was prime minister. Every time Mulroney brought up redress, George Hees would rebuff the idea. As minister for Veterans Affairs, Hees argued that Canadian veterans wouldn't support it and neither would he. However, George Hees became ill in the summer of 1988 and had to leave cabinet. With George Hees gone, the attitude within cabinet toward redress changed, allowing the prime minister to reconsider.

The government was now prepared to reopen negotiations but was concerned about how to proceed after the position taken earlier by David Crombie—the infamous "final offer" of July 1987. But the prime minister initiated action and asked the minister to arrange a negotiation meeting with the NAJC.

In late August 1988 we were hastened to a private meeting with government officials in Montreal. To ensure secrecy when we arrived at the hotel, all of us were ushered by a government official through a side door of the hotel, through the kitchen, and up several flights of stairs to a private meeting room. The interesting part of that meeting was that Lucien Bouchard was in attendance. He said that he had the ear of the prime minister and told us that the prime minister wanted the issue resolved. Mr. Bouchard was there to ensure that an agreement would be reached.

After two days of hard-nosed dialogue we reached agreement on the terms that included individual compensation of $21,000. People have asked why the sum of $21,000 was chosen. The American bill called for individual compensation of $20,000 for each Japanese American incarcerated in concentration camps in the United States, at the same time that Japanese Canadians were being forcibly removed. The NAJC argued—for very good reason—that our treatment in Canada was far worse and more severe than it had been in the United States and therefore it was important that Japanese Canadians should receive more. In a concession to this position the government agreed to pay $21,000 instead of $20,000 to each survivor—a symbolic victory of great importance to the NAJC negotiators.

At this point only four people knew about the redress agreement: The prime minister, the deputy prime minister, Mr. Lucien Bouchard, and the Honourable Gerry Weiner. When we left that meeting in Montreal, all of us were sworn to secrecy until the official announcement was made in the House of Commons. The reason we could not speak about the settlement was because these four key people still needed to convince the cabinet to support the agreement.

One of the key components of the NAJC redress proposal was the demand to either change the War Measures Act or to rescind it to ensure that what had been done to Japanese Canadians could never be perpetrated against any other group. Prior to the Ottawa Rally, the NAJC had appeared before a Parliamentary committee reviewing the War Measures Act offering a significant number of changes to the bill. Ann Sunahara, author of *Politics of Racism,* assisted the NAJC in drafting the amendments. In April 1988 the government adopted the Emergencies Act and rescinded the War Measures Act. The new act authorizes Parliament rather than just the Cabinet to take special temporary measures to ensure safety and security during national emergencies. Also, any temporary measures made by the act are subject to the Charter of Rights and Freedoms.

On 22 September 1988, the government of Canada acknowledged the injustices suffered by Japanese Canadians during and after the Second World War. Prime Minister Mulroney announced that a comprehensive redress package had been reached with the National Association of Japanese Canadians and issued a public apology. The announcement in the House of Commons was a great moment for human rights. For most Japanese Canadians the news was a shocking but pleasant surprise, but for those of us who had struggled through the redress campaign it was a dream come true. The signing of the Japanese Canadian redress agreement was an extraordinary achievement that was to become the beginning of a healing and renewal process for Japanese Canadians. This settlement was an uplifting experience and would be of immense importance to the Japanese Canadian community and have a far-reaching impact nationally. One gentleman, shortly after the announcement, said this to me: "I finally feel as if I'm a true Canadian." In his mind there had always been a doubt because of the way his government treated him. Others have told me that a great burden has been lifted, a feeling of guilt, thinking somehow they were responsible for what happened to them during the war.

I believe that the words of Bruce McLeod, former moderator of the United Church of Canada, puts redress into perspective as a human rights issue: "Acknowledgement of an imperfect past is a prerequisite for a future in which people live together in mutual respect, and self-righteous racism does not take us by surprise again."

The process of community involvement was an important factor for us in the implementation process and we urged the government to respect the offer of partnership. We pointed out that Japanese Canadians had no say when the forced relocation orders were passed and that now was the opportunity to correct those past actions by involving the community when it came to the implementation of the redress agreement. We wanted to be involved in the process. Minister Weiner recognized the importance for the NAJC to play a role in the implementation process and moved it along quickly, as many of the elderly internees were passing away.

The Japanese Canadian redress settlement secretariat was set up immediately; this was the office that was to receive the individual applications for compensation. This was done within a week, and three Japanese Canadians became part of the staff immediately. The NAJC worked with the government to develop the application form. We wanted the application form to be simple, unlike some government forms which are so detailed that the applicants must fill page after page. In the end the application form devised with the secretariat was one page, unlike the far lengthier and cumbersome application form now being used for residential school claimants. Once the secretariat received the application, the information could be checked very quickly to see if the applicant qualified, as the government kept meticulously detailed records on each family in the archives. The first person to receive a redress cheque for $21,000 did so in December, only three months after the secretariat office was first opened.

As part of the implementation, the government provided $3 million to set up offices in the major centres and hire local staff to assist individuals with the application process, to hold community information meetings, and to seek out possible recipients who might be living in institutions or remote areas. This service to the Japanese Canadian community was an important demonstration of the government's commitment to the process.

Some 4,000 people who were sent to Japan after the war were also eligible to receive compensation. A joint delegation of NAJC and government officials travelled to Japan to hold meetings in ten cities to provide assistance with the applications and to accept the form. The group met with the Japanese Ministry of Foreign Affairs officials to discuss how the redress settlement came about. During our stay there was much interest by the Japanese media as to why the Canadian government would send a delegation to give away money in another country. It was difficult for the Japanese to understand this concept. After one of the top officials heard the story he said to me that he didn't think the Japanese government would be able to admit a mistake or willingly compensate the victims. He stated sincerely, "You know, it takes a mature country to be able to do that." When I heard those words, I was extremely proud that I was Canadian, because even though our country is young, when it comes to human rights, we are mature. It was important for us to hear that comment.

Today, we have the Charter of Rights and Freedoms, and the Human Rights Act that rightfully protects citizens from losing their basic rights. Other legal changes have arisen since the advent of Japanese Canadian redress. All of these protections did not exist during the Second World War. However, we are able to explore the extent that Japanese Canadians were deprived of their basic rights and make comparisons to what is considered acceptable today. For example, fundamental freedoms such as freedom of peaceful assembly and freedom of association were not permitted outside the internment centres. Japanese Canadians were not permitted to meet as a group in public. Some leaders in Winnipeg resorted to meeting in different hotels to avoid being found out.

Democratic rights such as voting in an election were not permitted until 1948. My parents, both born in Canada, finally received their Canadian citizenship papers in late 1948. Under the War Measures Act, Japanese Canadians were not permitted to move freely in Canada and could not return to the West

Coast until 1949, four years after the war ended, in contravention of mobility rights that exist today allowing any person freedom to live and work in any province.

The greatest breach for Japanese Canadians was on the legal rights of citizens. Today everyone has the right to life, liberty, and security of person and the right not to be deprived thereof. Everyone has the right to be secure against unreasonable search or seizure. Everyone has the right not to be arbitrarily detained or imprisoned, and on detention the individual has the right to retain and instruct counsel without delay and to be informed of that right. All of those rights were overtly violated. During 1942 and 1948, Japanese Canadians were not allowed to purchase property. They were arbitrarily detained up to four years without ever being charged with a crime. These comparisons give measures as to the extent that rights of Japanese Canadians were dispossessed and denied.

Perhaps it was the denial of rights and internment experience that provided Japanese Canadians with the resilience and fortitude to overcome adversities. As I noted earlier, there is a saying in our community, "shikataga-nai," that translates into "it can't be helped," and therefore you accept what has happened and move on forward, the best you can. It was with this attitude that Japanese Canadians faced reality and began to re-establish themselves in their new environment by working hard and being exemplary citizens. The success of redress has had a profound impact upon the community. For many individuals redress helped them come to terms with their identity and their heritage. One person remarked that "since redress, my awareness has grown and also my sense of myself. I feel that it's easier to walk tall and talk about my culture."[37] Someone else said, "Redress was important because it had a psychological effect and helped our elders open up and gain peace of mind."[38] For many, redress was the beginning of a healing process, but one person told me this: "I felt the Redress Settlement was something of a closure for me."[39] These Japanese Canadians are now more willing to talk about the past and share their stories with the younger generation and with other Canadians. Pride in Japanese heritage and identity is more obvious amongst Japanese Canadians.

The $12 million community fund administered by the Japanese Canadian Redress Foundation has contributed tremendously to the revitalization and stimulation of the Japanese Canadian community. Prior to the redress settlement there were only two Japanese cultural centres in Canada. Today, we have twelve scattered across the country. Cultural and community centres have become focal points where cultural, educational, and social activities bring Japanese Canadians of all generations together. The increased level of participation demonstrates that there is renewed interest in Japanese Canadian culture and in being Japanese. Programs and activities are being accessed by other Canadians and this relationship has certainly created positive attitudes.

The face of the Japanese Canadian community is changing. The forced relocation has resulted in a generation of Japanese Canadians, the majority of whom are in mixed marriages. The intermarriage rate is over 95 percent. Today nearly 40 percent of the Japanese Canadian population is of multiple ethnicities and that is increasing each year.

The creation of the Canadian Race Relations Foundation or CRRF was one of the final terms of the Japanese Canadian redress agreement. The bill to establish the foundation was passed in 1990, but it took until 1996 for the bill to be proclaimed, with Honourable Lincoln Alexander as the first chairperson. The foundation survives on an endowment of $24 million, of which $12 million was contributed on behalf of the Japanese Canadian community. One of the important policy issues for the foundation is to provide moral and research support for groups who have suffered past injustices and or are facing discrimination presently.

One of the legacies of the Japanese Canadian Redress Agreement is the precedent that it has established for the government to resolve other past injustices. Since 2003, the Canadian government has issued apologies and compensation packages modelled after the Japanese Canadian redress settlement: to Indigenous veterans (2003); to Chinese Canadians for the head tax (2006); to the victims of Indian residential schools (2008); and to Ukrainian Canadians who faced internment during the First World War (2008). More recently, in 2016, an apology was given to the Sikh community by the prime minister for the Komagata Maru incident, and in 2019 the government apologized for its treatment of Métis veterans. The Japanese Canadian redress achievement has had a positive influence for other Canadians and is one that we as Canadians can be proud of. We still have some ways to go as a society, as Dennis Edney's important contribution to this volume underscores. He notes the wrongs Canadian Omar Khadr, a former child soldier, has endured, as a victim of what could be reasonably termed internment by other means or state outsourcing of internment. We must be vigilant in the face of injustice. It is through the recognition of past injustices that we as a country work to do better, trying never to make those mistakes again and growing to become more inclusive, understanding, and welcoming.

Notes

1 "The War Measures Act 1914," 22 August 1914, Government of Canada, 5 George V. Chap. 2.

2 For more information on internment in Canada during the Second World War, consult the related essays in this volume. See also Lubomyr Y. Luciuk, *A Time for Atonement: Canada's First National Internment Operations and the Ukrainian Canadians, 1914–1920* (Kingston: Limestone Press, 1988); and Bohdan S. Kordan, *No Free Man: Canada, the Great War, and the Enemy Alien Experience* (Montreal and Kingston: McGill-Queen's University Press, 2016).

3 For an overview of these operations, see Ken Adachi, *The Enemy That Never Was: A History of the Japanese Canadians* (Toronto: McClelland and Stewart, 1976); and Pamela Hickman and Masako Fukawa, *Righting Canada's Wrongs: Japanese Canadian Internment in the Second World War* (Toronto: James Lorimer and Company, 2011). See also essays by Thomson, Bjorge, and Fujiwara in this collection.

4 For a discussion of this, consult Anna Comer Sunahara, *The Politics of Racism: The Uprooting of Japanese Canadians during the Second World War* (Toronto: Lorimer, 1981), 66. See also Mona Oikawa, *Cartographies of Violence: Japanese Canadian Women, Memory, and the Subjects of the Internment* (Toronto: University of Toronto Press, 2012), especially note 3 on page 321.

5 Cassandra Kobayashi and Roy Miki, *Justice in Our Time: The Japanese Canadian Redress Settlement* (Vancouver: Talon Books, 1991); Sunahara, *The Politics of Racism*; Oikawa, *Cartographies of Violence*; Adachi, *The Enemy That Never Was*; Hickman and Fukawa, *Righting Canada's Wrongs*. On the experiences of sugar beet labourers, see Fujiwara and Bjorge's pieces in this collection.

6 Provincial Elections Act of British Columbia, 1885. For discussion of the law and challenges to it, consult Chapter 2: "Quong Wing v. The King," in James William St. G. Walker, *"Race," Rights, and the Law in the Supreme Court of Canada: Historical Case Studies* (S.l: Osgoode Society for Canadian Legal History [u.a.], 1997), 51–121.

7 Walker, *"Race," Rights, and the Law*, 76–77.

8 Erika Lee, "Hemispheric Orientalism and the 1907 Pacific Coast Race Riots," *Amerasia Journal 33, no. 2: 19–48;* John Price, "'Orienting' the Empire: Mackenzie King and the Aftermath of the 1907 Race Riots," *BC Studies: The British Columbian Quarterly* 156, no. 7 (2007): 53–81; Howard H. Sugimoto, "The Vancouver Riot and Its International Significance," *The Pacific Northwest Quarterly* 64, no. 4 (1973): 163–74.

9 For discussion of anti-Asian sentiment, its manifestations, and impact, see Patricia E. Roy, *A White Man's Province: British Columbia Politicians and Chinese and Japanese Immigrants, 1858–1914* (Vancouver: University of British Columbia Press, 1990); Erika Lee, "The 'Yellow Peril' and Asian Exclusion in the Americas," *Pacific Historical Review* 76, no. 4 (2007): 537–62.

10 Mitsui, as quoted in Kobayashi and Miki, *Justice in Our Time*, 44.

11 King, as quoted in Kobayashi and Miki, *Justice in Our Time*, 46.

12 Kobayashi and Miki, *Justice in Our Time*; Sunahara, *The Politics of Racism*; Oikawa, *Cartographies of Violence*; Adachi, *The Enemy That Never Was*; Hickman and Fukawa, *Righting Canada's Wrongs*.

13 Reid, as quoted in Japanese Canadian Centennial Project, *A Dream of Riches: The Japanese Canadians, 1877–1977* (Vancouver: Japanese Canadian Centennial Project, 1978), 77.

14 Mackenzie, as quoted in Stephanie Bangarth, *Voices Raised in Protest: Defending North American Citizens of Japanese Ancestry, 1942–49* (Vancouver: UBC Press, 2008), 28.

15 Sunahara offers a detailed discussion of these attitudes and their manifestations in legislation and other public officials' behaviour in *The Politics of Racism,* 18, http://www.japanesecanadianhistory.ca/Politics_of_Racism.pdf.

16 Stuart, as quoted in Maurice A. Pope, *Soldiers and Politicians: The Memoirs of Lt. Gen. Maurice A. Pope* (Toronto: University of Toronto Press, 1962), 177, as quoted in Sunahara, *The Politics of Racism,* 18, http://www.japanesecanadianhistory.ca/Politics_of_Racism.pdf.

17 Comments by Thomas Reid and Major General Ken Stuart are found in Kobayashi and Miki, *Justice in Our Time*, 24.

18 Reference to establishment of reparations committee is in Kobayashi and Miki, *Justice in Our Time*, 64.

19 The above statement came from "Minutes of the Proceedings and Evidence of the Special Joint Committee of the Senate and of the House of Commons on the Constitution of Canada, Wednesday, November 26, 1980." Referenced in Kobayashi and Miki, *Justice in Our Time*, 69.

20 United States, *Personal Justice Denied: Report of the Commission on Wartime Relocation and Internment of Civilians* (Washington, DC: The Commission, 1983), https://www.archives.gov/research/japanese-americans/justice-denied.

21 Kobayashi and Miki, *Justice in Our Time*, 65.

22 Japanese Canadians have named each generation in Canada by the following terms: Issei – these are people who came to Canada from Japan before World War II and are the first generation. Nisei – second generation, are Canadian–born children of the Issei. Sansei – third generation, are the children of the Nisei, largely born in the 1940s and '50s. Yonsei and Gosei are the fourth and fifth generations, respectively.

23 Kobayashi and Miki, *Justice in Our Time*, 66.

24 Maryka Omatsu, *Bittersweet Passage: Redress and the Japanese Canadian Experience* (Toronto: Between the Lines, 1992), 35.

25 Canada Special Committee on Participation of Visible Minorities in Canadian Society. *Equality Now!* (Quebec: Canadian Gov. Publ. Centre, 1984).

26 Portions of this exchange in the House of Commons can be viewed via this news story: "The Struggle Continues for Japanese Canadians," *The Journal*, 31 January 1985, http://www.cbc.ca/archives/entry/japanese-canadians-the-struggle-continues.

27 Ibid.

28 Ibid. An interview with the author—and his response to Murta's comments—follows Murta's interview on the clip.

29 That comment was made during an informal discussion between the minister and the author, Art Miki, who was then president of NAJC.

30 National Association of Japanese Canadians, *Economic Losses of Japanese Canadians After 1941: A Study Conducted by Price Waterhouse* (Vancouver). For a discussion of the study and its findings, see Kobayashi and Miki, *Justice in Our Time*, 92–93 (Winnipeg: NAJC, 1985).

31 Kobayashi and Miki, *Justice in Our Time*, 91.

32 Ibid., 97.

33 Roy Miki discusses the media's coverage of the redress fight in *Redress: Inside the Japanese Canadian Call for Justice* (Vancouver: Raincoast Books, 2000), 148–50.

34 This was signed by the leaders from the following organizations: the Korean Canadian Cultural Association of Metro Toronto, the German Canadian Congress, the International Sikh Organization – Federation of Sikh Societies, National Council of Jamaicans, Council of Muslim Communities of Canada, Canadian Lithuanian Community, United Council of Filipino Associations of Canada, Canadian Arab Federation, Pakistani Canadian Community Centre (Toronto) Inc., Canadian Polish Congress, Hellenic Canadian Congress, Canadian Jewish Congress, Czechoslovak Association of Canada, Canadian Hispanic Congress, National Congress of Italian Canadians, and the Chinese Canadian National Council. See Kobayashi and Miki, *Justice in Our Time*, 108.

35 For coverage of the event, see "Want Compensation for Internment," *The Globe and Mail*, 15 Apr 1988.

36 From "Japanese American Redress Settlement: The Civil Liberties Act of 1987," cited in Kobayashi and Miki, *Justice in Our Time*, 110.

37 Arthur K. Miki, *The Japanese Canadian Redress Legacy: A Community Revitalized* (Winnipeg: National Association of Japanese Canadians, 2003), 169.

38 Ibid.

39 Ibid.

ACKNOWLEDGEMENTS

This collection grew out of an international workshop held at the Ukrainian Labour Temple in Winnipeg, Manitoba, from 17 to 19 June 2015. The purpose of this meeting was simple—gather together community members, scholars, activists, public history professionals, students, educators, artists, and others with an interest in or experience of internment (most notably former internees, their descendants, and redress activists) and engage them in a dialogue on the history and continued impact of civilian internment in Canada from 1914 to the present. By bringing together this diverse array of discussants, the resulting conversation was by design explicitly cross-cultural, or perhaps more accurately, cross-internment. One of the most notable features of the workshop—especially the sessions devoted to survivor and "legacy" memories—was how often similarities (and some notable differences) in the camp experiences or family experiences of loss and betrayal associated with internment cut across ethnic, religious, and political lines. Indeed, this became a key theme that emerged from the workshop; with so many participants—survivors and scholars associated with the study of one particular group—proclaiming, "I didn't know that happened to your people, too."[1] We are immensely grateful to those who attended and shared their stories and research—we wish all could have been included in this book.

These conversations were both necessary and timely for a number of reasons. To begin with, we knew all too well that many of the former internees and other eyewitnesses were passing from the scene and that it was imperative that their stories be preserved before it was too late. Just as importantly, we were also keenly aware that the legacy of internment, with its sad record of violating the civil rights and liberties of Canadians (and non-Canadians as well), was a matter that has all too often been swept under the proverbial carpet, in spite of its continuation (in a variety of forms) and its direct relevance to many of the social, cultural, and political issues with which we grapple today.

The workshop was organized by the Canadian Society for Ukrainian Labour Research (CSULR) in collaboration with a number of other community organizations including the Manitoba Japanese Canadian Cultural Centre (MJCCC) and staff from the Canadian Museum for Human Rights (CMHR). It was made possible thanks to the generous financial and in-kind contributions from the following organizations: Brandon University, the Manitoba Japanese Canadian Cultural Centre, the Canadian Museum for Human Rights, the Association of United Ukrainian Canadians, the Ivan Franko Museum, the Joseph Zuken Memorial Foundation, the Endowment Council of the Canadian First World War Internment Recognition Fund, the University of North Dakota, the Manitoba Government Ethnocultural Support Program, the Social Sciences and Humanities Research Council, Brandon University Student Union, Past Perfect Productions, the Canadian Museum of History, Carleton University Public History Program, and University of Manitoba Press.

We appreciate the commitment and patience each of the authors in this collection demonstrated throughout the editorial and publication processes. Others helped move this book along, too, and several deserve singling out for their particularly contributions. Connie Humes provided diligent assistance with many aspects of the manuscript in the early phases of its development. Lily Stearns and Brent Stearns—who were key organizers of the internment workshop—remained passionate supporters of this book project. Not enough good can be said of the folks at University of Manitoba Press, including David Carr, Jill McConkey (whose tough editorial stance helped considerably improve the manuscript), David Larsen, Glenn Bergen, and copyeditor extraordinaire Gretchen Albers.

To those closest to us we owe an immense debt of gratitude. Rhonda would like to acknowledge her family (especially Aaron Floresco, Sebastian Hinther-Floresco, Evelyn Hinther, Glen Ash, Sophie Skolny, Lynne Onofreychuk, Helen Floresco, George Floresco, and Cathy Kennedy) and many friends who supported this project, sustaining her as they always have through yet another hilly book manuscript journey. She would also like to thank her colleagues at Brandon University for their ongoing interest in, support (both moral and financial), and encouragement of this project. Jim would like to acknowledge the support of his family, especially Mary Mochoruk—who has now helped him to survive through a PhD and four book manuscripts. His mother, Sheila Mochoruk, and his children, Kaitlin, Brendan, and Colleen—and the newest additions to the family, Hayley and Braylynn Mochoruk—have all made the process of writing and editing far more enjoyable and meaningful. He also needs to thank his colleagues at the University of North Dakota (UND) for their unflagging support, encouragement, and patience. Finally, he also owes a very real debt of gratitude to the College of Arts and Sciences at UND and its Scholarship Initiative Grants and to the Schulte family, whose generosity to the History Department at UND provides the sort of financial support that allows him to keep engaged in primary research.

Notes

1 Some of the most compelling of these testimonies from one of the workshop's most remarkable roundtable discussions focussed on the memories of internment survivors and their offspring and offer particularly compelling insight on the long-lasting and intensely personal impact of internment. We urge readers of this volume to read both the transcript and Jodi Giesbrecht's insightful introduction in Jodi Giesbrecht, "Conference Report: Panel 3, Civilian Internment in Canada, Winnipeg MB, 17–19 June 2015," in the *Oral History Forum d'histoire orale* 36 (2016).

CONTRIBUTORS

Mikhail Bjorge received his doctorate in history from Queen's University. He teaches economic and political history in Toronto, Ontario, and works primarily on the history of capitalism. He has just completed the manuscript for his first book, *The Workers' War*.

Ed Caissie is the curator of the New Brunswick Internment Camp Museum. He taught for thirty years and received two national awards for innovative teaching, including one for the creation of the New Brunswick Internment Camp Project. Caissie is a graduate of the Art Institute of Boston and the Nova Scotia College of Art and Design.

Todd E. Caissie is a PhD candidate in Art History and Cultural Heritage and Preservation Studies at Rutgers University, a member of the Board of Directors of the New Brunswick Internment Camp Museum, and author of "Not Too Old to Serve: Veterans Guard of Canada at the NB Internment Camp Museum," published by *Legion Magazine* (May 2018).

Emily Cuggy is a senior associate at Know History, a historical research firm based in Ottawa, Ontario. She holds an MA in public history from Carleton University.

Paula Draper, PhD, is an historian and educator. Her 1970s research into the story of Jewish refugees interned in Canada during the First World War led her to become an early advocate of memory history. She wrote the text for the exhibit *"Enemy Aliens": The Internment of Jewish Refugees in Canada,*

1940–43 (http://enemyaliens.ca), and has published widely on the topic of Canada and the Holocaust.

Dennis Edney, QC, is an Alberta lawyer practising human rights, criminal, and constitutional law. His is the recipient of numerous awards, including the 2008 National Pro Bono Award for his work on the Omar Khadr case, to which he devoted considerable personal resources, time, and energy.

Aya Fujiwara received her PhD in Canadian History at the University of Alberta. She is the Director of Prince Takamado Japan Centre for Teaching and Research and teaches both Japanese and Canadian history at the University of Alberta. Her research interests include the ethnic and immigration history of Canada along with Japan-Canada relations.

Jodi Giesbrecht, PhD, is the Director of Research and Head Curator at the Canadian Museum for Human Rights, where she oversees the museum's research, curatorial, and oral history programs. Her recent publications include articles on human rights and museology, oral history, and the history of redress movements in Canada.

Rhonda L. Hinther, PhD, is Associate Professor of History at Brandon University and an active public historian. Her most recent book is entitled *Perogies and Politics: Canada's Ukrainian Left, 1891–1991* (University of Toronto Press, 2018). Hinther is co-editor, with Jim Mochoruk, of *Re-imagining Ukrainian-Canadians: History, Politics, and Identity* (University of Toronto Press, 2011).

Franca Iacovetta is Professor of History at University of Toronto. Recent publications include *Beyond Women's Words* (Routledge, 2018) and articles on married women's nationality and migrant children's health. She is completing a monograph on women's pluralism and is involved in a collaborative project on Emma Goldman in Toronto (history and legacy).

Judith Kestler earned her MA in European ethnology/cultural anthropology from the University of Würzburg, Germany, and her PhD in cultural anthropology from the University of Hamburg. Her PhD thesis analyzes the internment of German merchant seamen in Canada during the Second World War as a cultural practice. Currently, she is a project coordinator at the University of Music Würzburg.

Kassandra Luciuk is a PhD candidate in the Department of History at the University of Toronto. She is the author of a forthcoming graphic novel based on the experiences of an internee held in the Kapuskasing internment camp from 1914 to 1917.

Marinel Mandres, PhD, is a member of the Department of Geography and Environmental Studies at Wilfrid Laurier University and the International Migration Research Centre. He recently completed a project on the internment of Serbs and Romanians in Canada during the First World War. His current research examines the wartime internment of Italians.

Arthur K. Miki, CM, OM, has had a distinguished career as an elementary school teacher, principal, and community activist. As president of the National Association of Japanese Canadians (NAJC) from 1984 to 1992 he led the negotiations to achieve a just redress settlement in 1988 for Japanese Canadians interned during the Second World War. In 1991 he received the Order of Canada.

Jim Mochoruk is a professor at the University of North Dakota where he teaches Canadian, U.S., British, and British imperial history. His publications include *The People's Co-op: The Life and Times of a North End Institution* (Fernwood Publishing, 2000); *"Formidable Heritage": Manitoba's North and the Cost of Development, 1870 to 1930* (University of Manitoba Press, 2004); and, with Rhonda Hinther, *Re-Imagining Ukrainian-Canadians: History, Politics and Identity* (University of Toronto Press, 2011).

Myron Momryk is a retired archivist from Library and Archives Canada where he worked for twenty-five years. He volunteers at the Canadian Museum of History's archives where he processed the Prokop (Prokopchak) Family fonds. His most recent publication is *Mike Starr of Oshawa, A Political Biography* (University of Ottawa Press/Canadian Museum of History, 2017).

Kathleen Ogilvie graduated from Carleton University's public history program in 2016. Currently she works for the Canadian Museums Association as a Program Officer for the Young Canada Works in Heritage Organizations Program. In her spare time, she blogs about museums on her website, http://www.presenting-past.com.

Sharon Reilly is a public historian living in Winnipeg. She worked at the Manitoba Museum from 1980 to 2011, curating numerous social history exhibits including Parklands Gallery displays on Japanese Canadian internment and the impact of war. From 2011 to 2015, Sharon worked at the Canadian Museum for Human Rights.

Clemence Schultze, daughter of a political refugee from Hitler's Germany, gained her doctorate on Greek historian Dionysius of Halicarnassus and had a career lecturing on Roman history at Queen's University Belfast and Durham University. She works on classical historiography and reception, and is preparing her father's archive for publication.

Grace Eiko Thomson holds a master's in the social history of art from the University of Leeds, UK. She is the founding executive director-curator of the Japanese Canadian National Museum and served as the president and past president of the National Association of Japanese Canadians. She has also served as an art advisor and curator for numerous galleries across Canada.

Travis Tomchuk, PhD, is a curator at the Canadian Museum for Human Rights. His work deals primarily with Canadian human rights history. He is the author of *Transnational Radicals: Italian Anarchists in Canada and the U.S., 1915–1940* (University of Manitoba Press, 2015).

Christine Whitehouse is a research grants facilitator at Dalhousie University. Her dissertation, which includes an earlier version of Chapter 7, won the 2017 German-Canadian Studies Doctoral Dissertation Prize.